A Bird in the Bush

Stephen Moss is a writer and television producer specialising in birds and other wildlife. He works at the BBC Natural History Unit, producing the television series *Birding with Bill Oddie*, *Bill Oddie Goes Wild*, and the forthcoming *Nature of Britain* with Alan Titchmarsh. He writes the 'Birdwatch' column in the *Guardian*, contributes regularly to birdwatching magazines, and is a regular voice on BBC Radio. His other books include *Birds and Weather*, *How to Birdwatch* and *The Garden Bird Handbook*. He lives with his wife and three sons in south-west London.

'A great book, putting together the history and development of birdwatching in a historical and social context, in a thoroughly readable style. It must have taken years of researching . . . It is thorough, well-researched and contains enough meat for many pleasurable evenings' entertainment'
Birds magazine

'A substantial read, packed with interesting snippets and not a little humour, and surely everyone who reads this book will learn something. In short, this is a fascinating book on our absorbing passion'
Ian Dawson, *Birdwatch* magazine

'I have to admit to being a bit of a weekend twitcher, so [one of] the two books that delighted me most in 2004 [was] *A Bird in the Bush* by that unfussy and rousing birder Stephen Moss'
Jim Crace, *Daily Telegraph* Books of the Year

'Fascinating and comprehensive . . . [an] enthralling book'
New Statesman

'You really ought to buy a copy. Or better still: buy copies for those people who still don't understand what birding is all about. They won't find a better explanation'
Gordon Hamlett, *Birdwatching* magazine

'A wonderfully detailed account that emphasises the history of bird studies and culminates with a searching analysis of the twitcher's black art . . . With 375 closely-packed pages this is a book for several long, rainy afternoons in the car at Cley'
Tim Birkhead, *BBC Wildlife* magazine

'A well-researched book and particularly good on the mid-twentieth century, when so many people took up the hobby, and found that it grew into a passion'
Derwent May, *The Times*

STEPHEN MOSS

A Bird in the Bush

A SOCIAL HISTORY
OF
BIRDWATCHING

Aurum

First published in Great Britain
2004 by Aurum Press Ltd
25 Bedford Avenue, London WC1B 3AT
www.aurumpress.co.uk

Reprinted twice

Published in this paperback edition 2005

A catalogue record for this book is available from the British Library.

ISBN 1 84513 085 5

1 3 5 7 9 10 8 6 4 2
2005 2007 2009 2008 2006

Designed and typeset in Fournier by Peter Ward
Printed by Bookmarque, Croydon, Surrey

For Suzanne,
with whom I shall spend the rest of my life
enjoying birds

For those who practise it bird-watching is not only a sport and a science, but also something near a religion, and after all its externals have been inventoried the essence stays incommunicable.

The Art of Birdwatching, Max Nicholson (1931)

CONTENTS

PREFACE

The observation of birds may be a superstition, a tradition,
an art, a science, a pleasure, a hobby, or a bore; this depends
entirely on the nature of the observer.

Watching Birds, James Fisher (1941)

THE LITTLE VILLAGE of Egleton in Rutland, in the very
heart of England, is for most of the year a calm and
tranquil place. But for three hectic days every August,
birders arrive in their thousands for the annual British
Birdwatching Fair. The 'Birdfair', as it is usually known,
occupies the middle ground between the Chelsea Flower Show
and the Glastonbury Music Festival – at least in terms of the age,
social class and background of its participants. And while it may
not be able to boast the cachet of the former, or the coolness of
the latter, it is still the unmissable event for birders; not just from
Britain, but from all over the world.

A whistle-stop tour of the Birdfair reveals much about the
nature of birdwatching at the beginning of the twenty-first century. People come here to meet old friends and make new ones,
attend lectures and sign up for foreign birding tours, or simply to
sit outside the beer tent and soak up the sunshine. From time to
time, if they get tired of the crowds, they can even wander
around the nearby nature reserve to watch the birds.

Many visitors head straight for the optics marquee, where
the latest top-of-the-range binoculars and telescopes from
companies like Leica, Zeiss and Swarovski are on display, offering stunningly bright vision and enormous magnification – and
little change from £1000. Others browse the second-hand book-
stalls, handling a fabulously rare copy of the New Naturalist
volume on British Warblers with a reverence normally shown to
the Dead Sea Scrolls. Faced with such an array of bird-related
paraphernalia, some simply rush from one stand to another to

end up with an armful of carrier bags and a large hole in their bank account.

However, all this commercial activity is only a small part of the Birdfair. There are well-known characters such as Bill Oddie, signing an autograph after showing clips from his latest TV series; and first-time visitors like Graham Mee and his son James from Essex, who only took up birding a couple of years ago – after watching an earlier series of *Birding with Bill Oddie*. There are huge white marquees, like something out of a society wedding. There are quizzes and slideshows, book signings and barbecues, everything imaginable related to birds and birding – even a Christian service and a five-a-side football tournament.

Despite its very English surroundings, the Birdfair is also a truly global event. Visit marquee number three, and you will see the unmistakable bearded figure of Marek Borkowski from Polish Wildlife Tours, one of the great pioneers of conservation and birding in eastern Europe. Marek, his wife Hania and his four young children have driven halfway across Europe in an ex-Russian army van to be here. Over the next three days they will shake hands with, and serve coffee and traditional Polish cake to, several hundred people, many of whom will be persuaded to visit their picturesque wooden house in the Biebrza Marshes, where they can watch White-backed Woodpeckers and nesting Hoopoes while enjoying even more Polish hospitality.

Or drop into marquee number four, and meet Gerard Ramsawak, from the Pax Guest House in Trinidad – a man whose whirring energy invites comparison with the hummingbirds that feed from the balcony of his famous establishment. Before you can even say hello, his wife Oda has handed you a glass of rum punch and a brochure outlining the delights of birding there. And in marquee number two, you can enjoy the unusual, and heart-warming, sight of the representatives from Israel and Palestine greeting each other with open arms. Wander around the rest of the fair, and in time you will come across the African Bird Club, the British Bulgarian Friendship Society, Fantastico Sur from Chile, Kiwi Wildlife Tours from New Zealand – people from every corner of the world, here to share their love and enthusiasm for birds. And if your birding horizons do not stretch quite that far, there is the domestic contingent: ranging from *British Birds* magazine to the Wildfowl and Wetlands Trust, and a great deal more besides.

For many visitors, the highlight of the fair is a visit to the art marquee. Here, every possible way of depicting a bird is on display: from an almost photographic representation of every fine plumage detail, to an impressionistic sketch capturing the indefinable quality of a flock of birds in flight. People stand and stare in awe.

They are not the first to do so: more than ten thousand years before the birth of Christ, our distant ancestors would have looked at the very first images of birds, and perhaps felt the same sense of wonder. People have been watching birds, in one way or another, since the first prehistoric hunter depicted his quarry on the walls of a cave. But for the vast span of human history, people were not 'birdwatching' in any modern sense. Going out to look for birds, with the primary purpose of watching them for pleasure, is a very recent phenomenon; and today's birder, as he or she is now known, is a typical product of modern Western society. The combination of factors that enables us to 'go birdwatching' – the capacity to appreciate nature for its own sake, and the financial means and leisure time to do so – has only been present for the past hundred years or so.

In August 2001, at the same time as that year's Birdfair was attracting thousands of devotees, reports appeared in the tabloid press claiming that teen pop idol Britney Spears was a birdwatcher. This turned out to be a typical 'silly season' story, based on the fact that she had pictures of birds on the walls of her Los Angeles home. It did seem too good to be true: after all, how could the coolest pop sensation possibly have anything to do with a pastime as monumentally untrendy as watching birds?

For birding has also always been an object of derision, especially in the popular media. Dismissed by one commentator as 'organic trainspotting', it has generally been treated with a mixture of affectionate ridicule and barely concealed disdain. The 1970 film *Carry on up the Jungle*, which featured Frankie Howerd

3

and Sid James as members of a 'bird-fancying expedition' captured by cannibals, was typical in its portrayal of birdwatchers as comical buffoons. Thirty years later, the image had hardly improved. In the very last episode of the ITV series *Inspector Morse*, the lugubrious Morse revealed to his long-suffering side-kick Lewis an interest in birds. Lewis's amazement at Morse's new hobby said it all: birding was portrayed as something people did when they had no other purpose left in life; a symbol of the detective's inevitable decline into old age.

Journalists love having a go at birdwatchers, too. Bernard Levin once described them as 'the incredible in pursuit of the inedible', while on Radio Four's *Midweek*, presenter Libby Purves could hardly conceal her amazement when faced with a mature adult who had joined his father on a birding holiday abroad: 'This is a major form of coming-out – saying, "I'm a grown man and I went on a birdwatching holiday with my father". It's wonderfully uncool, isn't it? It's so uncool it's cool!'

So despite the massive rise in the numbers of people taking up the pastime in recent years, birders are still regarded as either comical or eccentric. Yet as James Fisher pointed out at the start of World War II, all sorts of people watch birds:

> Among those I know of are a Prime Minister, a President, three Secretaries of State, a charwoman, two policemen, two Kings, two Royal Dukes, one Prince, one Princess, a Communist, seven Labour, one Liberal, and six Conservative Members of Parliament, several farm-labourers earning ninety shillings a week, a rich man who earns two or three times that amount in every hour of the day, at least forty-six schoolmasters, an engine-driver, a postman, and an upholsterer.

An up-to-date list, which I have compiled more or less at random, is equally diverse: a royal duke, three pop stars, a post-woman, a landscape gardener, several university lecturers, at least three former Conservative cabinet ministers, a trades union leader, four comedians (three living, one dead), a quiz show host, ITV and BBC weather forecasters, a fashion photographer, a nurse, a grandmother, two ten-year-old boys, the news editor of the *Daily Star*, an Australian musician, and a retired worker from Ford's of Dagenham.

So what have Prince Philip and Jarvis Cocker, Ken Clarke and Magnus Magnusson, David Bailey and Billy Fury, or Vic Reeves and Eric Morecambe, got in common? And what about the thousands of people at the Birdfair, or the millions who regularly tune in to watch Bill Oddie's television programmes on birds? They certainly don't share the same social class, income, political affiliation, sense of humour or age, that is for sure.

Perhaps they simply get pleasure from watching birds, like the singer Van Morrison, who sang: 'Spent all day bird-watchin' and the *craic* was good!' For while birdwatching may not be in quite the same league as gardening, cookery or DIY, it is still one of our most popular leisure activities. And whatever the cynics might think, birds do matter to most people: indeed, the ups and downs of bird populations have recently been included in the government's quality of life index.

The recognition that watching birds might increase our enjoyment and satisfaction is belated but welcome, and at last has begun to penetrate the normally cynical media. A *Guardian* newspaper feature entitled '100 ways you can make the world a better place', included 'Bring birds into your life; get a bird-table'. Birding has even been featured on Radio Four's *Thought for the Day*, where an Anglican bishop declared that our spiritual needs can be met by listening to birdsong.

So although the media has been slow to respond to a change in attitudes towards birding, this change is undoubtedly occurring. Perhaps, in the next decade or so, an interest in watching birds will be considered no more eccentric, sad or comical than a passion for listening to music, watching football, or gardening.

Although this book is mainly about the growth and development of birding in Britain, I have included a number of examples from elsewhere: particularly North America, where the pastime has often followed a similar path to that on this side of the Atlantic. Inevitably I have had to be highly selective: this cannot, and does not, attempt to be a definitive history of birding. Instead I have chosen specific examples and key people to tell the story and illustrate the wider picture. Ultimately I have tried to seek out the answer to an apparently simple question: *why* do we watch birds?

It is odd, perhaps, that no-one has thought to ask this question before. After all, birds come into our lives from our earliest years: through nursery rhymes, feeding ducks in the local park, and singing about 'two turtle doves and a partridge in a pear tree'. We read Puffin and Penguin books, watch Donald Duck cartoons, and sleep under eiderdowns. We give each other Easter eggs and fly kites – yes, the toy was named after the bird, not the other way around! As we grow up, we are exposed to an array of images in which birds are used to promote products as diverse as Swan Vestas matches, The Famous Grouse whisky and Kestrel lager. Our very language is full of phrases derived from the appearance or behaviour of birds: 'up with the lark', 'bald as a coot', and 'out for a duck'. Since they are such an integral part of our lives, perhaps we should be asking ourselves a different question: not 'why do people watch birds?', but 'why doesn't *everyone* watch birds?'

At this point, I must reveal my own hand: I too am a birder. Indeed, I cannot recall a time when I was not aware of birds, and fascinated by their presence. Like all the people featured in this book (and many of those who will read it), I too have got up at dawn, cycled through the wind and rain, been appallingly sea-sick, hitched lifts, gone twitching, trudged around my local patch, and travelled the world – all in pursuit of what Irish birder Anthony McGeehan described as 'a lifetime's consuming passion'. In recent years I have even managed, like some of the people featured in Chapter 15, to turn my hobby into my profession – I now earn a living by making television programmes and writing books about birds. Not that birds and birding are my whole life: I have a loving family, a rewarding job and many other interests. But they are always there, wherever I go, to remind me that there is another world which, although it sometimes intersects with ours, we can never truly understand. As Ted Hughes wrote, of the miraculous annual return of the Swifts:

> They've made it again,
> Which means the globe's still working . . .

I, and birders everywhere, watch birds for many different reasons: as a challenge, as a form of collecting, because it gets us out into the open air, because of their aesthetic appeal, to learn more about them, or simply for fun – or indeed for all these reasons put together. Ultimately, perhaps, our fascination derives from that which sets birds apart from the rest of creation. In the words of the American writer Donald Culross Peattie:

> Man feels himself an infinity above those creatures who stand, zoologically, only one step below him, but every human being looks up to the birds. They seem to us like emissaries of another world which exists about us and above us, but into which, earth-bound, we cannot penetrate.

Today, at the start of the twenty-first century, birding is one of the world's most popular pastimes, as the many visitors to the British Birdwatching Fair bear witness. It is pursued by millions of people, of different ages, cultures and social backgrounds, in every country on earth. And it brings an incalculable degree of pleasure and satisfaction to those who do it. How this extraordinary state of affairs came about is the subject of this book.

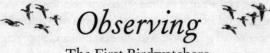

CHAPTER ONE

Observing

The First Birdwatchers

Man has always been aware of birds, and they still supply
material and inspiration for recreational, intellectual, and
scientific pursuits, as well as fresh eggs for breakfast.
Ornithology: an Introduction, Austin L. Rand (1974)

FOR 'the man who started us all birdwatching', in James
Fisher's memorable phrase, we must go back to the middle
of the eighteenth century. Here, in a rural English parish,
we find an individual who, despite spending virtually his whole life
tied to a single place, produced what is undoubtedly the best
known natural history book ever written. The place was the
Hampshire village of Selborne. The author was the Reverend
Gilbert White.

To regard Gilbert White as the first birdwatcher requires
some explanation. After all, human beings had no doubt been
aware of birds since prehistoric times, but if they had taken any
further interest in them, it was for three main reasons. For our
ancestors, birds could be objects of religious worship or superstition, used for ornament or decoration, or simply represent a good
square meal. So although there are many references to birds in
ancient literature and culture, as we shall see in the next chapter,
we must make a clear distinction between simply 'watching birds'
and 'birdwatching' in its modern sense. The latter – the subject of
this book – is fundamentally a recreational activity, undertaken
primarily for pleasure.

During the hundred years from the middle of the eighteenth
to the middle of the nineteenth centuries, four individuals represent this developing pastime of looking at birds in a new and
different way from before. These four men – Gilbert White, and

his three followers Thomas Bewick, George Montagu and John Clare – lived at the point in time when our relationship with birds finally began to shift from a one-way process of exploitation, into a new, more equal relationship of observation and appreciation. In part they reflected changes going on in society; in part they helped to shape those changes. Most importantly of all, White, Bewick, Montagu and Clare found a connection between human beings and nature at the very moment when a dislocation between man and the natural world was beginning to occur.

In the two hundred years since, the scientific study, aesthetic appreciation, and the various sporting and social aspects of looking at birds gradually developed into a more structured activity pursued by millions of people – the pastime we know today as birdwatching or birding.

L IFE FOR the vicar of a quiet country parish in the eighteenth century was not quite the pastoral idyll we might imagine, but it nevertheless had its attractions. For an educated young man, with a passionate interest in the natural world, it provided plenty of time to pursue the objects of his study. There was only one major drawback: it tied the incumbent to a single locality.

Born in 1720, Gilbert White lived and worked for virtually the whole of his life in the village of Selborne, and rarely travelled outside the parish borders for any length of time. But while other men might have become frustrated by this geographical limitation, White turned it to his advantage, by keeping meticulous records of his observations of local wildlife, especially birds.

At the time, an interest in wildlife was considered an unusual, even bizarre, pastime. Indeed, the majority of people simply would not have been able to watch birds on a regular basis. For a start, there were the demands of daily work, which took place from dawn to dusk, and left manual labourers too exhausted to contemplate any other activity – let alone something as apparently unproductive as looking at wildlife. But even for the leisured classes, there were barriers. The countryside was a very dangerous place, as social historian G. E. Mingay has observed: 'Up to the latter part of the nineteenth century the countryside was often far from being the haven of uninterrupted peace and pleasure that is sometimes supposed. True, there were village feasts and celebrations . . . But there were also highwaymen, footpads, housebreakers and armed gangs . . .'

Another restraining factor was other people's attitudes. Wandering aimlessly about the countryside would have been regarded as very peculiar, and could lead to hostility, violence or even arrest. Travel was also dangerous, expensive and uncomfortable, with most journeys taking place by coach or horseback on unmetalled roads, and taking several days or even weeks to complete.

The one person who was allowed to roam unmolested around the village and its surrounding countryside was the local vicar. Indeed, he was expected to do so, as it enabled him to enjoy the physical and spiritual benefits of being out and about, while at the same time allowing him to engage with his parishioners.

As a result, according to Patrick Armstrong, author of *The English Parson-Naturalist*, the Christian church actively encouraged an interest in natural history, as the later hymn 'All Things Bright and Beautiful' shows. Armstrong notes that many country parsons 'saw a delight in nature as an expression of Christian piety', with White being the archetypal example.

But inevitably, White's choice of vocation led to feelings of isolation and loneliness. In later life, he lamented the lack of a companion with whom to share his thoughts and theories: 'It has long been my misfortune never to have had any neighbours whose studies have led them towards the pursuit of natural knowledge; so that, for want of a companion to quicken my industry and sharpen my attention, I have made but slender progress . . .'

If White were not such a straightforward and honest man we might suspect him of being ironic. For if he had actually met such a person, and been able to discuss his observations of wildlife face to face, we might never have heard of him. That is because his most celebrated work, *The Natural History and Antiquities of Selborne*, is a collection of letters written in journal form to two distinguished scientific colleagues, both based in London: Thomas Pennant and Daines Barrington. It was finally published in 1789, just four years before White's death.

As *Selborne* reveals, White was a pioneering ornithologist, responsible for many important discoveries, including the first firm identification of the three species of leaf-warbler found in Britain. But more importantly, he was also a birdwatcher in the modern sense. He took immense pleasure simply from being out in the field looking at birds, as this observation shows: 'Black-caps mostly haunt orchards and gardens; while they warble their throats are wonderfully distended.'

He was, even by modern standards, a meticulous observer, whose writings (apart from the odd example of archaic language) could come from any modern book on bird behaviour: 'The yellowest bird is considerably the largest, and has its quill-feathers and secondary feathers tipped with white . . . it haunts only the tops of trees, and makes a sibilous grasshopper-like noise, now and then, at short intervals, shivering with his wings when it sings . . . '

Even today it would be hard to find such a clear, concise and evocative description of a Wood Warbler. Such careful and accurate observation of a living bird is way ahead of its time, especially considering the obsession with collecting specimens which was to dominate ornithology for the following century or more.

For the modern reader, the secret of White's appeal is that he looks at the natural world in the same way as we do. He saw nature as something to enjoy, which could provide recreation and renewal, rather than as a resource to be exploited for man's benefit. It is easy to take this for granted, but White is arguably the first person we know of who really did so, as Raymond Williams observed:

> Anyone who lives in the country can experience at times, or seem to experience, an unmediated nature: in a direct and physical awareness of trees, birds, the moving shapes of land. What is new in Gilbert White, or at least feels new in its sustained intensity, is a development from this; a single and dedicated observation . . . It is a new kind of record, not only of the facts, but of a way of looking at the facts: a way of looking that will come to be called scientific.

White's preoccupation with his 'local patch', and the seasonal and annual changes in the birdlife he observed there, also strike a chord with modern birders. Like Jane Austen, who lived in a country parsonage just six miles from Selborne, White understood that a specific example rooted in a single location and time can illuminate a greater truth than a more general observation:

> For many years past I have observed that towards Christmas vast flocks of chaffinches have appeared in the fields; many more, I used to think, than could be hatched in one neighbourhood. But, when I came to observe them all narrowly, I was amazed to find that they seemed to me to be almost all hens. I communicated my suspicions to some intelligent neighbours, who, after taking pains about the matter, declared that they also thought them all mostly females; at least fifty to one. This extraordinary occurrence brought to my mind the remark of Linnaeus; that 'before winter all their hen chaffinches migrate through Holland into Italy.' Now I want to know, from some curious person in the north, whether there are any large flocks of these finches with them in the winter, and of what sex they mostly consist? For, from such intelligence, one might be able to judge whether our female flocks migrate from the other end of the island, or whether they have come over to us from the continent.

This combination of local observation, discussion with fellow enthusiasts, and the setting up of a new line of enquiry is quite different from anything that went before. It establishes Gilbert White's credentials as the father of modern birdwatching.

It also goes some way to explain why, more than two hundred years after it was first published, *The Natural History of Selborne* is still widely read. But it does not fully account for the book's phenomenal popularity. Close observation on its own, however fascinating, is not enough – White's crucial insight was that he realized that watching wildlife can also have an aesthetic and spiritual dimension. Once again, this was utterly new: Gilbert White was the first person to combine accurate observation with a genuine love of birds for their own sake, a quality which ornithologist James Fisher suggested was the reason for the book's success:

This humane, tolerant, kindly and modest man must have delved into the nature of things with no other motive but that of inquiry or, as he probably thought of it, worship. There are many now who, in so far as they possess such motives, owe them to him. In White the nature-investigator and the nature-lover were inextricably confused; and many believe that the pursuit of truth in natural history will continue to be successful only so long as this benign confusion is preserved.

Gilbert White died four years after the publication of *The Natural History of Selborne*, at the age of seventy-two. More than two hundred years later, the book remains one of the best-loved classics of nature-writing. At the most fundamental level, White's continued fame rests on a simple truth: that even today we can identify with his desire to spend time engaging with the natural world, and gain spiritual refreshment from doing so. 'Selborne,' as social historian David Allen says, 'is the secret, private parish inside each one of us.'

ALTHOUGH it would eventually become one of the best-selling books of all time, *The Natural History of Selborne* was hardly a runaway success. Indeed, it did not really begin to sell in large numbers until the 1820s, thirty years after White's death.

In the meantime, in 1797, the first truly popular work on British birds had appeared. Thomas Bewick's *A History of British Birds* is often compared to *Selborne*, and indeed has been described as 'the other work . . . with a comparable claim on the hearts of bird-watchers.' It is certainly true that Bewick did more to make the general reading public interested in birds than anyone before him.

Bewick's work appeared in two volumes, arranged in systematic order: the first devoted to 'Land Birds' and the second, which appeared in 1804, to 'Water Birds'. Like many artists of his day, he used wood engraving to produce black-and-white illustrations. However, Bewick had pioneered a new engraving technique, which allowed him to work on material of a finer grain than before. This created much finer and more delicate illustrations, giving the illusion of light and shade – perfect for capturing the variations and subtleties of plumage.

Born in rural Northumberland in 1753, the eldest of eight children, Thomas Bewick was an unlikely candidate for subsequent ornithological fame. Indeed, as Fisher noted: 'Bewick was not a very good observer of natural history or a very original thinker on the subject. But when he died in 1828 . . . he had done for nature art what Burns did for poetry – put a little honest humanity in it.'

The ornithological bibliographers Mullens and Swann went further, describing Bewick as 'in the strict sense of the word, hardly an ornithologist at all'. But it was his skill as an artist which ensured that his *History of British Birds* would become a publishing phenomenon, running to no fewer than six editions in Bewick's lifetime, and many more after his death.

As a child, Bewick drew and sketched everything that moved: using pen and ink, and when ink was not available, juice from blackberries he had collected from the hedgerows around his home. After a seven-year apprenticeship in Newcastle upon Tyne, he became a printer and engraver, and also gained a reputation as a political radical. This combination of idealism and entrepreneurial skills found an appropriate outlet in his publishing ventures, which combined educational instruction with the opportunity to make a handsome profit. Having already produced a work on the world's quadrupeds, which had become a best-seller, he then turned his attention to a more familiar subject: Britain's native birds.

Although nowadays Bewick's engravings appear rather crude and old-fashioned, at the time they served a vital purpose: helping to foster an interest in birds amongst a broad cross-section of society. His books had a considerable influence on subsequent artists, his fame even crossing the Atlantic Ocean to North America. In 1827, a year before his death at the age of seventy-five, Bewick was visited by the American bird artist John James Audubon, who described him as 'a most agreeable, kind and benevolent friend'.

Later Audubon named a North American species, Bewick's Wren, in memory of the Englishman, while a familiar winter visitor to Britain, Bewick's Swan, also bears his name.

ALTHOUGH Thomas Bewick did more than anyone before him to make people aware of birds, he was not himself a bird-watcher. The next of White's 'disciples', George Montagu, undoubtedly was.

Today, if we are aware of Montagu at all, it is because Britain's rarest breeding bird of prey, Montagu's Harrier, is named after him. Yet he had a profound influence on the development of birdwatching – not least because he named and catalogued Britain's birds in his *Ornithological Dictionary*. First published in 1802, and extensively revised and republished by James Rennie in 1831 (sixteen years after Montagu's death), this had a profound influence on subsequent generations of ornithologists and collectors. These included the nineteenth-century American Elliott Coues, who described it as: 'One of the most notable of treatises on British Birds . . . which has held its place at a thousand elbows for three-quarters of a century.'

Born in 1753, the same year as Thomas Bewick, Montagu led a chequered but fascinating life. This saw him enlisting in the army just before his seventeenth birthday, rising steadily through the ranks to become a lieutenant, marrying at the age of twenty, and later serving in the American War of Independence. Afterwards, he returned to his native county of Wiltshire, where he became lieutenant-colonel of the county militia, and sired four sons and two daughters.

So far, so good – indeed a predictable attainment of respectability and success for a man of his background and class. But despite his achievements, Montagu was frustrated and unhappy in both his marriage and his career. In June 1789, around the time of his thirty-sixth birthday, he wrote to Gilbert White, who by this time had earned a reputation as one of Britain's most respected naturalists. In his letter, Montagu confessed that he had: 'delighted being an ornithologist from infancy, and, was I not bound by conjugal attachment, I should like to ride my hobby into distant parts . . . '

Montagu's frustration simmered for a decade, eventually coming to a head in a spectacular and scandalous manner. In 1797, he had embarked on an affair with Mrs Eliza Dorville, the wife of a London merchant. Two years later, he was court-martialled for allegedly conspiring against three of his fellow officers, and forced to resign his commission. To cap matters, he then became embroiled in litigation with his eldest son, which eventually led to the loss of the family fortune.

The army's loss was now ornithology's gain. Montagu and his mistress decamped to a cottage just outside the village of Kingsbridge in Devon, where he lived for the remainder of his life, finally able to devote himself to his obsession with birds. Much misunderstood by contemporaries, one of whom described him as 'a man of bad temper', he has in more recent times come to be acknowledged as one of our most influential and pioneering ornithologists. His rehabilitation was championed by James Fisher, who praised him as: 'That energetic army officer and field worker (who) in his efficient way . . . swept up almost the last of our birds that were unknown because unrecognised.'

In the fashion of the day, this mainly involved 'collecting' specimens (a euphemism for shooting them). Despite his apparently cavalier attitude to social convention, Montagu was in fact a very methodical man, and he now set about compiling an up-to-date and accurate account of the status of Britain's birds. He began by checking unusual or controversial specimens collected by others, often discovering that an apparently 'new' species was in fact simply a familiar bird in an unfamiliar plumage. So he demonstrated that the 'Greenwich Sandpiper' was simply a Ruff in non-breeding plumage, and that the 'Ash-coloured Sandpiper' was the same as the Knot. In doing so he was effectively creating the first proper 'British list' of acceptable species.

But Montagu went one step further than simply disproving the claims of others. He described and classified several hitherto unrecognized species of British bird. Among the flocks of

Yellowhammers in the fields and hedgerows around his south Devon home, he noticed certain birds which showed characteristic plumage differences, including a black throat and face mask, and olive instead of reddish-brown on the breast. These, he correctly deduced, were Cirl Buntings – hitherto thought only to be found in mainland Europe. Two centuries after he discovered it there, the Cirl Bunting's British stronghold is still around his adopted home.

His other major discovery was the bird which now bears his name. Until then, there had been much confusion regarding the Hen Harrier and the raptor then known as the 'Ash-coloured Falcon', whose males and females look very different from each other, but resemble their counterpart in the other species. When a male harrier was shot near his home in August 1803, Montagu examined the specimen and correctly pronounced that it was indeed a separate species from the Hen Harrier: being smaller and slimmer, with much narrower wings and several clear plumage differences. An extract from the description reveals his obsession with detail:

> Bill black, the base and cere greenish: irides and orbits bright yellow: crown of the head, cheeks, throat, under part of the neck, back and scapulars cinereous-brown . . . the eight prime quills are dusky-black . . . the first is very short, the third by far the longest: secondary quills cinereous-brown above, pale beneath, with three remarkable dusky bars, traversely placed, and nearly in parallel lines, each half an inch in breadth . . . legs orange-yellow, rather long and slender: claws small, and black.

This obsession with feather-by-feather detail is not all that far from the 'New Approach to Identification' proposed by Killian Mullarney and Peter Grant in the 1980s – with one important difference: Montagu was able to make his observations in the hand, rather than on a living bird in the field.

Soon afterwards, two continental ornithologists gave the species the name 'Le Busard Montagu', and in 1836 William MacGillivray used the term Montagu's Harrier for the first time, thus ensuring his immortality. Sadly, the rest of George Montagu's life was beset by tragedy. Three of his four sons were killed in the wars with France, and he himself died prematurely in 1815, when he trod on a rusty nail and contracted tetanus. By the time of his death, the number of bird species known to occur regularly in Britain had risen from about 215 in the mid-eighteenth century, to more than 240 – leaving only a handful of regular visitors still to be described.

To the modern birder, possessed of the latest field guide with its many hundreds of species, together with full-colour plates and distribution maps, Montagu's achievements may seem a mere footnote in ornithological history. But without him, and his *Ornithological Dictionary*, there is no doubt that the task of identifying and classifying Britain's breeding birds would have taken much longer. This was of vital importance to the rapid development of birdwatching: after all, it is not possible to watch birds, in the modern sense, if you do not know which species you are looking at.

By clearing up so many misapprehensions and errors, Montagu made it possible for those who came after him – notably the two great Victorian ornithologists William MacGillivray and William Yarrell – to build on his work with their seminal avifaunas of the 1830s and 1840s. These in turn laid the foundations for Harry Witherby's *Handbook of British Birds* (1938–1941) – a work which had a profound influence on many of today's older generation of birdwatchers, and on the development of birdwatching as a popular pastime.

O N A FINE spring evening, around the time Montagu died, a young farm labourer was walking in the fields around Shacklewell, on the outskirts of London. Passing a small spinney, he noticed a well-dressed lady and gentleman listening attentively to the song of a bird, and heard them 'lavishing praises on the beautiful song of the nightingale . . . which happened to be a thrush'.

The man so familiar with the difference between the song of a

Nightingale and the song of a thrush – and indeed with the songs and habits of all common birds – was the poet and writer John Clare. 'They listened and repeated their praise with heart felt satisfaction,' Clare recollected wryly in a letter to his publisher, 'while the bird seemed to know the grand distinction that its song had gained for it and strive exultingly to keep up the deception by attempting a varied and more louder song.'

This amusing tale has a deeper significance. Fifty years earlier, when Gilbert White was listening to the Song Thrushes of Selborne, it would have been highly unlikely for a well-dressed young couple to be out for an evening walk in the countryside, and enjoying the sound of birdsong. But by the early nineteenth century the idea of enjoying the sights and sounds of the rural landscape – indeed, the very notion of the 'countryside' – had, for the first time, entered British life; to such an extent that, as Clare observed, the lady was blithely unaware that her long dress was becoming soaked with the evening dew.

Once known rather patronisingly as the 'peasant poet', Clare's reputation has now been fully restored, and today he is regarded as one of our major writers. As well as being 'the finest poet of Britain's minor naturalists', he was also 'the finest naturalist of Britain's major poets': a first-rate birdwatcher and ornithologist, who contributed a vast amount to our knowledge of the distribution of birds at this period of time.

He is known to have observed at least 119, and possibly as many as 145 different species of bird in his local area – an outstanding achievement even by comparison with modern standards, and all the more so when we consider that he watched them without binoculars or a telescope. His sightings included several species which are now either very rare or no longer found in the area, such as the Bittern, Corncrake and Osprey, and one observation which until recently remained a mystery:

> There has been a strange bird seen about us . . . one that has not found a place in books yet was shot three or four Winters ago by a labourer . . . it was about the size of a large goose but more slender in the body . . . its wings was very long and its neck about

the length of a goose . . . its eye was large and black and its bill black and hookd exactly like an Hawk the upper mandible hooked over the other as if for tearing its food . . . its legs were red striped with black and its feet webbed with odd large claws . . . its general colour was white with light wavings of brown all over like the breast of the Heron.

Clare's reference to a hooked beak led most subsequent observers to assume this must be a bird of prey. In fact the webbed feet are more relevant: for this is an excellent description of a juvenile Greater Flamingo. It almost certainly refers to a wild bird from mainland Europe, giving Clare a good claim to the first record of this species for Britain.

Clare may not have as much direct influence on the development of birdwatching as White, Bewick or Montagu, but nevertheless he is a crucial figure in this story. For in his ability to make such accurate and detailed observations, he resembles the modern birdwatcher more closely than any other man of his time.

John Clare was born on 13 July 1793, just seventeen days after Gilbert White was laid to rest in Selborne's parish churchyard. His birthplace, and home for the first three decades of his life, was Helpston, to the north-west of Peterborough, which he described as 'a gloomy village . . . on the brink of the fens'. A precocious but lonely child, he took himself off on solitary nature rambles, frequently drawing accusations of lunacy from his fellow villagers. His ability to read and write also set him apart from the rural labouring classes among whom he lived, so it is hardly surprising that he preferred to find solace in the wildlife and landscape around him.

Like Gilbert White, Clare had no proper optical aids, so his observation all had to be done with the naked eye. This explains the emphasis in his writings on the behaviour of birds, rather than the modern obsession with fine plumage details, which he rarely mentions. In both his poetry and prose, he generally concentrates on the bird's actions rather than its appearance.

As well as writing his much-loved poems about birds, Clare also kept extensive notes and diaries of his observations, written in his characteristic punctuation-free style. These reveal an acute eye for detail which allows us to picture what he saw in forensic clarity, combined with some delightful bits of folklore, as in this description of the Long-tailed Tit:

> The long taild Titmouse calld with us Bumbarrel and in Yorkshire pudding bags and feather pokes is an early builder of its nest . . . it makes a very beautiful one in the shape of an egg leaving an entrance on one side like the wren . . . it forms the outside of grey moss and lines it with great quantitys of feathers . . . it lays a great number of very small eggs.

Clare goes on to muse on the bigger picture – what we might call ecology – and in doing so makes a passing reference to the widespread childhood practice of catching and killing small birds:

> One might think that by the number of eggs these birds lay they woud multiply very vast but on the contrary they are not half so plentiful as other birds for the small hawks make a terrible havock among their young broods as soon as they leave the nests – the young ones that escape the school boy and hawk live in familys and never forsake their parents till the next spring – they may be seen to the number of 20 in winter picking something off the twigs of the white thorn in the hedgerows.

As this passage reveals, Clare knew nature as a network of living animals and plants, not simply as a collection of skins and specimens in a museum: 'He did not shoot, stuff, dissect or arrange'.

Unlike his contemporaries, Clare wrote poems about real birds, not idealized poetic ones. This led to some friction between Clare and Keats, with the latter complaining that in Clare's poetry: 'the description too much prevailed over the sentiment . . .' Clare's response was curt and to the point: [Keats] 'often described nature as she appeared to his fancies and not as he would have described her had he witnessed the things he describes . . .'

A comparison between two poems by these respective authors, both about the Nightingale, confirms the view that while Keats may have been the finer poet, Clare was definitely the more acute observer of nature. Keats's *Ode to a Nightingale* is more about the author than the bird, which barely makes an appearance until the very final verse, and even then is perhaps merely a figment of the poet's fevered imagination:

> Adieu! Adieu! Thy plaintive anthem fades
> Past the near meadows, over the still stream,
> Up the hill-side; and now 'tis buried deep
> In the next valley glades:
> Was it a vision, or a waking dream?
> Fled is that music – Do I wake or sleep?

In the face of such magical language and profound emotion it may seem churlish to point out that Nightingales never sing in flight, so that Keats's description of the bird flying away from him could not be based on a real observation. In contrast, although still expressed in poetical language, Clare's sonnet *The Nightingale's Nest* is clearly rooted in actual experience:

> I hear the Nightingale,
> That from the little blackthorn spinny steals,
> To the old hazel hedge that skirts the vale,
> And still unseen, sings sweet – the ploughman feels
> The thrilling music, as he goes along,
> And imitates and listens – while the fields
> Lose all their paths in dusk, to lead him wrong
> Still sings the Nightingale her sweet melodious song.

Despite mistakenly crediting the female of the species with the power of song, Clare nevertheless manages to re-create the atmosphere of a specific experience in a particular location. As the literary critic John Barrell observed, Clare does not so much describe the landscape, or even each place, as evoke 'what it is like to be in each place'.

Ironically, Clare's life was ultimately devastated by his very attachment to this 'sense of place'. During the first few decades of the nineteenth century the process of enclosure altered the English countryside beyond imagination. Trees were cut down, fields divided and new hedgerows planted; and as a result the whole shape of the landscape around Clare's home radically changed. The familiar landmarks which kept him 'grounded', to borrow a term from modern psychology, were lost forever. He lamented the loss in one of his most famous poems, *The Flitting*, written in 1832:

> I've left my own old home of homes
> Green fields and every pleasant place
> The summer like a stranger comes
> I pause and hardly know her face . . .
>
> I sit me in my corner chair
> That seems to feel itself from home
> I hear bird music here and there
> From awthorn hedge and orchard come
> I hear but all is strange and new . . .

After writing this lament for a lost world, Clare descended into mental illness, and spent much of the remainder of his life confined in various asylums until his death in 1864. Neglected and virtually ignored by the literary establishment, he was eventually rehabilitated in the second half of the twentieth century when, thanks to his growing fame and reputation, his abilities as a close observer of birds and other wildlife were finally appreciated.

BEFORE we follow the events which led from such early pioneers as Clare, White, Bewick and Montagu to the world of birding we know today, we must now backtrack in time. Chapters 2 and 3 examine how birds were regarded during the period from prehistoric times to the end of the eighteenth century – a period when people may have been 'watching birds', but were not yet truly 'birdwatching'.

CHAPTER TWO

Believing

The Prehistoric World to the Middle Ages

And God said, 'Let the waters bring forth abundantly the
moving creature that hath life, and fowl that may fly above the
earth in the open firmament of heaven'.

Genesis (Chapter 1, verse 20)

TWELVE THOUSAND years ago, in a place known today as
Cresswell Crags in Derbyshire, a man engraved two
figures onto the wall of a cave. One was some kind of
water bird – possibly a crane or a swan; the other was a bird of
prey. When they were first discovered, in 2001, these images were
covered with graffiti left by modern visitors to the site. But when
this was removed their true significance became clear – as the only
surviving example of prehistoric cave paintings in Britain.

It has long been known that our ancestors depicted the birds
and mammals they hunted in art. At one cave, at Gargas in the
French Pyrenees, there is a picture of a tall, long-legged bird
(presumably a crane or heron), which dates from about 18,000
years ago, and is probably the oldest image of a bird in existence.
On the walls of a cave at Tajo Segura, in southern Spain, a later
civilization (roughly 6000–4000 BC) depicted up to a dozen recog-
nizable species, including Great Bustard, flamingo and White
Stork, which are accurate and clear enough to be identifiable today.

But why did the cave painters do their work in the first place?
The generally accepted theory is that the paintings were used as part
of a ritual between members of the tribe; and that when youngsters
reached adolescence they would be led into the caves to look at the
images, in order to strengthen the bonds between them.

The cultural historian Jacob Bronowski saw early man's urge
to depict the creatures around him as having an even greater

significance: a clear indication that for the first time, humankind was able to imagine the future:

> For us, the cave paintings re-create the hunter's way of life as a glimpse of history; we look through them into the past. But for the hunter, I suggest, they were a peep-hole into the future; he looked ahead.

This suggests that as well as a ritual use, the paintings had a more practical one. After all, to hunt an animal you first have to be able to recognize and identify it. While it would be going too far to compare these crude but arresting images to those in a modern field guide, they do show that from a very early stage in their development, human beings had the urge to identify and categorize the world around them.

Between 10,000 and 8000 years ago, watching birds was also of practical use to early Neolithic farmers, who observed the comings and goings of seasonal migrants so they could judge the best time to plant and harvest their precious crops. Some of this knowledge has survived until the present day, in the form of weather lore relating to bird behaviour. These include short-term forecasts:

> 'Swallows high, staying dry;
> Swallows low, wet will blow.'

As well as more long-term ones:

> 'If ducks do slide at Hallowtide, at Christmas they will swim;
> If ducks do swim at Hallowtide, at Christmas they will slide.'

The continued survival of such rhymes and proverbs shows both the power of folk memory, and the wider cultural importance of birds.

THE FIRST civilisations to build permanent structures incorporated birds into their design. The earliest example was made by the Sumerians of Mesopotamia (present-day Iraq). It depicted a row of birds (probably doves) on a mosaic frieze of a building near the ancient city of Ur, and was created around 3100 BC.

The Ancient Egyptians also took a keen interest in birds, the legacy of which can be seen in the engravings and hieroglyphics which decorate their surviving monuments. The earliest Egyptian bird painting (c. 3000 BC), on the tomb of Ne-fer-Maat at Medum, depicts six geese of three identifiable species. A study of Ancient Egyptian art by Reginald Moreau found at least ninety species of bird, many of which no longer occur in the region. Their significance was mainly religious: birds were considered to be 'winged souls', with different species assigned to particular gods. The hawk, for example, was the emblem of Horus, while the Sacred Ibis represented Thoth, the god of learning.

What appears to be the earliest written reference to 'watching birds' also comes from Ancient Egypt. One day, some three thousand years BC, an Egyptian official posted to some far-flung corner of the empire wrote a letter home, complaining: 'I spend the whole day watching the birds.'

We can tell, even from such a brief extract, that the writer gained very little pleasure from his encounters with the local birdlife – indeed, birds appear only to have emphasized the boredom of his existence, instead of enhancing its pleasure, as they do for modern observers.

In literature, too, birds are present in some of the earliest works. Homer's *Iliad*, composed around the eighth or ninth century BC, describes the Trojan hosts as shouting 'like the Cranes which flee from the coming winter and sudden rain'.

But the richest source of early references to people watching birds is the Bible. In the very first book of the Old Testament, Noah sends forth a Raven, 'which went to and fro, until the waters were dried up from off the Earth'. The Book of Genesis goes on to make explicit mankind's dominant relationship over the living world, which was to shape our exploitative and one-way attitudes towards wild creatures until relatively recent times:

> And God blessed them, and God said unto them, 'Be fruitful, and multiply, and replenish the earth, and subdue it: and have

dominion over the fish of the sea, and over the fowl of the air, and over every living thing that moveth over the earth'.

Written around the sixth century BC, the Book of Job contains the first direct allusion to bird migration. Like the rest of creation, it was regarded as a gift of God: 'Doth the hawk fly by thy wisdom, and stretch her wings toward the south?'

The natural rhythms of God's creation are further acknowledged in the Book of Jeremiah's oft-quoted reference to the migratory habits of birds: 'Yea, the stork in the heavens knoweth her appointed times; and the turtle [dove] and the swallow and the crane observe the time of their coming.'

This Biblical preoccupation with the travels of birds no doubt arose because of the geographical position of the Holy Land, on one of the major migration routes between northern Europe and Africa, where birds would have been difficult to ignore. The man who made the most detailed studies of birds in the ancient world was also exposed to the twice yearly movements of migrating birds, in Ancient Greece.

Born in Macedonia in 384 BC, Aristotle was arguably the last person who could attempt to assemble the sum of human knowledge in one place. In the eighth book of his great work *Historia Animalium* he made several references to bird migration, including reasonable guesses about the migratory routes of the Common Crane and White Pelican. He accurately observed that the Swallow and Turtle Dove are absent during the colder months of the year, and that the Cuckoo disappeared about the time the Dog Star rose, in July.

Aristotle also made some famous mistakes. There is, for example, his belief that the Redstart 'transmutes' into the Robin in winter, or that swallows hibernate – an idea which survived for more than two thousand years. But despite these minor errors it is hard to argue with Max Nicholson's verdict, that 'like everything else he touched, ornithology was permanently enriched by his fruitful and penetrating mind'.

After Aristotle, more than a thousand years passed during which the study of birds, though not entirely neglected, was far from the forefront of cultural and scientific enquiry. The Romans took a passing interest – though their knowledge was mainly related to culinary matters, with peculiar delicacies such as flamingo's tongues appearing at banquets. But like their forebears, the Romans continued to be fascinated by the religious or superstitious aspects of birds. For example, the modern word 'auspices' derives from the Latin words for 'bird' (avis) and 'to look at' (spicere), and comes from the custom of making divine prognostications from observing the flight of birds, or even examining their entrails! Birds figured prominently in Roman legend, too: it was said that cackling geese at Juno's Temple awoke the Roman guards and prevented the city falling into the hands of the invading Gauls.

The only Roman writer who considered birds in what we would now call a 'scientific' way was Pliny (AD 23-79), who wrote a comprehensive encyclopaedia of the natural world, *Historia Naturalis*. This classified birds into three categories, based purely on the shape of their feet: raptors, waterfowl, and everything else – a crude oversimplification which nevertheless stood, with a few variations, for many centuries afterwards.

FROM THE fourth to the fourteenth centuries, the period often known as the Dark Ages, birds were by and large ignored. Apart from trying to catch them for food, most people knew little about birds, and cared even less. This is hardly surprising: for the vast majority of Europe's population life was nasty, brutish and short, leaving little time for pursuits other than work. 'Peasants labored harder, sweated more, and collapsed from exhaustion more often than their animals', writes historian William Manchester:

> Surrounding them was the vast, menacing, and at places
> impassable, Hercynian Forest, infested by boars; by bears; by the
> hulking medieval wolves who lurk so fearsomely in fairy tales
> handed down from that time; by imaginary demons; and by very
> real outlaws, who flourished because they were seldom pursued. . .

> Beneath the deciduous canopy, most of them toiling from
> sunup to sundown, dwelt nearly 73 million people. . . Between
> 80 and 90 per cent of the population lived in villages of fewer than
> a hundred people, fifteen or twenty miles apart, surrounded by
> endless woodlands. . . Travel was slow, expensive, uncomfortable
> – and perilous.

The few references to birds which can be found in surviving
writings of the period are usually of secondary importance to
another purpose, such as telling the story of a great hero.
Nevertheless, a few more accurate descriptions do occur, proving
that at least some observers were watching the birds themselves,
rather than gaining their knowledge from second hand sources.

The earliest, and best known, example appears in a seventh-
century poem written in Anglo-Saxon, known as 'The Seafarer
poem'. James Fisher, who believed this referred to the Gannet
colony on Bass Rock near Edinburgh, described the verse as 'the
first bit of true-sounding, wild-inspired field ornithological record
since the Romans gave up their colony':

> There heard I nought but seething sea,
> Ice-cold wave, awhile a song of swan.
> There came to charm me gannets' pother
> And whimbrels' trills for the laughter of men
> Kittiwake singing instead of mead.
> Storms there the stacks thrashed, there answered them the tern
> With icy feathers; full oft the erne wailed round
> Spray-feathered . . .

This evocative verse was matched for accurate observation by
St Columba, who in the late sixth century watched migrant cranes
on the Scottish island of Iona. After releasing an injured bird,
he saw it: 'raising itself on high in the presence of its ministering
host, and considering for a little while its course in the air, it
returned across the sea to Ireland in a straight line of flight, on a
calm day.'

As Fisher noted: 'this might be from the notebook of a Bird
Observatory of today'. It appears that even when watching birds

was not ingrained in the culture of a society, the impulse to make an accurate observation still occasionally rose to the surface.

During the centuries of Viking occupation and Norman invasion, few descriptions of birds go beyond a passing reference. Nevertheless, Fisher noted a steady increase in the number of species mentioned in English literature, from just sixteen species by AD 700, to fifty-nine by AD 80, and seventy-five by the turn of the first millennium. The 'British list' finally reached the 100 mark in 1382, with the publication of Geoffrey Chaucer's *The Parlement of Foules*, an allegorical work in which the specific identity of the birds mentioned is secondary to their literary significance.

The Middle Ages produced many examples of human interaction with birds, but none that could be described as 'birdwatching' in the modern sense -- though in the early thirteenth century St Francis of Assisi became celebrated for his ability to make wild creatures flock around him and feed from his hand. The main interest in birds was falconry, or 'hunting with hawks', a major preoccupation of royalty and the nobility. William I ('the Conqueror') was an enthusiastic falconer, and the Domesday Book listed the detailed whereabouts of 'the eyries of hawks'.

As a result, birds of prey and gamebirds were the best known of Europe's birds. One of the keenest practitioners of the sport was Frederick II (1194–1250), Emperor of Germany. Known as 'Stupor mundi' – the wonder of the world – Frederick was a keen and educated observer. His treatise on falconry, *Concerning the Art of Hunting with Birds*, contained reasonably accurate information on the habits of many species, including the fact that the cuckoo lays its eggs in other birds' nests.

But references to species not used for hunting, or for hunters' quarry, are few. One of the best known is the account by the medieval monk Matthew Paris, who in 1251 observed an invasion of a hitherto unknown bird in the apple orchards of St Albans:

> About the fruit-season there appeared, in the orchards chiefly, some remarkable birds never before seen in England, somewhat larger than larks, which ate the kernel of the fruit and nothing

else, whereby the trees were fruitless, to the loss of many. The beaks of these birds were crossed. . .

The last phrase gives away the birds' identity as Common Crossbills – an invasive species which frequently appears at sites where it has never previously been seen.

Almost two-and-a-half centuries later, in the year that many historians regard as the bridge between the medieval and modern worlds, a single encounter between men and birds changed the course of world history. By October 1492, Christopher Columbus and his fleet were in trouble. They had been at sea for more than two months, the crew were becoming discontented and mutinous, and there were mutterings of an uprising against their leader.

Then, on 7 October, the sailors noticed large flocks of migrating birds, all heading south-west. As a result, Columbus decided to change course and follow them, so that 'from a state of despondency they passed to one of confident expectation'. This optimism was not misplaced: five days later, on 12 October, they finally sighted land – the island of San Salvador in the Bahamas. The conquest and settlement of the Americas had begun.

But although Columbus and his men were watching birds, what they did was still very far from anything we would recognize as 'birdwatching'. It would be a further three hundred years before human beings would begin to watch birds in the way we do today.

CHAPTER THREE

Understanding

The Dawn of the Modern Era

> She laments, sir . . . her husband goes this morning a-birding.
> *The Merry Wives of Windsor*, William Shakespeare (1602)

A T THE START of the seventeenth century, people's attitudes towards wild creatures were more or less the same as they had been for the previous thousand years. For the vast majority, birds existed for one reason only: to hunt and kill. So it is not surprising that the very first reference to the word 'birding', the oft-quoted line from Shakespeare's *The Merry Wives of Windsor*, in fact refers to the practice of 'fowling' – hunting birds with primitive guns. Cruelty towards birds was endemic: songbirds were frequently eaten ('Four and twenty blackbirds baked in a pie . . .'), or kept in cages for the beauty of their song.

During this period, the relationship between humanity and birds (and indeed other animals) was characterized by what Keith Thomas has called 'the cruelty of indifference', based on the long-standing belief that God's creation was put on this Earth at the service of mankind. But gradually, as a result of the huge social changes wrought by the Renaissance and Reformation, a more modern and less anthropocentric view began to emerge. The very first written work devoted exclusively to birds, William Turner's *Avium Praecipuarum*, was dedicated to the young Prince of Wales, who later reigned briefly as Edward VI. Written in Latin, although it was largely concerned with determining the various species named in the writings of Aristotle and Pliny, it also included details of birds Turner himself had observed in the wild.

During the seventeenth century, the number of known British bird species increased from 150 to more than 200. This was the result of work by pioneers of the new science of zoology, of whom the most important figure was undoubtedly John Ray (1627–1705), often described as 'the founder of modern zoology'.

John Ray came from humble beginnings. Born in Essex, he was the son of a village blacksmith. However, thanks to a grammar school education and the proceeds of a fund to support poor but bright boys, he attended Trinity College, Cambridge, where he became a fellow in 1649, at the age of twenty-one. He studied quietly there for the following thirteen years, during which time the English Civil War raged around him. But with the Restoration of the monarchy of Charles II, Ray's fortunes took a turn for the worse. As a Puritan, he refused to take the oath prescribed by the Act of Uniformity, and in 1662 he lost his college fellowship.

But there was a silver lining to this particular cloud. For the remaining forty or so years of his life Ray pursued his passion for nature, initially with his friend and companion Francis Willughby. Their relationship was founded on a shared interest rather than equality, for Willughby was a country gentleman of a fine family. Yet despite their differences in social class, they formed a close working partnership, travelling throughout Britain and Europe in search of specimens to collect and examine.

But in the summer of 1672, aged just thirty-seven, Willughby suddenly fell ill and died – 'to the infinite and unspeakable loss and grief of myself, his friends, and all good men', as Ray later wrote. As well as inheriting the guardianship of Willughby's two sons and an annuity of sixty pounds, Ray took over the task of publishing his friend's writings. In 1676 the posthumous work appeared in Latin, and two years later, in 1678, an English edition followed, with the grandiose title: *The Ornithology of Francis Willughby of Middleton in the County of Warwick; Fellow of the Royal Society. In Three Books. Wherein All the Birds Hitherto known, Being reduced into a Method suitable to their Natures, are accurately described.*

Willughby's *Ornithology* was a remarkable work, not least because it was the first book devoted to birds to be written entirely in English. It rapidly advanced the science of ornithology, and marked the change from a world in which most printed material was based on guesswork and assumption, to one where accurate observation was paramount. It noted, for the first time, the distinctions between similar species such as Yellow and Grey Wagtails, and between Redpoll, Linnet and Twite. For the rest of his long life Ray continued to push back the bounds of scientific knowledge, publishing works on subjects as diverse as botany and fishes. He justly deserved C. E. Raven's description of him as 'the English Aristotle . . . with whom the adventure of modern science begins'.

DURING the following hundred years or so, from the Glorious Revolution of 1688 to the birth of Queen Victoria in 1819, Britain underwent a series of major social and cultural changes.

The greatest was the transition from a mainly rural, agrarian society, where the vast majority of people worked on the land and lived in the countryside, to a mainly industrial society, where most people worked in factories and lived in towns and cities. During the same period, modern scientific disciplines arose, including ornithology. These two factors had a profound influence on the development of birding. The first created a section of society who began to feel cut off from their rural roots; the second fostered a sense of curiosity which led such people to explore wild places and the newly discovered 'countryside'.

Attitudes towards animals changed, too. The prevailing view, that nature was primarily created by God for the exclusive use of mankind, was gradually being displaced by a growing concern for the welfare of wild animals, and a desire to experience these creatures in the freedom of their natural surroundings. This coincided with the publication of several popular books on natural history, including those by Gilbert White and Thomas Bewick.

The most important change of all was the cultural transformation that bridged the gap between the Renaissance and the modern world, which we now know as 'The Enlightenment'. According to Roy Porter, author of the definitive history of the period, 'the key Enlightenment concept was Nature'.

By demystifying the natural world, and stripping away centuries of superstition and fear, the Enlightenment paved the way for a modern view of nature: as something from which we can take strength and sustenance, which can be enjoyed for its own sake. 'In the early years,' David Allen writes: 'we can watch people playing with nature, treating it like a newly purchased toy. Later, as they become accustomed to the novelty and learn to react with less and less unease, we see their boldness grow. Eventually, as the century ends, we find them helplessly in love with it.'

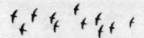

A<small>T THE</small> beginning of this period, in the year 1700, the vast majority of people in England lived and worked their entire lives on the land, in close contact with wild creatures: 'There was an overwhelming proximity – physical, mental and emotional – between humans, flocks and fields,' observes Roy Porter.

But by the end of the eighteenth century this had changed completely. The proportion of people living in towns and cities had doubled: from one in eight in 1700 to one in four by 1800. This was largely the result of two events: the Industrial Revolution, which gave people a reason to seek work in urban areas; and a simultaneous agricultural revolution, which gave them economic and social reasons to leave the countryside.

During the eighteenth century more than two thousand Enclosure Acts had been passed, affecting more than six million acres of land – equivalent to an area larger than Wales. This effectively removed the land from general use, and turned it to profit for a few wealthy landowners. An unintended consequence was to create the patchwork landscape of fields and hedges we know and love today – the English 'countryside' – which has a far shorter pedigree than is often assumed. The new landscape was described by a contemporary observer, Arthur Young, in his 1768 work *A Six Weeks' Tour through the Southern Counties of England and Wales*:

All the country from Holkham to Houghton was a wild sheepwalk before the spirit of improvement seized the inhabitants, and this glorious spirit has wrought amazing effects: for instead of boundless wilds and uncultivated wastes inhabited by scarce anything but sheep, the county is all cut into enclosures, cultivated in a most husbandlike manner, richly manicured, well peopled, and yielding a hundred times the produce that it did in its former state.

But enclosure had other, far less positive effects. By removing many rural people's opportunity to make a living, it drove them into the newly growing towns and cities, thus rapidly depopulating rural England. By the end of the eighteenth century, England had become one of the most urbanised countries in Europe, intensifying what historian G. M. Trevelyan called 'the harsh distinction between urban and rural life'.

More positively, enclosure also changed people's relationship towards nature. The English countryside was no longer wild and terrifying, but now more like an extension of the garden – a place to visit and enjoy.

Paradoxically, some of the keenest aficionados of the new craze sought out the wildest possible places to explore. Mountains were especially popular, and it soon became fashionable to tour the 'wilderness', partly because these places had not been changed by the hand of Man. As Lord Shaftesbury declared, 'the wildness pleases . . . we contemplate her with Delight'. It was, as historian Simon Schama has noted, an extraordinary shift in attitudes within a very short period of time: 'Educated late eighteenth-century Britons were prepared to go to places that no one in their right mind a generation ago would have dreamt of setting foot.'

It is not hard to explain the sudden lure of the countryside. People living in towns and cities no longer worked on the land, and had mostly lost contact with wild and domestic animals. Exploring the countryside put them back in touch with their rural roots; it provided a kind of 'controlled hardship' for the newly prosperous middle classes (just as hiking and camping do for city dwellers today); and was also consonant with new trends in science, which encouraged a fascination with all aspects of the natural world.

O N THE other side of the Atlantic, most people did not have time to watch wildlife for pleasure – they were too busy trying to make sure it did not kill and eat them. Eighteenth-century America was the land of the wild frontier, where survival was the first priority – and the need to subdue wild nature came far above the impulse to classify, describe or enjoy watching it.

Nevertheless, the early settlers tried to make sense of their new and unfamiliar world. One way was to transfer English names of common birds to the unfamiliar species they discovered in the New World. Even the vaguest similarity with a familiar bird from back home justified the reapplying of its name to an American species. So a large thrush with a reddish breast was named the 'robin', a small falcon the 'sparrow hawk', and a whole family of dazzling little birds, with colours so much brighter than their European counterparts, became the 'warblers'.

Fortunately, a handful of these early explorers attempted a more rigorous and accurate description of what they found. One of these was Mark Catesby (1682–1749), an English naturalist who spent many years exploring the south-eastern states of the USA during the early eighteenth century. Catesby illustrated 113 species of bird he discovered on his travels, and published his findings in the monumental *Natural History of Carolina, Florida and the Bahama Islands*, which appeared in two volumes in 1731 and 1743. Unlike most works of the period, which were based on a combination of museum specimens and hearsay, Catesby's descriptions were rooted in personal observation, as in this detailed description of the Goatsucker (now known as the Common Nighthawk):

> They are very numerous in Virginia and Carolina, and are
> called there East India Bats. In the evening they appear most, and
> especially in cloudy weather: before rain, the air is full of them,
> pursuing and dodging after flies and Beetles. Their note is only a
> screek; but by their precipitating and swiftly mounting again to
> recover themselves from the ground, they make a hollow and

surprising noise . . . like that made by the wind blowing into a hollow vessel; wherefore I conceive it is occasion'd by their wide mouth forcibly opposing the air, when they swiftly pursue and catch their prey . . .

Following in Catesby's footsteps came William Bartram (1739-1823), who found more than two hundred species in Pennsylvania, the Carolinas and Florida, and in turn had a great influence over his protégé Alexander Wilson – the man justly described by nineteenth-century collector Elliott Coues as 'the father of American ornithology'.

Apart from John James Audubon, Alexander Wilson (1766–1813) is surely the best known of all American ornithologists. Indeed, if the number of species named after him is any guide, he beats Audubon by four to two (Wilson's Storm-petrel, Plover, Phalarope and Warbler, as against Audubon's Shearwater and Oriole). Born in Paisley in western Scotland, Wilson emigrated to the USA in 1794, settling on the banks of the Schuylkill River in southern Philadelphia. Having learned to draw under the patronage of William Bartram, he undertook several long expeditions, including an epic trek to the Niagara Falls and back, a distance of some 1300 miles – all on foot!

The journey was to collect material – both by field observation and with a shotgun – for his epic work *American Ornithology*, which appeared in nine volumes between 1808 and 1814. This described 264 species – well short of the 600 or so species in a modern field guide to eastern American birds, but still a remarkable achievement. Unlike many of his contemporaries, he preferred field observation to collecting, and wrote: 'The greatest number of the descriptions, particularly those of the nests, eggs, and plumage, have been written in the woods, with the subjects in view, leaving as little as possible to the lapse of recollection.'

This was a new and enlightened attitude. But Wilson did not live to see the publication of the final volume of his masterwork, dying in 1813 at the relatively early age of forty-seven. After his death his reputation grew rapidly, with a contemporary, Joseph Sabine, writing that Wilson had: 'produced a work which, for correctness of description, accuracy of observation, and acuteness of distinction, will compete with every publication of natural history yet extant . . . the beauty of the style, and perspicuity of the narrative, add unrivalled charms to its scientific merits.'

By a remarkable coincidence, in May 1977, more than 160 years after Wilson's death, one of the species he had originally described – a Cape May Warbler – was discovered singing in Paisley Glen, within sight of his birthplace. It remains the only record of this North American species in Britain.

But in the history of birding in the New World, one figure towers above all others. John James Audubon (1785-1821) had an unusual background, even by the standards of his day. He was born in Haiti in 1785, the result of a liaison between a French naval captain and a poor servant girl. His mother died when he was only six months old, and he was brought back to France. At the age of eighteen he was sent to Pennsylvania, to avoid conscription in the forthcoming Napoleonic wars. However, instead of managing his father's plantation he spent his time sketching birds, until, in March 1810, a chance meeting with Alexander Wilson, who was touring the area seeking subscribers for his *American Ornithology*, changed his life.

Fired with enthusiasm, Audubon launched his career as a bird artist, eventually publishing his unique life-size works in the massive, four-volume *The Birds of America*, which appeared from 1827-1838. This was a truly extraordinary work: not only the world's largest published bird book (a new page size, 'elephant folio', was invented to describe it), but also the most expensive: in March 2000 a copy sold at auction for almost $9 million (then £6 million).

Audubon was a complex and ambiguous figure, and it is now hard to separate the man from the many myths that have grown up around him since his death. Motivated by a combination of fame, money and a love of wild adventure, he did more to advance knowledge and public appreciation of North American birds than any other man in history. He was a great artist and a great visionary, and like many Americans he was also a shameless self-publicist, as his biographers Barbara and Richard Mearns have pointed out:

One of his many skills was the ability to sell not only his books, but himself, and the image he promoted has caught the imagination of succeeding generations. But along with the paintings, the myths and the ornithological discoveries we have inherited another legacy in the names of the North American birds . . . No other ornithologist ever indulged in this habit as indiscriminately as Audubon.

Indeed, as Mearns and Mearns show, of the ninety-one species of bird named by Audubon no fewer than fifty-seven – almost two out of three – were named after people. Time has not been kind to Audubon, however, and only about one in three of his proposed names are still used today, as many turned out either to have been discovered and named before, or were not true species. In one bout of misguided enthusiasm, Audubon managed to name a single species – the Hairy Woodpecker – no fewer than five times, after a range of people including his field assistant, a friend in New Jersey, and even his family physician in London!

Eventually, a life spent collecting, painting and selling the 'Audubon brand' took its toll, and by 1846 his sight was failing, and his general health began to decline. He died aged sixty-five, in January 1851, at his home on Manhattan Island overlooking the Hudson River. More than 150 years later, his name lives on in the Audubon Societies, the bedrock of the bird protection movement in the USA.

ONE OF the key developments during the Enlightenment was the formalization of modern science. Of the life sciences, botany was the first to develop, swiftly followed by entomology and geology. Not far behind came ornithology – a subject which would eventually give a vital impetus and respectability to the pastime of birdwatching.

In *Discovering Birds: The Emergence of Ornithology as a Scientific Discipline*, Paul Farber has traced the development of attitudes towards birds during the eighteenth and nineteenth centuries. At the start of the period, he notes, birds occupied a central place in western European culture, but this was almost entirely in the 'cultural realms' of heraldry, gastronomy, agriculture, hunting, bird-keeping, taxidermy and fashion. But gradually, ornithology became a recognized scientific discipline, with a keen and growing band of followers.

One of the key figures in the new science of ornithology was the Swedish naturalist Carl von Linné (1707-1778) generally known as Linnaeus. Linnaeus created the system of binomial nomenclature which we still use today, in which every species of plant or animal can be distinguished from any other by its unique, two-part scientific name. Many of Linnaeus's original epithets have now been superseded, but one we still use today is *Fringilla coelebs* for the Chaffinch. 'Coelebs' derives from the Latin meaning 'bachelor', a reference to his observation that during the autumn female Chaffinches leave his native Sweden and head south, while the larger, hardier males remain. Other surviving Linnaean names include *Troglodytes troglodytes* for the Wren, a puzzling name, given that this means 'cave-dweller', which perhaps refers to the fact that Wrens occasionally nest in crevices in rocks.

In the second half of the eighteenth century, the baton was taken up by two Frenchmen: Mathurin-Jacques Brisson (1723-1806) and Georges-Louis Leclerc de Buffon (1707-1788). Both published important works on birds: Brisson's *Ornithologie* (1760) and Buffon's *Histoire naturelle des oiseaux* (1780). As one would expect, these relied heavily on museum collections, but were nevertheless of serious scientific standing. The English edition of Buffon's work, published in 1792-93, laid the foundation for subsequent study by Montagu and MacGillivray, and by popularizing the new science, also helped to spread a more widespread interest in birds. Looking back almost one-and-a-half centuries later, in 1929, Max Nicholson pointed out the crucial influence of Buffon's work on subsequent generations:

> It meant that natural history could no longer be the special preserve of a rather dull and pedantic set of men, but must (be) interpreted in terms of ordinary lay experience . . . ornithology

suddenly passed into the hands of a large corps of enthusiasts . . .
Birds, a comparatively small and limited class, rose rapidly to a
popularity which they have never had to yield.

BY 1789, when the first edition of *The Natural History of
Selborne* appeared, the practice of watching birds purely for
pleasure could truly be said to have begun. White's attitude
towards birds – with which the modern reader finds it so easy to
empathise – indicates a major movement away from that which had
held sway for the previous few thousand years, when in the words
of ornithologist Austin Rand, 'man's chief interest in birds was to
eat them', and towards our modern age, when, as Rand puts it:

> We have passed the time when they figured only in magic and
> appeared in stories chiefly to help teach a moral lesson, and have
> come to the time when a knowledge of birds has become a part of
> our culture in science, literature, and recreation. Ornithology has
> played a significant part in opening our eyes to the living world
> around us – its meaning and our place in it.

But before this could come to pass, another whole century
would elapse: an era when the battles between collecting and protecting birds would be fought out (sometimes literally) between
opposing factions; an era when developments in transport and
industry would transform the lives of millions, and in doing so
create a new appreciation of the countryside and its wildlife; and
an era when a growth in education and social awareness would
pave the way for modern social attitudes.

As the following three chapters will show, the developments
which occurred during the nineteenth century would eventually
lead to a point when – for the first time in history – mankind's
relationship with birds could primarily be defined by the pastime
of watching them purely for pleasure.

CHAPTER FOUR

Collecting

The Victorian Era, part 1

'To be a good Collector, and nothing more, is a small affair;
great skill may be acquired in the art, without a single quality
commanding respect.'

Handbook of Field and General Ornithology,
Elliott Coues (1890)

O NE DAY IN late October 1896, a young man was walking
along the sea wall at Cley in north Norfolk, a place
famed for its ability to attract rare migratory birds. As
always, he carried his shotgun, an indispensable tool of his trade –
for Ted Ramm was a professional bird collector and this was the
peak of the autumn migration. So when he saw a movement in the
long grass he took aim and let fly. At that moment, a small bird
weighing a fraction of an ounce, which had travelled many thousands of miles from its Siberian breeding grounds to this exposed
spot on the north Norfolk coast, reached the end of its long journey.

The bird was a Pallas's Warbler, the very first record of this
Asian species for Britain. As usual, Ramm took the corpse along to
the taxidermists' shop in Cley village, owned by his father-in-law,
H. N. Pashley. The prized specimen was stuffed and mounted, and
sold to a wealthy collector for the extraordinary sum of forty
pounds, equivalent to several thousand pounds today.

Pashley had taken up the art of taxidermy in 1884, at the
relatively late age of forty. He soon made a name for himself, and
had established a thriving business. Like thousands of similar
establishments up and down the country, his shop became a
favoured meeting point for locals and visitors alike. In his introduction to Pashley's memoirs, B. B. Riviere described the unique
atmosphere of the taxidermist's premises:

There can be few living ornithologists who have not, perhaps after a September day spent among the bushes, passed through into the warm, cheerful little workshop, with its countless stuffed birds occupying all the available wall-space from floor to ceiling . . . Outside, when at last one left, was the smell of the sea and the call of migrating birds passing overhead, and the memory of that small, enchanted room, with all its associations, will live long in one's pleasantest dreams.

Nor was Ted Ramm his father-in-law's sole supplier of rare and unusual birds. This was a time when practically every man, whatever his social status, carried a gun – and as well as shooting rats and rabbits, would be on the lookout for anything unusual that might be of interest to the local taxidermist. Taxidermy was sustained not only by the collectors themselves, but by the population as a whole. In both Britain and North America, people who were now living in towns and cities retained the desire to cling on to remnants of their rural heritage, and what better memento than a glass case containing a few stuffed birds on the sideboard or mantelpiece? Enthusiasm began early: future US President Theodore Roosevelt began his bird collection in 1867, at the age of eight. He eventually progressed from mere collecting to skinning birds for himself, at a taxidermist's on the corner of Broadway and Worth Street in New York.

Yet by the time H. N. Pashley's memoirs were published posthumously, in 1925, the era of the taxidermist – and with it the shooters and wealthy collectors – was coming to an end. Poor, working-class people still shot birds, and wealthy middle-class people still bought them, but the trade was a mere shadow of what it had been in its heyday.

Nowadays, it is tempting to view the passion for collecting as a temporary hiatus in the steady development of our interest in birds, but in fact the collecting era had a profound influence on the development of birdwatching. To understand why, we must go back to the earliest years of Queen Victoria's reign.

THE VICTORIANS were obsessed with accumulating natural objects. They collected fossils and fungi, bugs and beetles, shells and seaweed, microscopic organisms, all kinds of aquatic life, and of course birds and their eggs. These were proudly displayed in cabinets in Victorian drawing-rooms, where they allowed curious visitors to engage in stimulating conversation. By the mid-nineteenth century, collecting had established itself as a fashionable and socially acceptable pastime, though its proponents were still almost entirely from the male half of society.

This outbreak of popular enthusiasm was quite unprecedented. Until the beginning of the nineteenth century, the subject had been not only neglected, but positively despised. Indeed it was dismissed as a mere 'childish fancy' which, if practised at all by adults, turned them into figures of fun. Yet only a generation or so later, knowledge of nature – or at least of natural *objects* – had become as important a social accomplishment as painting, singing, or playing the piano. This change in attitude arose for several reasons, notably the practical and spiritual benefits the pastime was supposed to offer body and soul. The study of natural history was an ideal form of self-improvement, providing exercise, education and what Lynn Barber, in *The Heyday of Natural History, 1820-1870*, has called 'rational amusement'. It fitted in perfectly with the new philosophy, exemplified by Samuel Smiles' handbook for the upwardly mobile, *Self-Help*, in A. N. Wilson's words 'the ultimate self-defining bestseller of the mid-Victorian Age'.

Above all, nature study alleviated that great bugbear of Victorian middle-class life, boredom, caused by a new-found excess of leisure time amongst the upper classes. 'Natural history fitted the bill perfectly,' observes Lynn Barber:

> It was scientific . . . it was morally uplifting . . . (and) it was healthy. For gentlemen it offered new pretexts to go out and shoot something, and for ladies it offered new subjects for watercolours, for albums, or for embroidery . . . Other hobbies, such as music or painting, might alleviate indoor boredom, but only natural history could offer relief from outdoor boredom as well.

The Victorians may have taken collecting to new heights, but they were not the first to indulge in the practice. The first proper guns had been developed in the early sixteenth century – with their first successful use coming in 1533, when a Moorhen was shot and killed in Norfolk. The flintlock was invented in 1635, and by the end of the seventeenth century guns were the preferred means of hunting wild birds. Nevertheless, for the first three hundred years of their existence, firearms had been fairly inefficient killing tools. Then, in 1807, a Scottish church minister named Alexander Forsyth patented the percussion principle, which allowed guns to work much more effectively, even in wet weather. By 1851, the first breech-loading shotgun had been introduced from France, and guns had become lethal weapons capable of highly efficient killing.

Even though guns were now much more widely available, only men from the upper reaches of society could become accomplished collectors, for they alone had the freedom from work commitments and the private income to enable them to pursue their hobby. Edward Booth in Sussex, who had been left so well provided for by his late father that he was able to devote his entire attention to bird collecting, was one such.

Born in 1840, Booth enjoyed the conventional benefits of a traditional Victorian education at Harrow School and Trinity College, Cambridge. He also received a more practical schooling in taxidermy from a man named Kent, a bird stuffer and barber, of St Leonards-on-Sea. His early hunting-grounds were Rye Marshes in Sussex, but he soon ventured farther afield, to the Norfolk Broads and Scottish Highlands. Wherever he went, he shot every bird he could find. Today, the fruits of Booth's labours can be seen in the institution that bears his name, the Booth Museum of Natural History in Dyke Road, Brighton. Inside, in glass cases, are hundreds of specimens from Booth's massive collection. Though moth-eaten and faded by a century of exposure to light, they still retain an impression of their original splendour. This is a tribute to Booth's skill for displaying specimens in their 'natural' habitat, going to great efforts to recreate an impression of the surroundings in which they had been obtained.

IT IS TEMPTING to view men like Edward Booth as ruthless Victorians in tweeds, blasting away at everything within range, but the killing also had a practical purpose. Long before the days of binoculars and field guides, it was the only way to identify many of the birds people saw. As the oft-quoted saying goes: 'What's hit is history, what's missed is mystery.'

A collection was rather like a personal reference library, and was indispensable in discovering new species or identifying rare visitors. During the eighteenth and early nineteenth centuries, collecting had led to the discovery of many hitherto unrecognized species by ornithologists such as Montagu and MacGillivray. Indeed, despite his spotless reputation, even Gilbert White indulged in the practice, employing local men to obtain specimens of the three leaf-warblers in order to compare them in the hand. All serious ornithological works, up to and including the twentieth-century *Handbook of British Birds*, were based in a large part on knowledge gleaned from specimens in museums.

For the bird artist, attempting to portray the most accurate possible likeness of a bird, collecting specimens was simply essential. As Audubon wrote, 'I shot, I drew, I looked on nature.' Almost a century later, in 1896, artist and illustrator George Lodge was still asserting the benefits of collecting: 'In the cause of science and art one has no compunction in killing birds: the world at large benefits therefrom.'

But the most passionate defence of all came from a work which soon became the collectors' bible, written by a young American named Elliott Coues: 'The true ornithologist goes out to study birds alive and destroys some of them simply because that is the only way of learning their structure and field characters.'

The son of a wealthy New Hampshire shipping merchant, brought up in a comfortable middle-class home in the city of Washington DC, Coues nevertheless showed an intense passion for wildlife from a very early age. At the age of seventeen, he used his father's social connections to meet the celebrated Professor

Spencer Fullerton Baird, a leading ornithologist at the Smithsonian Institution, the national museum of natural history.

Following an expedition to Labrador, Coues qualified as a surgeon, learning his craft by treating wounded soldiers in the Civil War – an experience which left him with a healthy respect for firearms. Later, he rode five hundred miles on horseback alongside a supply train of wagons, collecting bird specimens as he went, as one contemporary observer described:

> Clad in a corduroy suit of many pockets and having numerous sacks and pouches attached to his saddle, he regularly rode out column every morning astride of his buckskin-colored mule . . . rarely did we see him again until we had been some hours in the following camp but we heard the discharge of his double-barreled shotgun . . . When he sat upon the ground and proceeded to skin, stuff and label his specimens, he was never without an interested group of officers and men around him.

Perhaps it was this interest from his fellow soldiers that gave Coues the idea of passing on his knowledge and experience to other enthusiasts. In 1872, he published his first and most influential work, *Key to North American Birds*, later issued in Britain in 1890 as the *Handbook of Field and General Ornithology*. Despite this innocuous-sounding title, the subtitle of the British edition gave away its true theme: 'With Instructions for Collecting and Preserving Specimens'. From the very opening lines, Coues left no doubt about his approach to ornithology:

> The Double-barrelled Shot Gun is your main reliance. Under some circumstances you may trap or snare birds, catch them with bird-lime, or use other devices; but such cases are exceptions to the rule that you will shoot birds, and for this purpose no weapon compares with the one just mentioned.

The following chapters provided a thorough course in the subject, and include: Dogs; Hygiene; Labelling; How to Make a Birdskin; Collection of Nests and Eggs; and Care of a Collection.

Coues was a committed enthusiast, who would spend every waking hour in the field, and encouraged others to do so:

Birds may be sought anywhere, at any time; they should be sought everywhere, at all times. Some come about your doorstep to tell their stories unasked. Others spring up before you as you stroll in the field, like the flowers that enticed the feet of Proserpine. Birds flit by as you measure the tired roadside, lending a tithe of their life to quicken your dusty steps.

He had no doubt as to the value of collecting specimens, placing the greatest emphasis on field experience, which he regarded as an indispensable prerequisite to scientific study in the museum. His gung-ho attitude has often been criticized: 'How many birds of the same kind do you want? *All you can get* – with some reasonable limitations; say fifty or a hundred of any but the most abundant species.'

But he did have a more sensitive side: 'Never shoot a bird you do not fully intend to preserve, or to utilize in some proper way. Bird-life is too beautiful a thing to destroy to no purpose.'

This concern for wildlife echoed the Christian ethos that pervaded every aspect of nineteenth-century life on both sides of the Atlantic and is also found in the moral messages Coues constantly strove to impart to his readers: 'Success hangs upon your own exertions; upon your energy, industry, and perseverance; your knowledge and skill; your zeal and enthusiasm, in collecting birds, much as in other affairs of life.'

Without Coues, and others like him, it is doubtful if the science of ornithology would have developed so rapidly and to such a level of expertise. Like Peterson's field guide more than sixty years later, his book influenced an entire generation, including Frank Chapman, a young man later to become one of America's greatest ornithologists, who 'for the first time learned that there were living students of birds . . . ' Coues' passion for being out in the field rather than cooped up in some dusty museum undoubtedly helped lay the foundations for the development of birdwatching during the following century.

WHAT EFFECT did the collecting boom have on the birds themselves? For some, it brought unexpected benefits: habitats were preserved and managed, especially for gamebirds and wildfowl. But birds of prey suffered the wrath of the sportsmen, as they had the unfortunate habit of killing birds before the collector could get to them. The slaughter was made worse by the increasing efficiency of firearms, and their rising popularity.

Views differ on the long-term impact of the collecting craze on bird populations. In their comprehensive review of the subject, *The Bird Collectors*, Mearns and Mearns argued that the number of birds killed by collectors through the ages 'was infinitesimal compared with the overall number of birds killed by man', for example as a result of changes in land use and habitat loss.

This may well be so, but there is no doubt that targeted collecting, especially of rare birds and their eggs, could and did have a significant effect on the populations of a declining species. Nowhere was this truer than for Britain's rarest birds of prey, such as the Osprey. In 1848, a Victorian gentleman named Charles St John travelled to Sutherland in the far north of Scotland in search of Ospreys, which at the time were in severe decline. Having collected birds and eggs from at least three nests, he ended his account with these deeply hypocritical words: 'There are but very few in Britain at any time ... As they in no way interfere with the sportsman or others, it is a great pity that they should ever be destroyed.'

The Osprey managed to hang on as a breeding bird for another sixty years or so, but eventually became extinct in Britain in 1916. Fortunately a more enlightened attitude towards birds has allowed it to recolonize Scotland from the 1950s onwards.

COLLECTING was not only lethal to birds. Wandering in wild and lonely places with a shotgun was a dangerous and potentially fatal pursuit for the collectors too. Many fell victim to their over-enthusiastic pursuit of a specimen, which would sometimes turn out to be their last. Hazards were many and varied: they might fall victim to wild animals, shotgun accidents, or poisoning from the arsenic powder used to preserve skins. They could fall down a cliff or from a tree, drown, or be trampled by wild animals. There were rumours that some collectors had been murdered by disgruntled employees, a jealous rival – or in the 'wild west', in an even more terrifying way, as Coues warned in a letter to his mentor, Spencer Fullerton Baird: 'The Apaches are so hostile and daring that considerable caution will have to tinge my collecting enthusiasm, if I want to save my scalp.'

But Coues' writings also show that he relished the danger – indeed, as this evocative passage shows, it may have been his main motivation:

> Birds crown the mountain-top you may lose your breath to climb; they sprinkle the desert where your parched lips may find no cooling draught; they fleck the snow-wreath when the nipping blast may make you turn your back; they breathe unharmed the pestilent vapours of the swamp that mean disease, if not death, for you; they outride the storm at sea that sends strong men to their last account. Where now will you look for birds?

There may be a more inspiring passage written about the single-minded pursuit of birds, but I have yet to find it. Here, surely, is a profound insight into why collecting could be, above all else, extraordinarily enjoyable.

For the vast majority of them – as for today's birdwatchers – the motivation was, as Mearns and Mearns have noted, sporting rather than scientific:

> Collecting provided a convenient and socially acceptable excuse for respectable grown men to climb trees, scramble down cliffs, go camping and roam freely out of doors, pitting themselves against the terrain, the weather and wary, elusive quarry. Success demanded physical fitness, endurance, patience, skill with guns and a level of fieldcraft now rare amongst birdwatchers. In short, it was considered good, manly fun . . .

Few pastimes provided such a perfect combination of physical and intellectual stimulation. 'What branch of science,' Philadelphia ornithologist Spencer Trotter asked, 'comes nearer to satisfying the primitive instinct that takes him into the woods to hunt and fish . . . and at the same time abundantly satisfying the acquisitive and classifying habit of mind?'

It was the *experience* of collecting that was so important: although some people could and did purchase their specimens from others, for the vast majority the motivation was the satisfaction of stalking and killing the bird, or collecting its eggs, themselves. As a result, collectors gained the kinds of skills so vital to the modern birdwatcher – what we know today as 'fieldcraft' – as well as an intimate understanding of the habits and behaviour of wild birds.

In many ways these purely amateur collectors had far more in common with today's twitchers than with the museum-based ornithologists of their own era. Like twitching, collecting was driven by the competitive impulse: to explore new places, to seek out and obtain new species, and to have a bigger and better collection than their friends and colleagues. This was a small world where everyone knew everyone else, and reputation was all. And as with finding a rare bird today, collectors needed a combination of natural ability and good fortune. No wonder it became so addictive and popular.

For some collectors, their passion took over their lives, as this entry from the diary of the naturalist and explorer Philip Henry Gosse amply confirms: 'Received green swallow from Jamaica. E. delivered of a son.'

Gosse's excuse was that he was currently working on his book *Birds of Jamaica*. Incidentally, the son relegated to such a cursory mention grew up to become an important literary figure in his own right: the writer Edmund Gosse.

IN AMERICA, the mania for collecting peaked in the second half of the nineteenth century, coinciding with the nation's own belated shift from an essentially rural, land-based society to an urbanized, industrial one. Between 1860 and 1900, the US population doubled, with more and more people living in towns and cities. As a result, many people there, too, for the first time in their lives experienced the luxury of leisure time that needed to be filled: not by sitting around doing nothing but, in accordance with their Protestant work-ethic, by taking part in something useful and fulfilling. But there was a deeper need, too: 'as civilisation loomed ever larger in their daily lives,' Mark V. Barrow observes, 'many Americans experienced an almost primordial yearning to re-establish some form of contact with nature.'

The same was undoubtedly true in Britain. Later this would find expression in the nineteenth century writings of Henry Thoreau and W. H. Hudson, who both promoted a less exploitative, more sympathetic attitude towards nature. But in the meantime, intimate contact with wildlife was still primarily satisfied through the barrel of a gun. And now, thanks to a revolution in travel by road, rail and ship, the collectors had the opportunity to cast their net even wider than before.

CHAPTER FIVE

Travelling

The Victorian Era, part II

Keep moving! Steam, or Gas, or Stage
Hold, cabin, steerage, hencoop's cage –
Tour, Journey, Voyage, Lounge, Ride, Walk,
Swim, Sketch, Excursion, Travel-talk –
For move you must! 'Tis now the rage,
The law and fashion of the age.

Samuel Taylor Coleridge (1824)

TODAY, DESPITE THE familiar grumbles about our road and railway networks, we take access to the remotest parts of Britain for granted. Birdwatching, like so many leisure activities, has been able to thrive as a result of this new-found mobility. But this is a relatively modern phenomenon: until about two hundred years ago most people spent their lives within a few miles of the place they were born. If they did venture away from home, it was usually out of necessity: for travel – on foot or by stagecoach – was difficult, uncomfortable, and often dangerous.

With the first railway journey, between Stockton and Darlington on 27 September 1825, all this changed. 'From west to east,' announced Henry Booth, secretary of the Liverpool and Manchester Railway, 'and from north to south, the mechanical principle, the philosophy of the nineteenth century, will spread and extend itself. The world has received a new impulse.'

In fact, despite Booth's hyperbole, the transport system had been gradually improving for some time before the coming of the railway. Since the middle of the eighteenth century, Britain's roads had undergone a steady upgrading to meet the needs of a rapidly growing population, which doubled from 10.5 million people in 1801 (the year of the first census) to just below 21 million in 1851.

So by 1830 a journey by coach between London and Edinburgh, which at the beginning of the eighteenth century had taken Daniel Defoe two weeks, could be done in just thirty-six hours. The improvements in the transport system also created an early tourist boom. The inauguration of a regular coach service between London and Carlisle in 1773 allowed the first excursions into the Lake District, a region previously out of bounds to all but the hardiest travellers. The contrast between the newly acquired trappings of modern life, and the potential difficulties of travel, only increased people's desire to explore the wilderness: a spell of hardship and the possibility of danger were part of the appeal.

Those keen to venture into the countryside were greatly assisted by the systematic mapping of Britain carried out by the Ordnance Survey between 1791 and the 1860s. Better roads brought another benefit: the mail service, which Gilbert White found so essential when communicating with his various correspondents, also improved rapidly during this period.

But the superiority of the roads was short-lived. The 1830s saw the dawn of the railway age. For the next eighty years or so the railways would be dominant, before they too were overtaken by the coming of the motor-car. The network of railways spread across Britain very rapidly indeed: from just 51 miles by 1830, to 666 miles by 1840 and almost 4000 miles by 1850. By 1875 most major lines had been built, and by the outbreak of World War I there were more than 23,000 miles of railway in Britain. The numbers of passenger journeys also increased enormously: from 5 million in 1838, to 603 million by 1880, and over 1100 million by 1901.

This had major social consequences, with third-class travel enabling all social groups to be mobile for the first time. Most importantly for the development of birdwatching, railways encouraged people to travel for leisure purposes. Cheap day excursions became very popular, with townspeople going for walks and picnics in the very countryside that their parents and grandparents had deserted only a few decades before.

Along with the rest of the population, naturalists made the most of cheap and easy travel to gain access to the countryside, either on weekend excursions or annual holidays. One popular trip was to the Isle of Wight, to see nesting seabirds. Queen Victoria and Prince Albert also helped popularize the habit, by frequent visits to their country estate at Balmoral in Royal Deeside. Botanising – excursions in search of wild flowers – was especially popular, as shown in this description of a trip to the Scottish Highlands, in the summer of 1847:

> Excursions may truly said to be the *life* of the botanist. They
> enable him to study the science practically, by the examination
> of plants in their living state, and in their native localities . . .
> and with the pursuit of scientific knowledge, they combine that
> healthful and spirit-stirring recreation which tends materially to
> aid mental efforts.

The author of this account, J. H. Balfour, went on to cite the recreational and spiritual benefits of a trip to the wilds with a group of like-minded enthusiasts:

> The companionship too of those who are prosecuting with
> zeal and enthusiasm the same path of science, is not the least
> delightful feature of such excursions . . . the pleasing incidents
> that diversified the walk, the jokes that passed, and even the very
> mishaps or annoyances that occurred – all became objects of
> interest, and unite the members of the party by ties of no
> ordinary kind. And the feelings thus excited are by no means of an
> evanescent or fleeting nature; they last during life, and are always
> recalled by the sight of the specimens which were collected.

Balfour may have been looking for rare flowers, but his sentiments are identical to those felt by anyone who has ever been on an expedition in search of unusual birds. They sum up a collective experience that was wholly new to this era, and would soon lead to a rapid growth in popularity for all forms of nature study.

A<small>T FIRST</small>, the coming of the railways, along with the other trappings of the industrial revolution, was regarded as entirely positive. 'We remove mountains, and make seas our smooth highway,' Thomas Carlyle wrote in *The Edinburgh Review* in 1829: 'Nothing can resist us. We war with rude nature; and by our resistless engines, come off always victorious, and loaded with spoils.'

The Poet Laureate, Alfred Lord Tennyson, agreed. 'Let the great world spin forever down the ringing grooves of change,' he wrote, still under the misapprehension that trains ran not on rails, but in grooves, like trams.

But despite the widespread view that the new method of transport was an example of progress, the railways were far from entirely beneficial. For at the same time as they opened up access to the countryside, they also began to destroy it. As the network of railway lines spread across the country, the process of habitat fragmentation which would eventually have such a negative effect on our breeding bird populations began; and what had once been a pristine wilderness was destroyed forever. William Borrer, author of the *Birds of Sussex* (1891), painted a sad picture of the destruction wrought by the railways in less than seventy-five years:

> The whole of Sussex is now intersected with railways, not only inland but along the coast . . the whistle of the steam-engine taking the place of that of the Wildfowl and the Wader. The estuaries, formerly abounding in these species, are now far more disturbed by traffic than they used to be, and much of the marshland has been brought under cultivation.

By the end of the nineteenth century, Britain had become an urban, industrialized nation, held together by the new network of railways. Along with another major social change – the creation of what we now call 'leisure time' – this was to have a profound effect on the development of watching birds as a mass participation activity.

O N A V I S I T to England in the 1830s, the Frenchman Alexis de Tocqueville wondered how the English managed to be so individual in their nature, yet so keen on forming clubs and societies. In *The English: a Portrait of a People*, Jeremy Paxman argues that this paradox is one of the defining characteristics of the English race:

> Instead of easy-going, random meetings of street life, the
> English do their socialising by choice and form clubs. 'Who
> runs the country?' asked John Betjeman rhetorically. 'The Royal
> Society for the Protection of Birds. Their members are behind
> every hedge.' And he was speaking long before the RSPB
> membership reached its present level . . . There are clubs to go
> fishing, support football teams, play cards, arrange flowers, race
> pigeons, make jam, ride bicycles, watch birds, even for going on
> holiday.

Paxman's list of modern-day organizations notwithstanding, the golden age of clubs and societies was undoubtedly the eighteenth and nineteenth centuries. During this period, the natural history field club had a far-reaching influence on the development of wildlife watching as a hobby.

There had been some local natural history societies as far back as 1710, but many more were founded during the 1820s and 1830s. Most dealt with natural history in general, rather than a specific area such as botany or ornithology. These early societies conformed to the rigid social divisions of the time, with different clubs catering for different social classes. Entomology – the study of insects – was open to all, because its adherents could find specimens to study any-where, without the need for special equipment. Ornithology, on the other hand, was still mainly pursued by country gentlemen, who, as Lynn Barber puts it, 'owned a gun and the right to carry it'.

As with so many other aspects of Victorian life, 'women were either left out, ignored, or only brought in on festive occasions because,' explains David Allen: 'Science was a man's business and the club a kind of intellectual stag-party where a male rattled his antlers: a place reserved apart for him, like his study, where women should never be allowed to intrude.'

The exclusion of women may not, however, have been entirely the men's fault: some women had been known to turn up on field excursions dressed in large hats and voluminous skirts, which may have been the fashion of the day but were hardly suitable for outdoor wildlife watching. Even when barriers to women were removed in the 1860s, few took advantage of the freedom to join. But during the 1870s and 1880s more women did begin to take part, no doubt in response to the growing interest in bird protection.

By 1873, according to Allen, there were 169 local scientific societies in Britain and Ireland, of which 104 were primarily field clubs, and at the end of the nineteenth century the total membership of natural history societies was almost 50,000. Although the primary motivation was a shared interest in wildlife, the social aspect of membership should not be underestimated. Victorian societies attracted members by offering tea and cakes, drinks, dinners, dances and even musical recitals.

However, the appeal of natural history went far deeper than mere socialising. Just as the growing popularity of association football gave the newly urbanized working man an annual cycle of 'seasons' to replace the one he had lost by leaving the countryside, so natural history societies, with their programme of excursions coinciding with seasonal changes in the natural world, provided a similar comfort and security. One of the prime movers in their establishment was Charles Kingsley, author of the Victorian children's classic *The Water Babies*. In 1871 Kingsley founded the Chester Society of Natural Science, Literature and Art, which organized field trips, some attended by hundreds of members. Another Liverpool-based club attracted 350 participants on a single excursion to north Wales. Fears were expressed about the negative impact of so many people descending on a single locality, especially as prizes were offered for the best bouquet of flowers collected on the excursion!

Several natural history societies founded in the Victorian era are still in existence today. In 1858 a small band of insect enthusiasts in east London founded the Haggerstone Entomological Society. By the end of the nineteenth century its interests and membership had broadened out, so the name was changed to the

London Natural History Society. Almost 150 years later, and confirming Jeremy Paxman's belief that the English prefer to do their socialising with like-minded people in a formal, structured setting, the society is still going strong.

THE SHIFT towards urban living that took place during Queen Victoria's reign enabled such clubs and societies to thrive. As early as the start of the nineteenth century roughly one in three British people lived in towns or cities, a far higher proportion than anywhere else in Europe. By the time of the queen's death in 1901, only one in five British people lived in 'rural areas': everyone else lived in a town or a city – many in the conditions of filth, poverty and degradation chronicled by Dickens.

Not everyone who lived in towns or cities was poor. Major reforms in housing, health and education had led to dramatic increases in life expectancy. The economy had prospered, and so had a burgeoning social stratum we would today describe as the middle-classes, who lived in a state of relative affluence. Ironically, they had only been able to achieve this new-found prosperity by leaving the very place where nature could be found – the countryside. By the end of the nineteenth century, town-dwellers – increasingly suspicious of venturing back to the place whence, just one or two generations earlier, their ancestors had come – were being satirized by Oscar Wilde in *The Importance of Being Earnest*:

> JACK: I have a country house with some land, of course . . . but
> I don't depend on that for my real income. In fact, as far as I
> can make out, the poachers are the only people who make
> anything out of it.
> LADY BRACKNELL: A country house! You have a town house,
> I hope? A girl with a simple, unspoilt nature, like Gwendolen,
> could hardly be expected to reside in the country.

In North America, the changes were even more dramatic. At the start of the nineteenth century most of the continent was barely explored, and those who did so suffered great hardship, danger, and the very real risk of premature death. Apart from a few pioneers such as Audubon and Wilson, most travellers' interest in birds was culinary rather than scientific. Yet by the end of the century, the American landscape had been more or less tamed, and ordinary Americans living in cities were able to venture into the wilderness for recreation and spiritual renewal. This growing interest can be gauged from the popularity of the 'Wilderness Discovery books' of John Muir (1838-1914), a native-born Scot whose family had emigrated and settled in Wisconsin when he was eleven years old. The new environment had a profound effect on the young Muir, who went on to become one of America's most widely-read and celebrated writers on natural history.

Muir's philosophy was a kind of 'new age' spirituality, a holistic communion with nature and its inner rhythms. It went firmly against the conventional wisdom of the time, which regarded birds and other animals as quarry to be hunted, caught and eaten, and woods and forests as infinite resources to be cut down for timber. Muir and his writings challenged the longstanding idea that nature was an endlessly renewable gift of God.

His lasting influence was to convince the newly urbanized American middle-classes that wilderness was not a dirty word, and that nature could be enjoyed for recreation and spiritual renewal, as he described in the opening chapter of *Our National Parks*, published in 1901:

> The tendency nowadays to wander in wildernesses is delightful to see. Thousands of tired, nerve-shaken, over-civilized people are beginning to find out that going to the mountains is going home; that wildness is a necessity; and that mountain parks and reservations are useful not only as fountains of timber and irrigating rivers, but as fountains of life.

Nevertheless, Muir himself recognized that the American public still needed educating about how to make the most of their encounters with wildlife:

> Travelers in the Sierra forests usually complain of the want of life.

'The trees,' they say, 'are fine, but the empty stillness is deadly; there are no animals to be seen, no birds. We have not heard a song in all the woods.' And no wonder! They go in large parties with mules and horse; they make a great noise; they are dressed in outlandish, unnatural colors: every animal shuns them. Even the frightened pines would shy away if they could.

Fortunately, as Muir pointed out, a minority of visitors to the American wilderness had learned how to behave:

> But Nature lovers, devout, silent, open-eyed, looking and listening with love, find no lack of inhabitants in these mountain mansions, and they come to them gladly . . . Every waterfall has its ouzel and every tree its bird: tiny nuthatch threading the furrows of the bark, cheerily whispering to itself as it deftly pries off loose scales and examines the furled edges of lichens . . . or some singer – oriole, tanager, warbler – resting, feeding, attending to domestic affairs.

MEANWHILE, at the same time as communications and transport were developing at home, the British were heading abroad in unprecedented numbers. Between 1880 and 1914 the British Empire grew in size by 4.5 million square miles, an area larger than the whole of the United States. At its height, at the end of World War I, Britain ruled more than a quarter of the world's land surface, embracing one in four of its people – truly an Empire 'on which the sun never sets'.

Built on the twin Victorian values of virtue and progress, and the assumption that these moral and material blessings should be shared with those less fortunate than themselves around the globe, the British Empire represented a golden opportunity for young men with an adventurous spirit. As doctors, soldiers and administrators, they were needed to oil the wheels of the vast imperial bureaucracy, keep the local people in check, and above all, as Asa Briggs puts it, 'to carry light and civilization to the dark places of the world'. In so doing, they found themselves with plenty of time on their hands – and what better way to spend it than watching, and of course collecting, birds? Thus men like Robert Swinhoe in China, Emin Pasha in Sudan, and a legion of Britons in India (including Jerdon, Hodgson, Blyth and Hume, all of whom gave their names to birds of the sub-continent) spent their ample leisure time collecting and observing the avifaunas of their new-found homes.

Army officers, too, were prominent; indeed, Mearns and Mearns have described them as 'by far the largest group of recreational collectors . . . in some of the remotest and least zoologically explored parts of the globe'. If it is true that war consists of ninety-nine per cent boredom interspersed with periods of intense activity, then *not* being at war was potentially even more soul-destroying; especially for those posted to some far-flung outpost. Some men sought solace in drink, gambling and the local women, while others expressed their urges in more wholesome ways, such as going out to collect the local birds. In this they at least had a head start over their civilian contemporaries: the ability to shoot straight.

One of the most prominent of this new breed of collectors was Allan Octavian Hume, son of a radical politician who later gained a well-earned reputation for statesmanship, decency and a genuine concern for India's rural poor. Beginning his career as a junior clerk, he rose rapidly through the civil service bureaucracy, gaining promotion for his adept handling of the Indian Mutiny of 1857-58. He combined his duties as a senior civil servant with frequent excursions around the sub-continent to collect birds. On one expedition he collected 1200 bird skins of 250 species, 18 of them new to the Indian avifauna – including the eponymous Hume's Wheatear – one of at least a dozen species which received his name as their epithet. By the time of his retirement in 1882 Hume had not only founded the Indian National Congress (an organization which, ironically, was instrumental in achieving that nation's independence from Britain) but could also be legitimately described by his friend and colleague C. H. T. Marshall as 'beyond all doubt the greatest authority on ornithology of the Indian Empire'.

In the spring of 1885, the fifty-six year old Hume returned to his home in Simla after spending the winter on the plains, intending to begin work on his greatest project, a series of books on all the birds of India. To his horror, he discovered that while he had been away his servants had gathered up several hundredweight of his manuscripts, papers and correspondence, carefully collected over the past twenty-five years, and taken them down to the local bazaar to be sold as waste paper.

The precious material was never recovered, and the dejected Hume never worked on Indian ornithology again. In a characteristically generous gesture, he donated his entire collection – more than 100,000 skins, eggs and nests, of over 250 species – to the Natural History Museum in London, before retiring in 1894, to the leafy suburbs of Upper Norwood in south London. He lived there quietly until his death in July 1912, at the age of eighty-three.

IN THAT SAME YEAR, other Britons were exploring quite literally to the ends of the earth. On his famous expeditions to the Antarctic, Captain Robert Falcon Scott was accompanied by two keen birdwatchers.

Had he survived the fateful journey to the South Pole, there is little doubt that Edward 'Bill' Wilson would have become one of the most influential birdwatchers and ornithologists of his day. Trained as a doctor, Wilson had accompanied Scott on his first expedition to the Antarctic in 1901. His skills as a bird artist had rapidly brought him to public notice, with his illustrations appearing in the popular account of the expedition. An ascetic and deeply religious man, he always strove to draw himself closer to God. It is said that once, while staying away from home in a hotel, he realized that he was beginning to prefer bathing in hot water to cold, and that 'something must be done to stop it'.

Despite a youthful bout of tuberculosis which had left him with scarred lungs, and a recent eye injury caused by a splash of boiling whale blubber, his determination secured him a place in Scott's party for the quest to reach the South Pole in the southern summer of 1911-1912. Along with his four companions, he perished in the attempt – thereby both ensuring his own immortality, and depriving the world of a talented ornithologist. At the end of his life, as they lay together in a frozen hut with no hope of rescue, Scott wrote a final letter to Wilson's mother: 'I can do no more to comfort you, than to tell you that he died as he lived, a brave, true man – the best of comrades and staunchest of friends.'

Another keen birdwatcher on the expedition did survive to tell the tale. Apsley Cherry-Garrard, or 'Cherry', as he was always known, was one of the party that went in search of Scott and his men, discovering their frozen bodies just eleven miles from food and safety. The failure to find them in time weighed heavily on Cherry's mind for the rest of his life.

Cherry cuts an unlikely figure either as hero, explorer or birdwatcher. He was kind, not very strong, and short-sighted to the point of virtual blindness (especially in Antarctica, where it was often impossible to wear spectacles because of driving snow). Yet his account of the polar expeditions published in 1922, *The Worst Journey in the World*, was an instant hit with the reading public, and has become a classic of the travel writing genre.

At its heart is the account of an extraordinary expedition, together with Wilson and 'Birdie' Bowers, during the winter of 1911. Their aim was to walk the sixty miles or so to the Emperor Penguin colony at Cape Crozier, in order to collect specimens of the eggs of this, the world's largest penguin, which they believed would reveal important facts about evolution. They eventually succeeded, though not without undergoing some of the worst hardships imaginable in temperatures which fell as low as minus 75 degrees Fahrenheit (minus 60 degrees Celsius). As Cherry later wrote: 'Antarctic exploration is seldom as bad as you imagine, seldom as bad as it sounds. But this journey had beggared our language: no words could express its horror.'

Thirty-five days after they had set out, the trio returned to base at Cape Evans, to a heroes' welcome. Scott described the expedition in his diary as 'one of the most gallant stories in polar history . . . a tale for our generation which I hope may not be lost in the telling'. Ironically, the scientific results of their suffering were of little or no importance: the penguins' embryos were too well developed to test out any scientific theories about evolution.

The polar expedition had an unforeseen impact on the development of birdwatching. Knowing that he was certain to die, Captain Scott wrote a final letter home to his wife Kathleen. He included firm instructions on how to bring up their infant son. 'Make the boy interested in natural history if you can,' he wrote; 'it is better than games.' Scott's dying wish had lasting consequences, for the young boy was none other than Peter (later Sir Peter) Scott, whose influence on natural history, conservation and birdwatching in Britain was arguably greater than any other twentieth-century figure. (See Chapter 11)

NOT EVERYONE had the opportunity to travel to distant parts of the world. But those who remained at home could still pursue their interest in birds. Indeed, as in the days of Gilbert White a century before, men of the cloth were still actively encouraged to do so. Partly this was due to the fortuitous combination of education and available leisure time, but as Patrick Armstrong observes, there was also a moral dimension to their pursuit:

> The nineteenth century was the heyday of the English parson-
> naturalist . . . through a diligent study of Creation, humanity may
> approach the Creator. Activity was preferred to the devil's aid,
> idleness; outdoor activity was particularly worthy and 'healthy',
> and well-directed outdoor activity such as collecting plants,
> observing geology or watching birds was especially to be
> encouraged − it was almost a moral duty.

One way to celebrate nature, and at the same time spread the word of God, was by writing books. A typical example was *A Familiar History of Birds*, written by the Bishop of Norwich, Edward Stanley. Posthumously published in 1865 by the Society for Promoting Christian Knowledge, this is a familiar blend of basic biology, anecdotal observation and Victorian prejudice. It contains such headings as 'Vultures – Loathsome feeders', 'Affectionate disposition of the Ostrich', and the usual old chestnut, 'Eagles carrying off children', and is intended above all for the reader's spiritual edification:

> The many anecdotes collected from the Author's own observation, the information of friends, or various respectable sources, will, it is hoped, excite others to register any facts within their reach, which may illustrate the mysterious economy whereby this beautiful portion of God's creation is enabled, in so many instances, to surpass the highest efforts of man's ingenuity, foresight, or philosophy.

Mankind was still seen as superior to the rest of creation, but human beings now had a duty of care as well: it was no longer acceptable to exploit nature without giving a thought to the consequences. This marked a halfway house between pre-Victorian attitudes and those of the twentieth century, when wildlife was finally granted its own intrinsic value.

Stanley's *Familiar History of Birds* was just one of a flood of popular natural history books that appeared during the latter half of the nineteenth century, a far cry from the expensive, subscription-only works of a generation before. Partly this was symptomatic of a general boom in popular publishing, brought about by innovations in printing such as the invention of lithography, which permitted the reproduction of colour illustrations at a reasonable price. Another reason was that far more people could now read. At the beginning of the nineteenth century most working class children only attended the occasional elementary school class, and even by 1861 only one in eight children attended school regularly. The Elementary Education Act of 1870 was a watershed, providing for all children to receive at least a basic education, whatever their age or class.

On the debit side, the growth in education and publishing was also responsible for a vast amount of inaccurate and sentimental twaddle. Notorious examples are the Revd C. A. Johns' *British Birds and their Haunts*, and The Revd F. O. Morris's *A History of British Birds* (1850-57), memorably defined by Lynn Barber as a work of 'quite stupefying dullness.' Unfortunately, although Morris was suitably humble and productive, he lacked one other vital quality – that of accuracy. In the withering verdict of Mullens and Swann: 'Morris was too voluminous to be accurate, and too didactic to be scientific. He accepted records and statements without discrimination, and consequently his book abounds with errors and mistakes.'

However, the general public at whom the books were aimed did not care whether they were accurate or not. It was enough that they were attractive and easy to read, qualities that kept them in print for many years. Even today, coloured pictures taken from Morris's works can be found in most second-hand book shops, reflecting their widespread popularity at the time.

A FEW MORE adventurous clergymen became pioneers abroad, as well as at home. From the late eighteenth century onwards, as the British Empire rapidly expanded, clerical naturalists also had the opportunity to exercise their passion for bird study, as the Biblical exhortation puts it, 'at the uttermost parts of the Earth.' One of the pioneers was Gilbert White's brother John, who was sent into exile as a chaplain at Gibraltar to avoid scandal and debt. Gilbert White himself encouraged his brother to take an interest in wildlife, and reaped the benefits when John sent him useful information on migratory birds.

The most notable of these clerical collectors was the redoubtable Reverend Henry Baker Tristram, an English clergyman who pioneered bird studies in North Africa and the Middle East, and who had three of the region's birds named after him: a warbler, a finch and a starling. His other claim to fame was that he was the first person to apply Darwin's theory of natural selection, when in 1859 he used it to explain the reasons for the coloration of various desert birds.

The son of a country vicar, and great-nephew of Daines Barrington, one of Gilbert White's original correspondents, Tristram continued the family interest in wildlife by amassing a suitably impressive collection of birds' eggs as a child. After following a conventional path into the clergy via public school and Oxford, fate intervened. Just after being appointed to a curacy in England, a weak chest required a warm climate in which to convalesce, and he was sent to Bermuda as naval and military chaplain. There his passion for birds grew, and continued once he returned home as rector of Castle Eden, in County Durham.

From that time onwards, Tristram led an extraordinary double life: alternating long periods as a clergyman in a quiet country parish, with long and arduous expeditions abroad. These included visits to Algeria, and to the land then known as Palestine (now Israel, the Occupied Territories and Lebanon). On one trip to Palestine in 1863-1864, he was accompanied by another Englishman, Henry Morris Upcher. The squire of a large country estate in Norfolk, Upcher soon won the admiration of his colleagues – earning the Arab sobriquet 'Father of two eyes' for his skilled marksmanship, honed by years of shooting gamebirds at home. After Upcher had returned to England in early June 1864, Tristram continued on to Mount Hermon, on today's border between Israel and Lebanon. There, he had a red-letter day by anyone's standards, shooting two birds which he believed were new to science: a large, plain, greyish-coloured warbler; and a small, yellowish-green finch. In fact they had both been discovered a few years earlier, but nevertheless both now bear his own name and that of his companion: Tristram's Serin and Upcher's Warbler.

Both Morris's and Tristram's lifetimes spanned the era between collecting and protecting birds. Like all bird artists of his day, Morris relied on mounted specimens – indeed, Morris's *History of British Birds* was widely used by taxidermists to work out the correct posture for each species. Yet later on he became a pioneer of bird protection, and in the 1860s he founded the Yorkshire Association for the Protection of Sea Birds, whose campaigning led to some of the first bird protection legislation.

This was not the only area in which he showed admirable fore-sight: he also wrote to *The Times* recommending that food be put out for birds during the winter months. And although Tristram was popularly known as 'The Great Gun' for his shooting and collecting exploits, later in life he supported early bird protection measures. In 1873, at a meeting of the British Association for the Advancement of Science in Edinburgh, he backed a motion condemning collectors, and calling for the preservation and pro-tection of British birds and their eggs. From 1904, until his death at the age of eighty-three in 1906, Tristram became vice-president of the newly-formed RSPB.

The eventual change of heart in both these men was sympto-matic of a radical shift in society as a whole. After dominating the scene for almost a century, the era of the bird collector was finally coming to an end, and that of the bird protector was about to begin.

CHAPTER SIX

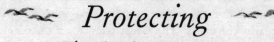

Protecting

The Victorian Era, part III

'A bird in the bush is worth two in the hand'.
Motto of *Bird-Lore*, magazine of Audubon
Societies of North America (1899)

'I do not protect birds. I kill them.'
Charles B. Cory, president-elect of the
American Ornithologists' Union (1902)

LIKE MANY great British institutions, the Royal Society for the Protection of Birds grew from humble and somewhat unlikely beginnings. In February 1889, a group of respectable middle-class women gathered in the Manchester suburb of Didsbury. Their mission was to put a stop to the widespread use of bird skins and feathers in the fashion and millinery trades, which was having such a devastating effect on bird populations. To show their commitment to the cause, they each paid an annual membership fee of 2 old pence (approximately 1p, but the equivalent of £2 today).

By 1899 the Society had over 150 branches and more than 20,000 members, the majority of them women. Just over a century later the Society's millionth member would sign up for the cause, and what had started out as a single issue pressure group would become the most successful conservation organization in Europe, embracing a wide range of issues from land use to hunting, and energy efficiency to climate change.

In 1989, to celebrate its one hundredth anniversary, the RSPB commissioned journalist and writer Tony Samstag to write a history of the organization. In the resulting work, *For the Love of*

Birds, Samstag was under no illusions as to the reasons behind the Society's enduring success:

> The RSPB . . . was born in and of cruelty, has thrived on it
> for a hundred years, grown prosperous and successful in fear,
> loathing and pain. Without the propensity of men to exercise
> their power in a wantonly destructive way, the RSPB would
> go out of business.

Along with the Audubon Societies, its counterparts in North America, the RSPB has spent the past century attempting to right the many wrongs which human beings – as individuals, corporations and governments – have inflicted on birds and their habitats.

IN THE WESTERN world at least, a willingness to prevent mankind's gratuitous exploitation of the natural world went hand in hand with the development of civilization. For most of human history it had been assumed that 'brute creation' was there for man to exploit and use at will – an attitude with backing from no less an authority than the book of Genesis, where it is written that: 'Every moving thing that liveth shall be meat for you.'

During the seventeenth and eighteenth centuries there had been a gradual shift away from seeing animals purely from this utilitarian point of view, to having their own intrinsic value. By the beginning of the nineteenth century it was widely accepted that human beings had responsibilities towards wild creatures, as well as rights over them. In the words of the poet William Blake: 'A robin redbreast in a cage, puts all heaven in a rage'.

The foundation of the Society for the Protection of Animals (later to become the RSPCA), in 1824, was a direct result of this change in attitudes. For the first time, a significant sector of society – the burgeoning middle class – had the resources and imagination to care for other creatures, thanks to greater prosperity and better education. But it was a concern still confined, as Keith Thomas has pointed out, to the higher social classes: 'kindness to animals was a luxury which not everyone had learned to afford'.

Despite its current unassailable position as 'market leader' in the field of nature conservation, the RSPB was not the first organization to be concerned with the protection of birds. The Yorkshire Association for the Protection of Sea Birds was founded sometime during the 1860s, and was arguably the first wildlife conservation society anywhere in the world. At the same time, a group of women in Croydon calling themselves the Fur, Fin and Feather Folk, took a pledge to avoid animal products in fashion.

The new movement had some influential supporters. In 1868, Professor Alfred Newton, the leading ornithologist of his day, addressed the British Association at Norwich: 'Fair and innocent as the snowy plumes may appear on a lady's hat, I must tell the wearer the truth – she bears the murderer's brand on her forehead.'

In a reflection of this gradual change in attitudes, the first bird protection legislation now began to appear on the statute book. In June 1869, Parliament passed the Sea Birds Preservation Act, prompted by the situation on the Yorkshire coast, where bird collecting had reached epidemic proportions. A report in the *Manchester Guardian* of 18 November 1868 refuted the collectors' claim that their harvest of seabirds was sustainable:

> On a strip of coast eighteen miles long near Flamborough Head, 107,250 sea-birds were destroyed by 'pleasure parties' in four months; 12,000 by men who shoot them for their feathers to adorn women's hats and 79,500 young birds died of starvation in emptied nests. Commander Knocker, there stationed, who reported these facts, saw two boats loaded above the gunwales with dead birds, and one party of eight guns killed 1100 birds in a week.

Such greedy exploitation of what appeared to be an infinite resource had already had devastating – indeed irrevocable – effects on one species. The Great Auk was the largest member of its family, and like the southern penguins was flightless, an undoubted factor in its downfall. Moreover, its breeding colonies were at lower latitudes than many other seabirds, making them more accessible to sailors eager to supplement their meagre rations with fresh meat. The last British record was from St Kilda, where a bird was captured and killed in 1840 by islanders who thought it was a witch; while the last Great Auk of all was clubbed to death off Iceland in June 1844.

Concern was also beginning to grow about the reckless shooting of wild birds for sport. In March 1888, just eleven months before the founding of the RSPB, the Breydon Wild Birds Protection Society was established at a public meeting in Great Yarmouth in Norfolk. Its purpose was to employ local men to watch over Breydon Water, a noted haunt of breeding and migrant birds. The plan was an immediate success: in June 1888, Albert Beckett, landlord of the Lord Nelson pub, was fined 40 shillings (about £400 today) for shooting two spoonbills. Illegal shooting rapidly declined, and by 1904 it could be reported that 'not a gun was fired on Breydon during the close season, notwithstanding the visits of many rare birds'.

Meanwhile, the newly formed Society for the Protection of Birds (the royal seal of approval was added in 1904) wasted no time in making its voice heard against the fashion trades. The task was made easier because the campaigners came from the same social class as those they were campaigning against. As Samstag has observed, the Society was an 'archetypal British voluntary organisation operating from a position of hereditary privilege, run mainly by and for women'.

Nevertheless, they had a fight on their hands: a taste for feathers in fashion went back to Greek and Roman times, and in the late Victorian era the trade was at its height. Between 1870 and 1920 20,000 tons of ornamental plumage, from many millions of birds, was imported into the UK. The estimated value of this trade was £20 million – as much as £4 billion at today's prices. Historian E. S. Turner has painted a graphic picture of what this meant in practice: 'At busy periods, the dealers of London and Paris nearly suffocated under their wares.'

Gradually, though, the Society's campaign began to hit home. Parliament continued to pass legislation, extending protection to many more species with the Wild Birds Protection Acts of 1880, 1894, 1896 and 1898. Little by little, the tide of opinion began to turn, with help coming from the highest level when, in 1899, Queen Victoria herself ordered that regiments in the armed forces should stop wearing plumes in their uniforms.

IN NORTH AMERICA, bird protection was developing in parallel to progress in Britain. Although an act to protect wildfowl in the Canadian province of Newfoundland had been passed as early as 1845, it was not until 1886 that the first official bird protection society in the United States was formed. The Audubon Society was the brainchild of George Bird Grinnell, and by the end of its first year boasted over 300 chapters and nearly 18,000 members. Its popularity undoubtedly benefited from its link with the most famous of all American bird artists, though there is a certain irony that the world's best-known bird protection society should be named after the man who took the killing of birds to new heights in pursuit of his art.

Like the RSPB, the Audubon Society was founded to protest against the wholesale slaughter of birds in order to supply skins and feathers for the fashion industry, in particular for ladies' hats. Ornate creations adorned with not just feathers but the whole skins of birds were now all the rage, with mail order companies advertising their wares at prices ranging from $1.19 to $3.69 ($30-$75 today). This bizarre fashion was encouraged by the social pages of the newspapers. 'Miss Brady looked extremely well in white,' noted one 1885 article, 'with a whole nest of sparkling scintillating birds in her hair, which it would have puzzled an ornithologist to classify.'

The grisly reality behind the glamorous façade was that millions of birds were being slaughtered simply to satisfy fashion. In 1886, a few months after this article appeared, Joel A. Allen, curator of birds at the American Museum of Natural History, called for controls on egg collecting and the plume trade, supporting his argument with statistics showing the scale of the carnage. He revealed that in a single season on Cape Cod, Massachusetts, 40,000 terns had been killed for their feathers; that a village on

Long Island had supplied 70,000 skins in just four months; and that a single millinery firm in New York was processing 30,000 birds every year. Unfortunately, despite the growing outrage, America's embryonic bird preservation movement ran out of steam, and by 1888, just two years after its foundation, Grinnell abandoned his society.

It took a further decade of killing before a new movement would begin. Harriet Lawrence Hemenway founded the Massachusetts Audubon Society in February 1896, 'to discourage the buying and wearing, for ornamental purposes, of the feathers of any wild birds . . . and to otherwise further the protection of native birds'. Mrs Hemenway was provoked to action when she read a no-holds barred account of the carnage left in the wake of a collecting expedition for the fashion industry, written by a young man named Gilbert Pearson:

> I had expected to see some of the beautiful herons about their nests, or standing on the trees nearby, but not a living one could be found, while here and there in the mud lay the lifeless forms of eight of the birds. They had been shot down and the skins bearing their plumes stripped from their backs. Flies were busily at work . . . This was not the worst; in four of the nests young orphan birds could be seen who were clamouring piteously for food which their dead parents could never again bring them.

By the end of 1896 two more states, West Virginia and Pennsylvania, had come on board, while the first decade of the twentieth century saw the addition of a further twenty-six – more than half the states in the Union.

This second movement succeeded when the first one had failed, partly because it was founded on smaller, state-based societies, and partly because bird protection had simply become a more socially acceptable cause. Women themselves were becoming sensitive to the fact that not everyone found the wearing of bird skins and feathers attractive, as contemporary nature writer Charles Warner acidly noted: 'A dead bird does not help the appearance of an ugly woman, and a pretty woman needs no such adornment.'

Nevertheless, many influential ornithologists continued to defend the collecting of birds for scientific purposes, so criticizing the plumage trade would lay them open to the charge of hypocrisy. For some, though, there was no moral dilemma – birds were there to be used. In 1902 Charles B. Cory, the president-elect of the American Ornithologists' Union (AOU), was invited to a meeting of the District of Columbia Audubon Society. His refusal was terse and to the point: 'I do not protect birds. I kill them.' The issue polarized opinion, with a heated debate on what constituted 'scientific collecting', reminiscent of the current dispute over 'scientific whaling'. In 1899 the nature writer Leander Keyser criticized the scientists, entreating them to 'study birds in all the varied phases of their lives'. 'What's the birds for,' countered one taxidermist, 'if they ain't to be used?!' No matter that the number of birds killed in the name of science was infinitesimal compared with the plumage trade, the criticisms hit home, and not without justification: one collector, W. E. D. Scott, called for a ban on commercial hunting while at the same time managing to shoot no fewer than seventeen specimens of Bachman's Warbler, which has since become extinct.

For another North American species, the bird protection movement had also come too late. At its peak, the Passenger Pigeon accounted for between one quarter and one third of all the birds living in North America – as many as two billion individuals. As late as 1870 flocks still darkened the skies as they passed overhead; yet once the bird's decline began, it was extraordinarily swift. The last wild bird was shot in Ohio in March 1900; the last surviving captive bird, named Martha, died at Cincinnati Zoo in September 1914.

There was human tragedy, too. In 1905 one of the Audubon Society's first wardens, Guy Bradley, noticed three men he suspected of shooting birds on a refuge at Oyster Key in south Florida. As he approached he noticed that they were carrying two dead egrets. When challenged, one of the men shot Bradley in the chest, killing him instantly. Because of a lack of witnesses, the culprit was never indicted for the crime.

IN JUST ONE or two generations, from the middle to the end of the nineteenth century, Americans had moved from the 'wild west' to the streets and avenues of the big city. In the process, their attitude had changed, from the insecure 'frontier mentality' of the pioneers, to the more mature, sophisticated ethos of the modern city dweller. Their view of the natural world changed too: 'One thing was clear,' Mark V. Barrow notes: 'the more Americans removed themselves from nature, the more they came to value it.'

The notion of watching birds for recreation and pleasure was still new, but as we have seen, it derived huge impetus from writers such as John Muir, and another figurehead of the nature conservation movement, Henry David Thoreau. In sharp contrast to men of the previous generation such as Audubon and Wilson, whose main aim was to categorize this new and unfamiliar avifauna, these writers sought to commune with nature in a more holistic, less analytical way.

The difference between Audubon and Thoreau is particularly striking. Born in 1817, just thirty-two years after Audubon, Thoreau spent his days wandering around his home neighbourhood of Concord, Massachusetts, and the nights writing up a detailed record of his thoughts and observations. This oft-quoted passage from his best-known work, *Walden, or Life in the Woods*, reveals that his attitude was one of co-operation with wild nature rather than domination over it:

> I found myself suddenly neighbor to the birds; not by having imprisoned one, but having caged myself near them. I was not only nearer to some of those which commonly frequent the garden and the orchard, but to those wilder and more thrilling songsters of the forest . . .

There is no doubt that Thoreau was ahead of his time: unlike most of his contemporaries, he far preferred watching birds to shooting them:

I wonder if it would not be well to carry a spy-glass in order to watch these shy birds such as ducks and hawks? In some respects, me thinks, it would be better than a gun. The latter brings them nearer dead but the former alive. You can identify the species better by killing the bird . . . but you can study the habits and appearance best in a living specimen.

The spy-glass he chose, presumably one designed for military use, cost eight dollars, an extravagant sum equivalent to perhaps one hundred times as much in today's money. Nevertheless, he got good use from it, and it confirmed his long-held belief that killing was not only pointless but destructive:

This haste to kill a bird or quadruped and make a skeleton of it, which many young men and some old ones exhibit, reminds me of the fable of the man who killed the hen that laid the golden eggs, and so got no more gold . . . Such is the knowledge you get from the living creature.

Thoreau's writings had a lasting effect on the attitudes of newly urbanized Americans, many of whose experience of nature was now limited to reading about it in his own accounts. Helped by this change in public attitudes, the protectionists began to make headway, and a new, moral tone appeared in the campaign literature. Writing in 1886, AOU President J. A. Allen was one of the first to put into words the aesthetic (as opposed to the scientific or commercial) value of birds:

Birds, considered aesthetically, are among the most graceful in movement and form, and the most beautiful and attractive in coloration, of nature's many gifts to man. Add to this their vivacity, their melodious voices and unceasing activity . . . and can we well say that we are prepared to see them exterminated in behalf of fashion, or to gratify a depraved taste?

Nevertheless, as late as 1905 a correspondent to a popular magazine, *American Ornithology for the Home and School*, was lamenting the continuing insensitivity of women who persisted in wearing plumes and skins:

As far as I can see, the continued agitation against the wearing of birds as ornaments, has had little effect here in Boston. Nearly half the hats seen on the street have on them various parts of what were once beautiful, happy birds. On some, heads; some, tails; some, wings; and on some the entire bird. Can you imagine anything more ridiculous than a young woman sporting an entire Herring Gull on her head? It seems a pity that women would cling to this barbarous fashion until actually forced to put it aside to escape prosecution. Perhaps they do not realize what they do.

I T IS IRONIC that one of the driving forces behind this growing bird protection movement in North America was a 'poacher turned gamekeeper' – a formerly enthusiastic collector who gradually came to see the merits in protecting wild birds against indiscriminate slaughter.

Frank Chapman (1864-1945) spanned the era from the nineteenth century, when collecting was still taken for granted, to the twentieth, when watching birds with optical aids finally became the custom. His interest in bird protection began in the summer of 1886, when he was working as a bank clerk in New York City. One summer's afternoon he took a stroll through an uptown shopping district, and counted 700 ladies in hats, three-quarters of which contained feathers. Using the skills he had gained as a keen collector, he managed to identify the plumes as coming from a wide range of species, including American Robin, Scarlet Tanager, Blackburnian Warbler, Cedar Waxwing, Bobolink, Blue Jay, Scissor-tailed Flycatcher, Red-headed Woodpecker, Northern Saw-whet Owl and Pine Grosbeak.

Chapman charitably observed that: 'It is probable that few if any of the women knew that they were wearing the plumage of the birds of our gardens, orchards and forests.'

Yet despite disapproving of the slaughter of birds in the name of fashion, Chapman continued to defend – indeed promote – the scientific collecting of birds throughout his distinguished career, and even went on expeditions to hunt them himself.

Today, the state of Florida is home to Disneyworld, the NASA centre at Cape Canaveral, and more than sixteen million people. But in 1889, when Chapman made his first expedition there, things were very different: Florida's population was less than 400,000, and the state's swamps, forests and coastlines were a veritable wilderness for birds.

Deep in the fetid swampland of the Indian River, Chapman discovered the last stronghold of a very rare species indeed, the Carolina Parakeet. He shot a total of fifteen birds, and liked the area so much that a few years later he came back again – this time on honeymoon with his bride, Fannie. Like many single-minded professional men, Chapman was understandably concerned that his newly acquired marital status would pose problems: 'When a man wedded to his profession takes a mortal wife he commits a very dangerous type of bigamy. If the two spouses do not agree there arises a three-cornered conflict to determine which one of them will be widowed.'

But to his delight, he soon discovered that his wife was not only enthusiastic about his passion for collecting birds, but also had a real aptitude for the craft. He tested her skills by asking her to skin a Marsh Wren:

> To my mixed astonishment, joy, and chagrin, her skilful fingers made so good a job of it that her second specimen was one of the [Dusky Seaside] Sparrows so rare that I handled them myself with caution. Thus her novitiate as assistant *preparateur* was as brief as it was satisfactory . . .

Sadly, two of the birds which Chapman and his wife were so keen to obtain subsequently became extinct: the last Carolina Parakeets were seen – and shot – at Lake Okeechobee, Florida, in April 1904; while the Dusky Seaside Sparrow managed to hang on along the Atlantic coast near Titusville until as recently as 1987.

There can be no doubt that the decline and final demise of these rare species was hastened by collectors like Chapman. But we can also thank him for helping prevent the shameful tally of North America's extinct birds from becoming even longer. For he became an avid campaigner for the protection and preservation of wild birds, curator of birds at the American Museum of Natural History, and founding editor of *Bird-Lore*, the official publication of the Audubon movement, which he began in 1899 and continued to own, publish and edit for the following thirty-five years.

Chapman's life sums up the dichotomy between collecting and protecting during this important transitional period: seeking to protect birds while at the same time defending the right to collect them for scientific purposes.

Another collector turned protector was the man who, as a young boy in the 1870s, had enjoyed bird collecting so much he worked in a taxidermist's shop on New York's Broadway and Worth Street. President Theodore Roosevelt was a key figure in the creation of bird protection laws in the US, creating fifty-one Federal Wildlife Refuges, including one at the site where Frank Chapman had slaughtered his Carolina Parakeets. By the time of his death in 1919 Roosevelt had accomplished more for the protection of wild birds than all the twenty-four US Presidents who had gone before. While governor of New York during the 1890s, he had closed down factories using bird feathers and skins, and joined the early Audubon movement. Roosevelt's great gift was vision: at a time when the general assumption was that natural resources would last forever, he made this appeal to the people of Sacramento, California: 'I ask that your marvellous natural resources be handed on unimpaired to your posterity. We are not building this country of ours for a day. It is to last through the ages.'

IN BRITAIN, another visionary was at work. Although the credit for eventual victory in the battle against the plumage trade cannot be given to any single individual, the campaign's most prominent figurehead on this side of the Atlantic was the popular nature writer W. H. Hudson.

Hudson was born in Argentina in 1842. Almost constant illness marked his early years, which meant he spent much of his childhood wandering the open pampas grassland, and studying its plant and animal life. After the death of his parents, he emigrated to England, and began his career as a writer of books, pamphlets and polemics against the plume trade, on behalf of the newly formed RSPB.

Like Thoreau, Hudson held views rooted in a deep spiritual appreciation of wild nature. 'One of the greatest pleasures in life – my life I mean,' he wrote in *Adventures Among Birds* (1913):

> . . . is to be present, in a sense invisible, in the midst of the domestic circle of beings of a different order, another world, than ours. Yet it is one which may be had by any person who desires it.

> Little birds are vertebrates and relations, with knowing, emotional, thinking brains like ours in their heads, and with senses like ours, only brighter. . . Thus we love and know them, and our more highly developed minds are capable of bridging the gulf which divides us from them . . .

But he never underestimated the difficulty of the task – when so many collectors had close connections with the British establishment:

> The law does not protect our birds and country from these robbers; they have too many respected representatives in high places, on the benches of magistrates, in the Houses of Parliament, and among important people generally. For are they not robbers and of the very worst description? . . . depriving the country . . . of one of its best possessions – its lustrous wild life.

Hudson was both an old-fashioned romantic and a forward-thinking visionary, his foresight revealed by his belief that actual possession of bird skins or eggs should be made a criminal offence. A law achieving this aim was finally passed – but not until 1982, sixty years after his death.

He did have one notable victory to celebrate, however. In 1921, Parliament passed the Importation of Plumage (Prohibition) Act, finally putting an end to the grisly exploitation of bird feathers and skins for the gratification of fashion. Hudson died in August 1922, having seen his views begin to prevail, and with his literary reputation at its height. But his fame was short-lived: by the 1950s his particular brand of sentimentality and spirituality had gone out of fashion, and today he is rarely read.

THIS GRADUAL change in attitudes, from an era when collecting birds was the normal practice to one where protecting them was paramount, came just in time in both Britain and North America. Sweeping urbanization and industrialization in the twentieth century would bring unprecedented habitat loss, leading to many bird species being under threat for the first time. The eleventh-hour arrival of the bird protection movement meant it would now play a vital part in safeguarding some of our rarest and most valuable birds.

From now on, more and more people would study living birds using optical aids, rather than dead birds obtained by looking down the barrel of a gun. The collectors had become, in Barbara and Richard Mearns' words, a 'mistrusted minority', and the era of bird watching – in its modern sense of a mass leisure activity – was about to begin.

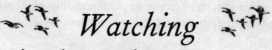

CHAPTER SEVEN

Watching

The Early Twentieth Century, 1901-1914

> The simple and intense delight in seeing and watching birds was always coupled with the desire to understand what we were seeing. Birdwatching is not only an intense aesthetic experience, but also a stimulus to the mind and to the imagination, as one tries to understand the nature of a bird's world.
>
> *Seventy Years of Birdwatching*, H. G. Alexander (1974)

ONE JULY DAY in 1908, a young man took a bicycle ride around Romney Marsh in Kent, in search of birds. As he was riding past the sand dunes by the coast at Littlestone, he saw three odd-looking birds sitting on the turf in the distance. Not sure of their identity, he got off his bicycle and walked across the grass towards them:

> I got near enough to identify them as Pallas's Sand Grouse ... A few days later the newspapers announced that a fresh invasion of Sand Grouse had taken place – the last of a series beginning in 1863. I knew nothing of the invasion when I found my three birds, and did not then even possess binoculars. At age nineteen I still relied on my eyes and a small telescope, which I think magnified four times, but its field [of view] was very small.

This was the very last invasion of this Central Asian species into Britain, and Pallas's Sandgrouse did not appear here again until a single bird was seen briefly in December 1964. Even today it remains one of the rarest and most sought-after visitors to our shores.

The young man's experience might have gone unrecorded, were it not for the fact that he went on to become one of the twentieth century's best-known birdwatchers. His name was Horace Alexander, but he was always known simply by his initials, as 'H. G.' Sixty-six years after his encounter with the sandgrouse, he published his memoirs under the intriguing title *Seventy Years of Birdwatching*. This was no idle boast: as the book's dust-jacket bore witness, H. G. 'began birdwatching in 1898 and has never stopped'. He continued to do so past his hundredth birthday, before his death in 1989, in his adopted home in a Philadelphian suburb. In between he led an extraordinary life, which included becoming a close advisor to the Indian leader Mahatma Gandhi, who described him as 'one of the best English friends India has'. Throughout his life he maintained a reputation for innocent enthusiasm, an impression reinforced by his rather childlike facial expression.

According to the doyen of today's birdwatchers, Ian Wallace, H. G. Alexander was 'one of those remarkable gentlemen who virtually founded the hobby and science of birdwatching'.

Though this comment could be applied to several figures in this book, it is particularly appropriate in this case. H. G.'s life coincided with the seismic shift in the pastime, which during the twentieth century went from being a minority interest pursued by a handful of eccentrics, to a mass participation activity followed by millions.

Brought up on the borders of rural Kent and Sussex, H. G. Alexander was one of four brothers, three of whom later became eminent ornithologists. Young Horace's interest in birds was first awakened on his eighth birthday on 18 April 1897, when his elder brother Gilbert gave him a book on natural history. Horace, and his brothers Wilfred and Christopher, soon became obsessed by their new craze, each trying to outdo the others in a spirit of friendly rivalry.

Looking back, Horace ascribed the brothers' interest in nature to their Quaker upbringing, which denied them access to music and the arts. So, by way of compensation, Quakers became students of natural history, of the world of nature, and they got a great deal of pleasure from this pursuit.

Bear in mind that when Horace and his brothers took up

watching birds for pleasure, the pastime was not yet known as 'birdwatching'. That phrase first appeared in print in 1901, the year Queen Victoria died, as the title of a book by Edmund Selous, younger brother of the celebrated big-game hunter F. C. Selous. *Bird Watching* was an unremarkable work: a miscellany of anecdotes, popular science and sentimentality, written in an ornate, florid style, of which this opening passage is typical:

> If life is, as some hold it to be, a vast melancholy ocean over which ships more or less sorrow-laden continually pass and ply, yet there lie here and there upon it isles of consolation on to which we may step out and for a time forget the winds and waves. One of these we may call Bird-isle – the island of watching and being entertained by the habits and humours of birds – and upon this one . . . I will straightway land, inviting such as may care to, to follow me.

Looking back more than a century later, it seems extraordinary that a phrase which we now take for granted was created by a man who did not even publish his first paper on birds until the age of forty-one, and whose death in 1934 went largely unnoticed by the ornithological establishment.

In 1905, Selous published an account of his expedition to the northern isles, *A Bird Watcher in the Shetlands*, which was given to the young Horace as a Christmas present by his Uncle James. It had the valuable effect of drawing him away from the temptations of egg collecting, and towards careful field observation of birds:

> None of our uncles ever used a gun. But Uncle James had a collection of eggs, and Wilfred followed his example. At first I wanted to do the same; but my parents discouraged the idea. By the time I acquired his book, Selous, supporting Hudson, confirmed me in accepting this way of bird study as the best.

Yet incredible though it may seem, H. G. did not actually own a pair of binoculars until his twenty-first birthday in 1910, by which time he had been a serious birdwatcher for at least twelve years. During this period he had to share a pair with his older brother Christopher, which could be frustrating, as he recalled when they caught sight of a kingfisher: 'Christopher would whip his binoculars off in a split second so that I could see the vanishing bird.'

Even those who did own binoculars still faced problems: it is said that a Sussex vicar switched his attention from birdwatching to botany because whenever he went out carrying a pair of binoculars his parishioners thought he was off to the races!

By the time H. G. Alexander died in 1989, he had witnessed unprecedented change in the world of birdwatching, from a time when shooting and collecting a rare bird was not only acceptable but almost inevitable; to the start of the twitching era in the 1960s and 1970s.

The seeds of this transformation can be found in the years from 1901 to 1914. During this time, birdwatching went from being a narrow, specialized and somewhat eccentric pastime pursued mainly by scientists, to a hobby in its own right – something ordinary people did purely for pleasure. More specific areas of interest, including feeding birds, migration studies and bird ringing, also emerged during this period.

In turn, these activities led to the emergence of a science of practical field ornithology, and gave a new respectability to the study of birds. This chapter will examine how this happened, during the brief period from the death of Queen Victoria to the start of World War I.

DESPITE H. G. Alexander's lack of optical aids during his childhood and early youth, binoculars were beginning to become more widely available.

According to Dr Fred Watson, an astronomer who has researched the history of early optics, the very first 'pair of binoculars' was constructed in 1608 by Dutch spectacle-maker Hans Lipperhey. His instrument was simply two telescopes joined together, and though it conferred a marginal advantage on the user, it was too difficult to manufacture for practical use. During the following century several people, including the Italian philosopher Galileo Galilei, the German astronomer Johann Kepler, and the English scientist Sir Isaac Newton all spent time investigating the properties of lenses. The biggest problem was how to achieve magnification without its attendant problems such as chromatic aberration, which created ghost images fringed with colour, and made the instruments all but useless for practical purposes.

During the eighteenth and early nineteenth centuries, meanwhile, optical instruments were being developed for a very different purpose: to allow opera buffs and theatre-goers to watch a performance through what soon became known as an 'opera glass'. At first these were small and very simple telescopes, decorated with gilt and ivory, and magnifying two or three times – more a fashion accessory than a useful optical aid. But gradually they improved, especially after the Austrian Johann Friedrich Voigtländer joined two tubes together to make 'opera glasses'.

These instruments were soon adapted for outdoor use: not for recreational purposes such as watching wildlife, but for a far more utilitarian reason – to spy on the enemy during wartime. During the Crimean War, from 1853-56, field glasses (as they had come to be known) were issued to the British forces, though their poor optical quality led one officer to dismiss them as 'useless toys'.

In 1854, came the breakthrough which led directly to the binoculars we still use today. That year, the Italian inventor Ignatio Porro registered a patent for a compact prismatic system, which used transparent blocks of glass with flat, highly polished surfaces to transmit or reflect light. This was a major advance, as by 'folding up' the path of light through the instrument, telescopes could be made much shorter than before. Porro himself did not attempt to construct a binocular version of his instrument, but within five years several manufacturers did – though poor materials and inferior workmanship still meant that these were inadequate for use in the field.

Finally, in 1894, Ernst Abbe – an optical designer based in the German city of Jena – joined forces with the scientific instrument maker Carl Zeiss to produce the first truly effective pair of prismatic binoculars: the Zeiss Feldstecher (German for field glass). Two years later they went on sale in Britain, selling for the princely sum of £6 10 shillings to £8 (equivalent to several hundred pounds today). With their 8x magnification and 20mm objective lens, they bore a remarkable resemblance to instruments used by birdwatchers for much of the following century.

Other manufacturers, including Bausch and Lomb in the USA, Voigtländer in Germany and Ross in the United Kingdom, soon entered the market, and by the first decade of the twentieth century prismatic binoculars became the standard instrument for civilian as well as military uses – including birdwatching.

Meanwhile, the introduction of optical aids had led American nature writer Florence Merriam to produce her best-selling book *Birds through an Opera Glass*, in 1889. It was a guide to seventy of the commoner North American species, and although poorly illustrated, it can be regarded as the precursor of the modern field guide, almost half a century before Roger Tory Peterson. With its no-nonsense approach, it inspired many Americans to take up birdwatching:

> The first law of field work is exact observation, but not only are you more likely to observe accurately if what you see is put in black and white, but you will find it much easier to identify the birds from your notes than from memory.

The improvement in optics was also a major influence on the growing acceptance of 'sight-records' – field observations of a rare bird, supported by notes – which meant that unusual visitors no longer needed to be shot to be accepted by the ornithological establishment.

Two men almost single-handedly changed the attitude towards sight records in Britain. One was H. F. Witherby, founding editor of *British Birds* magazine. The other, ironically, was a noted egg-collector – the Revd F. C. R. Jourdain.

From an early age Harry Forbes Witherby had devoted his spare time to studying birds. Later, he had travelled extensively through the Middle East and Africa, a journey he described in *Bird Hunting on the White Nile*, published in 1902. His enthusiasm for birds was single-minded: it is reported that on their honeymoon in

Algeria he taught his wife Lilian the art of skinning and preparing specimens.

Witherby soon became converted to a less brutal method of studying birds, which he described as 'systematic investigation' – using the growing army of amateur birdwatchers to help answer scientific questions about birds. This was a revolutionary approach, which eventually led to the founding of the British Trust for Ornithology, and would transform the way birdwatching was to develop during the twentieth century.

The first stage in this revolution was to establish a new monthly magazine in which Witherby could spread the gospel to a wider public. The inaugural issue of *British Birds* appeared in June 1907. From the very first page, Witherby laid out his manifesto in clear and explicit terms:

> We hope, with the co-operation of our readers, to embark upon a series of more systematic investigations than have hitherto been attempted . . . Could observations on such points be conducted on a common basis and made contemporaneously in different parts of the country, results of great interest and of very considerable scientific importance would be achieved.

About the same time, his friend and colleague Jourdain began to create a set of 'field-characters', in the manner of a military drill, to be used by observers to test their sightings. This enabled records to be checked against original field-notes, and rejected if they failed to pass this rigorous inspection. It is ironic that this new approach, developed by one of the most notorious egg-collectors of his day, would become one of the prime weapons against the practice of collecting specimens. Barbara and Richard Mearns have given a mixed verdict on this complex man:

> The Revd Jourdain was no ordinary egg-collector; he had one of the largest and most scientifically useful egg collections in Europe. After forty years of ransacking the more important West Palearctic habitats there was no-one to rival his immense knowledge of the region's breeding birds. Since he worked through the period when egg collecting became unfashionable,

if not unpardonable, he never received proper recognition for his profound contribution to ornithology.

M EANWHILE, ordinary people continued to become bird watchers after going through the egg-collecting phase as schoolboys – where it was popularized in children's books such as *Tom Brown's Schooldays*. Looking back in 1950, popular nature writer E. W. Hendy recalled his childhood initiation into the ritual:

> At my first private school we were the usual rout of birds-nesting boys, for in those Victorian days interest in birds was confined to the collection of their eggs. In fact, the first book on birds which I possessed consisted of detailed instructions as to how to find nests and how to blow eggs . . . The approved method of preserving these trophies was to stick them with gum on a stiff sheet of paper attached to the bottom of a cardboard box; naturally most of them got broken.

Collecting also brought an extra thrill – the very real danger of being caught:

> I remember that my elders instilled into us a healthy dread of the Police, for the earliest Wild Bird Protection Acts were then in force, and we were quite unaware that they applied only to birds and not to their eggs. I well recollect how, on my return from an Easter holiday, spent chiefly in birds-nesting forays on the Mendips, I was careful to conceal my thorn-scratched hands when in the vicinity of a policeman!

But as with many young collectors, Hendy's initial kleptomaniacal impulse soon turned into a wider appreciation of birds for their own sake, and he graduated to become a keen birdwatcher.

By now, birdwatching was being practised by people from all kinds of backgrounds and social status. In *Adventures Among Birds*, published in 1913, W. H. Hudson described encounters with two 'typical' birdwatchers, from opposite ends of the social scale. The first was in the town of Buxton, Derbyshire, with:

. . . a tradesman of the town, a Mr Micah Salt, who had studied the birds of the district all his life. But not in books; he did not read about birds, he observed them for his own pleasure and it was a pleasure for him to talk about them, but it went no further. He did not even make a note; bird-watching was his play – a better outdoor game than golf . . . (which) does not make you swear and tell lies and degenerate from being a pleasant companionable being to an intolerable bore.

Hudson met the second individual in Hampshire, where he was searching for a Dartford Warbler's nest:

He is one of those strange but not very uncommon persons who lead a double life. To some of us he is known as an ornithologist; to the theatre-going public he is an finished actor, and those who know him only as an actor would, I imagine, hear with surprise, perhaps incredulity, that, off the boards, he is a haunter of silent, solitary places where birds inhabit, that in these communings he has a joy with which the playgoer intermeddleth not.

Not everyone was content with simply pursuing their hobby for pure enjoyment. Others saw an opportunity to make a living from it. One such was an ambitious young man named W. Percival Westell, whose prolific achievements included writing more than fifty books by the time he was in his late thirties. A self-made man, Westell had to combine writing with paid work to earn a living: 'In 1904 my little library consisted of six books, all written by myself . . . Leaving town, I accepted a commercial engagement by day and went on writing by night'.

One of his most widely-read works was *British Bird Life*, first published in 1905, in which he forcefully made the argument for protection rather than collecting:

The day for the wanton shooting of birds is now fast passing away; in the place of the gun, trap and catapult, one sees substituted on many sides the field-glass, note-book and camera, and it has been my aim in these sketches to set forth the delights of stalking with a bloodless intention, to observe them as animate beings, and to learn something of their interesting lives and habits.

The introduction to *British Bird Life* was written by the Right Hon. Sir Herbert Maxwell, Bart, MP, who had been responsible for pushing several Bird Protection bills through Parliament. Sir Herbert praised Westell's efforts to educate the 'tens of thousands of children who have no early acquaintance of country life', and in a passage reminiscent of the Victorians' obsession with self-improvement, he examined the use of such knowledge:

> What advantage is it to a lad who has his living to work out in the shop or counting-house, the factory or the mine, the railway service or the post office, to know that a Robin eats worms and insects, while the staple food of a Chaffinch is hard seeds? . . . My answer is that what distinguishes man above all other living creatures is his superior intelligence. It is not desirable that every clerk, railway porter or factory hand should be an ornithologist; but every human being of every station and calling is the better of understanding something of matters outside his daily routine. Knowledge is not only power, it is pleasure; and many a dreary life has been brightened . . . by the habit of watching and inquiring into the operations of Nature.

DURING the same period as birdwatching was beginning to reach a wider audience, developments were also occurring in the more serious areas of bird study, such as migration studies and bird ringing.

Birds had been 'marked' as early as 1740, when Johann Leonard Frisch proved that Swallows did not hibernate under water. He did so by tying coloured threads to their feet, and when the birds returned the following year, showed that the threads had not lost their colour. In 1890, a private landowner in Northumberland was the first to use aluminium rings, placing them around the legs of young woodcock to study their movements; while in 1899 a Danish ornithologist, Christian Mortensen, put numbered rings on the legs of birds, in order to discover more about their movements and migrations.

In 1909, Sir Landsborough Thomson in Scotland and Harry Witherby in England took up the challenge, the latter's work eventually becoming the official British scheme. Although the advent of war brought bird ringing to a temporary halt, the practice grew again rapidly between the two world wars, developing into the national scheme now run by the British Trust for Ornithology.

The same was true in North America, where bird 'banding', as it is known, also began in 1909. In its early days it was an ad hoc affair, with one participant even marking wildfowl with rings carrying Biblical quotations instead of serial numbers! But it soon became highly organized: by 1933 there were 2000 licensed ringers banding a total of 1.5 million birds, while in the 1940s over 5 million birds were being ringed each year, providing more than 300,000 recoveries.

At the same time, the study of visible migration was also becoming more popular. first in the field was the German pioneer Heinrich Gätke who spent long periods observing migrating birds on the North Sea island of Heligoland in the mid-nineteenth century, publishing his findings in his seminal work *Heligoland as an Ornithological Observatory: The result of Fifty Years Experience*, in 1895.

In 1905, a Briton took up the baton. William Eagle Clarke was a Yorkshireman by birth, and had taken up a post in the natural history department at the Royal Scottish Museum in Edinburgh in 1888. He made many contributions to ornithological journals, taking a particular interest in the occurrence of unusual migrants and rare vagrants on outlying islands of the British Isles. But it was not until he was in his early fifties, in the autumn of 1905, that he stumbled across the location that would prove to be the most important place for sightings of vagrant birds not only in Britain, but the whole of Europe: 'On consulting a map of Scotland, with a view to selecting a bird-watching station in which to spend my autumn vacation in 1905, I was much impressed with the favourable situation of Fair Isle for that purpose . . . '

Fair Isle lies to the north of the British mainland, roughly halfway between the island groups of Orkney and Shetland. In less than a century since its discovery by Eagle Clarke, over 350 different species have been recorded there, more than any other location in Britain. This is largely due to its unique geographical location at the crossroads of several major migration routes. Fair Isle also holds the record for British 'firsts' – of the eighty-three species new to the 'British list' from 1946 to 1980, one in five were recorded from this tiny speck of land.

In September 1905, Eagle Clarke finally made the long journey north by train and boat to Fair Isle, and was immediately overwhelmed by the number and variety of migrants. He went back for the following four autumns, each time staying for five weeks; and for three springs (1909-1911). He was often accompanied by his companions Norman Kinnear, and by the Duchess of Bedford, one of the few women ornithologists of the time. Because of his full-time post in Edinburgh, Eagle Clarke could not be on Fair Isle all year round, so he employed one of the islanders, George Stout, as a bird-recorder. By paying him a small sum he thus made Stout the first ever professional birdwatcher. Stout proved to be a fine choice: 'Through his assiduity and excellent work most satisfactory results were obtained.'

From autumn 1905 to spring 1912, Eagle Clarke and his companions recorded no fewer than 207 species of bird on Fair Isle – roughly half the British total of the time – including several great rarities, such as Blyth's Reed Warbler (seen by the Duchess of Bedford, and later captured following a 'great hunt', in September 1910), Thrush Nightingale (shot by Eagle Clarke behind the south lighthouse in May 1911), and Pine Bunting (obtained by islander Jerome Wilson in October 1911). All three were the first records of these eastern European species for Britain.

In 1912 Eagle Clarke published his life's major work, the two volume *Studies in Bird Migration*, in which he made this justifiable boast:

> My forecast of the importance of Fair Isle as a bird observatory
> has been more than realised. Seven years investigation have made
> it the most famous bird-observatory in our islands; indeed it has
> become the British Heligoland.

Eagle Clarke's pioneering observations had put Fair Isle well and truly on the ornithological map. This previously obscure lump of rock soon became a place of regular pilgrimage. Although many of the rarest specimens were still shot, people were now visiting the island to watch birds rather than kill them. Imperceptibly, the driving impulse to collect birds with a shotgun was turning into a desire to record them using binoculars and a notebook. Eagle Clarke himself, meanwhile, continued to visit Fair Isle regularly: on his final stay there, in 1921, it was said that he and his companions 'lived on bad food and good whisky for a fortnight!'

As MORE people began observing birds in the field rather than the museum, the first stirrings of a new science began to occur. Ethology, or the study of bird behaviour, was pioneered by two amateur ornithologists, Eliot Howard and Edgar Chance, both of whom had to combine their studies of birds with a demanding career in business.

Henry Eliot Howard (1873-1940) was a professional businessman, whose birdwatching activities were thus restricted mainly to the early hours of the morning during spring and summer. As a result he chose to concentrate his study on a group of birds he could easily see at that time and season, the warblers. This eventually resulted in one of the earliest monographs of a family: *The British Warblers – A History with Problems of their Lives*, was issued in nine parts from 1907-1914, and remains a much-sought-after work to this day.

Edgar Chance (1881-1955) was another full-time businessman who devoted his spare time to bird study – recording the extraordinary breeding habits of the Cuckoo. When he began his studies, it was widely believed that the female Cuckoo carried her egg in her beak before depositing it in the host's nest. Chance dismissed this as nonsense, offering the sum of £100 to anyone who could prove him wrong. He kept his money, and eventually showed beyond doubt, using the new medium of cine-film, that the

Cuckoo lays her egg directly into the nest like any other bird. His book on the subject, *The Truth about the Cuckoo*, published in 1940, remains a classic of twentieth century ornithology.

During the early years of the twentieth century men like Howard and Chance were isolated figures, working outside the official scientific establishment. It was not until after World War II that the study of bird behaviour would achieve scientific respectability, and would come to involve many thousands of ordinary birdwatchers keen to understand more about the objects of their passion.

One man who played a key role in attaining that respectability was Sir Julian Huxley. Born in 1887, Huxley came from an extraordinary family, which combined literary and scientific achievement in equal measure. He was the elder brother of novelist Aldous (author of *Brave New World*), and grandson of Darwin's defender, the redoubtable Victorian scientist T. H. Huxley.

Huxley later had an extraordinary career in public life, which included serving as the first director-general of UNESCO (the United Nations Educational, Scientific and Cultural Organization). Not only an eminent scientist, he was also a great popularizer: he set up 'pets' corner' at London Zoo, and appeared regularly as a panellist on radio's *Brains Trust*. He was also an extraordinary raconteur, who in his seventies regaled the members of Guy Mountfort's 1963 expedition to Jordan with what Mountfort later described as lavatory humour.

Huxley's fascination with bird behaviour had begun at an early age, but his lifelong involvement in intensive bird study really took hold just before World War I. In the summer of 1912 he spent a fortnight's holiday watching Great Crested Grebes on a reservoir near Tring in Hertfordshire, which he wrote up in *British Birds* in 1914:

> Both zoology and photography would profit if naturalists for a little time would drop the camera in favour of the field-glass and the notebook, some patience, and a spare fortnight in the spring – with these I not only managed to discover many unknown facts about the Crested Grebe, but also had one of the pleasantest of holidays.

Considering the rapid growth of interest in watching birds during the first half of the twentieth century, it is extraordinary that between the years of 1890 and 1940 hardly any outstanding scientist apart from Huxley took an interest in birds. Indeed, during the first half of the twentieth century, the only aspects of birds studied by zoology students were the anatomy of pigeons and chicks – the other nine thousand or so species of bird were dismissed, in T. H. Huxley's memorable phrase, as 'glorified reptiles'. As a later ornithologist, David Lack, noted: 'Ornithology, like the collecting of butterflies, was dismissed as a dilettante pursuit for "mere amateurs".'

However, as a contribution to serious science, birdwatching had one major thing going for it – lots of participants. The only way to study all aspects of birds' lives, such as migration and distribution, was to mobilize a small army of amateur observers to collect records. As Frank Chapman observed in 1905: 'In no other branch [of science] are the professionals so outnumbered by the amateurs.'

NOT ALL birdwatching was being done in the name of science. For the first time, it was now possible to enjoy watching birds as a mass participation sport. On Christmas Day 1900, Frank Chapman organized the first in what would, during the following century, become one of the largest mass gatherings of birdwatchers anywhere in the world: the annual Audubon Christmas Bird Count.

Today, there are almost 2000 separate bird counts, involving over 50,000 participants, from Alaska to Hawaii and from California to Florida – and every state in between. Over the years, participants have become ever more ingenious in their approach, as an article in the Audubon magazine in 1980 revealed:

> For transportation they rely mostly on their feet, but anything that will get you there is legal. And in past years they have used dog-team, helicopter, canoe, airboat, hovercraft, horse and

golf-cart. In 1979-80 . . . the birding team at Grandfather
Mountain, North Carolina, logged a mile and a half by
hang-glider.

The first Christmas Bird Census, as it was originally called,
was a more modest affair, involving just twenty-seven observers in
twenty-five different locations, all on foot. Chapman published the
results in his new Audubon Society magazine, *Bird-Lore*.

Together, the new magazine and the idea of counting birds at
Christmas provided an outlet for American's new-found obsession with watching and listing birds. By 1909 the annual count
involved more than 200 participants, who logged a total of more
than 150,000 birds. In 1913, a team in California achieved the first
count of 100 species. By 1939, 2000 observers recorded over 2
million birds. Nevertheless, although ostensibly a scientific study,
the Christmas Bird Count is really more of a social event, eagerly
looked forward to by its army of regular participants.

Christmas Bird Counts encouraged the making of lists, another
characteristic obsession of the modern birder. Back in Britain,
H. G. Alexander and his brothers were probably the first birdwatchers anywhere in the world to keep a New Year's Day list –
begun on 1 January 1905. It was not a very ambitious start: the
fifteen-year-old boy simply counted the birds seen from his
window, then added Wren and Goldcrest on a short walk –
making a grand total of seventeen species! The following year,
Horace and Christopher reached a total of thirty-three species,
which at the time they thought was reasonably good. Bear in
mind, however, that their transport was limited to their own two
legs – they did not even use bicycles until 1915. The pursuit of
birds was far less frantic than it is today:

> . . . though we did our best to get a good list, we did not go to the
> extreme lengths of rising before dawn and searching for owls, or
> continuing after dark. Indeed, for some years we did not even take
> a sandwich lunch out with us. Having eaten a normal family
> breakfast, we would set off soon after 9 a.m. and return home for
> lunch at one o'clock, with the possibility of going out again for a
> short walk before darkness fell.

This early obsession with listing birds developed into a life-long habit for H. G. Alexander, though unfortunately many of his records were lost when a suitcase containing his precious bird notebooks was stolen in India in 1946.

Listing soon grew in popularity, probably because it acted as a substitute for the now unfashionable practice of physically collecting specimens. Just like a collection of skins or eggs, it provided a tangible record of achievement for the owner.

At the same time, people were beginning to enjoy watching birds to learn more about their habits and behaviour. This practice led to one of the great ornithological works of the twentieth century, Arthur C. Bent's celebrated *Life Histories* of North American birds. By the time of his death in 1954, Bent had produced 20 volumes, thanks to help from a nationwide network of over 800 amateur contributors, who sent in their observations – from the regular and mundane to the highly unusual – for Bent to include in his books. Many of his keenest contributors were women who, being limited by their social situation, mainly concentrated on the lives of songbirds, found in and around gardens and towns, rather than the species of more far-flung and exotic locations. Bent himself admitted that he was only as good as his continent-wide network of amateur observers: 'If the reader fails to find mentioned in these pages some things which he knows about the birds, he can blame himself for not having sent them to me.'

Another activity much beloved of middle-class nature lovers was feeding birds. According to James Fisher, the first man to feed wild birds for altruistic reasons (as opposed to fattening them up for the pot!) was the sixth-century monk St Serf of Fife, who tamed a robin by giving it food. The practice had been revived in Victorian times, though perhaps because it appeared to contravene the values of 'waste not, want not', it did not become a popular pastime.

Then, in 1890-91, Britain was plunged into a long hard winter. As the freezing weather tightened its grip, national newspapers began to encourage readers to put out food for the birds. According to W. H. Hudson, 'hundreds of working men would take advantage of the free hour at dinner time to visit the bridges and embankments, and give the scraps left from their meal to the birds.'

By 1910, *Punch* magazine was referring to feeding birds as a 'national pastime', in which even serious ornithologists got involved. At a meeting of the British Ornithologists' Club in February 1900, Ernst Hartert suggested planting 'thick bushes, especially those with thorns and berry-bearing species as were liked by birds, instead of foreign evergreens and shrubs'. He also gave his distinguished colleagues a brief lecture on providing alternative nest sites using the new nestboxes designed by Baron von Berlepsch in Germany. These were manufactured by a firm in Westphalia and available for about sixpence each (2.5 pence – just over £1 in value today). During his talk, Hartert also referred to habitat destruction due to changes in land-use – possibly the first time this had been identified as a cause of species decline in birds.

WE HAVE already seen how the expansion of the railway network enabled people to explore the wider countryside for the first time. By the end of the nineteenth century, another mode of transport provided even greater mobility and access to new places: the bicycle. This transformed the practice of nature study, providing a cheap, accessible and flexible means of personal transport for virtually everyone.

The bicycle was also relatively silent, a great asset when trying to get closer to wild birds, and although it could not give access to everywhere that could be reached on foot, this was more than balanced by the greater distances that could be covered. In America, the development of the 'safety bicycle' in the 1880s had equally revolutionary consequences, allowing riders to cover a far greater area than on foot, while being more flexible than railway or horseback. One enthusiast, Neil F. Posson, waxed lyrical about combining his favourite pastimes:

> I think the most healthful, instructive and pleasing exercise one
> may take, is to roam the country . . . in pursuit of the study of

birds; and I think the second most healthful and pleasing exercise is bicycling . . . and now combining these two pleasures, we have the sum of total health and happiness.

The rapid rise of birdwatching in the United States during this period may not, however, be simply the result of improvements in technology and mobility. One distinguished observer, the ornithologist and conservationist Robert Porter Allen, suggested that it was also a result of a fundamental change in values, which pervaded all aspects of American life: a backlash against an increasingly urbanized, industrialized society. Around the turn of the century, Americans appear to have stopped perceiving birds as mere objects, and begun to see them as individuals, with feelings not very different from their own. 'Birds have not only a beauty which appeals to the eye', wrote Frank Chapman in 1915;

> . . . but often a voice whose message stirs emotions to be reached only through the ear . . . and humanlike attributes which go deeper still, arousing in us feelings which are akin to those we entertain toward our fellow human-beings.

As a result of this change in attitudes, more and more middle class Americans sought an escape from the hustle and bustle of their increasingly busy lives. It is hardly surprising that many chose to do so through birdwatching.

DURING the first decade of the new century the private car also emerged on both sides of the Atlantic as a means of transport – albeit only amongst the upper classes who could afford to buy one. Less than one hundred years later it is almost impossible to imagine the sense of freedom those early motor travellers must have felt, and the private car's almost disorienting ability to devour the landscape in even a short journey. In his novel *Howards End*, published in 1910, E. M. Forster evokes 'this craze for motion':

A motor-drive, a form of felicity detested by Margaret, awaited her . . . The chauffeur could not travel as quickly as he had hoped, for the Great North Road was full of Easter traffic. But he went quite quick enough for poor Margaret, a poor-spirited creature, who had chickens and children on the brain.

'They're all right,' said Mr. Wilcox. 'They'll learn – like the swallows and the telegraph-wires.'

'Yes, but while they're learning –'

'The motor's coming to stay,' he answered. 'One must get about. There's a pretty church – oh, you aren't sharp enough. Well, look out, if the road worries you – right outward at the scenery.'

She looked at the scenery. It heaved and merged like porridge. Presently it congealed. They had arrived . . .

The return journey is even more extraordinary:

In a few minutes they had stopped, and Crane opened the door of the car.

'What's happened?' asked Margaret.

'What do you suppose?' said Henry.

A little porch was close up against her face.

'Are we there already?'

'We are.'

'Well, I never! In years ago it seemed so far away.'

Such a dramatic telescoping of time and space was to have profound effects on British society, allowing people to contemplate – and indeed undertake – journeys to places much farther afield than before. For birdwatchers it opened up the possibility of travelling to places significantly beyond the scope of a journey on foot or by bicycle. But ironically, along with the new found freedom came the potential for destruction of the countryside that was to occur during the remainder of the twentieth century. Forster himself had an inkling of this: later in the novel he referred to 'London's creeping', the gradual spread of the towns and cities into the countryside that would soon occur as a result of the rise of the motor-car.

DESPITE the rapid growth of motor transport, there were still parts of the English countryside where it was possible to walk for hours at a time without encountering the trappings of modern civilization.

On the morning of 9 June 1910, an Englishman and an American took an early train from London to the little Hampshire village of Itchen Abbas, just a few miles from Gilbert White's Selborne. Dressed in the standard country uniform of stout shoes and tweeds, they embarked on a long walk, through woods and fields, past streams and rivers, across valleys and hills. By the end of the day, they had seen or heard some forty species, and as the Englishman later remarked: 'for some twenty hours we were lost to the world'.

The remarkable thing about this encounter is that the two men involved were the British Foreign Secretary, Edward Grey (later to become Viscount Grey of Fallodon); and the recently retired American President, Theodore 'Teddy' Roosevelt. Both men were keen birdwatchers, so when the President arranged his visit to Britain an important priority for the Foreign Secretary was to organize a day out in the Hampshire countryside.

In retrospect, it seems extraordinary that the two men were able to wander around for a whole day on their own. Imagine the same happening today, with Kenneth Clarke (himself a keen birdwatcher) taking George W. Bush on a country walk, and it is easy to see how much the world has changed in the intervening ninety years or so. But this was an age of innocence, and if two of the world's most senior politicians wanted to put the cares of their office behind them for a day, that was perfectly acceptable.

Grey was highly impressed with his companion's field skills, remarking:

> He had one of the most perfectly trained ears for birdsong I have every known, so that, if three or four birds were singing together, he would pick out their songs, distinguish each, and ask to be told

their name . . . But I think Colonel Roosevelt still believed that one or two of the American bird songs were better than anything we had in England.

Roosevelt's enthusiasm for birds was not merely a casual one: in his youth, he had been a keen collector, and his poor eyesight only increased his powers of identifying birds by song. He once commented wryly on people's reaction to his interest in birds: 'People looking into the White House grounds and seeing me stare into a tree no doubt thought me insane.'

His passion continued into his retirement: in 1916, six years after his walk with Edward Grey, he signed the Migratory Birds Treaty between the USA and Canada. This was the earliest piece of international bird conservation legislation, and the first time it was acknowledged that birds do not belong to any one country, but cross international boundaries on their travels.

Many years later, Grey wrote what was to become one of the best-loved books on birdwatching, *The Charm of Birds*. But for now he had other things on his mind, as Foreign Secretary during one of the most turbulent periods in British history, ending with the seemingly inevitable slide into the horrors of World War I.

Yet despite – or possibly because of – Grey's heavy responsibilities as Britain's longest-serving Foreign Secretary to date, he still found time to indulge in watching and listening to birds. This is not as unusual as it might appear, for although someone with a lifelong commitment to public service, Grey was a reluctant performer on the political stage. As the great Liberal Prime Minister Gladstone remarked: 'I never knew in a man such aptitude for public life, and such disinclination for it.'

Grey and his wife Dorothy built a country refuge by the River Itchen near Winchester, within easy reach of London, to allow them to indulge their passion for birds. They went there every weekend, and made careful observations of the local birdlife, including Red-backed Shrike and Cirl Bunting, both long since vanished from the area. Edward and Dorothy looked forward to their weekend excursions with what Grey described as 'a rapture of anticipated pleasure'.

In the preface to *The Charm of Birds*, Grey explained, in his colloquial, unaffected style, what motivated him to set down his experiences in words:

> This book will have no scientific value. Those who have studied birds will not find in it anything that they do not already know; those who do not care for birds will not be interested in the subject . . . My observations have been made for recreation; in search of pleasure, not of knowledge; and they have been pursued only in so far as the ministered to the pleasure of holidays and home life . . . One who reviews pleasant experiences and puts them on record increases the value of them to himself; he gathers up his own feelings and reflections, and is thereby better able to understand and to measure the fullness of what he has enjoyed . . . Thus even those of us who have nothing new to tell, may have something that is fresh to say.

First published in 1927, the book struck an immediate chord with the general public, rapidly becoming a best-seller; new editions were still being published in the twenty-first century. However, Grey's life was marked by tragedy. In 1906, his wife Dorothy died after falling from her horse and cart; then, after he had achieved fame for a second time through his writings on birds, the degeneration of his eyesight and hearing meant he could no longer enjoy the sights and sounds of his beloved countryside. He died at Fallodon in September 1933, at the age of seventy-one.

Edward Grey's legacy was to have articulated a new way of looking at birds that still resonates today. The central message of *The Charm of Birds* was that watching or listening to birds could bring solace and spiritual regeneration to the world-weary, putting day to day troubles in perspective.

This theory was to be tested, almost to destruction, in the four years to come.

CHAPTER EIGHT

Fighting

World War I, 1914-1918

Hushed is the shriek of hurtling shells: and hark!
Somewhere within that bit of deep blue sky –
Grand in his loneliness, his ecstasy,
His lyric wild and free – carols a lark.

I in the trench, he lost in heaven afar,
I dream of Love, its ecstasy he sings . . .

'A Lark Above the Trenches', John William Street (1916)

O N THE EVE of World War I, Edward Grey stood at the window of the Foreign Office at dusk, and uttered some of the most memorable words ever spoken about that terrible conflict: 'The lamps are going out all over Europe; we shall not see them lit again in our lifetime.'

For Grey, the onset of war was particularly painful. For many years he had pursued a policy of *entente cordiale* towards the very nations whose squabbling over territory and power in the Balkans had now dragged the whole of Europe into armed struggle; and, in the last days before war was finally declared, had done more than most to try to preserve the peace.

To assuage his pain, he continued to seek solace and comfort in his love of birds, and in the continuity of their place in the wider scheme of things. 'In those dark days', he wrote in 1928, ten years after the war's end:

. . . I found some support in the steady progress unchanged of the
beauty of the seasons. Every year, as spring came back unfailing
and unfaltering, the leaves came out with the same tender green,
the birds sang, the flowers came up and opened, and I felt that a

great power of Nature for beauty was not affected by the War. It was like a great sanctuary into which we could go and find refuge for a time from even the greatest trouble of the world, finding there not enervating ease, but something which gave optimism, confidence and security. The progress of the seasons unchecked, the continuance of the beauty of Nature, was a manifestation of something great and splendid which not all the crimes and follies and misfortunes of mankind can abolish or destroy.

This passage hints at the profound sense of dislocation felt by everyone involved in the Great War. For this was not only of a different order from all previous conflicts, it also marked the end of an era when Britain ruled the land and seas, and everything was right with the world. It was as though the only constant that remained was the passage of the seasons and the natural process of renewal that accompanies them.

This sense of disorientation was powerfully evoked by the writer who today is synonymous with British power and imperialism, Rudyard Kipling. It is notable that he uses the natural world, rather than human affairs, as a metaphor for the end of hope and the onset of autumnal decay:

> There's a whisper down the field where the year has shot her yield
> And the ricks stand grey in the sun,
> Singing – 'Over then, come over, for the bee has quit the clover,
> And your English summer's done'.

Summer was over, metaphorically speaking, for everyone.

LOOKING BACK almost a century on, it is difficult to imagine what day-to-day life was actually like for the servicemen involved in the Great War. What we do know is that for the first time in history whole sections of the British male population, from the labourer in the fields to the lord in his stately home, were uprooted and dumped down into a foreign land to fight for King and Country.

For the vast majority of these young men, this was the first time they had travelled any distance from home, let alone abroad. At first, many must have been comforted to discover that the fields and hedgerows of Flanders were not very different from the familiar countryside they had left behind. But as the horrors of war began to take their toll, and the pastoral landscape was turned into a scene resembling a medieval depiction of Hell, it is hardly surprising that they grasped at anything which might give them even a small reminder of the comforts of home.

So just as Edward Grey found sanctuary in the passing of the seasons, so ordinary men fighting on the Western Front took pleasure in watching the local birdlife: some of it familiar, some not. Charles Raven, later to achieve eminence as a Cambridge don and author of several works on the history of ornithology, recalled one such event:

> A small incident happened which brought back my love of
> birds with a rush. We were in the fighting for Vimy, and cut to
> pieces in front of Oppy Wood in April 1917. The battalion was
> sent back to rest, 150 instead of 800 strong. We marched back
> from Roclincourt to La Comté, and settled down, to my joy, on
> the edge of a wood where Golden Orioles were nesting. I had just
> spent a first morning watching the gorgeous cock, when the
> colonel announced that we had to return at once to the line.

Raven and his comrades were, as can be imagined, far from happy with this development – indeed he describes their mood as 'venomous . . . too sore even to grumble'. But then, as he put it, 'a miracle happened' – the men discovered that a pair of Swallows was building their nest in the entrance to their temporary HQ, an old signalling station:

> These birds were angels in disguise. It is a truism that one touch
> of nature makes the whole world kin: those blessed birds brought
> instant relief to the nerves and tempers of the mess . . . we all
> regarded the pair with devoted affection.

From then on, the whole battalion became obsessed with the Swallows' fortunes. They began by placing bets on when the first egg would appear, organizing a daily inspection using an elaborate trench-periscope. When the battalion was relieved, the incoming soldiers were given strict instructions on guarding the nest from harm, while during a particularly heavy German bombardment, 'our chief anxiety was lest a stray fragment might "casualty" the birds'.

For Raven himself, these nesting Swallows seemed to offer him a new sense of purpose, enabling him better to withstand the privations of war. He even dreamed about birds:

> In the thick of that year's fighting, and my crowd had their share of it, sleep meant for me a visit to one of the bird-crowded islets that my mother had pictured in my nursery days. From the restless horror and hideousness of the war-zone I could slip away to the imagined wonder of wave-washed rocks and the clamour of sea-fowl . . . I knew them in those days as I know my home, though till the year after the Armistice I had never seen them with the bodily eye.

Others reported similar experiences, though in less lyrical terms. A father wrote to *British Birds*, passing on news from the front line:

> My son, 2nd Lieut. Eliot Wallis, writes to me that, seeing a Swallow come out of a deserted German dug-out in north-east France, he looked and found a nest 'with four spotted eggs'. As every chimney, house and shed had been levelled by the retreating enemy, the birds had evidently returned to the usage of an earlier day, for few of us have seen a Swallow's nest in a cave.

Such behaviour, though unusual, was by no means unique. Despite the huge disruption along the front lines of the conflict, birds appeared to adapt remarkably quickly. Patrick Chubb, another correspondent to *British Birds*, added his observations to 'various articles in the papers regarding birds in the war-stricken parts of France':

> These include the House-Sparrow, Swallow, House-Martin, Chaffinch, Yellow-Hammer, Sky-Lark, Willow-Wren [Willow Warbler], Magpie, Kestrel and Wood-Pigeon. All of these I have

seen flying about in front of our own and the French artillery during an artillery duel. The House Sparrows continue to sit on the house-tops of this village (I cannot name it) which is about ¾ mile from the French trenches, although the shells are continually knocking large holes in the roofs. So far I have only seen one of these birds killed at all.

Under the eaves of two of the cottages three pairs of House-Martins have already built their nests. (I may add that this village has had about twenty shells fired over and on it each day for the last two days. In fact it is only left standing because there are so many spies in it. We have caught three of them.)

Affection for the local birds was not confined to the British side: Chubb relates how a German was discovered in an attic in the village with six pet Wood Pigeons. On being found, he swore that he was English!

In response to this note, and also to articles in the newspapers which suggested that the fighting was causing serious disturbance of bird life, *British Birds* received several more letters from serving soldiers. These pointed out how well birds had adapted to the presence of the war, with accounts of Willow and Sedge Warblers singing during an artillery duel, and a Kingfisher appearing next to a trench. Perhaps most extraordinary of all was a pair of Song Thrushes which built their nest in a tree right next to a large artillery gun – though the birds eventually deserted, and 'moved to a presumably quieter neighbourhood'.

The presence of birds moved some servicemen to philosophical flights of fancy, as in this letter home from soldier and writer Alexander Gillespie in May 1915, quoted in Paul Fussell's book *The Great War and Modern Memory*:

Presently a misty moon came up, a nightingale began to sing . . . It was strange to stand there and listen, for the song seemed to come all the more sweetly and clearly in the quiet intervals between the bursts of firing. There was something infinitely sweet and sad about it, as if the countryside were singing gently to itself, in the midst of all our noise and confusion and muddy work.

Gillespie was not himself a birdwatcher, yet he immediately found both solace and a poignant regret in hearing the Nightingale's song. In doing so he was following in a long Romantic tradition, typified by poets such as John Keats. And like Keats a century earlier, it was the mood evoked by the bird's song, rather than the bird itself, that motivated him to more melancholy reflection:

> So I stood there, and thought of all the men and women who had listened to that song, just as for the first few weeks after Tom was killed I found myself thinking perpetually of all the men who had been killed in battle . . . Gradually the night wore on, until the day began to break, and I could see clearly the daisies and buttercups in the long grass about my feet. Then I gathered up my platoon together, and marched past the silent farms to our billets.

In a letter to *The Times* in July 1917 J. C. Faraday, another front-line soldier, found greater comfort in the Nightingale's song:

> You will have a terrific tearing and roaring noise of artillery and shot in the dead of night; then there will be a temporary cessation of the duel, with great quietness, when lo! and behold and hear! Hearken to his song! Out come the nightingales, right about the guns . . . And another kind of love music is introduced to our ears and souls, which does us good. Think? It makes you think – and beautiful thoughts come along to relieve you from the devilment of war and the men who cause it . . .

In his autobiographical work *Memoirs of an Infantry Officer*, published almost twenty years after the end of the war in 1937, poet and writer Siegfried Sassoon wrote of another encounter with a Nightingale. At the time (spring 1916), he was serving at an Army school in France, thirty miles from the front line of the war:

> With half an hour to spare after breakfast, I strolled up the hill and smoked my pipe under a quick-set hedge. Loosening my belt, I looked at a chestnut tree in full leaf and listened to the perfect performance of a nightingale. Such things seemed miraculous

after the desolation of the trenches. Never before had I been so intensely aware of what it meant to be young and healthy in fine weather at the outset of summer. The untroubled notes of the nightingale made the Army School seem like some fortunate colony which was, for the sake of appearances, pretending to assist the struggle from afar.

A devoted birdwatcher himself, Sassoon later returned to the trenches. His main regret was saying goodbye to a fellow officer, also keen on birds:

Allgood was quiet, thoughtful, and fond of watching birds . . . Allgood never grumbled about the war, for he was a gentle soul, willing to take his share in it, though obviously unsuited to homicide. But there was an expression of veiled melancholy on his face, as if he were inwardly warned that he would never see his home in Wiltshire again. A couple of months afterwards I saw his name in one of the long lists of killed, and it seemed to me that I had expected it.

The other bird which appeared in several memoirs of life in the trenches was the Skylark. Partly this was because it would have been very familiar to any soldier brought up in the English countryside; but also it was because, like the Nightingale, it had long been part of the canon of English Romantic verse. The soldier-poet John William Street followed in this literary tradition:

Hushed is the shriek of hurtling shells: and hark!
Somewhere within that bit of deep blue sky,
Grand in his loneliness, his ecstasy,
His lyric wild and free, carols a lark.
I in the trench, he lost in heaven afar;
I dream of love, its ecstasy he sings . . .

The song of Skylarks at the start of the day evoked mixed emotions of nostalgia and profound sadness for another serving soldier, Sergeant Major F. H. Keeling:

Every morning when I was in the front-line trenches I used to hear the larks singing soon after we stood-to about dawn. But those wretched larks made me more sad than anything else out here . . . Their songs are so closely associated in my mind with peaceful summer days in gardens or pleasant landscapes in Blighty.

While for others in the front line, larks could cause unnecessary confusion and panic, as Patrick Chubb noted: 'Sky-Larks are continually up in the air, and are continually being mistaken at first sight for aeroplanes.'

The association of Skylarks with the horrors of the trenches is an enduring one: in 2004, the West End production of R. C. Sherriff's play *Journey's End* ended with the poignant sound of the Last Post played on a bugle, accompanied by a single Skylark's song.

Other observers – especially those who had been keen bird-watchers before the conflict – attempted a more methodical survey of the birds of the area in which they had been stationed. These included Harry Witherby, who during the last year of the war was posted to the area around Dunkerque, 'a country . . . not attractive to bird-life'; and Captain Arthur Sowerby, who made most of his observations while being driven around in his staff car, and who noted in *British Birds* the unexpectedly beneficial side-effects of war on birds:

> As time goes on, and Nature clothes the shell-torn and naked earth of the battlefields, these areas, which cannot possibly be populated again by human beings for a long time to come, must inevitably become wonderful bird sanctuaries . . .

Wartime observations of birds were not confined to the near Continent. Temporary Royal Naval Surgeon J. M. Harrison was posted to the Greek province of Macedonia, 'a veritable Paradise to the ornithologist.' He also reported his experiences in *British Birds*, in an account remarkable for its restraint under the circumstances:

> The above condensation, memorised as far as has been possible from my ornithological diary – which was lost, with the rest of my effects and some interesting specimens, with my ship M 28 in the action of January 20th – will give some idea of the attractions

offered to the field naturalist in Macedonia, and may be of interest to others about to embark O.H.M.S. for that quarter, and help to send them on their way one degree cheerier, and hold out some consolation for Foreign Service in war-time.

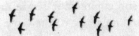

Consolation was certainly required. Hopes of a quick end – 'it will all be over by Christmas' – rapidly receded, and by 1915 the armed forces had grown from a peacetime strength of four hundred thousand men to more than two-and-a-half million. A year later, with active conscription, it reached three-and-a-half million, and towards the end of the war it peaked at over four million – one in three of the entire male workforce. As Peter Clarke has noted: 'Whichever way it added up, the Western Front was, for a large proportion of men born during the last decade of the nineteenth century, the experience of a lifetime, sometimes the ultimate experience.'

The statistics of dead and wounded are almost impossible to contemplate. On a single day – 1 July 1916, the first day of the notorious Battle of the Somme – the British suffered 60,000 casualties, with more than 21,000 deaths, mostly in the first hour of fighting. And this was only the worst of many similar days, at the end of which three quarters of a million Britons had lost their lives.

From early 1915 onwards, the pages of *British Birds* were regularly given over to reports of the birdwatchers and ornithologists who would never return. The first of these was devoted to Lieut. Francis Monckton, who had been killed in action on 8 November 1914, at the age of twenty-four. Editor Harry Witherby added a short postscript drawing attention to Monckton's observations of autumn migration, made only a couple of weeks before his death.

During the next four years a dozen more obituary notices appeared. These ranged from young men just embarking on an ornithological career, such as Austin Leigh; to experienced officers such as Lieutenant-Colonel H. H. Harington. Killed in action in

Mesopotamia in March 1916, in his late forties, Harington was a typical soldier of the British Empire. Indeed, he had first taken up an interest in birds when posted to Burma during the early 1890s, and had discovered several races new to science while serving there. His name is still commemorated in the scientific names of several species, including a race of the Grey Bushchat.

These accounts were written in the gung-ho style which prevailed at the time, before the true conditions of the war had become widely known. Typical is the final line in the obituary of The Hon. Gerald Legge, second son of the Earl of Dartmouth: 'He was last seen lying mortally wounded on the ground, and cheering on the men of whom he was so proud. That was Gerald Legge.'

At 11 a.m. on 11 November 1918, World War I finally came to an end with the declaration of the Armistice. Later that day, in his speech to the House of Commons, Prime Minister David Lloyd George attempted to put the four years of hostilities into a wider historical context: 'At eleven o'clock this morning came to an end the cruellest and most terrible war that has ever scourged mankind. I hope we may say that thus, this fateful morning, came to an end all wars.'

Britain had changed forever. A generation of British birdwatchers had been cut down in the prime of life before they had a chance to make a major contribution to the new science of bird study. This tale of unfulfilled potential was repeated throughout that 'lost generation', whose absence would have far-reaching effects on British society for many decades. The scale of the carnage is illustrated by the experience of Landsborough Thomson, the pioneer of bird ringing who went on to become one of the twentieth century's leading ornithologists. He managed to get through the war, serving with the Argyll and Sutherland Highlanders. But as his *British Birds* obituary in 1977 revealed, of a group of nine contemporaries studying zoology at Aberdeen University, he was the only survivor.

More than half a century after the war, in 1974, H. G. Alexander wrote of his own loss of enthusiasm for the rigorous discipline of studying birds: 'The slaughter of the innocents in Flanders dried me up, and I had little heart for such efforts. To go out for a few hours, as one watched birds, was very comforting; but serious ornithological work, whether in the field or in the study, was too difficult.'

Among the young men who had died a pointless death in the fields of Flanders, where Skylarks and Nightingales sang, was Horace's elder brother Christopher. In the obituary he wrote for *British Birds*, Horace recalled happier pre-war days when the brothers had shared their love of birds. He noted that Christopher had preferred to enlist as a private soldier: 'Most of his training was at Dover, where he had chased Dark Green Fritillaries and watched Shrikes in his first school-days, eighteen and twenty years before.'

Very different from the bombastic heroics of earlier obituaries, this was a restrained and poignant tribute to a life 'devoted to the study of Nature', and to a dear brother with whom he would never speak, share a joke or watch birds again.

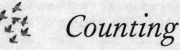

CHAPTER NINE

Counting

Between the Wars, 1918-1939

> For those who practise it bird-watching is not only a sport
> and a science, but also something near a religion, and after
> all its externals have been inventoried the essence stays
> incommunicable.
>
> *The Art of Birdwatching*, Max Nicholson (1931)

THE 'war to end all wars' had finally come to an end, and the world was counting the cost. The figures spoke for themselves: Britain alone had lost 750,000 men – roughly one in six of the younger generation. Several million more had sustained physical injuries or disabilities, or were suffering from 'shell-shock'. Relief was another widespread emotion, expressed by Siegfried Sassoon:

> Everybody suddenly burst out singing,
> And I was filled with such delight
> As prisoned birds must find in freedom . . .

But as his fellow writer Robert Graves pointedly noted in his 1929 memoirs *Goodbye to All That*: '"Everybody" did not include me.'

For the generation born just after the turn of the century, which had been too young to take part in the conflict, there was a widespread feeling of guilt at having 'missed out' on doing their duty. In 1940, George Orwell, born in 1903, summed up the feelings of his contemporaries:

> As the war fell back into the past, my particular generation, those
> who had been 'just too young', became conscious of the vastness
> of the experience they had missed . . . men a little older than

myself, who had been through the war . . . talked about it unceasingly, with horror, of course, but also with a steadily growing nostalgia.

Max Nicholson, born a year after Orwell in 1904, was also deeply affected by memories of the war, which broke out when he was just ten years old:

> I saw all these young men, marching through the streets of Portsmouth to their deaths. They were not much older than me – and so few of them came back. I had a very deep feeling that I had to take their place – I had this mission that I must make up for the loss, and do the things that they were unable to do. This was not a choice – it was imposed on me.

Nicholson went on to fulfil his mission: indeed on his death in 2003, in his ninety-ninth year, he was hailed as the most important environmentalist, conservationist and ornithologist of the twentieth century.

Endlessly energetic, deeply articulate, and impatient of others who did not share his Messianic views, Nicholson was that rare being, a practical visionary. The list of his achievements during a long and busy life almost defies belief. He ran (and in many cases founded) almost all the key ornithological organizations of today, including the British Trust for Ornithology (BTO), the Edward Grey Institute at Oxford, the Nature Conservancy Council (later split up into various bodies including English Nature) and *British Birds*. During the war itself, as a senior civil servant, he organized the North Atlantic shipping convoys which kept the supply line open between America and Britain. Afterwards, he attended the post-war conferences at Yalta and Potsdam, where as Churchill looked on in frustration, Roosevelt and Stalin carved up Europe between the two new superpowers of East and West.

Despite his busy life, Nicholson also found time for watching birds. Not the least of his many achievements was to help turn birdwatching from an essentially casual, amateur pastime into something more organized, structured and above all, rigorous.

It was during this brief period between the two world wars

that birdwatching finally emerged from the shadows of the Victorian obsession with collecting, and became a definable 'sub-culture' in British society. Although still practised by relatively few people, it gradually began to insinuate itself into all sectors of society, and to come to the attention of a wider public.

LIKE SO many people whose lives have been shaped by their passion for birdwatching, Max Nicholson's first encounter with wild birds came about purely by accident. Living in Ireland in the first decade of the twentieth century, his parents kept hens, and there was a little yellow chick of which he was particularly fond.

One day he was sitting outdoors when a Sparrowhawk appeared out of nowhere, grabbed the chick, and flew off. His devotion to the chick forgotten, the young Max was hooked. Later, after a visit to the bird galleries at the Natural History Museum in London, his parents bought him a copy of White's *Natural History of Selborne* and a notebook. He began keeping notes of his bird sightings at the age of seven, in 1911, and continued to do so for the rest of his life. At the time of his death, ninety-two years later, it could justifiably be said that he had been watching birds for longer than anyone who has ever lived.

Until he was seventeen, Max hardly met another birdwatcher, though he did join and later run the natural history society at his school at Sedbergh, in the West Riding of Yorkshire (now Cumbria). But his real introduction to serious bird study came when he went up to Oxford in 1926.

1920s Oxford was hardly the place where an ornithological revolution seemed likely to begin. The prevailing mood was one of hedonistic self-interest, characterized by a shallow cynicism about anything seen as 'meaningful' or 'worthwhile'. In his 1945 novel *Brideshead Revisited*, Evelyn Waugh painted a vivid picture of undergraduate life for the 'bright young things':

The party assembled. There were three Etonian freshmen, mild, elegant, detached young men who had all been to a dance in London the night before . . . Each as he came into the room made first for the plovers' eggs, then noticed Sebastian and then myself . . .

'The first this year', they said. 'Where do you get them?'

'Mummy sends them from Brideshead. They always lay early for her'.

Life, for the privileged classes at least, was an endless round of balls, champagne for breakfast and the consumption of plovers' eggs (though these may in fact have come from Black-headed Gulls!). But at the same time, another group of Oxford undergraduates was engaging in a rather more wholesome and productive activity. For these young men, mornings were not spent sleeping off a hangover or punting lazily along the River Cherwell, but on dawn excursions in search of birds.

These were men with a mission. They believed that watching birds should have a clearly defined purpose beyond that of simple enjoyment, and that by introducing a more rigorous approach to their activities they could make a contribution to building a new and better world. As a result, in 1921 the Oxford Ornithological Society (OOS) was founded. The Society would have an extraordinary impact on the future of birdwatching – one that has lasted to the present day.

One of its first members was a young don named Bernard Tucker, who would become editor of *British Birds*, and also one of the editors of the influential *Handbook of British Birds*, before his early death from cancer in 1950. Both Tucker and Nicholson had the rare ability of being able to get on and do things, while maintaining a broader vision of why they were doing them. Between them, these two men recreated the link between scientific ornithology and popular birdwatching, so that instead of drifting further apart the two disciplines came together, each gaining strength from the other.

Nicholson was recruited by Tucker soon after his arrival at Oxford. It was an auspicious time to have an interest in birds:

In one of numerous lucky accidents in my life, just after I went to Oxford they needed a new Chancellor, and they appointed Lord Grey of Fallodon. The University picked on me and said we must do something to please the Chancellor – so passed the word down that anything to do with birds should be encouraged. This was the first time that ornithology became a recognised academic activity – until then they didn't care about it!

With characteristic zeal, Nicholson went straight to work organizing the Oxford Bird Census. He also began his extraordinarily prolific career as a writer, publishing his first book in 1926, when he was still only twenty-two years old. *Birds in England* laid down the ground rules for the future development of ornithology and birdwatching in Britain, in the confident tones of a young man who no longer had any respect for his elders – whom he described as 'an elderly and passive group of amateurs'.

Nicholson was determined to lead ornithology away from what he called 'the Victorian leprosy of collecting'. He aimed to reduce the dominance of the British Ornithologists' Union (BOU), and its concentration on the classification and distribution of birds, or what has been called 'museum ornithology'. In its place, he called for a revolutionary new approach: one that would eventually develop into the sciences of ecology and ethology.

He had carried out his first bird survey in 1925, when he counted the birds in Kensington Gardens, near his London home. The final total of almost 5000 included 2600 House Sparrows – over half the total bird population of the gardens. In November 2000, seventy-five years after the original count, Nicholson and his colleagues returned to Kensington Gardens. This time they found only eight House Sparrows: a decline of 99.7 per cent.

Back in 1925, much still remained to be discovered about the habits of even the commonest birds. Determined to discover where the gulls which fed in the central London parks spent each night, Nicholson took advantage of a reliable bus service:

Leaving Kensington one afternoon as soon as the first parties came over I got on top of the first bus to Barnes, towards which the line

of flight apparently pointed . . . At Castlenau I got off and walked
along the right bank of the Thames towards Barn Elms Reservoirs
till I came in a few minutes to the lower tanks, of which the
nearest was filled with swarming gulls making an indescribable
clamour . . . I now began to see gulls coming in across the River
from the direction of inner London . . . sometimes a hundred or
two at a time . . . The total number that I saw come in was
certainly to be reckoned in thousands.

Incidentally, the story behind the book from which this extract
is taken is almost as amazing as the discoveries documented inside.
Having written the draft of a book on London's birds during
the mid 1920s, Nicholson took it around several booksellers and
publishers. Unfortunately, at a time of economic depression and
civil strife their verdict was that there was no market for such a
volume. A disappointed Nicholson put the manuscript in a bottom
drawer in his house in Chelsea and promptly forgot about it. More
than sixty years later, his wife Toni came across the manuscript,
and the book, now entitled *Birdwatching in London: A historical
perspective*, was finally published in 1995!

By 1927, when his second book appeared, entitled *How Birds
Live*, the OOS began the Oxford Bird Census. The following year
Nicholson launched the first ever national survey of a single
species carried out anywhere in the world: a census of heronries.
In an inspired move, he dramatically increased coverage by
publishing appeals for help in local and national newspapers,
including the *Daily Mail*. Almost 400 people officially joined the
census (at least another 400 unofficially took part), with much of
the fieldwork made possible by the extensive use of a relatively
new arrival on the scene, the private car. It was a huge success,
setting the standard for surveys to come.

More than sixty years later, in the early 1990s, Max Nicholson
attended the press launch of the *New Atlas of Breeding Birds*, the
definitive survey of our avifauna. He must have been amazed, and
very proud, of the fact that today Britain's birds are more closely
surveyed and studied than any other comparable fauna in the
world.

Nicholson continued to produce manifestos for his new approach, including *The Study of Birds* (1929), and *The Art of Bird Watching* (1931). Both were relentlessly practical, yet written with dry humour, forensic precision and remarkable foresight. In *The Study of Birds*, he expounded his core philosophy:

> One cannot observe without a theory, and what seems the simplest of ornithological tasks – to go out of doors and look out for something worth recording – is in reality one of the hardest . . . It is a mistake to imagine that complete impartiality and freedom from preconceived ideas is the qualification for the perfect observer. The cow (has) a remarkably open mind, yet it has never been found to reach a high degree of civilisation.

Despite its title, *The Art of Bird Watching* was almost entirely concerned with the science of the hobby, with chapters on equipment, census work and ecology. He also summarized the recent changes in birdwatching:

> The older bird-watcher was essentially an individual who might aspire to have at his finger-tips everything that there was to be known: the new bird-watcher is more frequently a member of some sort of organisation . . . concentrating on special questions, and renouncing any attempt at all-round knowledge. The older bird-watcher . . . would seek to draw from each observation the most sweeping deductions not only about birds in general, but about man and Nature and the works of God. The new bird-watcher adopts a more cautious and humble, and also a more scientific standpoint: the more he sees of wild birds the less knowledge he feels inclined to claim about them. (This is) the inevitable development from an amateur and chaotic towards a professional and organised foundation characterised of most civilised activities.

Nevertheless, he still managed to find room for a more spiritual approach, delivered with characteristic tongue-in-cheek irony: 'For those who practise it bird-watching is not only a sport and a science, but also something near a religion, and after all its externals have been inventoried the essence stays incommunicable.'

From the early 1930s, the pioneering Oxford group found that its growing workload was making severe demands on its amateur organizers and limited resources. Things came to a head in 1931, when Tom Harrisson and P. A. D. Hollom (later co-author of *A Field Guide to the Birds of Britain and Europe*) organized the Great Crested Grebe Inquiry. This time there was a huge press campaign, including an appeal on the BBC's Home Service, which recruited 1300 volunteers, requiring huge organizational effort. *The Times* newspaper described the report on the survey, published in *British Birds*, as 'one of the fullest accounts of life-history which are so far available for any wild bird in any country', noting the significant fact that it was the slaughter of Great Crested Grebes which had eventually led to the rise of the bird protection movement in Britain.

Nicholson realized that to fulfil Witherby's 1907 vision of a national census of all bird populations, a new organization would be needed, along the lines of his own proposal in *The Art of Birdwatching*: 'A Society of Bird-watchers on a national scale . . . linked under a single inspiration bird-watching would undoubted-ly be in a position to enter a period of intense creative effort.'

However, things were particularly bad economically at the time, and funds to set up such a body were simply not available. Fortunately Nicholson had another bright idea. If the government could be convinced that birds were a weapon against insect pests, perhaps they would fund such an organization. He duly organized a census of Rooks, convinced the Ministry of Agriculture of its usefulness, and a full-time research biologist, W. B. Alexander (H. G.'s brother), was appointed.

The embryonic organization struggled on for a year or two. Then, in 1932, Nicholson proposed to create a 'British Trust for Ornithology', but because of the Depression funds were not available from Oxford University. Witherby came to the rescue, selling his large collection of bird skins to the British Museum, and donating the £1400 proceeds (equivalent to more than £50,000 today) to the fledgling British Trust for Ornithology (BTO). Max Nicholson became its first secretary, and the trust's work began in earnest. Its aims could be summed up in a phrase from *The Art of*

Birdwatching: to bring to an end the 'old fashioned splendid isolation of the birdwatcher'.

Another organization was set up at the same time. Lord Grey of Fallodon died in September 1933, and it was suggested that his name should be given to a new organization at Oxford, the Edward Grey Institute of Field Ornithology. Today, the EGI has grown to become the home of scientific ornithology in the United Kingdom.

The movement towards 'organized birdwatching' was not without its critics. Throughout the 1930s the RSPB opposed the 'scientification' of the pastime, criticizing migration studies as 'undesirable', and promoting its own agenda of bird protection. But the tide was turning inexorably in favour of the new approach, with leading ornithologists such as Julian Huxley rebuking the Society for its 'blindness to the intellectual, as opposed to the emotional side of the bird-lover's activities'. Eventually, in 1936, this resulted in what has been described as a 'hostile takeover' of the RSPB, in which the forces of the new science finally triumphed over the old sentimentalism.

The forgotten figure of this revolution went on to have an influence far beyond the confines of the ornithological world. Tom Harrisson, co-organizer of that pioneering Great Crested Grebe survey, was an extraordinary, charismatic figure. He was full of ideas, which were described by his friend and colleague K. E. L. Simmons as: 'four-fifths totally impractical, one-fifth brilliant'. Like many geniuses, he was not an easy man: it is telling that Judith Heimann's biography of Harrisson is entitled *The Most Offending Soul Alive*.

As a result of taking part in bird surveys, Harrisson turned his attention to an even more widespread group of animals: his fellow human-beings. In the late 1930s he set up an organization called Mass-Observation (M-O), which set out to do for ordinary British people what the BTO was doing for birds: to carry out detailed scientific studies on contemporary society, using a body of amateur observers to collect the data. M-O really came into its own during World War II, with its observations of the behaviour of ordinary Londoners during the Blitz.

Harrisson's approach to observing humans was virtually identical to his way of looking at birds: to watch them without preconceptions, note down their behaviour, and resist interpreting their actions. So it is hardly surprising that many well-known birdwatchers, including Max Nicholson, James Fisher and Richard Fitter, became involved with M-O. In her biography of Harrisson, Judith Heimann quotes his own acknowledgment of the vital influence his early work on birds had on the techniques he later used to study people: 'You don't ask a bird any questions. You don't try to interview it, do you?'

Tom Harrisson went on to have a colourful and varied career in a wide range of fields, including social anthropology, before his life was cut short by a motor accident in Thailand in 1976. Ironically, as K. E. L. Simmons noted in 1992, the very multiplicity of his pursuits and achievements led to his pioneering ornithological work being forgotten:

> It is one of the absurdities of our science that T. H. Harrisson –
> who as ornithologist, anthropologist, sociologist, biologist,
> museum curator, conservationist, and adventurer became one
> of the great polymaths of his time – is largely unknown to
> birdwatchers today.

Yet without Harrisson and his contemporaries, the way in which we look at birds today might have been very different. They finally discarded the anthropocentric Victorian approach of writers such as W. H. Hudson, and instead looked at birds as living creatures – connected with human beings, but nevertheless independent of them.

THE GROWING number of serious birdwatchers needed books to help them to identify and understand the behaviour of birds. The first of these came from an unlikely source: a Cheshire-based journalist named T. A. Coward. Unlike most birdwatchers and ornithologists of his day, Coward came from humble, working-class origins, as his 1935 obituary in *British Birds* pointed out: 'He was a short, thick-set, knickerbockered figure, topped by a cloth cap . . . '

Like his appearance, Coward's writing style was no-nonsense and accessible – endearing him to generations of birdwatchers. He is best-known for his three-volume *The Birds of the British Isles and their Eggs*, first published in 1920. This remained one of the standard works for birdwatchers until the 1950s, when it was finally superseded by the arrival of the 'Peterson, Mountfort and Hollom' field guide. Though the three volumes were too bulky to be easily carried around in the field, the clear and detailed text, and colour plates showing the birds in their natural habitat, ensured the books' success.

In 1922 Coward defined, for the first time, a concept still in widespread use today: that of 'jizz', the way in which an experienced birder can identify a species on even a brief, distant view, because of some indefinable quality of its appearance. In Coward's own words:

> Jizz may be applied to or possessed by any animate and some
> inanimate objects, yet we cannot clearly define it . . . as a rule, it is
> character rather than characteristics . . . something definite yet
> indescribable, something which instantly registers identity in the
> brain, though how or what is seen remains unspecified. It is its jizz.

He also took an uncompromising and forward-looking view against killing for killing's sake: 'The history of the Hoopoe as a British bird is a long, disgraceful obituary . . . it would be a regular summer visitor if stupid and greedy collectors and gunners would leave it alone.'

This plain-speaking, forthright approach was unlikely to endear him to the ornithological establishment of the day, many of whom still regarded collecting as an acceptable – and indeed necessary – pastime. So Coward never attended meetings of organizations such as the British Ornithologists' Club, and was destined to spend his life on the fringes of British ornithology, despite (perhaps even because of) the popularity of his books amongst the general public.

In 1985, more than half a century after Coward's death,

ornithologist Bill Bourne (himself a thorn in the flesh of the British ornithological establishment) asserted that he had been unjustly neglected in his own time. In the pages of *British Birds*, Bourne asserted that Coward was a victim of social snobbery, which affected our opinion of his legacy:

> It is time he received more recognition for his work in bringing ornithology back to ordinary people and out into the field. It seems doubtful whether anyone has ever written better about birds, and it seems high time for a revival of his simple, clear, and original style.

This may be an exaggeration of Coward's qualities, but there can be no doubt that he was one of the great popularizers of bird-watching, helping to make it more accessible to the non-expert and beginner. He was also a kind and generous man, who despite his busy life (he wrote a regular column for the *Manchester Guardian*) made time to help his fellow birdwatchers, as this anecdote in his obituary revealed:

> A hundred stories might be told of his love for his neighbour . . . but one must suffice. Years ago, a friend who lived alone in rooms at Knutsford was stricken by typhoid. Every day for more than a month, Coward, putting his work aside, devoted time he could ill spare to cycling the seven miles out, and back again, because the sick man itched for news of the countryside and to know how the spring migrants were coming in.

One feature which helped make Coward's books so popular was their illustrations, by the Victorian bird artist Archibald Thorburn. Originally painted for a work commissioned by Lord Lilford in the late nineteenth century, Thorburn's illustrations were later used in a modest little pocket-sized volume which influenced thousands of people to take up birdwatching: *The Observer's Book of Birds*.

For anyone who grew up any time from the 1930s to the 1970s, the 'Observer's Books' were an integral part of childhood. The series, which covered subjects as varied as aircraft and heraldry, wild flowers and churches, was the indispensable companion of generations of young boys and girls, many of whom gained a life-long interest as a result of reading one of these little books. That is particularly true in the case of the post-war generation of bird-watchers: after its first publication in 1937 *The Observer's Book of Birds* sold an astonishing three million copies, and had a shelf-life of almost half a century.

Publishers Warne & Co. chose birds as the subject of this, the very first Observer's book, by pure chance. Having acquired the copyright of Thorburn's plates, re-using them to produce a cheap, popular bird book during the depression of the mid-1930s made sound economic sense. The book itself was also the product of an unlikely pen. In 1923, at the precociously early age of thirteen, S. Vere Benson and her sister had founded the Bird-Lovers' League, to discourage the international trade in wild birds and their skins. Despite the sisters' tender age, the project was a huge success, persuading thirty thousand people across the world to help protect wild birds by boycotting the plumage trade. When she came to write her pioneering book on birds, Miss Benson had clear and modest ambitions:

> For many years I have, from time to time, been asked by birdlovers to recommend a really inexpensive pocket textbook of British birds. Usually I could recommend nothing that was not either too bulky, too expensive or inadequate to the needs of the would-be ornithologist. I think no one will be able to say that this one is either too large or too expensive, or that it is inadequately illustrated.

By including all the species regularly found in the British Isles, but omitting scarce migrants and rarities, Benson achieved her aims of clarity and portability. Originally priced at half a crown (roughly £2.50 today), the first edition of *The Observer's Book of Birds* has since become a collector's item, with one in its original dust-jacket recently selling at auction for £100. But for anyone pricked by a nostalgic desire to seek out a copy, later editions can still be picked up from most second-hand bookshops for just a few pounds.

MEANWHILE, across the Atlantic, a true revolution had begun. In 1934, a slim volume had appeared entitled *A Field Guide to the Birds*, written and illustrated by a young New York bird artist named Roger Tory Peterson. In the three quarters of a century since its publication, the 'Peterson Guide' has had more effect on the growth and development of birdwatching as a mass participation pastime than any other book in history. As Elliott Richardson wrote in the foreword to John Devlin and Grace Naismith's biography of Peterson in 1977:

> It has been said that my old friend and teacher, Roger Tory Peterson, has done more than any other person to make the field identification of birds a science. I am sure that is true. But it is fair to say that Roger Tory Peterson has also done more than any other man to make field identification a sport.

Peterson's was not the first field guide: as well as Florence Merriam's *Birds through an Opera-glass* in 1889, Frank Chapman had written several popular works on bird identification around the turn of the century. In 1906, a young bird artist named Chester Reed began publishing a series of guides which were in use for over thirty years, sold more than half a million copies, and had a lasting influence on the young Roger Peterson.

But this was the first time that a systematic attempt had been made to make bird identification in the field a more rigorous and accurate process. Peterson's subtitle – 'A Bird Book on a New Plan' – gave a clue to the revolutionary nature of the book. And like many revolutions, what Peterson had done was deceptively simple. Unlike previous guides, which had shown the birds in a variety of 'natural' poses, he chose to portray the birds in identical postures, to make it easier to compare similar species. The illustrations were utilitarian rather than aesthetic, and depicted the birds in the way birdwatchers were most likely to see them: for example ducks were shown swimming, while raptors were portrayed in flight, viewed from beneath. Key field marks, such as a white patch on the wing or a dark crown, were indicated by the use of arrows, and there were line drawings in the text to help identify difficult species. This was light years ahead of *The Observer's Book of Birds*, whose design and illustrations belonged to a bygone era.

What is most surprising to the modern birder is that of a total of thirty-five plates, only three (showing warblers, finches and buntings) were painted in colour. Peterson defended this approach on the dust-jacket:

> The book is made on an entirely new plan, which recognises the fact that color-values rather than the actual colors are most important in identifying birds at a distance. The text is entirely without frills and is devoted strictly to giving information to help the student to identify birds in the field. This book will at once take its place as an indispensable pocket companion for Eastern bird-students, both beginning and advanced.

For once, the hype was justified. Having been rejected by several publishers, the first edition of two thousand copies – published on 27 April 1934, and priced at $2.75 – sold out during the very first week. Since then well over three million copies have been sold, and today you can buy a Peterson field guide to almost every aspect of the natural world, including astronomy and the weather.

With characteristic modesty, Roger Peterson put the book's success down to the fact that he was a 'home-made ornithologist', trained in art rather than the academic discipline of biology, which prompted him to adopt a visual approach to the problems of bird identification. He also understood that his book was only a guide, and not the 'holy writ' it was sometimes regarded as by his disciples. He concluded his introduction with this warning for over-eager rarity hunters: 'One should always use a certain amount of caution in making sight identifications, especially where rarities are concerned . . . A quick field observer who does not temper his snap judgement with a bit of caution is like a fast car without brakes.'

In one review of the Guide, quoted in *Neighbors to the Birds*, the writer used humorous irony to reveal how the book had fundamentally changed the way people looked at birds, compelling them to attempt to identify them instead of simply enjoying them from an aesthetic point of view:

> We never used to identify songbirds, we used to lump them together and listen to them sing. But my wife, through a stroke of ill fortune, somehow got hold of a book called 'A Field Guide to the Birds' . . . and now we can't settle down to any piece of work without being interrupted by a warbler trying to look like another warbler and succeeding admirably . . .

Another far-reaching effect of Peterson's new guide was to give momentum to the drive to persuade the ornithological establishment in the US to accept 'sight records' of rare birds. This built on the work already done by Peterson's mentor, Ludlow Griscom – known as 'the dean of North American birdwatchers'. Griscom had shot birds himself as a young man, but had then fought against the 'specimen fetish' of scientific ornithology to develop the art and science of field identification.

However, the most extraordinary result of the Peterson revolution took place almost a decade later, during World War II, when his bird identification techniques were used for a very different purpose. The United States Air Force drew up charts to differentiate allied and enemy aircraft, using Peterson's simple technique of arrows pointing to important 'field marks'. As a result the number of 'friendly fire' incidents, in which an aircraft is downed by shots from its own side, was dramatically reduced.

Ultimately, Roger Tory Peterson's influence went far beyond the bounds of birdwatching. His stunning artwork, combined with his avuncular personality and easy charm, endeared him to generations of Americans, some of whom had only the vaguest interest in natural history. As the environmentalist Paul Ehrlich wrote in the 1980s, when a facsimile of the original edition of Peterson's guide was issued:

> In this century, no one has done more to promote an interest in living creatures than Roger Tory Peterson, the inventor of the

modern field guide . . . His greatest contribution to the preservation of biological diversity has been in getting tens of millions of people outdoors with Peterson Field Guides in their pockets.

Elsewhere, the revolution took a little longer to arrive. *A Field Guide to the Birds of Britain and Europe*, also illustrated by Peterson, appeared in 1954, and from the 1970s onwards hardly a year went by without a new guide to one of other of the world's regions appearing.

Most birders welcomed the portable, easy to use field guides, though to a select few, it hardly mattered, as British ornithologist David Bannerman discovered when he met a young district commissioner in West Africa. The young man casually mentioned that he always took Bannerman's own work on West African birds with him on safari. 'Not all eight volumes?!' exclaimed Bannerman; to which the gentleman casually replied: 'It only means another porter!'

Britain may have fallen behind North America in terms of field guides, but in one area of publishing it still reigned supreme: that of the definitive 'handbook' providing comprehensive coverage of all aspects of bird identification, behaviour and distribution.

The prime movers behind the *Handbook of British Birds*, which appeared in five volumes between 1938 and 1941, were two grand old men of British ornithology, H. F. Witherby and F. C. R. Jourdain. Like Peterson and Griscom in North America, Witherby and Jourdain had already done much to promote the acceptance of 'sight-records' by developing the concept of 'field-characters': the rigorous code by which species might be identified without first having to shoot them.

Now they joined forces with two other key figures in mid twentieth century ornithology, B. W. Tucker and N. F. Ticehurst, to produce what would become the definitive work on Britain's birds for the following forty years or more. In the preface to the *Handbook*, they outlined their intentions:

> Our aim in this Handbook . . . has been to produce a work of real practical utility, not only to the professional ornithologist, but to the beginner. We have sought to make it as complete as possible as a book of reference on British birds, and to arrange it in such a systematic and uniform way that it can be consulted on any point about any species with ease.

The notes on field characters and general habits, written by Bernard Tucker, were a model of clarity and brevity – as in this description of the Treecreeper (italics as in original):

> Creepers are the *only small British Passerines with relatively long, decurved bills*. Chief characteristic of soberly coloured Tree-Creeper is its behaviour. Constantly hunting for insects, it ascends trunks or limbs of trees, and more rarely walls, in succession of little jerks, then flies, generally obliquely downwards, to trunk or branch of another tree and again ascends. Upper-parts brown, streaked pale buff; rump more rufous; whitish eye-stripe; underparts silvery-white; wings barred buffish. Young have more rufous-yellow tinge and more spotted appearance than adults. Length c. 5 ins.

This blend of accuracy and insight inspired several generations of birdwatchers, from the 1940s until the 1970s, to go out and look more closely at our native birds. It was finally superseded by the elephantine *Birds of the Western Palearctic*, which owed its existence to the knowledge gained by a generation brought up on the *Handbook*.

THE CHANGE in attitudes brought about by Witherby and his disciples also had an effect on the declining but committed band of serious egg-collectors. Back in 1908 the BOU had passed a resolution condemning the taking or destroying of British birds or their eggs, yet two years later, in October 1910, leading oologist

P. F. Bunyard had exhibited a series of rare birds' eggs at a meeting of the British Ornithologists' Club.

A fellow member, J. L. Bonhote, was prompted to take action. While not condemning collecting *per se*, he called for a new perspective:

> How many of us owe our interest in birds to the egg-collections we made as boys at school, and where would our knowledge of the science of ornithology be were it not for our collections? But the good of collecting lies in its use and not in its abuse, and I do not hesitate to say that no scientific purpose is served by the accumulation of masses of clutches or by the destruction of a single clutch of one of our very rare breeding species. Such acts only pander to a collector's greed, and bring the scientific study of birds into bad repute.

Bonhote went on to propose a resolution condemning this aspect of collecting. Following what the minutes, with characteristic understatement, call 'a somewhat animated discussion', the motion was carried almost unanimously.

Finally, in April 1922, the Club members went the whole way. After a complaint by Lord Buxton at the annual meeting of the RSPB, condemning the actions of oologists as 'constituting a distinct menace to the effective protection of wild birds . . .', the BOC decided to cease publishing details of proceedings at dinners held by the Oological Club, and dissociated itself from its activities.

Even so, the standard introduction for most young people to birds was still via collecting their eggs – though most stuck to the unwritten rule of taking only a single egg from each clutch. Books such as *Birds Nesting*, by J. G. Black, sought to impart a moral superiority to the 'proper' egg collector:

> Every egg in your collection should remind you of the nest it came from, the bird that laid it, the search for it, the finding of it, and all sorts of pleasant things. Eggs that don't remind you of anything at all are not a *collection*; you might as well have an album of stamps given you by your big brother when he got tired of it.

But gradually, things were beginning to change. A more

restrained approach was reflected in the introduction to E. W. Hendy's *The Lure of Bird Watching*, published a few years later, in 1928. The writer, J. C. Squire, noted recent changes in attitudes towards birds and their protection:

> Even with regard to the common birds there is a perceptible change in the public attitude. Village children may still 'pug' nests and stone or torture nestlings. But wanton torture is diminishing; the young egg-collector is gradually being trained to take one egg rather than the whole clutch; birds are protected by law which used to be slaughtered like vermin. A growing respect for bird-life is perceptible ...
>
> To-day there are a host of observers who would watch birds with enthusiastic affection, never kill a bird, and would never dream of killing a rare bird. The modern man who kills a rare bird is not regarded as the hero of an exploit, but as the perpetrator of an unpunishable crime. The collectors, the hoarders of eggs, the stuffers of skins are now a furtive race.

The shift away from egg-collecting as the primary reason for searching for birds' nests is demonstrated in the life of Desmond Nethersole-Thompson. Nethersole-Thompson was one of the great characters of twentieth-century ornithology, though because of his early days as a collector he never quite received the recognition he deserved.

He had been persuaded to give up collecting by, of all people, F. C. R. Jourdain, and found a substitute in his quest to understand the breeding behaviour of birds such as the Greenshank and Snow Bunting, which he regarded almost as a 'battle' to outwit the object of his study. Nethersole-Thompson's obsession with these species was undoubtedly due to a combination of their extreme rarity, the difficulty of finding their nests, and most of all the wild and inaccessible places in which they bred. Thus is was that in 1933, he decided that the only way to really understand these birds was to go and live alongside them for an entire breeding season, using funds saved from his annual salary of £120 as a schoolmaster. He described his preparation in his monograph *The Snow Bunting*, written thirty years later in 1966:

All that winter I lived like a monk and by the end of March I had saved the large sum of just over £50. I had thought of little else but Greenshanks and Snow Buntings, and had counted the days of winter and early spring with the eagerness of a convict in prison.

In early spring 1934, Nethersole-Thompson was finally ready to go, and after taking the night train from King's Cross to Aviemore, was reunited with his wife Carrie, a Highland naturalist whom he had met on a previous birds-nesting expedition to the Highlands. They headed up to the high tops, where they were to spend a total of sixty-six days and nights living in a small tent, observing the breeding Snow Buntings. To say that this was no easy undertaking is a profound understatement:

> A July cloudburst nearly washed us out. Water ran off the hills and poured like a burn right through the tent. Clothes, blankets, and bread were wet and sodden . . . We huddled close in misery and growing hopelessness. How eagerly we welcomed the first greyness of dawn, although outside the mist was grey and clinging. Then, almost like a miracle, the mist vanished; and by noon we had begun to dry out.
>
> . . . Sometimes big winds blew up in the night . . . The small tent often seemed about to rise and fly, but somehow it always held. For whole weeks the wind roared against the canvas, dulling our wits and condemning us to passive inactivity . . . We lost count of days – each often seemed more miserable than the one before – and had to shout against the roar of the wind.

Despite these privations, the couple stuck to their task. Looking back, Nethersole-Thompson recalled the effects of their long vigil: 'I came down from the hill, older in experience, possibly a little wiser, and certainly over two stone lighter.'

Fortunately the effort was worth it: in a single season the Nethersole-Thompsons had discovered more about the breeding behaviour of this charming and fascinating bird than all the people who had gone before them. During the next few years, they continued to spend their summers watching their beloved 'snow birds', despite an addition to their own family:

Although our son, Brock, was born in August 1935 this did not stop us going to the hill. Carrie used to put Brock into a gamebag and hump him to camp on the tops along with our stores and gear. When he was less than ten months old he was listening to a snow bird singing in a rough corrie and trying to crawl over the moss and stones to get his hands on a clutch of dotterel's eggs.

To a later generation brought up to watch birds on reserves in the comfort of heated hides, or on guided tours, this may seem like an extraordinary – indeed almost masochistic – dedication to the cause; and the Nethersole-Thompsons were perhaps not wholly typical of their own contemporaries. But from today's perspective, it is hard not to feel a frisson of envy for a time when ordinary bird-watchers could go out and discover new and extraordinary things about Britain's breeding birds.

Nethersole-Thompson's experiences of life in the Highlands had other, unexpected consequences. Brought up in the comfortable surroundings of the London middle-class, but now appalled by the deprived lifestyle of the local people, he eventually became a county councillor for Inverness, and stood unsuccessfully for election to parliament as a Labour candidate. For the rest of his life he functioned equally effectively as a thorn in the side of the Scottish political powers that be, and as one of our greatest field observers. He died in May 1989, still on the fringes of the British ornithological establishment despite his achievements, no doubt due to the stigma attached to his early days as an egg-collector. With hindsight, we can now accord him his rightful place as a pioneer of close field observation of birds, and as a genuine popularizer of birdwatching, especially in Scotland.

As EGG-COLLECTING gradually declined, another, more benign form of 'collecting' became popular: bird photography. This had begun in the final years of the nineteenth century, with such men as R. B. Lodge, who took the first close-up of a bird at the nest in 1895. Other pioneers included brothers Richard and Cherry Kearton, whose book *British Birds' Nests*, also published in

1895, was the first to feature pictures taken only in the wild. These pioneers used large, cumbersome plate cameras, which were heavy and awkward to carry about in the field, but by the start of the twentieth century mass-market portable cameras gradually began to become available.

One of the most popular was the Kodak 'Box Brownie'. Launched in 1901, and costing just one dollar in the US or five shillings in Britain, the Box Brownie made photography available to a mass market for the very first time. The original slogan – 'You press the button and we'll do the rest' – captured the imagination of the general public, and the camera went on to become a world-wide best-seller, making Kodak's founder George Eastman a millionaire in the process.

But there was more to the Box Brownie than cheapness and convenience. Photographer Arthur Steiglitz described it as 'an art form for the masses', and it inspired many young people to take up photography – first as a hobby, then, in some cases, as a profession.

One man inspired by this little camera went on to become the world's best-known bird photographer. Eric Hosking was born in 1909, and like many sickly and undernourished children at the time, his survival in early years was touch-and-go. Perhaps to encourage him to venture outdoors, when he was aged seven or eight his parents bought him a Box Brownie. Fired with enthusiasm for his new hobby, the young Eric saved his pocket money for something better. By the age of ten he finally had the thirty shillings required to buy a plate camera – much better quality than the little Kodak model. In his autobiography, he recalled the excitement of that first purchase:

> Immediately I got home, I loaded three plates and hurried to a song thrush's nest I had found and took my first bird 'photograph'. Back home again I persuaded my elder brother Stuart to help me develop it. I was so excited I could hardly wait for the light to be switched on, but as we looked at the negative my heart sank – it was just a misty blur. I had not realised that it was necessary to focus a camera and had merely rested the lens on the edge of the nest and pressed the shutter release!

With practice and experience, the young Eric soon became proficient at photographing birds. After leaving school aged fifteen, with the parting words of his headmaster ringing in his ears – 'Hosking, you'll never make anything of your life' – he became an apprentice in the motor trade. Long hours and a salary of only ten shillings a week, most of which he spent on commuting, meant he had little time or money available to pursue his interest in photography. He also sustained a serious foot injury in an industrial accident, so that for the rest of his life he suffered considerable pain when walking over rough ground. Then, in 1929, Britain's economy went into freefall as a result of the Wall Street crash. Hosking's employer went into liquidation, and at the age of twenty, along with millions of his fellow workers, he found himself on the dole.

What must at the time have seemed like a disaster turned out to be the event that would transform Hosking's fortunes: 'It was the most degrading, depressing period of my life. Yet it also led to the best thing that ever happened to me. I did not know it then, but I had finished with regular employment for ever . . . For me, the depression brought release.'

Hosking needed a stroke of luck, which came in a phone call from an old school-friend working as a sub-editor on the *Sunday Dispatch* newspaper, who asked him to go along to London Zoo to photograph their newest acquisition: a baby elephant seal. Hosking had the bright idea of taking along the four year old daughter of a friend, and putting her next to the seal to show its huge size. The resulting photograph was published the following Sunday, covering half the back page, and earning him the princely sum of two guineas (£2.10 – about £100 today). Eric Hosking's career as a professional photographer had begun.

One of his first attempts to photograph birds ended in disaster. Having found a Goldcrest's nest containing the egg of a Cuckoo, he rather naïvely told a fellow lensman, George Boast, and his companion of this unique discovery. Five days later, on inspecting the nest, Hosking discovered to his horror that the eggs and nest had been taken. Several years afterwards he discovered that a clutch of Goldcrest's eggs with a Cuckoo's egg had been exhibited at a meeting of the British Oologists' Association – by George Boast's companion. At the time there was still no law against egg-collecting, so all Hosking could do was regret his lost chance of a famous ornithological scoop.

Hosking's fortunes took an upturn when he was called by an advertising agency requesting a photograph of a swan. Finding nothing suitable in his files, Hosking cycled off to his local park in north London, threw the swans some bread, and took a roll of photographs. A drawing made from one of them soon appeared on advertising hoardings all over Britain – and the image has been the logo for Swan Vestas matches ever since.

This success launched Hosking in his new career, and soon afterwards he even won a commission to photograph the young royal princesses, Elizabeth and Margaret Rose, for *Country Life* magazine. But for the first time a young photographer like Hosking was able to make a living taking portraits of birds rather than people, thanks to a rapidly growing demand from book publishers, advertisers, newspapers and magazines. In turn, the prominence of these pictures helped to promote an interest in birds and birdwatching amongst the wider public.

Then, the day after the coronation of King George VI in May 1937, tragedy struck. While climbing a pylon hide he had erected in order to photograph a pair of nesting Tawny Owls, he felt a heavy blow strike his face. One of the owls, approaching on silent wings, had sunk its sharp claws into his left eye.

He was rushed to Moorfields Eye Hospital in London, where surgeons struggled to save the sight of his eye. But after a fortnight, a dangerous infection had set in, and now threatened the sight of his other, good eye. In these days before antibiotic drugs, he was given a stark choice – do nothing, and risk going blind, or have the injured left eye removed: 'It was an awful decision to make. In my profession sight is everything. Obviously I could not risk going blind, yet what good would a one-eyed naturalist-photographer be? It looked as though the career I loved so much was to end. I was twenty-seven.'

Hosking did opt for the removal of the injured eye, and despite his misgivings, he continued to take photographs. Indeed, he went on to become the best-known bird photographer in the world, his pictures gracing books, magazines, galleries and private homes. More importantly for the development of birdwatching, perhaps more than any other person during the years between the two world wars, he helped bring birds to the forefront of public consciousness. And just to show that he bore the owl no ill-will, when he wrote his best-selling autobiography in 1970, he called it, with typically wry humour, *An Eye for a Bird*.

Yet despite the interest in bird surveys, the growing availability of bird books, and the rise of bird photography, birdwatching itself was still regarded as a minority pastime, as one of the last survivors from that era recalls.

Brought up in the south London suburbs during and just after World War I, Richard Fitter's very first memory of any kind was sitting in his pram on Tooting Bec Common watching the ducks on the pond. Later he recalls his governess showing him his first Song Thrush's nest – which he remembers as being 'extraordinarily beautiful'. Typical of his generation, he had a childhood interest in egg collecting, though in deference to the ethics of the day, he only took a single egg from each nest. The urge to collect may have been because like many young birdwatchers he did not own a pair of binoculars until he was about sixteen years old. This was far from unusual: 'If you were seen carrying a pair of field-glasses people shouted at you, "Are you off to the races?" That was the only respectable purpose you could have field-glasses for!'

Fortunately for the young Richard, he was sent away to boarding school at Eastbourne College in Sussex. There, he came under the guiding influence of headmaster E. C. Arnold, whose memory is commemorated in the name of Arnold's Marsh at Cley in Norfolk. Arnold was one of those unusual figures who spanned the eras of collecting and protecting – although he wrote a book on bird reserves, Fitter described him as 'the sort of person who would prowl around Blakeney Point shooting Willow Warblers, hoping that they would prove to be something rarer!'

By the time Fitter came under his wing, Arnold had somewhat mellowed. At a meeting of the school natural history society he casually revealed that Black Redstarts could be found during the late autumn and winter at the foot of Beachy Head. One Sunday afternoon (their only free time during the whole week) Fitter and a school friend went to see them.

His enthusiasm was fired; after acquiring one of Max Nicholson's books, and subscribing to *British Birds*, he became active in bird surveys, driving round London with James Fisher to count Starling roosts. In 1935, having persuaded a friend to borrow his father's motor-car, he ventured farther afield to Tring reservoirs in Hertfordshire. It was a destination that four years later would become the location for a meeting that changed Fitter's life. (See Chapter 10.)

Richard Fitter was not the only birdwatcher taking advantage of the greater availability of motor transport to go birdwatching. In the half century since it had first appeared on Britain's roads, the spread of the motor-car had continued apace. In 1914, there had been 150,000 cars in Britain, and by 1922, they had become a normal attribute of the middle-class family. By the start of World War II in 1939, there were 1.5 million cars on the road.

We tend to think of motorized birding as something new; yet as Max Nicholson recalled, during the 1920s those birdwatchers who owned cars would flit from place to place, and bird to bird, 'in the manner of young people visiting different night-clubs'. Just as in the nineteenth century rail travel had opened up the countryside to people yearning to escape the cities, so the motor-car catered for a basic human need for fresh air and contact with nature. In 1939, in his book *The Countryside Companion*, Tom Stephenson looked back on the changes between the two world wars:

> In recent years there has arisen a widespread recognition of the need for contact with the land from which many of us have been too long uprooted. Never have there been so many people taking every opportunity to escape from town to seek recreation in places where rural peace still endures. Much of this is, no doubt, to be explained by shorter working hours and increased facilities for travel.

Ironically, the places that proved most popular with bird-watchers were not 'places where rural peace still endures', but the rather unsalubrious surroundings of reservoirs and sewage farms, which regularly turned up the most extraordinary records of rare birds.

However, the continued spread of the motor-car had its downside. By allowing people to commute between their home and place of work, it led to a rapid exodus from cities into the newly created suburbia. As the network of roads spread further and further out into the countryside, so houses, shops, offices and factories were built to meet the needs of the people who had moved there, turning England, in the words of the historian G. M. Trevelyan, into 'one huge unplanned suburb'.

Richard Fitter's old headmaster E. C. Arnold was particularly outspoken in his criticism of the effects of the motor-car on wildlife. In his 1940 book *Bird Reserves*, referring to a proposed set of road 'improvements' close to a bird sanctuary, he asserted that it was ridiculous that money should be used to provide 'lethal facilities for a selfish and self-assertive class'. He also predicted, accurately as it turned out, that unregulated building would cause major problems for birds in the future: 'Bird protection is nowadays far more a matter of preserving bird haunts than of making laws to protect birds, which may easily, like the Kentish Plover, be exterminated by progress in the form of bungalows, though officially protected by the law.'

Less than two decades later his prediction sadly came true, when as a result of habitat loss and disturbance the Kentish Plover was lost as a British breeding bird. It is ironic that private motor transport, the single biggest factor in allowing successive generations access to the countryside to watch birds, would also destroy so many important bird habitats, and threaten the birds that lived there.

The final factor that made birdwatching more popular during the 1920s and 1930s was a change in social attitudes towards 'hobbies'. 'Leisure time', something that had always been available to the privileged few, was now emerging as something which the majority of working people could enjoy.

As American sociologist Steven M. Gelber has pointed out in *Hobbies:Leisure and the Culture or Work in America*, during the first half of the twentieth century average working hours declined dramatically, and by 1920 industrial workers had eight hours more free time per week than in 1900. Moreover, they no longer had to work six days a week – most people now had Saturday afternoons off as well as Sundays.

This time needed to be filled, and one of the most satisfying ways of doing so was with a hobby. In 1913, the author of an article on hobbies (quoted in Gelber's book) had asked his readers this rhetorical question: 'What, you have no hobby? In these days of drive, push and worry how can you recreate yourself without the aid of a hobby?'

This question was based on the premise that hobbies literally restored energy to the participant, improving both their work and home life. In an increasingly mechanized world, a hobby also gave life a sense of meaning and purpose, advocating a new 'leisure ethic' that made self-fulfilling leisure an end in itself, not just something to fill up spare time.

In the USA, participation in all kinds of hobbies continued to increase. A 1933 survey found that more people increased the time they spent on hobbies than on any other form of leisure time, and did so more intensively. By 1938, hobbies were even being advanced as an antidote to dullness and a way of improving your social life: 'Do you know a person who is so bubbling over with enthusiasm that everyone around him catches the kindling spark? Have you noticed how interesting he is, how easily he attracts friends? Would you like to know his secret?'

The secret, of course, was a hobby. Birdwatching is perhaps not what the writer had in mind – the most popular interests were still collecting objects and making handicrafts – but the effects on the individual and their self-esteem were undoubtedly the same. In a rapidly changing society, birdwatching helped give people a foundation around which to build the rest of their life. From now on, this would increasingly become the central reason for watching birds.

B Y 1939, at the end of two decades of fragile peace, people had begun to get used to the idea of 'freedom of choice' – the notion that they could decide for themselves what to do in their spare time. In his essay on the English, *The Lion and the Unicorn*, George Orwell noted:

> Another English characteristic which is so much a part of us that we barely notice it, and that is the addiction to hobbies and spare time occupations . . . We are a nation of flower-lovers, but also a nation of stamp-collectors, pigeon-fanciers, amateur carpenters, coupon-snippers, darts-players, crossword-puzzle fans . . .
>
> It is a liberty to have a home of your own, to do what you like in your spare time, to choose your own amusements instead of having them chosen for you from above. The genuinely popular culture of England is something that goes on beneath the surface, unofficially.

This new-found ability to do what you liked was about to be severely curtailed during six further years of wartime. But the seeds had been sown: the freedom to enjoy watching birds had been given to people, and nothing – not even Hitler's mighty war machine – was going to take that freedom away.

CHAPTER TEN

Escaping

World War II, 1939-1945

In a way war encouraged birdwatching. It is often said that war consists of five per cent wild excitement and fear, and 95 per cent boredom. Stationary soldiers and, still more, prisoners of war need a hobby.

Peter Marren, *The New Naturalists*

O N SUNDAY 27 August 1939, exactly one week before Britain went to war with Germany, two young men met for the very first time on a London Natural History Society (LNHS) field trip to Tring Reservoirs in Hertfordshire.

After the war, Richard Fitter and Richard Richardson would collaborate as author and illustrator of the first full-scale field guide to British birds, but at the time of this first meeting they were poles apart in their experience. As we saw in the last chapter, Richard Fitter had begun birdwatching at boarding school in Sussex, influenced by his headmaster, the redoubtable ornithologist E. C. Arnold. Later, in the 1930s, he had become active both in bird surveys and in applying the same techniques to studying human beings, in the Mass-Observation movement. At the early age of twenty-six he was already a force to be reckoned with in British ornithology.

Richardson, on the other hand, was a callow youth of seventeen, who still did not own any field-glasses and had to borrow a pair from his companion. His diary (quoted in Moss Taylor's biography) reveals it to have been 'the most interesting day that I've ever experienced'. But though a successful day's birdwatching, the outing was tinged by the imminence of conflict. 'All of us,' Fitter recalled, more than sixty years later, 'realised that war was coming, and that this might be the last field trip for some time.'

On Sunday 3 September, Prime Minister Neville Chamberlain declared war on Hitler's Germany, and for the second time in a quarter of a century, the world was plunged into chaos. The LNHS party's forebodings were soon realized: many people were called up into the forces, key coastal sites were declared out-of-bounds for the duration and consequently opportunities for birdwatching at home were few and far between.

Like everyone else, birdwatchers and ornithologists made their own contribution to the war effort. But unlike World War I, when a whole generation of young men was wiped out on the fields of Flanders, this time casualties were much lower – especially among the fighting men. As a result, the vast majority of the young bird-watchers who had come of age during the 1930s survived unscathed.

The war also had more long-term consequences. Barriers between social classes, while hardly collapsing overnight, began to break down. This eventually allowed the majority of the post-war generation, rather than a privileged elite, to become more socially mobile than their forebears. This in turn increased people's disposable income and leisure time, enabling them to participate in hobbies such as birding.

The war brought another unexpected bonus: many thousands of people (mostly men in the armed forces) were sent to parts of the world they could not have dreamed of visiting in peacetime – where they discovered a whole new range of exotic birds. After the war this widening of horizons was to have a profound effect on the development of birdwatching as a mass activity.

RICHARD RICHARDSON spent the first year of the war living in London, with most of his birdwatching confined to the London parks and reservoirs. He noticed some changes to the capital's birdlife almost straight away, as his diary entry for 14 September 1939 reveals:

Since the war began, people have been unable to spare much bread and other food for the birds in St James's Park, and I wondered if it's this that has caused the marked decrease in the gull visitors, who knowing that no food is available here have gone elsewhere to find it. Mr Hinton says it's difficult to get fish for the pelicans now!

In late 1940, Richardson joined the Royal Norfolk Regiment, and spent the next three years at various postings in East Anglia. Then in September 1943, he and his battalion were finally sent abroad, on a troop ship bound for India.

It was his birding experiences back home, however, that first gave him consolation on the long outward journey. Like many young soldiers, most of whom had never travelled further than the English seaside, he experienced mixed feelings of excitement and homesickness, but during a brief train stop on the way from Bombay to Deolali, he heard a familiar sound – the call of a Common Sandpiper: 'The silvery whistle struck a chord in my memory, for it was one of the treasured sounds of London, where the waders often pass over on foggy September nights . . . '

Richardson was not alone in taking consolation from birds. Just as in World War I, the sound of familiar birds offered serving soldiers not only inspiration and comfort but also a priceless sense of continuity and permanence. Fighting in Italy in 1944, Alex Bowlby first assumed the sound he heard coming from the direction of the enemy lines was a German soldier imitating the song of a bird:

> But as the bird sang on I realized that no human being could reproduce such perfection. It was a Nightingale. And as if showing us and the Germans that there were better things to do it opened up until the whole valley rang with song . . . I sensed a tremendous affirmation that 'this would go on' . . .

The familiar song of the Skylark also prompted a pensive Bowlby to reflect on the absurdity of his situation: 'In the lulls between explosions I could hear a lark singing. That made the war seem sillier than ever.'

Just as in the previous conflict, when singing Skylarks would sometimes be mistaken for enemy aircraft, similar incidents would occasionally occur. The most notorious, known as 'The Battle of Barking Creek', took place in late 1939, when a flock of geese in the Thames Estuary was misidentified as a formation of enemy aircraft. As a result, two squadrons of fighters were scrambled, and in the resulting confusion, attacked each other. It is thought that this was the first time that birds had been detected by radar – a process that after the war would make significant contributions to our knowledge of bird migration.

Meanwhile, soon after Richard Richardson arrived at Deolali, a serious skin problem confined him to hospital for the next eight months. Although this afforded him ample opportunity to watch the local birds, his lack of binoculars proved greatly frustrating: 'So far I've seen four different kinds of shrike in India, but as yet, don't know the names of any of them!'

Perhaps to compensate for his inability to identify the smaller birds, he turned his attention to the behaviour of the larger ones, such as the ubiquitous Pariah Kite: 'They are bold enough to snatch food from a plate carried by a human being; usually approaching from behind and clutching the tit-bit with the feet as they pass rapidly over the shoulder of the astonished victim.' To accompany his notes, Richardson added sketches to his diary, including an illustration of this very incident – with the added note: 'No, this isn't just a yarn! Just a daily occurrence.'

Like so many birdwatchers of his generation, Richardson's interest was considered somewhat eccentric by his fellow soldiers:

> Always I long for someone with whom I could share each little interesting discovery, each little triumph and the many little failures. Someone who feels the same about birds & things as I do . . . I've only met one fellow in the Army who really enjoyed watching birds & the strange thing about it was that his name was Richardson too. Sometimes when I'm elated by a new discovery I cannot help telling one or two of my pals here. They are very decent about it & try to be interested but their often ill-concealed boredom brings me down to earth again.
>
> Once or twice a mess-mate has asked me what kick I get out of studying birds & often, as I pause to find an answer, I detect a tiny

gleam of triumph in his eyes when he sees I cannot answer straight away.

Nevertheless, Richardson persisted in his observations and sketches; his experience serving him well after the war, when he became one of Britain's best known bird artists. His almost permanent presence on the famous East Bank at Cley – one of the key meeting places during the post war years – gave him a special place in the memories of generations of birdwatchers, until his death in 1977, at the age of just fifty-five.

AFTER THE WAR, many British servicemen wrote accounts of their wartime experiences, of which Guy Gibson's *Enemy Coast Ahead* is one of the best-known examples. But another young RAF man, albeit with a rather less glamorous job as a wireless mechanic, was the only one to write a memoir specifically about his birdwatching experiences.

Published in 1946, *Wing to Wing: Bird-Watching Adventures at Home and Abroad with the R.A.F.*, came from the pen of E. H. Ware. A leather factor in civvy street, Ware had joined up in 1940, and after various postings in England and Scotland he was sent abroad to North Africa and Corsica.

Wing to Wing is a brisk, workmanlike account, rarely ascending to the heights of the classic nature writers, or rivalling the outlandish humour of his contemporary Spike Milligan. Yet in some ways this makes it a more realistic portrayal of the typical life of the serviceman, with all its petty annoyances, as in this description of the long voyage by troopship out to Africa:

> Life on a trooper, as I soon found out, is no pleasure cruise; far
> from it. Your day starts at a much-too-early hour with 'Show a leg
> there!' and your own N.C.Os see that there is no turning over and
> going to sleep again. The fortunate occupants of the top bunks
> climb out, treading on the faces of any unfortunates still lying in
> the lower ones, and force a space to dress in the crowded deck

beneath by the simple expedient of dropping into it . . . That over, queuing commences. Queue No. 1 is for wash-bowls, queue No. 2 for latrines, queue No. 3 for breakfast. Breakfast over, you have about half an hour to get into any queue you missed before, to clean out your accommodation, to tidy up your bunk, and generally get ready for ship's inspection.

After a long and tedious journey, the ship finally reached Algiers, and Ware's foreign birdwatching adventure could begin. The modern birder, who has long since left the Mediterranean behind in search of ever more exotic destinations, may find his struggles to identify birds amusing. For example, it takes him 'a fortnight's patient work' before he finally identifies a mysterious skulking bird as a Sardinian Warbler – a common and now familiar bird of the region. But this was well before the era of reliable field guides, and Ramsay's *Birds of Europe and North Africa*, published in 1923, on which he had to rely, proved far from adequate:

> The trouble was that the only available book on the birds of North Africa, which my wife had sent out to me as soon as I had been able to let her know where I was, merely consisted of a museum description of the skins, with no plates, and no notes on signal marks, song or habits, three pointers which so often help to separate difficult species.

With hindsight, Ware's memoirs unwittingly reveal just how much birdwatching changed during the decades following the war. By the 1970s, reliable field guides, improved optics and the boom in cheap foreign travel would make his experiences seem parochial and insignificant by comparison. But for Ware and thousands of others like him, the war offered unparalleled opportunities to develop their interest in and knowledge of birds.

ALTHOUGH subject to the whim of the RAF in terms of where and when he was able to watch birds, at least E. H. Ware had some freedom of movement. That did not apply to those unfortunate prisoners-of war, who were confined to a single location, sometimes for virtually the whole of the war.

One of these was John Buxton, who five years after the war ended published a slim volume on the Redstart, as part of the Collins 'New Naturalist' series. What made this book different from the others in the series was that the research and study had been carried out almost entirely in a POW camp in Bavaria.

A Fellow of New College, Oxford, before the war a tutor in English Literature and occasional poet, Buxton cuts an unlikely figure either as a hero or ornithologist. But at the outbreak of war he joined the Commandos, and in early 1940, was involved in the ill-fated Norwegian campaign, one of the greatest military disasters of the early years of the conflict, and taken prisoner by the Germans.

He was to remain captive for the remainder of the war, at Eichstätt in Bavaria. Five years is a long time to lose your liberty, particularly for a man as active in mind and body as Buxton. But in one small way he was fortunate: Eichstätt was in an attractive, rural setting, and birds were plentiful. As Peter Marren, author of *The New Naturalists*, has observed, this had its advantages: 'In some ways, prisoner-of-war camps offer rather good opportunities for bird-watching. It is hard to imagine any other circumstances in which so many intelligent, active people would have so much spare time on their hands, nor so much incentive to find a distracting pastime.'

So while his fellow-inmates spent their time dressing up as chorus-girls or digging escape tunnels, Buxton, as he recalled in the opening chapter of *The Redstart*, experienced a moment of epiphany:

> In the summer of 1940, lying in the sun near a Bavarian river, I saw a family of redstarts . . . going about their ways in cherry and chestnut trees. I made no notes then (for I had no paper), but when the next spring came, and with it . . . the first returning redstarts, I determined that these birds should be my study for most of the hours I might spend out of doors. It seemed to me that we prisoners might watch some bird together, and that

several of us working on one kind might discover more than if we
tried to make our notes on all the birds that should visit us . . .

Buxton immediately set about organizing his colleagues with
characteristic military efficiency. Regular observations began in
April 1941, and soon took up virtually all the prisoners' free time.
In just three months, from April to June 1943, Buxton and his team
of 'volunteers' spent a total of 850 hours watching a single pair of
Redstarts – an average of over nine hours a day!

The results of their observations are summed up in the title
chapters of Buxton's book: 'Arrival in breeding Area – Song –
Territory', 'Egg-laying and Incubation', 'Growth of the Chicks' and
so on. But what makes the book so fascinating to the modern reader
is the author's thoughts on the spiritual feelings of a captive man
watching free birds – emotions that go right to the heart of why
people get so much pleasure and satisfaction from birdwatching:

> My redstarts? But one of the chief joys of watching them in
> prison was that they inhabited another world than I; and why
> should I call them mine? They lived wholly and enviably to them-
> selves, unconcerned in our fatuous politics, without the limitations
> imposed all about us by our knowledge. They lived only in the
> moment, without foresight and with memory only of things of
> immediate practical concern to them . . .

Buxton returned to academia after the war, but remained active
in the birdwatching world, promoting bird observatories and
ringing, and introducing the mist-net into Britain from Germany at
a BTO conference during the mid-1950s. He died in 1989.

JOHN BUXTON was not the only birdwatcher who ended up as a
prisoner-of-war at Eichstätt. The camp also played host to
Peter Conder, later to become the director of the RSPB, and
George Waterston, subsequently the founder of Fair Isle Bird
Observatory and head of the RSPB's Scottish office. This fortu-
nate coincidence was later described by the New Naturalist editors

as 'a minor ornithological congress . . . where plans for post-war development were laid which had a far-reaching effect on ornithology in the British Isles.'

Conder had been captured at St Valery-sur-Somme in June 1940, and like Buxton spent five long years incarcerated in Eichstätt. When he died in 1983 his friend and colleague Bob Scott recalled his wartime experiences: 'His German captors soon became used to his activities to such an extent that he became a useful look-out during escape attempts. He made detailed observations on Goldfinches, recording his results on whatever material was available, including German toilet paper.'

Peter Conder also took the opportunity of his enforced sojourn in Germany to study a species common in mainland Europe, but only a very rare vagrant this side of the Channel: the Crested Lark. After the war, in 1947, he and two fellow prisoners-of-war set down their observations in *British Birds*, written with typical British understatement:

> Crested Larks were seen wherever we stayed and often bred within a hundred yards of us, but always outside the wire. So in each succeeding year we were able to see but little of their breeding behaviour. Add to this repeated disappointment the necessity for carrying food and not mountainous piles of bird notes when we were set marching in the last winter and it will be understood why so few written notes survive.

Conder and his fellow POWs did retain one bizarre observation: that the most common call of the Crested Lark sounded uncannily like 'God Save the Queen'! Presumably this was regarded as a small but significant act of defiance against their Nazi captors.

Conder's imprisonment was a life-changing experience. The man who described himself as an 'academic failure' and 'a bit of a loner' was to become one of the leading conservationists of his day. After the war, instead of returning to a career in advertising with the family firm, he became warden of Skokholm Bird Observatory off the Welsh coast. Later, he joined the RSPB, and under his thirteen-year stewardship as director from 1962 the membership increased ten-fold, from 20,000 to 200,000.

Ironically, the best-known film version of life in German prison camps, *The Great Escape*, released in 1963, has a wonderfully stereotyped portrayal of an English birdwatcher. Donald Pleasance plays Blythe, 'the Forger', a modest, unassuming non-combatant who has only become a prisoner-of-war by unfortunate accident.

In one of the quieter moments of an otherwise action-packed film, he meets the brash American Hendley, 'the Scrounger', played by James Garner. When the topic of birds comes up, the following dialogue ensues:

HENDLEY: Birds? I used to do a little hunting myself.

BLYTHE: Oh! Not hunting, watching.

HENDLEY: Oh, a birdwatcher . . .

BLYTHE: That's right. Watching them, and drawing them.

    I assume you have birdwatchers in the States?

HENDLEY: Yes [he hesitates]. Some.

What makes this scene even more absurd is that Blythe is so short-sighted he is almost blind, his eyes worn out by the close work required for forging, so presumably he would have found watching birds rather a challenge.

IN CONTRAST to those incarcerated and frustrated POWs with so much time on their hands, the men running the military operations of the war had little time for any other activity, let alone one as apparently unproductive as watching birds.

Nevertheless, the irrepressible Max Nicholson managed to do so, even in the most unlikely surroundings. One night during the Blitz, while working as a volunteer air-raid warden near his Chelsea home, he heard a Redshank calling high in the sky above. He also interrupted an important Whitehall meeting to listen to a Black Redstart singing outside the office window. But his most fabled birding exploits came on an ocean crossing to Washington on the *Queen Elizabeth*, during his wartime work in organizing the Atlantic convoys. His son Piers recalls the story:

The exact position of the ship was a matter of top security, and known only to the Captain and the navigating officer. There was therefore consternation when Max announced to the Captain that they were 300 miles south-west of Iceland. 'How did you know?' they asked, fearing a damaging security breach. 'Well I have just seen a bird which has a 200 mile radius from Greenland but is unknown in Iceland, while I saw another bird earlier today which has a 300 mile range from Iceland, but they have now vanished'.

Even more remarkably, the chief of staff of Britain's armed forces, Field Marshal Lord Alanbrooke, kept up his hobby of bird-watching despite the onerous and at times almost unbearable responsibility of his post.

Born in 1883, Alan Brooke charted a steady rise through the military hierarchy between the two world wars. In May and June 1940 he was put in charge of the evacuation of 330,000 troops from Dunkirk, and, as a result of snatching success from a mission that had seemed doomed to failure, was promoted in December 1941 to chief of staff. He was later hailed by Field Marshal Montgomery as 'the greatest soldier, sailor or airman produced by any country taking part in the last war'. Though the post-war publication of his diaries caused controversy, with their trenchant criticism of both Churchill and General Eisenhower, during the war itself Alanbrooke maintained excellent relations with the American general. In part this was thanks to his passion for birds, as Alex Danchev and Daniel Todman explain in their introduction to his war diaries:

> During the African campaign Eisenhower and Alanbrooke were in close professional accord, but while their personal relations were friendly enough, they had a touch of formality about them. Then one day Alanbrooke happened to mention to Eisenhower that he had tried to get the *Book of Birds* [a two-volume work published by the National Geographic Society] but had been told it was out of print . . .
>
> Within two days a copy of the book had been located in the States, flown across the Atlantic, and delivered to Alanbrooke with Eisenhower's compliments. That was the end of any trace of

formality between these two great soldiers; from then on it was 'Brookie' and 'Ike'.

Even at the height of the war, Alanbrooke found time for birdwatching. In June 1942, as a break between Cabinet meetings to discuss the possibility of retaking Rangoon and the threat posed by Rommel in North Africa, he made the journey north to visit the seabird colonies off Northumberland. Unfortunately, the trip ended in disappointment and near disaster:

> A day I had been looking forward to for months, namely
> visit to Farne Islands. Unfortunately weather foul and heavy
> sea running. In trying to load up dinghy overturned . . . and
> *all* my camera gear fell into the sea!! Luckily Captain rescued
> camera before it sank . . . But camera, films, lenses and all were
> swimming in sea water! Impossible to use camera, opportunity
> missed, most depressing. Anyhow weather very poor and
> drizzling. Finally flew back from Acklington, landing Hendon
> about 8.15 p.m.

A year later, on 11 June 1943 – less than a month after the Dam Busters raid – he tried again. This time he had better luck with the weather:

> Left 9 a.m. for Seahouses, where Admiral met us with a ship to
> proceed to Farne Islands. Practically the same naval party as last
> year with bird watchers . . . We had a delightful day and took
> many photographs of eider duck, fulmar petrel, kittiwakes,
> guillemots, razor bills, puffins and shags. Weather held up well.

Alanbrooke's interest in bird photography eventually led to his close friendship with Eric Hosking. The bond between the upper middle class army officer and the working class photographer was not typical of the era; but a shared interest, especially in birds, helped break down social barriers. Nor was Hosking overawed by the status of his companion: when, on one occasion, the Field Marshal was making too much noise in a hide, he was told in no uncertain terms to shut up!

The two men first met in the summer of 1945, following the

German surrender, and just before Alanbrooke's historic trip to Potsdam for the conference that was to lay the foundations for the post-war world: 'While I was home on Saturday afternoon, I was told that there was a car with some gentlemen who wished to see me. [I was introduced] to Mr Eric Hosking, the great bird photographer . . . Apparently they had found a hobby's nest with young in a Scotch fir . . . and wanted to put up a hide.'

In his autobiography *An Eye for a Bird*, Hosking himself had a rather different recollection of the meeting: 'We drove to Lord Alanbrooke's house and, with some trepidation, knocked at the front door. It was answered by a man wearing an old, open-necked shirt, vivid red braces and old khaki trousers. I was just about to ask for the great man himself when I realised that this was he.'

Undoubtedly Alanbrooke used bird watching and bird photography as a temporary release from the immense pressure and frustration of his work, as his war diaries, with their intriguing juxtaposition of his role as war leader with his passion for birds, frequently testify. Characteristic is his interruption of an entry about photographing the Hobby's nest with a deeply personal confession, written many years later, about his relationship with Churchill (shown in brackets):

27 JULY 1945

. . . during dinner Eric Hosking turned up to fix details about my using his hide to photograph hobby tomorrow.

(The thought that my days of work with Winston had come to an end was a shattering one. There had been very difficult times, and times when I felt I could not stand a single more day with him, but running through all our difficulties a bond of steel had been formed uniting us together . . .

On reading these diaries I have repeatedly felt ashamed of the abuse I had poured on him, especially during the latter years. It must, however, be remembered that my diary was my safety valve and the only outlet for all my pent up feelings . . .

I shall always look back on the years I worked with him as some of the most difficult and trying ones in my life. For all that I thank God that I was given an opportunity of working alongside of such a man, and of having my eyes opened to the fact that occasionally such supermen exist on this earth.)

28 JULY

Met Hosking at 8.30 at the White Lion and went on to the hide at once. A huge erection 26 feet high! but within 12 feet of the nest. There are 3 young birds. By 9 am I was established. At 10.45 the hen came for the first time and was at nest feeding for 10 minutes. At 12.15 she returned and was again there for close on 10 minutes. I took a lot of photographs and only hope that they may be good. It was a wonderful chance, and I believe the first time that a coloured cine picture of a hobby has been taken!

As Labour MP and *Tribune* journalist Raymond Fletcher wrote in 1959, four years before Alanbrooke's death: 'Viscount Alanbrooke, I am quite sure, would prefer to be remembered as an ornithologist than as a soldier.'

YOU DID NOT have to be Britain's chief of staff, a prisoner-of-war, or posted to some far-flung outpost of the Empire, to watch birds. Those who remained in Britain, even though restricted by wartime travel regulations, could still do so. Richard Fitter was sent round Britain's airfields to do aircraft surveys, and recalls cadging a flight from Wick around the northernmost outpost of the British Isles, Muckle Flugga in the Shetland Isles, where he had aerial views of the famous Gannet colony.

Others had to make do with more down-to-earth surroundings. Norman Moore, later to become one of Britain's leading ecologists, was an undergraduate at Trinity College, Cambridge in the early 1940s. In between his studies and college life, he volunteered as a lookout for enemy aircraft, and recalled one night in May 1942 when he heard 'the strident call of a Corncrake on the Trinity Backs'. Birdwatching was still regarded as a rather eccentric pastime, as he revealed in an essay to commemorate the seventy-fifth anniversary of the Cambridge Bird Club in 2000:

People with binoculars were a rare sight outside race meetings. On 21st November 1940 I was intently watching a bird which was flying up and down the Cam by the gasworks. 'What are you looking at?' asked a passer-by. 'A Little Gull', I replied. 'You are a one!' he said with a snigger.

Two other unusual species seen by Norman Moore were in the process of becoming new colonists as British breeding birds: a Black Redstart heard from the top of St John's College tower, and a Little Ringed Plover observed at Cambridge Sewage Farm.

These two species were also being observed elsewhere. In a 1943 paper in *British Birds*, Witherby and Fitter reported on the colonization of towns and cities in southern England by the Black Redstart. This Continental species had gained a toehold in Britain in the early 1920s, nesting mainly on coastal cliffs. But it was the sudden appearance of bomb-damaged sites, especially in London, which enabled it to colonize permanently. Witherby and Fitter reported several unusual sightings, including one nesting in a fireplace of a bombed house in Wandsworth. Max Nicholson also heard a singing male on an office block at St James's Park station, and the authors concluded that the species was perhaps three or four times as common as the previous year. However, they also noted that one reason for this apparent increase might be that the great reduction of traffic noise since before the war made them easier to hear!

Another great ornithological event at this time was the colonization as a British breeding bird by the Little Ringed Plover. The very first pair had nested at Tring Reservoirs a year before the outbreak of war, in 1938. Six years later, in 1944, three more pairs bred: two at Tring and one at a newly excavated gravel pit at Shepperton in Middlesex.

Five years later, in 1949, Kenneth Allsop was working as a cub reporter on a weekly newspaper at Slough in Buckinghamshire, when he published his first novel. *Adventure Lit Their Star* was a fictionalized account of the colonization by the Little Ringed Plover – perhaps the first time a bird had been used as the focus of a novel's plot.

The story is a simple one. Richard Locke is invalided out of the RAF with tuberculosis, and while on the slow road to recovery he discovers a pair of nesting Little Ringed Plovers. He decides to keep a vigil against egg-collectors, and foils two young boys who are hoping to take the clutch. After he has convinced them that guarding the eggs is better than stealing them, the trio come up against a really serious collector – a dastardly fellow named Colonel E. R. Goodwin. After a suitably dramatic stand-off, they finally win the day, saving the precious eggs from pillage.

Adventure Lit Their Star is in many ways a remarkable piece of writing. It has a very real charm, and includes some extraordinary and forensically detailed passages, which convey the perils of migration from the 'bird's-eye-view'. It is also very revealing about the attitudes of the day – a modern reader may be surprised to discover that taking the plovers' eggs was not against the law:

> 'The colonel . . . looked annoyed. "You and the reservoir people can go to the devil, and I would remind you that little ringed plovers aren't private property."'

One factor that had motivated Allsop to tell the story was the fact that these rare birds had chosen to nest in such a familiar, unprepossessing place, as he revealed in his introduction to the novel:

> It was, I think, the setting that heightened my desire to write this story. It is a happy event if a rare bird nests in a Norfolk sea-marsh, in a Scottish forest, on a Welsh mountain. If it nests on the outskirts of a large city, in the messy limbo that is neither town nor country, where suburban buildings, factories, petrol stations and trunk roads sprawl and blight, the event takes on an extra piquancy.

The most important legacy of *Adventure Lit Their Star* is that perhaps for the first time a writer created a character who gained spiritual comfort, and even the will to go on living, through his interest in birds. Here is Locke returning home immediately after his discovery of the Little Ringed Plovers' nest: 'The journey back along the hissing, dull-shining roads, with the rain stinging his face and misting the skyline of sagging hedgerows, was one of joy and sweetness for Locke. He thought he had never been happier.'

Richard Locke may be fictional, but his discovery of the therapeutic value of birdwatching makes him a key figure in explaining its sudden boom in popularity after the end of the war.

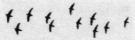

LIKE MANY other birdwatchers at the time, Allsop's hero relies on his trusty bicycle to get around. During and even after the war, petrol rationing meant that travelling even a short distance to see an unusual bird was out of the question. In the early days of the war, Eric Parker (the editor of *The Field* magazine) received a telephone call from a fellow birdwatcher, telling him that a Grey Phalarope – a rare wading bird rarely seen inland – had been sighted at Cutmill Pond, near Godalming in Surrey:

> If I wished to see it the sender . . . would try to let me know whether it was still there. My first thought was how to get to Cutmill Pond, which meant a journey of some eight miles . . . It was towards the end of the month and I had hardly any petrol left . . . I could get no message through; air-raids day and night blocked the telephone and on the top of air-raids came a storm which broke the line. At last the message came through: the bird had gone.

With travel so difficult, the only option was to watch birds in your local neighbourhood. Ornithologist Stuart Smith studied Yellow Wagtails on a vegetable plot in a Manchester suburb, and published the results in one of the earliest New Naturalist monographs, *The Yellow Wagtail*. The Revd E. A. Armstrong found inspiration even closer to home, in the garden of his Cambridge rectory. He evocatively described his moment of epiphany in another New Naturalist monograph, *The Wren*:

> Darkness was falling on a November evening in 1943 and the bombers were roaring off into the gloom when, happening to look

out of my study window, I saw a small bird . . . A couple of evenings later the wren was there again . . . My interest was again captured by a bird which had fascinated me as a boy. Here was a species about which I should like to know more.

One notable aspect of this wartime boom in the close study of birds was that so few of the participants were professional ornithologists – indeed some were not even scientists. John Buxton, as we have seen, was an Oxford don, while Stuart Smith trained as a textile chemist and Edward Armstrong as a philosopher and theologian. They were very much part of the English amateur tradition, which rates enthusiasm and sceptical enquiry as high as formal training. Indeed, the very phrase 'New Naturalist' was coined to acknowledge this approach.

However, there was still room for the trained scientist who could also write for the general public. Without doubt the most influential and best-known single-species study of the period – indeed perhaps of any era – was David Lack's *The Life of the Robin*, published in 1943. Later to win fame as a leading ornithologist, and pioneer the use of radar to study bird migration (see Chapter 11), Lack had begun his career as a schoolmaster at Dartington Hall in Devon. He began studying Robins there in the mid-1930s, originally simply to keep the school's boarding pupils amused and occupied in their spare time. He soon realized that the popular belief that the Robin was one of the best known British birds was deeply erroneous, and that much that had been published about the species was quite simply wrong. In a methodical, scientific way, he set about observing the birds without prejudging their behaviour.

The finished book was a major best-seller, with a second edition appearing in 1946, a Pelican paperback in 1953, and was still in print in the 1970s. A passage was even used as part of the GCE 'O' Level English examination. Unlike many popular writings on birds, *The Life of the Robin* was also very well received by the ornithological establishment. In his review in *British Birds*, Bernard Tucker wrote:

It is everything that a popular exposition by a scientific writer should be, clear, readable and told in straightforward language, yet losing nothing in accuracy and precision. It is written with great charm and humanity and frequently enlivened with apt and often entertaining quotations or 'curious information' from other writers, zoological and otherwise.

N OT EVERYONE interested in birds had the time, inclination or ability to produce scientific monographs based on long hours of field observation. For the more casual observer, nevertheless eager to escape the rigours of wartime, a young man named James Fisher had the answer.

In 1941, while studying Rooks for the Ministry of Agriculture, Fisher had brought out a Pelican paperback, entitled simply *Watching Birds*. Printed on thin wartime paper, and priced at two shillings, this modest little volume went on to sell over three million copies, and turned on a whole new generation to the joys and pleasures of birdwatching.

James Fisher was an unlikely man of the people: the son of the headmaster at the public school Oundle, and educated at Eton, he was a typical product of the British upper middle class. Like many men of his background, he combined an overweening self-confidence, at times bordering on arrogance, with the ability to get on with people from every walk of life.

At Oxford he began reading medicine, and might have been expected to take up a career as a doctor. Instead, inspired by his uncle Arnold Boyd, himself a well-known ornithologist, Fisher switched to zoology, and set out to proselytize on behalf of birds and birdwatching – a crusade that was to become his life's work.

After Fisher's untimely death in a car crash in September 1970, his friend and colleague Roger Tory Peterson paid tribute to 'a vivid personality, a dynamo of energy and purpose':

> James took the view that scholarship is barren unless the fruits of
> its labours are communicated to the public . . . Versatile and

prolific, his writings had a profound influence on popular ornithology, and he bridged the gap between the academic and the layman more effectively than any of his contemporaries.

After the war, Fisher would go on to write many more books, and appear in over one thousand radio and television broadcasts. He believed passionately that anyone could make a contribution to the study of birds, and that all they required was a little guidance and encouragement. *Watching Birds* was written to provide just that:

> To the ordinary human being, birds are certainly the most fascinating living creatures of the countryside . . . 'Watching Birds' is written by a scientist for just such amateurs; its object is to introduce the study of birds to those who have no zoological training . . . and, having made the introduction, to persuade them to join the army of bird-watchers who . . . have made our knowledge of British birds greater than that of the bird-life of any other country.

Despite his background, Fisher was committed to improving the lives of ordinary people at a time when less hopeful souls might have thought this impossible. Writing in November 1940, just after the famous victory in the Battle of Britain began to turn the corner for the Allied forces, he stoutly defended his optimistic approach:

> Some people might consider an apology necessary for the appearance of a book about birds at a time when Britain is fighting for its own and many other lives. I make no such apology . . . Birds are part of the heritage we are fighting for. After this war ordinary people are going to have a better time than they have had; they are going to get about more . . . many will get the opportunity, hitherto sought in vain, of watching wild creatures and making discoveries about them. It is for these men and women, and not for the privileged few to whom ornithology has been an indulgence, that I have written this little book.

This found a willing and eager readership. Despite the strictures of wartime, *Watching Birds* was an immediate success, reaching a whole new audience for whom birdwatching had not previously been a possibility. Children who had been evacuated to the countryside, soldiers serving for long periods abroad, and those left behind at home, all bought and read this little paperback, and as a result gained a lifelong interest in birds.

Watching Birds even made the term 'birdwatching' the standard phrase for this activity, according to Richard Fitter: 'Until then we weren't birdwatching as such – we were just going out to look for birds!'

In the 1945 edition, Fisher tried to explain the book's continued popularity, pointing to the growing desire amongst the general public to educate themselves through reading and other activities: 'I believe this is because the *study* of birds (a business somewhat different from an *interest* in them or an emotional love for them) concerns a very large number of the ordinary people who meet each other in the street and buy Penguins to read in trains . . . '

Meanwhile, Britain was changing, and birdwatching would change with it. In July 1945, Clement Attlee won a landslide election victory for Labour. The British were tired of privilege and the rigid social class system, and wanted to enjoy the freedom for which they had fought so long. They were eager for learning, and would now get it: either as a result of the 1944 Education Act, or through evening classes for those who had already left school.

Cheap paperbacks like *Watching Birds*, and more expensive but still affordable illustrated works such as the New Naturalist series, would enable the post-war generation to learn more about natural history. Once petrol rationing finally ended in the early 1950s, the rapid spread of the private motor-car would allow them to put this learning into practice. By 1951, Fisher was able to remind readers of a further new edition of his book of his foresight at a time when optimism had appeared futile: 'In the first paragraph of my first preface (1940) I was rash enough to make some prognostications. As far as I can make out, these have come quite true.'

On 8 May 1945, VE Day, Germany finally surrendered. The war in Europe had lasted six long years; millions had been killed, millions more had their lives changed forever. The celebrations went on through the night, and no doubt many people spent the next day at home, recovering quietly from the excesses of the night before.

Two young men marked the end of the hostilities in a rather more healthy and invigorating manner. With Richard Richardson still thousands of miles away in Ceylon, Richard Fitter arranged to go birdwatching with another London birdwatcher, John Parrinder. They caught a train down to All Hallows on the North Kent Marshes, which for the first time in five years was no longer out-of-bounds to visitors. There, in a pool by the sea wall at Cooling, they found two Black-winged Stilts, rare wanderers from the continent. That spring, what may have been the same pair of stilts settled down to nest in the unlikely surroundings of Nottingham sewage farm – the first ever breeding record for Britain.

For Britain's birdwatchers, this was a timely reminder that although Britain, society and its people might have changed, the birds were still there: oblivious to humanity, and simply waiting for a new generation of birdwatchers to find, watch and enjoy them.

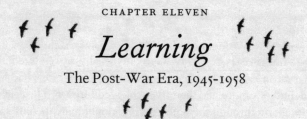

CHAPTER ELEVEN

Learning

The Post-War Era, 1945-1958

Many of us were old enough to remember the disaster of the
early twenties, following the first World War, when there was
a dismal failure to produce the promised world fit for heroes.
All during the years of the Second World War was the
determination to be ready for the peace.

   The better life must include not only food, clothing and
homes . . . but also the satisfaction of the less obvious
demands of the spirit . . .

> Sir Dudley Stamp, *Nature Conservation in Britain* (1969)

IN THE YEARS immediately following the end of World War II,
two companions would meet regularly during the breeding
season to go searching for the nests of rare birds in Sussex.
The younger man was James Ferguson-Lees, only in his late teens,
but already showing the promise that would lead him to a career
as one of the twentieth century's most influential ornithologists.
The older man, who at the age of seventy was still fit enough
to shin up trees and clamber up cliff faces in search of Peregrine eyries, was John Walpole-Bond – known to the world of
ornithology as Jock.

   Just the sight of Jock Walpole-Bond (1878-1958) would make
onlookers stop and stare. He was described in his *British Birds*
obituary as 'the very embodiment of an Old Testament prophet',
and his habit of making personal remarks in a loud voice
about passers-by made him an embarrassing companion. Other
observers likened him to a tramp, and it is said that he was twice
offered his bus fare, and once given a florin and told to buy
himself a square meal. In his earlier years, at Oxford, he used to
take on travelling prize-fighters at fairs – and beat them!

However, Walpole-Bond's eccentric appearance and behaviour concealed a fine ornithological mind, and a desire to find nests that bordered on obsession. He once claimed to have seen, *in situ*, the eggs of every regular British breeding bird, and he had a comprehensive egg collection – at a time when this was still legal, if not perhaps socially acceptable. In the spirit of the day, however, he and Ferguson-Lees had a gentleman's agreement that the great oologist would not return to take the eggs from any nest they found on their outings.

His younger companion could hardly have been more different. In 1952, at the age of just twenty-three, James Ferguson-Lees became assistant editor of *British Birds*, taking on the full-time post of executive editor two years later. In his time there, he founded the Rarities Committee, and along with Max Nicholson, unmasked the notorious 'Hastings Rarities' as a fraud.

Later he served for many years on the council of the RSPB, was chairman and president of the British Trust for Ornithology, planned and chaired major international conferences, played a key role in planning and setting up *The Birds of the Western Palearctic*, and still found time to join Guy Mountfort on his expeditions to southern Spain, Bulgaria and Jordan. He also spent eighteen years writing the definitive, 1000-page guide to the world's raptors. In *Who's Who in Ornithology* he lists his other interests as 'crosswords, gardening, very amateur photography, watching rubbish on TV'.

They could not have realized it at the time, as they travelled around the Sussex countryside from Rye to Chichester and Ashdown Forest to the South Downs, but these two men were at a crossroads in the history of birdwatching. During the years immediately following World War II, from 1945 to 1958 or so, one era ended and another began.

The chapter finally closing – of which Jock Walpole-Bond was one of the last representatives – was the world of the Victorians: when egg-collecting was an acceptable 'sport'; amateur naturalists roamed the countryside, describing its delights in rambling, flowery prose; and birdwatching was still the mildly eccentric pastime of a few enthusiasts, most of whom knew each other by reputation, if not by face and name. It was also a time when old-fashioned courtesies held sway: as Ferguson-Lees recalls, the older generation of birdwatchers spent considerable time acting as mentors to younger ones, encouraging them and teaching them the 'rules' of fieldcraft and bird identification.

The new era – typified by the young, go-getting Ferguson-Lees – was one of rapid change and growth. It saw the arrival of proper field guides and the widespread availability of decent optical aids; the development of organized structures to run the hobby on a more rigorous and professional basis; and the rise of ethology, the new science of bird behaviour. Meanwhile, thanks to the relatively new media of radio and television, millions of listeners and viewers could enjoy birdwatching vicariously from the comfort of their sitting room.

Technology became a key factor, too, with the wartime invention of radar being used not just to track enemy aircraft, but also to follow flocks of birds on their epic migratory journeys. At the same time, a growth in the study of 'visible migration' and bird-ringing led to the flourishing of a nation-wide network of bird observatories. Although at first these were beyond the access of many, by the mid 1950s it was at last becoming easier to visit these far-flung places thanks to a rapid rise in car ownership, a result of the consistent economic growth that would eventually prompt Prime Minister Harold Macmillan's famous remark that: 'Most of our people have never had it so good'.

The social structure of birdwatching had also changed. Before the war it was largely the preserve of what we would today call the 'upper middle classes': those with the time, money and opportunity to go out into the countryside. After the war, like so many British pastimes and institutions, it became more socially and geographically inclusive, with many town and city dwellers developing an interest in birds for the first time.

Most important of all, the relative insularity of British bird-watchers, and an unwillingness to look beyond these shores, was finally challenged, as they tentatively began to explore not only continental Europe but also the wilds of North America. The 1950s also saw the first stirrings of an obsession that was to dominate birding during the latter decades of the century: the desire to see as many species of birds as possible, quaintly known as 'tally-hunting', which would eventually develop into the full-blown competitive sport of twitching (see Chapter 14).

During this short period of a dozen or so years, birdwatching changed in more ways than anyone would have thought possible at the end of World War II. By the end of the 1950s, on both sides of the Atlantic, it was finally set to become the mass-participation activity it is today.

JAMES FERGUSON-LEES'S experiences, if not perhaps quite typical, are certainly evocative of a period when becoming a birdwatcher required a long and often arduous process of apprenticeship. Like most of his schoolboy contemporaries, he started by collecting eggs: the regulation one for each species. But his interest in birds really began in earnest when he joined Bedford School's natural history society at the age of thirteen. A year later, he began to make regular Sunday morning visits by bicycle to Northampton Sewage Farm (a round trip of some forty miles), where he met the man who was to have the greatest influence on his development as a birdwatcher, Bernard Tucker.

A modest and gentle man, slight of build and stature, Tucker was nevertheless one of the driving forces behind the revolution in birdwatching and ornithology that had taken place during the 1920s and 1930s. Early on in his career, he had helped found the Oxford Ornithological Society, recruiting the young Max Nicholson to the cause. He spent the rest of his professional life at Oxford, becoming Reader in Ornithology in 1946 – the first at any British university. In 1943, on the death of Francis Jourdain, he had become editor of *British Birds*; he was also one of the editors of *The Handbook of British Birds*, where he pioneered the use of field characters in identification (see Chapter 9).

Every Sunday, Tucker would also make his way to Northampton Sewage Farm, travelling by train and bicycle. Despite the age gap (Tucker was in his early forties), the two birdwatchers became firm friends: 'Although I was only fourteen', Ferguson-Lees recalls,

> . . . and he to me an icon as editor of *British Birds*, he took me
> under his wing and encouraged me to send my observations to
> him. He taught me a lot about field-identification, and in 1946 he
> and his wife took me for a memorable trip to Speyside, which gave
> me my first experience of the birds of the Scottish Highlands.

Through Tucker, Ferguson-Lees began to meet other leading birdwatchers, including James Fisher. Despite a seventeen-year age gap, they became firm friends, travelling to Wales to search for Red Kites, along with the writer and humorist Stephen Potter. In 1949, they went on an expedition to the remotest place in Britain – the islands of St Kilda – an extraordinary journey for those days.

By then, however, Bernard Tucker had fallen ill; and the following year, aged just forty-nine, his life was cut cruelly short by cancer. His legacy was to have seen through a quiet but extraordinarily effective revolution in the way people watched birds in Britain, not least because he helped to create a more exact, rigorous and methodical approach to identifying birds. In Ferguson-Lees's view: 'I still believe that he should be regarded as the father of modern field-identification techniques in Britain.'

In his willingness to devote time and attention to encouraging younger birdwatchers, Tucker also typified an attitude and practice that has since fallen by the wayside. It is hard to imagine the parents of one of today's fourteen year olds allowing their son to wander around a sewage farm in the company of an older man, however noble his intentions.

For at least a decade after World War II had come to an end, Britain still languished in the economic doldrums. Rationing – of meat and petrol, and even sweets – continued far beyond the war itself, finally coming to an end in 1954. Foreign holidays were virtually unknown, especially for the vast majority of working class or lower middle class families. Looking back, the era seems infinitely more distant than the colourful 'swinging Sixties' which were soon to follow.

However, there was one beacon of light in the darkness. Queen Elizabeth's Coronation, in June 1953, brought a huge surge in sales of television sets, and by the end of the decade two out of three British homes had a television. Even so, the 'goggle-box' was treated with disdain by many adults. But for the intelligent, inquiring child, television offered an escape into new and exciting worlds: almost unimaginably distant at times, yet through the magical power of the cathode-ray tube, tantalizingly within reach.

In adult life, Richard Porter was to work for the RSPB and BirdLife International. His most successful role was as the RSPB's investigations officer, pursuing egg-collectors with a ferocious and single-minded zeal that led one frustrated oologist to describe him as 'that horrid little man'. He also became one of the best-known figures in modern Middle Eastern ornithology, following in the footsteps of such illustrious forebears as Philby, Tristram and Hollom, thanks in part to his ability to sleep anywhere, at any time, and also to his swarthy complexion, which led one distinguished observer to remark that 'He speaks very good English for a Turk.' But it was the impact of one particular natural history film on television which launched this distinguished ornithological career.

Born in London in 1943, during the latter stages of the war, Porter was given a book of bird poems as a child by a next-door neighbour. This aroused his interest in birds, which grew when he became hooked on collecting the series of *I-Spy* books, filling in all the little boxes as he saw each species of bird.

Then, in 1953, the young Richard watched *The Great Adventure*, by a Swedish film-maker named Arne Sucksdorff. Already a well-established film director, Sucksdorff was an early influence on the young Ingmar Bergman, and in 1949 had won an Oscar. Seen today, *The Great Adventure* seems rather old-fashioned, though it has moments of charm, and undeniably excellent photography. The film tells the story of two young farm boys as they explore the Swedish countryside, and though it sometimes verges on the sentimental, it is redeemed by stunning landscapes and wildlife. No wonder it had such an effect on a young, impressionable lad, whose wildlife experiences had until then been confined to the London suburbs.

Birdwatching in Britain during the 1950s was about as far removed as you could get from the wide open landscapes, filled with the cries of geese, of *The Great Adventure*. At first, all Porter could do to recapture the magic of the film was to cycle or hitch a lift to Walthamstow Reservoirs, to scan through flocks of wintering ducks using a pair of World War II binoculars. Then, in August 1958, he attended a bird ringing course at Dungeness Bird Observatory, where he met Tony Marr.

At first sight, Tony Marr and Richard Porter are an odd pair. Marr is well over six feet, and beanpole thin; Porter is on the short side, and stocky. Then there are the differences in their lifestyles: Marr pursued a successful career as a civil servant, while serving unpaid on numerous ornithological committees; while Porter gave up the prospects of a steady job in the catering trade to travel in search of birds, then spent his working life directly involved in conservation.

Today, almost half a century after they first met, they are near neighbours, living in the north Norfolk village of Cley next the Sea. As best friends for nearly fifty years, and lifelong birding companions, they have from differing perspectives both witnessed – and indeed acted out in their own lives – the evolution of birdwatching throughout the second half of the twentieth century and beyond.

Their recollections differ on several things, including society's attitude towards birders back in the 1950s. Porter does not recall ever being made to feel odd or unusual, or people teasing him about his hobby. Marr, on the other hand, remembers that:

> It is difficult to appreciate just how basic and low-key was the birdwatching scene of fifty years ago. The pursuit itself was regarded as highly eccentric and open to ridicule. 'Oh, you watch birds, do you? The sort with two legs, I suppose. Ha, ha!' was the

usual gibe. Walking around with binoculars you were regarded as either a nutter or a peeping tom.

Marr finally discovered the existence of other birdwatchers when he joined the local bird club in Shoreham-on-Sea, in Sussex. He also recalls how being given a 'real' pair of binoculars transformed his birdwatching:

> In 1955, when I was 15, my parents bought me a pair of Barr and Stroud 10 x 50s costing £55 – I don't know how they afforded it. That was the greatest incentive to go out watching birds. I can still remember opening them when they arrived and smelling the leather case – it was a magic moment!

Like so many of the post-war generation, Porter's first pair of binoculars was handed down from his father's war service, though he too eventually got a decent pair:

> Mine were my father's air force binoculars, with the old webbing strap. I had those for years, and then my first proper pair was in 1959, when I bought a pair of Barr and Stroud, costing £46. I had to save up for them with my paper round money.

Another great influence on Marr and Porter's generation was the Junior Bird Recorders' Club – the forerunner of the YOC (Young Ornithologists' Club), and the junior branch of the RSPB. Founded in the middle of the war, in 1943, it started slowly at first, though after the name change to YOC in 1965 it grew apace, and by 1988 had almost 90,000 members. The JBRC held conferences in which its teenage members got to meet each other and make a name for themselves. Another way to do that was to get your initials beside a record of a rare bird in the county bird report – both Marr and Porter remember competing to get their name in print as many times as possible!

An acquaintance made one day in a local park enabled Porter to broaden his horizons considerably. He and some friends were looking at a Mallard's nest when the park keeper approached them to tell them off. But when he realized that they were not planning to take the eggs, he relented, and soon he and the eleven year old Porter were birdwatching colleagues.

His name was Fred Lambert, he was aged just nineteen, and best of all he owned a motorbike. Two years later he took Porter up to Cley in Norfolk, where the two of them slept together in a double bed: 'Imagine that – and my parents weren't even worried about it! It was a very innocent time!'

Lifts on motorcycles apart, lack of transport was a major problem. Few birdwatchers had access to a private car; so on weekend birding trips Marr and Porter developed a strategy to avoid the long bus journey home. As soon as they arrived at bird-watching hotspot Pagham Harbour, along the Sussex coast, they would immediately seek out an older, wealthier member of the Shoreham Ornithological Society, and latch on to him for the rest of the day. The relationship was symbiotic: the older man would gain the benefit of the youngsters' sharper eyes and expertise in identification; while as Marr remembers, they would enjoy a more tangible benefit: 'This meant you didn't stand at a freezing cold bus stop for twenty minutes, and then wait another hour for the train at Chichester, and get home late at night. You'd get whisked home in a warm comfortable car, and get dropped off at your own front door.'

Pagham was also a place where rare birds would regularly turn up. But this presented a further problem – one of communication. In the days when still very few people owned a private telephone, the postal system was the primary way to circulate news of a rarity. Tony Marr recalls getting a letter in October 1957, containing dramatic news: there was a Pectoral Sandpiper – a scarce American vagrant – at Pagham. Unfortunately this was a Monday, and at the time he was working in a nine-to-five job. He duly travelled there the following weekend, and to his amazement, actually saw the bird. But this was an exception, as he recalls: 'Modern birders will never believe this, but quite often the first inkling you had that there had been a rare bird in your area was when you read about it in the county bird report a year or so later!'

The *Sussex Bird Report*, and in particular its formidable editor D. D. Harber, were an important influence on the young Marr.

Harber seemed to enjoy rejecting any record which he – and he alone – considered dubious, causing a degree of friction with other birdwatchers. This was not helped by his lack of tact: he dismissed a paper on diver identification written by the young Richard Porter as 'largely nonsense', and wrote to an observer who claimed to have seen a Snowfinch at Newhaven (which would have been the first British record), that 'it was of course a Snow Bunting, you bloody fool!'

Others, including James Ferguson-Lees, recall that behind Harber's stern exterior was a remarkable man who, as one of the founding members of the British Birds Rarities Committee in 1958, did much to produce a more rigorous approach to records of rare birds. He had a flair for languages, and had learned enough Russian as a young man to read the six-volume *Handbook of Birds of the Soviet Union* and summarize its contents for the readers of *British Birds*. In his youth he had also been a member of the Communist Party of Great Britain, which he had joined while studying at the London School of Economics, although following a three-month visit to Russia in 1931 he became disillusioned with the system.

As Tony Marr remembers, Harber acquired a reputation as something of an autocrat, who would wield the editorial red pen with obvious relish: 'The relationship between Harber and contributors to "his" bird report was definitely that of headmaster and pupils: many of them recalcitrant and out of order, as he saw it, and needing education and enlightenment.'

Some younger, less respectful birders from Hampshire, collectively known as 'the Portsmouth group', decided to get their revenge. When Harber rejected their record of a Long-tailed Duck off Eastbourne, they sent him a brown paper parcel containing a pair of plastic binoculars from Woolworth's, with a note suggesting he would see more clearly if he used them. Unfortunately they gave away their identity by wrapping the offending item in a copy of the *Portsmouth Evening Post*!

As the 1950s came to a close, the new broadcasting media was having an ever-increasing influence on the post-war generation of birdwatchers in Britain. First there was radio, with programmes including *Nature Parliament* on the Home Service, which had a panel of experts answering listeners' questions about the natural world. Regular panellists included James Fisher and Peter Scott (son of the celebrated Scott of the Antarctic), who was rapidly establishing a reputation as one of the world's leading conservationists.

A good example of the tone and content of this enormously popular programme is Scott's answer to Fisher's question on what thrills him about birdwatching:

> Three things: first, watching the familiar and finding out
> something new about it; secondly the search for something special
> . . . and thirdly, and I suppose the most simple and obvious –
> seeing a rare bird. I'm very slightly ashamed of getting such a kick
> out of seeing rare birds – after all, what's much more interesting
> to science is what the majority of birds do. It is nevertheless very
> exciting and I defy any ornithologist to remain quite unmoved
> when he sees a rare bird.

Major developments were also occurring in television. In response to the growing interest in wildlife, the BBC Natural History Unit was founded in 1957. It soon began broadcasting some of the most popular and best-loved programmes on the box, featuring passionate amateurs such as schoolmaster Ernest Neal, who studied badgers, film-maker Eric Ashby, who brought the wildlife of the New Forest into millions of homes, and the retired Lord Alanbrooke who, inspired by his friendship with Eric Hosking, had begun to make his own films on birds. A young man named Tony Soper was also making a name for himself behind the scenes as a studio manager and cameraman. Later he would become one of the best known faces on wildlife television, and in 1983 presented the first series dedicated specifically to bird-watching, *Discovering Birds*, on BBC2.

The most popular natural history programme during this period was *Look*, presented live by Peter Scott, which was to run for fourteen years from 1955 to 1969, and regularly attracted five million viewers. One young fan, watching from the Liverpool suburbs, was the future Beatle Paul McCartney. Half a century later, interviewed for the *Beatles Anthology*, he recalled his childhood enthusiasm for the programme: 'Peter Scott had a TV show and he used to draw various birds every week. I wrote to him, "Can I have the drawings of them ducks if you're not doing anything with them?" I got a polite reply.'

One episode of *Look*, on an unlikely subject, captured the public imagination as never before. It seems incredible now that a short, black-and-white film about Europe's woodpeckers, shot on location in Germany by film-maker Heinz Sielmann, should have been such a sensation. Yet following the first transmission of the programme the BBC switchboard was inundated with requests to see it again, and it was repeated several times due to popular demand. Indeed, the film's audience 'appreciation index' was as high as the figure for that year's F.A. Cup final. In 1959, the book on the making of the film, *My Year with the Woodpeckers*, was published to considerable sales and critical success.

'Some people say that the popularity of natural history books, television and sound radio programmes derives from the wish of many of our industrialised population to escape; some even call this an escape from reality', wrote James Fisher in the foreword to Sielmann's book. 'If it is an escape then it is an escape *to* reality, and one of the best signs that the human race is capable of conquering grave problems and making our overcrowded world fit to live in.'

BBC RADIO was also becoming a medium for talks on various aspects of ornithology. In October 1958 Dr David Lack, author of *The Life of the Robin*, opened his talk on the study of migration with an evocative account of the perils facing migrating birds:

> As I speak at this moment, on an October evening, there are probably thousands of larks, starlings and thrushes crossing the

North Sea from the Continent into England . . . The migration of birds is a challenge to the imagination, especially when it involves small land birds crossing several hundred miles of sea . . . Now, suddenly, speculation can be replaced by direct observation, for migrating birds can be detected and tracked for a long time by high-powered radar.

The practice of using radar to observe the movements of migrating birds was less than a decade old. During the war, Lack himself had taken a break from the study of ornithology at Oxford to help run a chain of coast-watching radar stations, intended to give early warning of a German invasion. From about 1940, radar operators often reported 'echoes' in areas of the sea where there were no ships or aircraft to be found. Eventually one biologist suggested that they came from seabirds; and after much opposition, this theory was accepted.

There matters rested until the early 1950s, when a new, much higher-powered type of radar was developed. Now, as the operators watched the display screen, they sometimes saw a series of tiny echoes which they christened 'angels'. At first, these were thought to be some kind of weather factor, but closer analysis revealed obvious peaks in spring and autumn, unrelated to meteorological events. It was finally realized that the 'angels' were flocks of migrating birds.

It might be thought that the use of radar to study bird migration would be the death-knell of observers watching migrating birds with their binoculars and notebook. Yet the opposite was the case: discoveries by the radar watchers encouraged many bird-watchers to take up migration studies with renewed vigour. This was a subject which, as James Fisher noted in *The Shell Bird Book*, had long fascinated birdwatchers: 'All this seems a far cry from Gilbert White's simple log of Arrivals and Departures . . . but it is an evolutionary extension.'

This obsession with migration becomes easier to understand when you consider the unique geographical advantages of Britain and Ireland: on the edge of the vast Eurasian landmass, at a critical crossroads for migrants, and in an excellent position to

Gilbert White, 'the man who started us all birdwatching'. The Hampshire vicar wrote the best-selling *Natural History of Selborne*, the first book to treat nature as something to be observed, investigated and enjoyed. (Chapter 1)
Mary Evans Picture Library

Thomas Bewick, engraver and publisher, in his workshop. Bewick produced another great popular work, *A History of British Birds*, illustrated using a revolutionary new technique. (Chapter 1)
Mary Evans Picture Library

Despite spending much of his early life confined to a single locality, the nineteenth-century poet John Clare managed to observe well over 100 different species of bird in his Northamptonshire neighbourhood. (Chapter 1)
Mary Evans Picture Library

JOHN CLARE.

'What's hit is history, what's missed is mystery' – collecting birds became a major craze amongst the Victorians, for whom a display of stuffed birds in a glass case was an essential part of the furniture. This collection is kept at the British Museum of Natural History in Tring.(Chapter 4)
Natural History Museum, London

The Victorians also collected birds' eggs, justifying the practice as the pseudo-science of 'oology'. Ironically, their carefully assembled collections proved useful to later ornithologists. (Chapter 4)
Natural History Museum, London

'A dead bird does not help the appearance of an ugly woman, and a pretty woman needs no such adornment'. The nineteenth-century craze for using feathers in fashion (below) may have contributed to the extinction of birds such as the Passenger Pigeon (below left), here portrayed by the great American bird artist Audubon.
Mary Evans Picture Library

Edward Grey, who as our longest-serving Foreign Secretary still managed to pursue his interest in birds, and wrote a best-selling book on the subject. Here he feeds Mallards and Mandarin Ducks in his garden at Fallodon. (Chapters 7 & 8)
Seton Gordon

Binoculars now and then: the latest model from Austrian manufacturers Swarovski (left), and a pair of Barr and Stroud's dating back to the 1930s. The arrows denote naval use by the Ministry of Defence.
Courtesy of John Hullah, Cley-Spy

'Where now will you look for birds?' Elliott Coues (below) braved dangers in America's Wild West, while Apsley Cherry-Garrard (below right; standing right of picture) trekked across the Antarctic ice with Wilson and Bowers – both men driven by an obsession with birds. (Chapters 4 & 5)
Natural History Museum, London; and Scott Polar Institute

Two pioneers of modern 'field birdwatching': Harry Witherby (right) and Francis Jourdain (left), photographed in Corsica in 1937. Witherby was the driving force behind *British Birds* and *The Handbook*, to both of which Jourdain made a major contribution. (Chapters 7 & 9)
Eric Hosking Trust

Max Nicholson, whose life spanned the twentieth century, and who had a huge influence on the development of birdwatching as a mass-participation activity. (Chapter 9)
Eric Hosking Trust

Three other men who were instrumental in popularising bird-watching: Julian Huxley (below left) in the Jordanian desert; and Peter Scott (below right; on left of picture) with James Fisher in Iceland. (Chapter 11)
Eric Hosking Trust and courtesy of Philippa Scott

Field Marshal Lord Alanbrooke (with cine-camera) and bird photographer Eric Hosking on Guy Mountfort's pioneering expedition to the Coto Doñana in southern Spain during the late 1950s. (Chapter 11) *Eric Hosking Trust*

'Y'know, I guess these Oystercatchers eat most any mollusc . . .' The great American bird artist Roger Tory Peterson, sketching waders for the forthcoming *Field Guide to the Birds of Britain and Europe*, one of the best-selling bird books of all time. (Chapter 11) *Eric Hosking Trust*

Two ways of watching birds in the years after World War II: Desmond Nethersole-Thompson (below) hiking in the mountains of Scotland; Guy Mountfort (below right) using one of the first mist-nets to catch small birds for ringing. (Chapter 11) *Eric Hosking Trust*

Phoebe Snetsinger, world lister extraordinaire, who saw more than 8400 species of birds in her lifetime – despite at one stage having been given only a year to live. (Chapter 16)

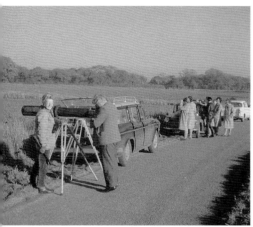

Early twitchers with a telescope of prodigious dimensions gather to look for a Houbara (now known as Macqueen's) Bustard, at Westleton, Suffolk, in December 1962. The man in the background is the Norfolk birder Richard Richardson. (Chapter 14)
Philip Stead

An epic overland birding trip to India in late 1978. Left to right: Nigel Redman, Frank Lambert, Chris Murphy, Dick Filby and Richard Grimmett. With luxury transport (below left) and watching Black Kites in the Golden Temple at Amritsar (below). (Chapter 13)
Courtesy of Nigel Redman

Some of the most influential bird books
of the mid-twentieth century, including field
guides, traveller's tales and even a novel –
Kenneth Allsop's *Adventure Lit Their Star*.
(Chapters 10 & 11)

Driven birding: Lee Evans, twitcher extraordinaire, checks the map before another lengthy odyssey, in his quest to see as many rare birds as possible. (Chapter 14)
Press Association

The changing face of the RSPB in two views of its flagship Minsmere reserve: a sparsely-populated car park in 1967 (above left), and the latest array of birding accessories on sale in the spacious visitor centre in 2004 (above). (Chapter 15)
Eric Hosking Trust and David Hosking

Birds get the celebrity treatment: TV presenter Bill Oddie endorses bird feeding products, an essential part of today's birding scene. (Chapter 15)
Courtesy of J. Haith Ltd.

attract rare vagrants. Having been confined to their home patches during the six long years of wartime, it was hardly surprising that people acquired the urge to explore far-flung localities in search of rare and exciting birds.

Migration watching was encouraged by the new bird observatories, most of which were on coastal headlands or far-flung islands, such as Spurn Head on the Yorkshire coast, the Isle of May in the Firth of Forth, or Lundy Island off the north coast of Devon. Their purpose was primarily to trap and ring birds in order to discover more about their migratory movements. Such romantic locations attracted a new generation of birdwatchers keen to seek out new challenges – happy to cope with the difficulties of getting there, and to put up with discomfort when they arrived. 'Migration study', observed Fisher, 'always will depend on the observatory and field-man, the island-lover, the cape-cliff haunter, the bunk-sleeper and the sandwich-eater.'

The rapid post-war spread of the bird observatory network owed much to one man: a Scot named George Waterston, who had been in Eichstätt prisoner-of-war camp along with John Buxton and Peter Conder (See Chapter 10).

At daybreak on a chilly October morning in 1943, Waterston had been on a Red Cross ship heading west from Norwegian waters towards the north of Scotland. The vessel was carrying sick and injured prisoners home to Britain after years of incarceration by the Germans. As dawn began to break, a lookout shouted the words everyone wanted to hear – 'Land ahead!' Every man who was able to walk, hobble or stand rushed up on deck to catch sight of their homeland.

But for George Waterston, there was something even more magical about the sight. For this was Fair Isle, that little speck of land lying between Orkney and Shetland, which since the turn of the century had been known as a magnet for migrating birds. Waterston had first visited the island in 1935, when he and his colleague were the only new faces the islanders saw all year. Now, as he looked out over the grey ocean, he made a vow to himself: that when the war was over, he would open a bird observatory on Fair Isle. And in 1948, he did.

Although it was not the very first bird observatory in Britain (the one on Skokholm, off Pembrokeshire, had been founded in 1933), the establishment of Fair Isle set the trend. In the following decade ten new observatories were set up, including such famed locations as Dungeness, Bardsey and Portland, as well as the now defunct observatories at Cley in Norfolk and Great Saltee off the Irish coast. All fulfilled a vital function for a generation of birders eager to get out in the field: by providing rudimentary accommodation at a low cost (typically a few shillings a night) they allowed birdwatchers to spend a week's holiday in a bird migration hotspot, amongst like-minded enthusiasts, and with the services of an expert warden and bird trapping equipment.

In the 1950s, before telephone information lines and pagers, and when travelling long distances to 'twitch' a single rarity was difficult if not impossible, staying at an observatory was the only way to have a real chance of seeing rare birds. Indeed, in some ways this became a self-fulfilling quest: the concentration of observers inevitably led to the discovery of rare vagrants that might otherwise have gone unnoticed. These included Britain's first American Robin on Lundy in October 1952, the first Siberian Thrush on the Isle of May in October 1954, and the first Thick-billed Warbler, also from Siberia, trapped on Fair Isle in October 1955. Indeed the importance of bird observatories at this time is shown by the fact that of the thirty new species added to the 'British list' between 1946 and 1960, more than half were found at or near bird observatories.

Writing in 1976, in *Bird Observatories in Britain and Ireland*, British Trust for Ornithology stalwart Robert Spencer noted the gulf between the public perception and the real thing: 'To the uninitiated, the term 'bird observatory' evokes a picture of a building with a massive telescope, through which one looks at birds. The reality is at one and the same time less splendid, and infinitely more exciting.'

To illustrate his point, he quoted an evocative passage from the Fair Isle log-book, dated 27 October – presumably sometime during the 1950s:

That blend of ritual and perpetual optimism which motivates observatory enthusiasts would not have allowed us to lie in, anyway, but this morning we were astir earlier than usual for the wind last night came steadily from the SE, and the stars were sharp. Someone put the kettle on the Calor gas for a quick cuppa, but we dressed silently, not wakeful enough to talk . . . Padded out in anoraks and duffel coats, binoculars obligatory for all . . . we stepped out into the uninviting dawn.

The writer's anticipation turned out to be well-judged, and the day was a classic one:

It was 3 o'clock before anyone could take time off for lunch, and indeed the traps were manned continuously until dusk . . . Now it is 9.30 p.m. The table is spread with log books, ringing schedules and field notebooks as the day's history is recorded in more permanent form. The driftwood fire crackles and flares intermittently, and a thin skin forms on the neglected mugs of cocoa. It's been a good day, and with the wind still in the SE, who knows what tomorrow will bring?

The sense of hard work, camaraderie and sheer excitement can rarely have been captured so well, leading me to suspect that the author was the leading migration enthusiast of his day, Kenneth Williamson. Before his death in 1977, at the age of sixty-three, Williamson had done more than anyone to popularize migration studies. He was the first warden of Fair Isle, developed early theories on 'drift migration' (later overshadowed by Lack's work with radar) and wrote several evocative books on Scottish islands. Like many of his contemporaries, he did so without having had any formal scientific training.

During the 1950s, Williamson's knowledge and enthusiasm made him a regular guest on BBC radio programmes, including a memorable outside broadcast in autumn 1959 during which he made live telephone calls to bird observatories up and down the country, getting up-to-the-minute reports on bird movements.

Many of today's leading birders look back on this period with great affection. Veteran birdwatcher Ian Wallace sometimes re-reads his diaries, recalling great days at places like Fair Isle, with the 'adrenaline rush' of witnessing migration spectacles at first hand. Richard Porter has equally fond memories of an encounter which fired his interest in rare birds, on 29 August 1959, at the observatory at Dungeness in Kent.

That day, the fifteen-year-old Porter encountered for the first time an older birder named Howard Medhurst, then editor of the *London Bird Report*:

> He arrived from London on his motorbike in the early morning, quickly lit up a Bristol cigarette and joined us on the morning round of the traps. As we approached the entrance to one of the traps a smallish bird flew up from the bushes giving us all a momentary glimpse. I hadn't a clue what it was and wouldn't even have given it a second thought if a whisper hadn't come down the line, *Howard Medhurst thinks it's a Barred Warbler!* We rapidly retraced our steps, drove the bushes again, and into the trapping box went our bird – and indeed it was a Barred Warbler. A juvenile identified on a glimpse in flight – and with no previous experience. A first for him and, I was told later, his 250th species for Britain.

It was a defining moment, with life-changing consequences – Porter decided there and then that he wanted to emulate Medhurst, in his approach not just to birding, but to life itself:

> My note taking became more detailed and I tried to look at everything I saw more carefully. Not surprising then that when I got home to North London I started begging my parents for a motorbike and that when I started smoking, my first cigarettes had to be Bristol!

Another regular visitor to Dungeness in the 1950s was Roger Norman, who had to rely on a bicycle for transport, often cycling more than forty miles in order to visit several sites in the area. He recalls one journey with particular horror:

> I still remember one very windy day when we had struggled against the wind on the way out and by the time we returned in

the evening it had gone round almost 180 degrees so we struggled again. For some reason I was desperately tired and had to be constantly encouraged to keep going by my companion. At one point I momentarily fell both asleep and off my bike!

Despite the occasional gap between expectation and reality, the bird observatories were very popular places to visit. Writing at the height of the boom, in 1963, Richard Fitter predicted a bright future: 'In a few years' time there will probably be as dense a network [of observatories] inland as there is now on the coast.'

Even in 1976, by which time ten of the original twenty-four observatories had closed down, Robert Spencer was equally positive: 'Fulfilling, as they do, the needs of both recreation and education, the observatories seem assured of their future . . . a renewed sense of direction and optimism is in the air.'

Yet today, just over a quarter of a century later, and despite the efforts of pioneers at new observatories such as North Ronaldsay on Orkney, bird observatories are languishing. The network has now been reduced to a rump of just a dozen: six in England, three in Scotland, one in Wales and two in Ireland. Many of these are struggling to survive on tiny budgets, in a world where faster and easier travel means that a birder can drive several hundred miles and back in a day, and has no need to stay overnight at place like Dungeness or Portland. Another reason for the decline is a practical one: in the early days of the bird observatories, before mist-nets had been invented, ringers would bring their trainees in order to train them; nowadays, portable catching equipment means there is no longer a need to do so.

Meanwhile, cheaper foreign travel has reduced the thrill of watching migrants close to home, and the actual number of birds appears to have declined too, so that observatories rarely experience the massive 'falls' that so excited the pioneers back in the 1950s. Just half a century after the golden age of bird migration studies, the subject is languishing in the doldrums.

IN THE YEARS after World War II, ethology, or the study of animal behaviour also had its heyday. Ethology first emerged from the dull and dusty culture of museum-based studies, when pioneers such as Konrad Lorenz, Niko Tinbergen and Julian Huxley began to look at the actual behaviour of living birds, instead of studying anatomy and physiology using dead ones.

As well as a keen eye and impressive intellect, these men had the ability to convey the complexities and subtleties of their observations to ordinary readers. Books such as Lorenz's *King Solomon's Ring* (1952), and Tinbergen's *Curious Naturalists* (1958), put across the thrill of watching ordinary birds, and discovering new insights into their behaviour. *King Solomon's Ring* is a scientifically accurate yet highly readable account of animal behaviour, with a fascinating chapter on the social life of Jackdaws:

> Remarkable and exceedingly comical is the difference in eloquence between the eye-play of the wooing male and that of the courted female: the male jackdaw casts glowing glances straight into his loved one's eyes, while she apparently turns her eyes in all directions other than that of her ardent suitor. In reality, of course, she is watching him all the time, and her quick glances of a fraction of a second are quite long enough to make her realize that all his antics are calculated to inspire her admiration; long enough to let 'him' know that 'she' knows.

Lorenz went on to become a television star – David Attenborough recalls having to produce a live show during which one of the subjects, a Greylag Goose, became so irritated that it defecated all over the great scientist's lap! However, his later career was marred by controversy after it emerged that before the war he had been a Nazi sympathizer; though when he accepted the Nobel Prize in 1973 he publicly apologized for his flirtation with National Socialism.

Julian Huxley, one of the very first people to study living birds, agreed that Tinbergen and Lorenz had shed 'a flood of new light' on the subject of bird courtship. Describing Tinbergen as 'a natural naturalist', Huxley pointed out another huge advantage of the new discipline: that even the ordinary field birdwatcher could now make genuinely useful contributions to our knowledge and understanding of birds.

It might be thought that this scientific approach would have little effect on day to day birding. But such was the popularity of the new books on animal behaviour that youngsters did try to follow their elders' example. Growing up in Middlesex, a young birdwatcher named Bruce Coleman took his bike, binoculars and brass telescope to Perry Oaks Sewage Farm, on the outskirts of the new airport at Heathrow: 'The sewage farm gave me my first Ruffs, Little and Temminck's Stints, Green and Wood Sandpipers, Greenshanks and godwits. And in quiet summer months I aspired to be a Niko Tinbergen by watching the "forward threat postures and head flagging" of the Black-headed Gull colony.'

In 1956, Edward Armstrong, the Cambridge curate who had watched Wrens from his study window during the war, published an important paper in *British Birds*, entitled 'The Amateur and the Study of Bird Display: suggestions for further work'. He traced the development of the new science of ethology from the pioneering observations of men like Edgar Chance and Edmund Selous, 'the initiators of bird-watching in the modern style', via the publication of *The Handbook of British Birds* before World War II, to the post-war years, when ethology established itself as a serious, professional science.

He pointed out that the amateur birdwatcher's contributions were now even more important than before: 'The outstanding advantage enjoyed by the amateur . . . is that he is much commoner than the professional . . . It is hoped that the historian of ornithology 25 or 50 years hence will not have to record the virtual disappearance of the individualist observer.'

As BIRDWATCHING became more and more popular, it was inevitable that conflict would arise between the 'old guard' of scientific ornithologists, and the new wave of amateur birdwatchers.

In the very first issue of the BTO journal *Bird Study*,

published in March 1954, the Revd P. H. T. Hartley – a leading figure in the ornithological establishment – wrote an article with the unassuming title 'Back Garden Ornithology'. He encouraged readers to concentrate on the birds of their local area rather than following the trend of going travelling far afield in pursuit of rarities:

> The years since the war have been notable for the currency of the strong illusion that ornithology can be followed at its best only on distant islands or the most inaccessible of sea-marshes . . . The summer population of bird-watchers in famous bird-haunts is so dense that, in the words of a friend of the writer's, 'A bird can't yawn but nine people write it down . . . '

Perhaps expecting a reaction, Hartley tried to pre-empt his critics:

> There may be those who say 'But I don't want to go in for scientific ornithology', not realising that this is another way of saying 'But I'm quite content with the second-rate in my bird-watching' . . . Non-scientific bird-watching is not splendid and adventurous bird-watching: it is simply lazy, incompetent and slovenly bird-watching.

Readers did not have to wait long for the backlash against Hartley's views. In the following edition of *Bird Study*, in June 1954, Denis Summers-Smith passionately defended birdwatching purely for pleasure:

> The scientist must realise that there are other objects in watching birds as laudable as the collection of facts and the expansion of the frontiers of knowledge: their aesthetic appeal; the satisfaction of the collector's instinct in adding new species to a tally; relaxation to the tired mind. This is no more 'slovenly bird-watching' than going to a concert without a score is slovenly listening. While it is not denied that deeper satisfaction may be obtained from deeper study, many are not suited to carry out scientific studies or read scores. Should we criticise them for the pleasure they get from birds or music?

In fact despite these views, Summers-Smith was one of the twentieth century's greatest 'amateur' ornithologists. Working full-time as an industrial chemist, and with post-war travel restrictions limiting his scope, he had selected the House Sparrow as the most suitable subject for practical study. This proved to be an inspired choice, and led him to become the world expert not just on the familiar *Passer domesticus*, but on two dozen other species of sparrow found around the world. The only drawback was that sparrows tend to live in close association with people, which presented unexpected problems, as he recalled in his New Naturalist monograph *The House Sparrow*:

> The peculiar difficulty of the house sparrow is its predilection for occupied buildings, the occupiers of which at times resent being looked at through binoculars . . . The problem was largely overcome by carrying out most of my observations on houses in the early hours of the morning before my neighbours had risen, though on occasions when they did get up early their suspicions were even greater and led once to a visit from the police. Another time . . . I was questioned by the police when I was carrying out a census in a village where I was not too well known. Both times, I must say, they were most courteous and sympathetic once I had overcome their initial disbelief.

But the debate about whether birdwatching should have any kind of ulterior purpose would not go away. Heated views were exchanged in a series of letters under the heading 'Science and Bird-watching' published during 1958 in *British Birds*. Now it was the amateurs who led the way, with G. L. Scott and D. K. Ballance criticizing the journal for including 'articles which are incomprehensible or of little interest to the ordinary bird-watcher': 'Birdwatching is a hobby as much as golf or tennis; the week-end golfer does not expect, on opening his sporting journal, to find a paper on . . . the behaviour of golf-balls in thermal air-currents.'

Elsewhere, others were taking an even more relaxed attitude to birdwatching. In 1951, in the wake of the popular works on *Lifemanship* by humorist Stephen Potter, Bruce Campbell wrote a spoof on the subject of 'Birdsmanship' for the RSPB's *Bird Notes* magazine. He laid down the rules of playing a complex game of one-upmanship with one's fellow birders, which required being as badly dressed as possible, and carrying the most battered pair of binoculars. He also gave advice on how to annoy both the tally-hunter and the serious ornithologist:

> Find out your potential rival's line, and play the opposite for all you're worth.
> Thus, if he is an acknowledged tally-hunter, you must use the scientific gambit, 'After all, it's only the common birds that really count, isn't it?' and continually hold up the party by calling their attention to Robins or House Sparrows . . . If after five minutes observation the Robin gives a perfunctory peck at its plumage, you murmur 'Ah, an intention movement!' make profuse notes, and add, to the air in general, 'I must write to Tinbergen about this.' A slight hesitation before the Tinbergen should make it clear that among your real associates you would say 'Niko'.
> On the other hand, if your rival is a serious ornithologist . . . you cry 'I'm frankly pot-hunting today; leave the sparrows alone for once, old chap and come and see some real birds! Tally-ho!' . . . You should manage to convince the party that your rival is an introverted spoil-sport living in an ivory tower.

It is interesting that the same period should produce two such opposing schools of thought about birdwatching: Campbell's inability to take it too seriously; and Hartley's view that it should be strenuous, edifying and self-denying – good for you even if it hurts. Perhaps this oversimplifies their personalities: Hartley reputedly enjoyed birdwatching as much as anyone, while Bruce Campbell took his fieldwork very seriously indeed. Nevertheless, the argument reflected the underlying tensions between the austere, self-sacrificing spirit of the post-war age, and the lighter, more carefree approach to life which would emerge during the following decade.

NOTWITHSTANDING the widening interest in watching birds for their own sake, there was still an interest in 'bird nesting' – searching for nests without taking the eggs. This was reflected in the sales of another book in the *Observer's* series, on *Birds' Eggs*, which appeared in 1954, and eventually sold more than 1.5 million copies – even more than the companion volume to *Wild Flowers*. The publishers clearly had their conscience pricked by the possibility that they were encouraging an illegal activity, and the 1969 edition included this warning: 'This book has been compiled in the hope that . . . the observer will be content to study eggs and nests in their natural surroundings – and to leave them there.'

As early as 1953 it was becoming clear that an interest in nest finding was on the wane, as James Ferguson-Lees noted in his *British Birds* review of Bruce Campbell's *Finding Nests*:

> In an age when so many ornithologists are for ever watching the
> coastal marshes and the sewage farms, and when those that do
> look seriously for nests are for the most part either undertaking
> the special study of a single species or belong to the happily
> decreased ranks of egg-collectors, how stimulating it is to find a
> book written by one who would obviously derive great pleasure
> from finding any nest even if there was little to be gained apart
> from the satisfaction of having found it.

In answer to the question 'Why find nests?' Bruce Campbell pointed out that, sixty years earlier, the only aim had been to take the eggs for one's collection. He gave four other reasons for doing so: photography, bird-ringing, the making of a 'case-history', or observing the behaviour of the young; all of which fitted in with the new approach to watching birds. Another incentive was to fill in cards for the BTO's Nest Record Scheme, which had begun by Julian Huxley and James Fisher as the Hatching and Fledging Enquiry in 1939. This grew rapidly in popularity in the 1950s, and led Bruce Campbell and James Ferguson-Lees to produce their pocket-sized *Field Guide to Birds' Nests* in 1972. By the end of the twentieth century the scheme could boast over one million records, and had become a vital historical database enabling scientists to measure, among other things, the effects of global warming.

But despite Campbell's efforts, fewer and fewer people set out to go looking for birds' nests, because of the practice's unfortunate associations with the pariah activity of egg collecting. This had become even less acceptable once the Protection of Birds Act was finally passed by Parliament on 1 December 1954. The new Act gave complete legal protection to all wild birds and their nests and eggs; with a few minor exceptions such as agricultural pests, and gamebirds during the shooting season. Breaking the law was punishable with fines of up to £5, and there were also special offences with a penalty of £25 and up to three months imprisonment.

Ultimately, the Protection of Birds Act was a major step in protecting Britain's birds. But it did have one loophole: for a while it continued to allow schoolboy birdwatchers to collect eggs, which did have the unintended by-product of teaching them important fieldcraft skills. In an article in *BBC Wildlife* magazine in 1998, Bill Oddie suggested that 'the hobby that dare not speak its name' was the driving force behind his lifetime's obsession with birds: 'The honest truth is if I hadn't been an egg collector, I very much doubt if I would have become a birdwatcher. What's more – and this is even more contentious – it was my egg-collecting experiences that taught me all sorts of skills and techniques. I actually learnt an awful lot. Of course, this isn't a justification, but it is a fact.'

But egg collecting also had its drawbacks, as Oddie discovered when, at the age of ten, he attempted to add three Pheasant's eggs to his growing collection. Unbeknownst to him, the eggs were addled, making them impossible to 'blow' to remove the contents. 'It was quite a challenge', he recalled in his autobiography *Gone Birding*: 'The foul and rancid contents had begun to thicken and I had to half suck as well as blow in order to empty the shell. But eventually I did it. I placed the third egg with the other two, carefully washed out the sink – and then threw up in it.'

As aversion therapy, his unpleasant experience was completely successful, launching him on a distinguished career as a birdwatcher, writer and television presenter: 'The taste has stayed with me forever . . . But good came of evil. I never took another egg again! I even destroyed the "evidence" and threw away my collection.'

However, serious egg thieves were still a major problem. In 1954, Ospreys had finally returned to nest in Scotland after an absence of almost half a century. The nest site, at Loch Garten, was watched round-the-clock by volunteers from the RSPB, but despite this, in June 1958, an egg-collector staged a daring night raid and took the eggs.

In response, the RSPB took a far-sighted decision, which would have major consequences for the development of bird-watching as a mass activity in Britain: they decided to make public their failure to protect the birds. As a result, they managed to turn the area around the nest site into a bird sanctuary. Then they took an even braver step: inviting members of the public to come and see the nesting Ospreys.

This was an immediate success: during spring and summer 1959 more than 14,000 visitors came, creating so much traffic that the RSPB put up road signs, which are still there today. According to social historian David Allen, this soon gave rise to comments that bird protection was now 'a matter of protecting the birds from their admirers'. Indeed, going to see the Ospreys became an excursion in itself: not all that different from visiting an historical monument or a day out at the seaside.

Thousands of visitors required dozens of volunteers to make sure the birds came to no harm. Writing in the RSPB's *Birds* magazine in 2002, Mike Everett (who recently retired from the Society's press office after almost forty years service) recalled being asked to run the Osprey Voluntary Warden Scheme back in the early 1960s:

> There were no purpose-built accommodation and hot showers like today. Almost everyone lived under canvas, things were fairly primitive and there was an almost military organisation and atmosphere about the place.
>
> We always had such a wonderful cross-section of people helping out, from retired service people to Marxist students, so you can imagine that in our off-duty hours the level of political debate was fantastic.

Everett also remembered the key decision to publicize the Osprey nest in the first place, especially considering that nest-robbers had taken the eggs in 1958: 'Now we think nothing of it, but in those days allowing the public to get on intimate terms with one of the country's rarest breeding birds had never happened before. It was completely revolutionary and proved a massive success.'

It certainly was: in 2002 the number of visitors finally passed the total of 2 million, while the Ospreys have successfully recolonized Scotland and recently begun breeding in England. The growth of the RSPB's membership from just 20,000 in the early 1960s to well over 1 million today, believes Everett, is in a large part due to the Ospreys: 'There is no single dynasty of birds that for 40 years has generated such affection, such emotion, such interest amongst people . . . So while the Ospreys owe us a lot, we owe them just as much. In every sense, it has been a true partnership.'

THE NEW LEGIONS of birdwatchers would not have been able to see – let alone identify – the birds they were looking at without the considerable advancements in the quality and availability of optical aids such as binoculars and telescopes.

Binoculars had been improving since World War II, owing to technical advances made by the Allied and Axis powers in the quest to observe and identify military vessels and aircraft. German manufacturers Zeiss had led the way, developing a process of coating the lenses with fluoride which dramatically reduced unwanted reflections and improved the light-gathering powers of the instrument. The company remained the market leader throughout the 1950s, despite competition from established British firms such as Ross, and later from Japanese manufacturers including Nikon and Pentax.

Many older birdwatchers still recall being handed down a weighty pair of ex-Army or ex-Navy binoculars by their father or uncle, to encourage them in their new hobby. Others were given a brand-new pair for their birthday or Christmas, such as the Barr and Stroud 8 x 32 model which the thirteen-year-old Bill Oddie received in 1954:

> I'm not sure if I had any binoculars at all before that and if I had they must have been ex-opera glasses or plastic toys from a Cornflakes packet . . . That Christmas Day I feverishly worked my way down a pillowcase full of boys' annuals, games and jigsaws, hurling them aside ungratefully in my anxiety to discover my 'big present' . . . Dad suddenly gave in and guided me to a brown-paper parcel hidden behind the settee. Inside it was a pair of 'real' binoculars. I was so grateful I put them on, jumped on my bike and went out for the rest of the day, leaving him to enjoy his Christmas dinner in peace.

One schoolboy birdwatcher, Ian Collins, recalls cycling to Staines Reservoirs to watch birds with a friend who had a telescope obtained from the *Eagle* comic, while Collins himself had to make do with World War I 'field-glasses'. Another, Roger Norman, remembers his first visit to Sandwich Bay, during his last year of school in 1950. He paints a vivid picture of the reality of the typical schoolboy birding experience of the time:

> I walked four miles to the nearest railway station and caught a train to Sandwich. From there I walked out past Stonar and Pegwell Bay. Apart from green-keepers on the nearby golf course I saw no-one all day. I had borrowed a school friend's father's opera glasses – magnification 2½ times. I was 'over the moon' as they say. I imagine that a youngster today would chuck the opera glasses in the nearest lake in disgust.

The same year he finally acquired a second-hand pair of 6 x 24 binoculars, with a chipped eyecup, which lasted him until 1956, all the way through his national service in the Middle East.

Perhaps the most unorthodox way of obtaining a decent pair of optics falls to Chris Mead, who later became hugely influential in his role at the BTO. 'My first binoculars were given to me by my father who was a grocer in Brighton', he told BBC Radio's *The Archive Hour* in the late 1990s, 'because somebody had been to the races and lost all their money, and they desperately needed some food, and so they swapped their binoculars for food at the grocers!'

Mead also remembered just how isolated new birdwatchers felt at the time: 'It was about six months or so before I met any other birdwatcher – in fact I thought I was almost unique . . . it wasn't until I went up to Cambridge that I found other bird-watchers and I spent so much time birdwatching I failed my maths degree!'

Mathematics' loss was ornithology's gain. Until his death in January 2003, at the age of sixty-two, Mead devoted his life to practical ornithology. Based at the BTO, first in Hertfordshire and later in Norfolk, Chris Mead threw himself with customary enthusiasm into bird ringing – over forty or so years he caught and ringed more than 400,000 individual birds of 350 species in Britain and on expeditions abroad. He was also the driving force behind the BTO's *Migration Atlas*, which appeared just before his death, and appeared frequently on radio and television to popularize birding. His finest epitaph is the last of his many books, *The State of the Nation's Birds*, a thoughtful analysis of the changes in Britain's birdlife during the course of the twentieth century.

Although good quality binoculars were in widespread use when Chris Mead began birdwatching, telescope design was still in its infancy, as Max Nicholson noted in a guide written for bird-watchers:

> Telescope-makers appeared to cling to the belief that what was good enough for Nelson was quite good enough for them . . . It is evident to anyone who glances at a party of ornithologists trying to use telescopes . . . that sooner or later either the telescope or the bird-watcher will have to be entirely redesigned. The former would be more convenient.

Until the first 'tripod-and-scope' combination appeared in the early 1970s, British birdwatchers had to rely on old-fashioned draw-tube telescopes, usually made of brass. Although pretty good optically, these had to be propped up against a convenient tree, wall or rock to enable the observer to hold the instrument steady. In the absence of these, you were forced to lie down, cross your legs and balance the telescope on your knee! One great ornithologist of the pre-war generation, Seton Gordon, used a small, three-draw, deer-stalking telescope for most of his life. 'In the 1970s, well into his senior years', remembers James Ferguson-Lees 'he could still hold this telescope as steady as a rock, without the tip moving at all. Marvellous sight!'

THE 1950s saw a boom in book publishing: new reproduction techniques made possible for the first time accurate colour illustrations in bird books and field guides. Whether a new enthusiasm for wildlife led the boom in book sales, or the other way round, is not easy to ascertain. But people were buying natural history books, especially those which encouraged field study, in far greater numbers than before.

The revolution in post-war natural history book publishing was led by William Collins & Co, and driven by the indefatigable energy of James Fisher. Back in June 1942, just as Rommel was celebrating his victory over the Eighth Army at Tobruk, four men had met for lunch at a French restaurant in London's Soho. They were Fisher, Julian Huxley, an expert in colour printing named Wolfgang Foges (who had fled to Britain to escape Hitler's regime), and the head of the firm, Billy Collins. At a time when, in Collins's words, 'this country's fortunes were at their most perilous hazard', the four men discussed a new publishing venture – 'something to take people's minds off this carnage'.

In 1945, in the wake of the Allied victory, the very first 'New Naturalist' volume appeared. Simply entitled *Butterflies*, it was written by a mildly eccentric Oxford zoology professor named E. B. Ford. It was not a field guide as such, but a masterful summary of almost everything that was known on butterfly biology. Titles on an eclectic range of other natural history subjects – from *British Game* to *London's Natural History*, and *Wild Flowers* to *A Country Parish* – followed thick and fast during the next few years, and by the mid 1950s there were more than thirty books in the series.

The New Naturalists were an instant success, rapidly acquiring a reputation for combining fine writing with scientific accuracy, and selling tens of thousands of copies each. They provided a gateway to a new world of nature study in the field, rather than in the laboratory or classroom, and stimulated people to go and take a fresh look at the natural world. Packed with colour illustrations and photographs, and with eye-catching dust-jackets, the series stood out on the bookshelves. For two decades, until the advent of colour television in the mid 1960s, they were the only way the average wildlife enthusiast could experience the natural world in all its glory from the comfort of their armchair.

Max Nicholson, whose own New Naturalist entitled *Birds and Men* was published in 1951, had no doubt the series would be a runaway success: 'People had been taken away from their homes and interests by the war, and returned to an absolute famine of books. The New Naturalists were very well written, on well-chosen subjects. They stood out from the crowd – and I think they still do.'

The series' most prolific author, with four books to his credit, is Eric Simms. Like most New Naturalist writers he describes himself as a 'gifted amateur', though this does not do justice to his career popularizing natural history via hundreds of BBC radio and television programmes, and his many books and articles. As a former pilot in Bomber Command, Simms also recalls the impact of the first volumes on a generation of men and women jaded by their wartime experiences: 'At the end of the war, people like myself wanted a complete change – tranquillity, comfort, a place to escape. These books were well-written, never patronising to the reader, and could be read again and again. They were just what we needed.'

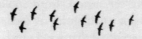

THE NEW NATURALISTS were attractive and fascinating, but they were not intended to help people identify birds and other wildlife in the field. For this, a new kind of book was required. Yet the first post-war field guide did not appear until 1952. *The Pocket Guide to British Birds* was the eventual result of the meeting of Richard Fitter and Richard Richardson at Tring Reservoirs on the eve of World War II (See Chapter 9).

Richardson was an entirely self-taught artist with a remarkable talent, who did most of the illustrations using a standard paint box in his landlady's kitchen at Cley. 'He seldom took a notebook or pencil with him in the field', explains Richard Fitter, 'but when an unusual bird appeared he would study it closely with those penetrating blue eyes that missed nothing. Within an hour or so of returning home he would have produced a painting that omitted no detail of plumage or attitude, and was also an excellent picture.'

Fitter also remembers Richardson's ability to draw and paint anywhere: 'He didn't even use a table – all he needed was a stool, and he would do it on his knee! He had an incredible talent to produce lifelike drawings at will.'

Richardson was praised by no less an authority than Peter Scott, who announced in the guide's Foreword that 'clearly a new bird painter of great skill has entered the field'. However, the excellence of his artwork was let down by poor printing, which made the plates appear washed out and insipid. Another problem was the book's layout. Unlike the Peterson guides, which were presented in 'systematic' order (i.e. placing related birds and families next to each other), Fitter took the revolutionary step of grouping birds by two artificial criteria: habitat and size. Although this appealed to novices, it was not well received by more experienced observers, who regarded it as potentially misleading. In a *British Birds* review, James Ferguson-Lees was scathing in his criticism:

> This is a disappointing book. It is original and ambitious . . . but on examination it fails to fulfil this early promise – attempts at great simplification have resulted only in complication . . . These criticisms must not lead the reader to regard this book as anything but a prodigious piece of work that is the best thing of its kind in Britain so far – but how much better it could have been.

Poor reviews did not hinder sales, however: *The Pocket Guide* sold more than 100,000 copies, and was still in bookshops well into the 1990s, more than forty years after its first publication.

The book that would change the face of birdwatching in Britain appeared two years later, in 1954. Like the Fitter and Richardson book, *A Field Guide to the Birds of Britain and Europe* was the result of another chance encounter, this time on Hawk Mountain in Pennsylvania. There, in 1949, artist and author Roger Tory Peterson met British ornithologist Guy Mountfort, and they agreed to collaborate on a European version of Peterson's celebrated *Field Guide to the Birds*.

Born in 1905, Mountfort had been interested in birds since childhood, but his passion really took off when, as a young man in the 1920s, he went to Paris to work as a salesman for the General Motors Corporation. There, he watched Crested Tits and Hawfinches in his garden, learned to ring birds, and even travelled to the fabled Camargue in an old Chrysler roadster. Back in Britain at the start of World War II, he enlisted in the Royal Horse Artillery and within just three years rose to the rank of Lieutenant-Colonel. He served in Europe, Africa, the Pacific and Asia, where he ate Great Hornbill – 'It didn't taste too bad!' His wide ornithological experience made him the obvious candidate to write the text of the new field guide.

The third member of the team was P. A. D. Hollom: one of the great unsung heroes of British ornithology. A deeply modest man, Phil Hollom helped pioneer the survey work initiated by Max Nicholson in the 1930s. After serving as a pilot with the RAF during the war, he took on the task of condensing the five volumes of *A Handbook of British Birds* into a single book. Published in 1952, *The Popular Handbook of British Birds* was concise, readable and affordable to a new generation of avid birdwatchers, for whom the larger work's price of five shillings per volume put it out of reach. *The Popular Handbook* soon became the definitive reference work, and a new edition – the fifth – was published more than a third of a century later in 1988. Hollom's deep knowledge and understanding made him the ideal third member of the team.

The guide took five years to come to fruition – during which time the authors and artist travelled all over Europe in order to get field experience of more than 500 species. On one trip, in October 1952, Roger Peterson visited Hilbre Island in Cheshire, in the company of Eric Hosking and the now ennobled Lord Alanbrooke.

Peterson's one-track mind was revealed one evening, after a long day in the field studying Oystercatchers. Gradually the conversation turned, as it often did in those days, to the war. Hosking recalled Alanbrooke vividly describing one of the tensest scenes he had ever witnessed, during negotiations in the Kremlin:

> We were enthralled. Alanbrooke vividly described the night before the British delegation was to fly home. He, Churchill and Stalin, with an interpreter, were sitting round a table sipping vodka when, suddenly, Stalin shook his fist at Churchill, swore, and demanded to know when the British were going to start fighting.
>
> The effect on Churchill was explosive. He crashed his fist on the table and lit into Stalin with a burst of impassioned oratory. Stalin listened for a minute or two, then, with a broad grin on his face, stood up, stopped Churchill's interpreter, and through his own said: 'I do not know what you are saying, but by God I like your sentiment!'
>
> While the rest of us hung on his words I happened to glance over at Roger and there seemed to be a glazed look about his eyes ... When Alanbrooke's wonderful story was done, and there was a slight pause, Roger spoke – 'Y'know, I guess these oystercatchers eat most any mollusc'.

Such single-mindedness clearly paid off: *A Field Guide to the Birds of Britain and Europe* was light years ahead of its rival. Peterson trademarks included pointers showing the bird's distinctive field marks, thumbnail distribution maps, and a concise, clear text; while features to appeal to his new, international audience included the birds' vernacular names in Dutch, French, German and Swedish. In 1997, forty-three years after it was first published, it was still selling strongly; and had passed the extraordinary mile-stone of one million sales, in thirteen different languages.

For the post-war generation of young British birdwatchers the new guide was a godsend. Ian Collins vividly recalls the day in 1954 when, with the princely sum of ten shillings and sixpence in his pocket (equivalent to about ten pounds today), he cycled to Kingston-upon-Thames to pick up his copy of the new guide. Until then, Collins had used an obscure little book called *Name That Bird*, by Eric Fitch Dalglish. This used an old-fashioned 'key' system of identification, in which the reader had to answer a series of questions in order to diagnose the identity of the bird. For Ian Collins, as for so many of his generation, *Name That Bird* was sadly inadequate. No wonder that he immediately took his precious new Peterson guide to school, where his envious class-mates eagerly gathered round to study it.

THE NEW FIELD guide had finally opened British bird-watchers' eyes to the possibility of venturing beyond these shores to watch exotic birds. Meanwhile, as Europe emerged from the social and economic turmoil of World War II, it was becom-ing easier to travel abroad. The post-war Labour government had established two national airlines (BEA and BOAC) in 1945, and in 1952 the first jet-powered airliner, the De Havilland Comet, had entered commercial service, reducing journey times dramatically, and making inter-continental travel a viable option for the first time.

British birdwatchers had travelled abroad to watch birds before, but mainly while serving the British Empire or during times of war. Now, people began to venture regularly across the Channel to watch birds in places such as France, the Low Countries and Austria. In 1961, one such expedition was recounted in the RSPB magazine *Bird Notes*. The author, Philip Brown, was at the time Secretary of the RSPB. He described the ups and downs of a nine-day trip in the summer of 1960, by car and air-ferry from Lydd Airport in Kent via Calais to the Netherlands.

During their visit the three companions tallied a total of 139 species, including many not found at all back home, such as Short-toed Treecreeper, Crested Lark and Middle Spotted Woodpecker.

They also enjoyed the delights of their new surroundings, including Amstel beer, crisp (not greasy) chips, and beef steaks that actually tasted of beef – a far cry from the horrors of post-war English cuisine. On the down side, the car (presumably a British model) broke down on numerous occasions, requiring frequent and regular pushing to get it going again.

Others did the European birding experience in rather more style. The ultimate European birding destination was the Coto Doñana in southern Spain, a huge tract of marshland south and west of Seville which was simply a paradise for birds. The businessman and field guide author Guy Mountfort had been entranced by the prospect of visiting Doñana since the early 1930s, when he had read Abel Chapman's *Wild Spain*, an account of a hunting trip to the region first published in the late nineteenth century.

Mountfort finally achieved his ambition in 1952, accompanied by Roger Peterson. It was while taking a short break from bird-watching, to visit the famous cathedral and mosque at Cordoba, that he too witnessed Peterson's single-minded absorption with birds:

> The scene was one of almost medieval beauty in a superb
> setting. We visited the thousand-year-old cathedral, with its
> strange mixture of ornate Moorish, Byzantine and classical
> Corinthian architecture . . . We returned outside to gaze up at
> the ancient spires. Roger silently gazed upwards with us.
> Finally he pronounced judgement.
>   'There are Lesser Kestrels nesting in that tower', he said.

Following this preliminary reconnaissance visit, Mountfort applied his brilliant organizational skills to planning two major expeditions to the Coto Doñana. The roll-call of participants reads like a *Who's Who* of twentieth century ornithology, with Eric Hosking, James Ferguson-Lees and James Fisher on the 1956 expedition; and Phil Hollom, Max Nicholson and Sir Julian

Huxley on the 1957 one. Mountfort also enlisted the services of a young Spanish ornithologist named Antonio Valverde, known to all as 'Tono', who continually amused the party with his 'irrepressible schoolboy humour'. Another celebrated participant was Lord Alanbrooke.

James Ferguson-Lees recalls the sense that they were exploring uncharted territory. Although born in Italy, he had only travelled abroad as an adult a couple of times before, to the Netherlands and briefly to Spain, so when Guy Mountfort invited him to become the youngest member of the first Doñana party it was too good an opportunity to miss. However, language barriers proved something of a problem. As they rode around on horseback, Tono Valverde, whose English was very limited, would ask Ferguson-Lees to test him on birds and other wildlife using their English names: 'His classic one was when I asked him what was making the noise of a frog. He thought for a bit, and then answered: "Adult tadpole"! Later on his English did improve . . . '

The Doñana expeditions were chronicled in the first of Mountfort's trilogy of travel books, *Portrait of a Wilderness*, published in 1958. Most of the book is a brisk account of the ups and downs of the expeditions, with fascinating information about the birds of the region, as well as some amusing anecdotes. Underlying this, however, is one man's journey of discovery:

> Sadly I rose and knocked out my pipe. Night was crowding
> swiftly over the marismas and the trees were now etched black
> against the sky. I walked slowly back down the silent trail.
> Tomorrow I would return to England by a twentieth-century
> turbo-prop airplane, to the hurly-burly of overcrowded London,
> to neon lights, telephones and relentless clocks, to constant noise
> and the reek of petrol fumes, to newspapers, recurrent crises and
> talk of the hydrogen bomb. Tomorrow my footprints in the
> Martinazo trail would begin to silt over. In a few days or weeks no
> trace of our expedition would be visible . . . Most of the birds we
> had been watching would soon depart and the winged multitudes
> from northern lands would pour into the Coto to replace them for
> the winter . . . Seasons would come and go, but our beloved

wilderness, the Coto Doñana, would dream on through the years, its solitude and beauty remaining, please God, unblemished.

Following the Doñana expeditions, Mountfort organized several further trips: to the Danube delta, described in *Portrait of a River* (1962); to Jordan, in *Portrait of a Desert* (1965), and later to Pakistan (featured in Eric Hosking's autobiography *An Eye for a Bird*). These books were vital in extending our knowledge of the breeding birds of these regions, but with their accounts of unforgettable days in the field they also opened the eyes of readers to the delights of birdwatching abroad.

Guy Mountfort died aged ninety-seven in April 2003, the same month as his friend and contemporary Max Nicholson. Like Nicholson, he was lauded as one of the true giants of twentieth century ornithology, who had done so much to extend the horizons of British birdwatchers.

IN 1955, a different kind of book captured the imagination of the British and American public. *Wild America* told the story of two men's 100-day, 30,000 mile trip around the North American continent, during spring and summer 1953. It was written by arguably the two greatest all-round birdwatchers of the twentieth century: James Fisher and Roger Tory Peterson.

The pair travelled around the continent like a modern Don Quixote and Sancho Panza, with almost as many trials and tribulations. The contrast between the staid, upper middle-class Englishman, sporting a collar and tie, and the laid-back artist from New York State in his open-necked shirt, was bound to produce some culture clashes. There was the added dimension that Fisher was seeing North America's birds for the very first time, while Peterson was one of America's most experienced and well-travelled birders.

In his opening remarks, Peterson explained the motivation behind their trip:

So much had I seen of wild Europe, and especially of wild Britain in the company of my colleague . . . that I had a growing desire to reciprocate, to show him my own continent.

'If you come to America,' I suggested, 'I will meet you in Newfoundland and conduct you around the continent . . . you will see a more complete cross section of wild America than any other Englishman, and all but a few North Americans, have ever seen.'

A sense of how difficult an undertaking this was came in the opening pages, when Fisher's arrival on the North American continent was disrupted by fog, with his plane diverted from Gander in Newfoundland – where Peterson was waiting for him – to the air base at Stephenville, almost 300 miles away. Fisher also complained about the pedestrian nature of air, as opposed to sea travel:

> Transatlantic travel is now reduced to a quick succession of unromantic waiting rooms, with polite female voices echoing through loud-speakers, all of which are permanently off adjustment. The Atlantic passage itself is a period of coffee, shiny magazines, coffee, conversation with neighbours, coffee, meals in elaborate cardboard boxes, coffee, sleep, and coffee.

Nevertheless, he did manage to catch a glimpse of a Gannet far below the plane – his first New World bird. Things soon picked up, and by the time they reached Texas, a month or so later, they were on a roll: 'Birds-birds-birds! Luther Goldman and Roger showed me more birds today than I have ever seen in one day before.'

By the end of a very long day in the field they had run up a final tally of 132 species – 30 of them 'lifers' for Fisher. As Peterson pointed out, every time Fisher saw a new bird he would shout, in a dreadful pun on the phrase 'tally-hunting', 'Tally ho!'

In three months Fisher and Peterson travelled from Newfoundland down the east coast to Florida; across to Texas, New Mexico and Arizona; then up the west coast to Seattle; before finally flying up to Alaska for an unforgettable trip to the Pribilof Islands and their vast colonies of seabirds.

Their aim was ostensibly to break Guy Emerson's North

American year record of 497 species, set in 1939. They did so easily, and Fisher even stole a march on his companion by sneaking out of the hotel at Anchorage to tot up an extra five species. However, his triumph was short-lived: after his return to England Peterson went on to achieve a total of 572 species for the year.

By the end of the year Fisher had more than doubled the number of species he had ever seen, yet his 'world list' was still well below one thousand species, a total even the novice birder can achieve nowadays with three or four trips abroad. But the result of their efforts was far more impressive than mere 'tally-hunting'. Fisher and Peterson went in search of several species and races which are now extinct, or almost certainly so. These included Dusky Seaside Sparrow at Cape Canaveral, Florida (later the launch site for the US space programme); a fruitless quest for Ivory-billed Woodpecker at one of its last remaining roosting sites, also in Florida; and a trip to look for North America's mightiest, and rarest, raptor, the California Condor.

Fisher's account of this episode is a typically gung-ho evocation of the drama and excitement of birdwatching. Having spent a fruitless day searching for this legendary bird, they are about to go home:

> We finally had to give up. Regretfully, we turned to the car.
> 'Why the hurry?' said Sidney Peyton, quietly, from behind his binoculars. We followed the slant of them, to a speck in the sky. The speck was a California Condor, and it was coming our way.
> It came right over. I could not estimate its height, but we had a perfect view . . . For five minutes we watched its monstrous ten-foot span, its primaries spread like fingers. It made a couple of slow flaps, as if it had all the time in the world, caught a new thermal, and soared away to the southeast until it had become a tiny speck and disappeared.
> 'Tally most incredibly ho!' I said as I ticked it off my checklist.
> 'Quite a bird,' commented Roger. 'Exhibit A.'
> 'Worth seeing, actually.'
> It had been worth seeing, actually, worth travelling ten thousand miles to see.

Wild America was published in the mid-1950s, when for most British birdwatchers intercontinental travel remained about as feasible as a trip to the moon. Not surprisingly the book was a huge success, while Roger Peterson's cine-film of the expedition played to packed houses at the Royal Festival Hall in London, and entertained millions more when it was later shown on television.

In the book's final passage, Fisher recounted a meeting with one of America's greatest ever statesmen; a man who twice, in 1952 and 1956, came within a whisker of entering the White House as president:

> Sometime later Herbert Agar brought a distinguished visitor into the club – one who was relaxing, after a strenuous campaign, with a tour of the world that made Roger's and mine look like a picnic. I was introduced to the great man. Proudly, and not to be out-travelled, I told him I had just been twenty or thirty thousand miles in his country.
>
> 'Good heavens,' said Adlai Stevenson, 'what were you running for?'

B Y THE END of the 1950s, the world of birdwatching had changed out of all recognition. Coach-loads of people were making the annual pilgrimage to the Ospreys at Loch Garten, and, as a result of their visit, joining the RSPB. The post-war generation of schoolboys had grown up, and were now making their own contribution to our knowledge of birds by visiting bird observatories up and down the country. Books like the Peterson, Mountfort and Hollom field guide and the New Naturalists had raised the level of knowledge and expertise amongst ordinary birdwatchers. And influential men such as James Fisher and Guy Mountfort had begun to explore the wider world in search of new places to watch birds.

Almost unnoticed amongst all this activity, a great British birdwatcher had died, in his eightieth year. Jock Walpole-Bond, the last of the great Victorians, was no more; and with him ended an era in which egg collecting and nest finding had been the driving forces of ornithology in Britain.

The swinging Sixties were about to begin.

POSTSCRIPT

THE HASTINGS RARITIES AFFAIR

Before we finally leave the old era behind, one more story needs to be told: the notorious 'Hastings Rarities Affair'. Although the major events occurred almost a century ago, the truth was only finally exposed in the early 1960s.

O N ITS JOURNEY along the Sussex coast from Bexhill to Hastings, the A259 passes through the seaside resort of St Leonard's-on-Sea. It was in these unlikely surroundings that the biggest ornithological fraud of all time had its headquarters. Today, number 15 Silchester Road is a unisex hairstylist; but for almost a hundred years, from 1845 to 1943, it was a taxidermist's shop.

There is not much call for taxidermy nowadays. But at the turn of the twentieth century it was a thriving and profitable trade. There was hardly a saloon or public bar in the country that did not have a couple of dead animals above the bar. The real bread-and-butter of the taxidermist's art was birds: large or small, colourful or dull, familiar or – especially – rare.

For it was rare birds – the avian equivalents of a Penny Black or a Dickens first edition – that were most in demand: waifs and strays that, by some migratory error or freak of nature, had reached our shores. A single specimen of a genuine rarity, obtained in the British Isles, might be worth several guineas, at a time when the average weekly wage for a farm labourer was barely two pounds. The Holy Grail was a 'first for Britain' – a species which had never before been recorded here – which could sell for as much as fifty pounds (several thousand pounds today).

So when George Bristow, the taxidermist at 15 Silchester

Road, began to get a reputation for being able to obtain such prized specimens it is hardly surprising that rich collectors beat a path to his door. He, in turn, did them proud. For a period of almost forty years, from 1892 to 1930, an incredible collection of rare birds passed through Bristow's little shop, were skinned, stuffed and mounted, and then sold to adorn the drawing-rooms of country houses for miles around.

HOWEVER, the ornithological establishment of the day, led by Harry Witherby, gradually began to harbour suspicions about the provenance of Bristow's rare specimens. Bristow claimed that they were 'obtained' by local gamekeepers and market gardeners, who would then pass them on to him, sometimes via an intermediary. Although bird protection laws were in their infancy, shooting rare birds might attract unwelcome attention, so Bristow took care not to identify the sources of his specimens. To confirm the bird's identity, he would usually call on the services of a local ornithologist, such as N. F. Ticehurst or M. J. Nicoll, men with an apparently spotless reputation for honesty.

Even so, Witherby and others had their doubts. The sheer number of records – and the very high proportion of extremely rare species including several first records for Britain – seemed incredible. But the apparent honesty of Bristow, and the impeccable credentials of Ticehurst and Nicoll, made it hard to prove that any wrongdoing had occurred. Nevertheless, when Witherby wrote to a local ornithologist about yet another first for Britain (an Olivaceous Warbler obtained 'near St Leonard's' on 20 May 1915) he expressed his doubts:

> I suppose this will be another new British bird in which case I had perhaps better send it to Hartert for confirmation . . . Did you see it in the flesh? I am very glad that you are taking up some of these records and I do wish you would do more. It is most important that someone entirely independent should examine them in the flesh. Do you know anything about a *Lusciniola melanopogon*

which F. Lindsay sent to me for examination – of course stuffed. I suppose that will have to be accepted and also a *Totanus brevipes*. Did you see the Black Larks in the flesh? I cannot understand all these rarities being got at Westfield – it seems to me most fishy.

A word of explanation is required here. '*Lusciniola melano-pogon*' refers to Moustached Warbler, a southern European species which has only occurred a handful of times in Britain. '*Totanus brevipes*' is the Grey-tailed Tattler, an Asiatic wader with only two modern sightings. But the records which really beggar belief are the series of multiple sightings of birds which had never before been seen in Britain, such as Black Larks, which included groups of four together on two separate occasions.

Bristow soon responded to the growing murmur of accusations. In June 1916, he wrote a letter to Witherby: 'For some considerable time now I have had hints that you and other ornithologists entertain doubts as to the authenticity of some of the rare birds I get, and I must admit not without reason.'

Whether or not these words constitute a tacit admission of guilt, there is no doubt that following this correspondence, and Witherby's attempt to tighten the process of official judgement and acceptance of records, the number of specimens began to decline, and by 1930 had dried up altogether. By the time George Bristow died in 1947, aged eighty-four, the vogue for collections of stuffed birds was in rapid decline, and taxidermy itself had become a dying art.

THAT WAS not the end of the story, however. During the 1950s and early 1960s, as new bird books appeared, the question of whether or not to include the Hastings records was becoming a matter for heated debate. In 1960, P. A. D. Hollom (one of the authors of the Collins *Field Guide*) made the controversial decision to omit them from *The Popular Handbook of Rarer British Birds*.

David Bannerman, one of the most respected ornithologists of his day, took a very different view. In 1961, in the Preface to volume nine of his monumental work *The Birds of the British Isles*, he defended the integrity of the records:

> It seems to me the gravest mistake once again to raise this controversial issue unless concrete evidence can be produced that the records were unreliable. Surely we should trust to the mature judgement and undoubted integrity of the first editors of *British Birds* and of *The Handbook* whose caution in accepting records was proverbial. They were in a much better position to judge than the present generation of ornithologists who may seek to discredit events which took place before they were born.
>
> For the reasons I have given I have decided at the outset to include the Hastings/Romney Marsh records of 1900-1916 in *The Birds of the British Isles* and shall continue to do so. It must be borne in mind that some of the birds obtained in this area between 1900 and 1916 were shot and recorded by Michael Nicoll himself, and to discard them now is unthinkable.

Just a year later, the unthinkable happened. The August 1962 issue of *British Birds* was entirely devoted to the repudiation of the Hastings Rarities. In all, 542 specimens and 43 sight-records of almost 100 species, including no fewer than 16 species which had never occurred anywhere else in the country, were deleted from the 'British list'.

The investigation was the work of *British Birds'* highly respected editors, Max Nicholson and James Ferguson-Lees. Their approach was, as Nicholson later admitted, somewhat unusual. Rather than make direct accusations of fraud and wrong-doing, and name names, they used statistics to make their case. A professional mathematician with a good knowledge of birds, J. A. Nelder, was enlisted to test the statistical validity of the records as a whole, and concluded that it was simply impossible that such a large number of unusual sightings could occur in a limited geographical area in this relatively short period of time.

The response to the *British Birds* exposé was immediate, with the scandal splashed across the front pages of the next day's newspapers. The location, just a few miles away from Piltdown Man, the most famous hoax in British history, did not go unremarked. That fraud, involving the supposed discovery of the 'missing link' between man and the apes, had been exposed just a decade earlier. Now, the Hastings Rarities Affair was being compared to Piltdown, as another nail in the coffin for Britain's scientific establishment.

Many people felt that the *British Birds* editors had taken the right decision. Fraud and dishonesty cannot be ignored for ever, and the truth was bound to come out in the end. The title of their editorial, 'Setting the Record Straight', said it all.

Amongst birdwatchers, the immediate reaction to the revelations was a mixture of shame and relief. At least things were now out in the open: the skeleton in the closet of British ornithology had finally been cleared out. But then came the recriminations. How, it was asked, could eminent local ornithologists like N. F. Ticehurst have been duped for so long? After all, he had actually examined many of the corpses at first hand, without, it seems, becoming suspicious.

THE MOST PRESSING questions were: how did the fraud occur, why was it done, and who was the perpetrator? *Why* was easy to answer: almost certainly for financial gain. As to *who* was behind the hoax, the finger of suspicion was pointed firmly at George Bristow, the taxidermist through whose shop so many of the specimens passed. It was hinted that Bristow would have made a tidy profit from selling off foreign specimens as the genuine, British-shot article.

But if this was the case, and Bristow was operating such a scheme, a vital question remained: *how* did he do it? Nicholson and Ferguson-Lees suggested that the new science of refrigeration was sufficiently advanced for the specimens to be brought to Britain by ship, in a deep-frozen state, from the Mediterranean and Middle East. Once ashore, the smuggled bird would be skinned and mounted. Then it would be presented as yet another victim of a conveniently anonymous market gardener, whose keen eye and accurate shot had supposedly obtained it in some remote hamlet high on the Kent or Sussex downs.

Later on, evidence surfaced to suggest that this hypothesis may have been correct. In 1970, a letter appeared in *British Birds*, from Robert Coombes. He recalled boarding a ship in Liverpool in 1939, and meeting an elderly steward named Mr Parkman. During their discussion, Parkman revealed an extraordinary secret:

> 'Before the first war', as a hobby and as a side-line, he had collected birds at ports of call and brought them back to England in the cold storage of his ships . . . He said that on arrival at a British port he always handed the birds over to his brother, who disposed of them 'at Hastings'. He mentioned 'Bristow, the taxidermist', as the destination for the birds . . .

Although some people questioned the reliability of the freezing process at the time, scientists have since confirmed that it was possible to transport the frozen skins of recently shot birds, even using the fairly primitive technology of the time. In 1995, two radio programmes from the BBC Open University examined the affair, interviewing Robert Heap, technical director of Cambridge Refrigeration Technology:

> The use of mechanical refrigeration on ships, as distinct from the long-established use of natural ice, started in 1879 with shipments of chilled beef and frozen mutton. And by the year 1900 there were no less than 356 mechanically refrigerated ships plying their trades around the seas of the world.

Another scientist confirmed that this could have been done without the specimens showing noticeable ill-effects.

Meanwhile, although the majority of ornithologists and bird-watchers supported the editors of *British Birds*, there was one notable dissenting voice. Dr James Harrison possessed excellent qualifications to judge the Hastings Rarities Affair. Brought up in Hastings, the author of the monumental two-volume *Birds of Kent*, and a pillar of the community, he was also the owner of one of the finest collections of stuffed birds in the country. Not surprisingly, a large proportion of that collection had come via the taxidermist's shop of George Bristow. Now Harrison fired his guns, metaphorically speaking, at the *British Birds* authors, criticizing the time-lapse between the alleged fraud and its public revelation: 'I suggest that the time is long past when such action should properly have been taken, and opinion, both as to the wisdom and the infallibility of the report . . . is bound to remain divided.'

Six years later, in 1968, Harrison privately published his own book on the subject, *Bristow and the Hastings Rarities Affair.* He made a spirited defence of Bristow, finding flaws in Nelder's statistical analysis, noting the subsequent appearance of rare birds in the Hastings area, and pointing out that Bristow himself 'never appeared to the writer as if he was in the big money!' Yet ultimately his increasingly weak arguments came across as those of a desperate lawyer defending a criminal who has been caught red-handed.

Yet in one aspect of the case he raised some important questions. How could one man, operating in a quiet seaside town, perpetrate such a large-scale fraud over so many years, without getting caught? To suggest that this provincial shopkeeper had the contacts, financial acumen and organizational ability to master-mind such a mammoth operation is stretching credulity.

Before he died, Max Nicholson was asked whether he suspected that someone else was behind the Hastings Rarities. He indicated that he and Ferguson-Lees had their suspicions at the time, but that without absolute proof they were not willing to name names. James Ferguson-Lees, now the sole survivor of those involved in the exposé, is also keeping silent.

IF ONE LOOKS at the evidence, albeit almost a century after the events occurred, one name keeps cropping up. Not Norman Ticehurst, who right up to his death at the age of ninety-six in 1969 could still not accept that fraud had occurred. Not James Harrison, who continued to defend the integrity of his friend

George Bristow, despite the evidence to the contrary, out of a deep-seated sense of loyalty and fair play. In fact, the name of the man who may have been behind the whole scheme was once used as proof that the records must be genuine. We only need to recall David Bannerman's indignant assertion: 'It must be borne in mind that some of the birds obtained in this area between 1900 and 1916 were shot and recorded by Michael Nicoll himself, and to discard them now is unthinkable.'

So who was Michael Nicoll? According to his obituary in *British Birds* (written by Norman Ticehurst), he was:

> . . . a delightful companion, his keenness, knowledge and skill both as field naturalist and museum worker earned him a high place amongst ornithologists of the day, while his kindly unselfishness, straightness of character and staunchness were the outstanding qualities that will be sorely missed by the numerous friends he has left behind him.

Fine words, but we know for sure that at least one of Nicoll's own specimens was fraudulent. On 9 September 1905 he allegedly shot a Black-eared Wheatear, near Pett Level in East Sussex. Later, the specimen was purchased (along with other items in Nicoll's collection) by the Booth Museum in Dyke Road, Brighton, where it still resides, along with many other examples of the Hastings Rarities. A letter in the museum's catalogue revealed that the skin had been prepared in 'the unmistakably oriental manner', and went on to make an astonishing assertion: 'It was only the fact that the skin had been prepared by an oriental, and not a European, naturalist, that enables us to realise that even Mr. Nicoll's warranty is in this case untrustworthy.'

The *British Birds* obituary revealed the connection that would have allowed Nicoll to procure such a specimen for himself. From 1902-1906, Nicoll made three voyages to collect birds, travelling around the world on a yacht owned by a British aristocrat, Lord Crawford. He published an account of his travels in 1908, in a book entitled *Three Voyages of a Naturalist*. Meanwhile, in 1906, he had been appointed to a job as assistant director of the Zoological Gardens at Giza in Egypt, where according to Ticehurst:

... with the exception of the usual intervals of leave, he spent practically the rest of his life in a congenial occupation with abundant opportunities for the advancement of the science which he had made his life's work ... He devoted his energies to the formation of a representative collection of the birds of Egypt ...

In 1923, already a sick man, Nicoll returned to England, where he set up home at Wittersham in Kent, only a stone's throw from Hastings and itself the location of several of the discredited records. Two years later, in October 1925, he died at the age of forty-five. He was laid to rest on the slope of the hill overlooking the marsh where he had shot so many birds for his collection.

It does not take a huge leap of the imagination to suppose that while travelling the world, or later when assembling his collection of the birds of Egypt, it might have occurred to Nicoll that he could make a tidy profit from passing on some of these specimens as genuinely obtained in Britain. There was certainly no shortage of wealthy collectors, some of whom may have turned a blind eye to the provenance of the specimens, while others were almost certainly duped. Bristow could have been just a convenient go-between: a basically honest man who could legitimately be supposed to obtain the birds from various casual gunners who preferred to remain anonymous.

WE SHALL PROBABLY never know the full truth about the Hastings Rarities Affair. And now, almost a century after its occurrence, and more than forty years after it was finally exposed, it may not seem to have much relevance. But as well as the need to rewrite the ornithological record books, in which genuine specimens were almost certainly thrown out along with fraudulent ones, it also had lasting consequences for the bond of trust on which records of rare birds depend, raising questions about whether or not similar frauds and hoaxes could have occurred anywhere else.

Most importantly of all, it revealed something about the moral codes of early twentieth-century Britain. The fact that the Hastings Rarities Affair could be perpetrated for almost forty years without serious doubts being aired, and go another thirty years before finally being exposed, tells us much about the nature of society at that time. In sharp contrast to the free and easy 1960s, it was a society where people knew their place, and acted accordingly. A society which was the very epitome of conformity. And most important of all, a society where a man's word was his bond. Under such circumstances, it is perhaps not all that surprising that the perpetrators got away with their fraud for so long.

They could not be allowed to get away with it forever. By the time the fraud was finally exposed, not only society had changed, but also birdwatching with it. The rapid rise in participation in the years following World War II, the travel boom, and the increased use of field guides, had all contributed to a new air of professionalism and rigour. With the establishment of the Rarities Committee in 1958, which critically examined every single sighting of a rare bird in Britain, the anomaly of the Hastings records could no longer be swept under the carpet. Although the unmasking of the affair was painful, it was absolutely necessary if the 'British list', and the records of rare birds it contained, was to have any credibility in the years to come.

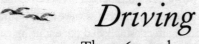

CHAPTER TWELVE

Driving

The 1960s and 1970s

If you can remember the Sixties, you weren't really there!

Proverbial saying (attributed to, among others,
Timothy Leary and David Crosby)

WHEN PEOPLE THINK of the 1960s, what do they remember? Well, at the risk of contradicting the famous saying, all sorts of things. The classic images of this turbulent decade have been so widely broadcast that they are part of most people's consciousness, whether they were alive at the time or belong to a later generation. For many, they will always be the 'swinging sixties': the era of the Beatles and the Stones, the Kennedy assassination and the moon landings, David Bailey and Twiggy, *That Was The Week That Was* and the Profumo Affair, Flower Power and Free Love.

But beneath the surface, the 1960s do not seem quite so straightforward. Even today, historians argue about the lasting effects of an era when revolution was in the air: a revolution that eventually led to a permanent change in society, though perhaps not quite in the way its protagonists imagined.

Historian Arthur Marwick, author of the seminal work on the decade, is ambivalent when it comes assessing the lasting impact of the 1960s: 'For some, it is a golden age, for others a time when the old secure framework of morality, authority and discipline disintegrated. . .'

What cannot be denied is that compared with the humdrum and predictable 1950s, major social changes did occur. Marwick contrasts the idealism, rebellion, and changes in sexual behaviour of the 1960s, with the 'rigid social hierarchy; subordination of women to men and children to parents; repressed attitudes to sex

. . . unquestioning respect for authority. . . and a dull and cliché-ridden popular culture' of the previous decade. He concludes: 'The consequences of what happened in the sixties were long-lasting: the sixties cultural revolution in effect established the enduring cultural values and social behaviour for the rest of the century.'

People were better off in material ways too – especially compared with their parents' generation, who had lived through the deprivations of World War II. Sustained economic growth combined with low unemployment and smaller family size to produce a surge in people's disposable income. People lived longer, and were healthier, thanks to the National Health Service. They were also better educated, especially those who had passed the eleven-plus exam and attended grammar schools – and in some cases university, often the first members of their family ever to do so. Working hours were reduced too, allowing people more time to enjoy leisure activities, while a greater awareness of issues such as the environment and nature also helped fuel the popularity of outdoor pastimes including birdwatching.

But what was life really like at the grass roots? In fact, for those who were not part of the charmed circle of pop stars, fashion icons, and self-proclaimed children of the revolution, life in Britain went on more or less as normal. People continued to pursue a variety of leisure interests – and a significant and growing minority chose to spend their spare time watching birds.

Like everyone else alive at that time, no doubt they were affected by the major social and cultural changes happening all around them. However, it is likely that the most dramatic changes in their lives derived more from the greater freedom and mobility which resulted from better private transport and higher standards of living, than the more esoteric aspects of the cultural and social revolution. Besides, the 'tune in, turn on, drop out' hippie ethos was pretty much incompatible with the self-disciplined and ordered lifestyle required to become a serious birdwatcher.

For although the media perpetuated an image of 'sex, drugs and rock'n'roll', the reality was rather more mundane, especially for the vast majority of young people still living at home with their parents.

Today, Tim Cleeves is a highly respected birder, with a long career in conservation at the RSPB, and the principal claim to fame of having found what is arguably the rarest bird ever seen in Britain: the Slender-billed Curlew at Druridge Bay, Northumberland in 1998.

As a schoolboy, Cleeves and a classmate would collect injured birds and animals and keep them in their garden shed until they either recovered or died. His companion soon lost interest in birds, and joined the school football team instead. But in 1962, at the age of eleven, Tim noticed an advert for the junior section of the Bristol Naturalists' Society in a newsagent's window in his home town of Hanham, near Bristol. A week or two later, having made the laborious journey by two buses from his home into the city, he attended his first meeting:

> It was a talk by a fairly weird looking bloke on plants, and I was not too impressed. The Junior Section had three members: a fat lad from Westbury-on-Trym who did quite passable Dalek impersonations, a suave-looking early Mod called Jonathan Savoury, and me. Everyone seemed posh and went to posh schools where they did prep (whatever that was!), and had to go in on Saturdays, which seemed like hell.

Despite this inauspicious start, Tim soon became an active member of the society, going on coach trips to distant locations such as Portland Bill, the New Forest and the Exe Estuary. His abiding memories are not the birds, but the antics that he and the other junior members got up to at the back of the coach. These included a dubious scam in which by moving up and down the vehicle they could confuse the society's treasurer into giving change for their tickets twice, which ill-gotten gains they then spent on sweets and cigarettes.

By their mid-teens, this growing gang of Bristol-based school-boy birdwatchers had begun to take their own trips, meeting every Sunday morning at the bus station and heading off to Chew Valley

Lake, the local birding hotspot. It is worth noting that despite their youth, they were allowed to go wherever they liked without parental supervision. Inevitably they also teamed up with adult birdwatchers – mainly older men – who would offer them lifts and accompany them on days out. It is hard to imagine parents of teenage boys being quite so tolerant today.

This may have been an age of innocence, but birdwatching could still lead young lads into trouble. In May 1965, a postcard arrived through Tim Cleeves' letterbox. It came from another local birdwatcher, Bernard King, and informed him that two Black-winged Stilts had been sighted at Chew. After school, Tim and a friend named Peter Roscoe (nicknamed 'Emperor Roscoe' after a prominent disc-jockey of the period) caught the 375 bus from Bristol to Chew Stoke, where the birds were supposed to be.

Unfortunately, they were the victims of inaccurate information – what birders call 'duff gen' – and ended up having to tramp down to the other end of the lake on foot, a distance of three miles. The good news was that the stilts were still 'showing', and they were able to get brief but decent views. The bad news was that it was now 9 p.m. on a Monday night; they were at least ten miles from home; and, using a common schoolboy ruse, they had each told their parents that they were at the other boy's house. To make things even worse, the last bus to Bristol had left a few minutes earlier.

However, salvation was at hand, in the unlikely shape of a Vauxhall Cresta parked in a lay-by. Undeterred by the fact that the car had steamed-up windows and was rocking rhythmically back and forth, Emperor Roscoe tapped gingerly on the window. This was wound down to reveal what Tim describes as 'a Greaser, with a bootlace tie, white frilly shirt, leather jacket and cowboy boots.' It was the moment of truth for the young birders: 'I thought he was going to flatten us, but after Roscoe asked if he was going to Bristol he said "Yeah – 'op in the back". He drove back like a maniac – no doubt to impress his "bird" – and we got back just in time before our parents called the police!'

To today's generation, a Vauxhall Cresta may not seem like a symbol of freedom; but for those growing up in the 1960s, the rapid growth of the private car changed their lives more than any other factor. Car travel grew dramatically during the period, doubling from 1952 to 1960 and again from 1960 to 1974, at the expense of the railway system which was undergoing major cutbacks and line closures at the time. Following the opening of Britain's first full-length motorway (the M1) in 1959, the network grew rapidly, from less than 200 miles in 1963, to almost 1000 miles by 1971, about half today's figure.

Even those who did not own a car could still get the benefit from one. Cars could be borrowed from a friend, a colleague, or a nervous father. People cadged lifts from fellow birders: those who had their own vehicle suddenly became very popular amongst fellow enthusiasts. And those at the bottom of the heap, with no access to a car from parents, friends or fellow birders, took the last resort – hitch-hiking.

Today, hitch-hikers are viewed with such deep suspicion that the practice has virtually died out, but in the innocent days of the 1960s things were very different. Hitching was seen as part of normal life, and though some drivers might have been a little reluctant to pick up a gang of binocular-toting scruffs, many were public-spirited enough to stop, at least often enough to make standing by the side of the road and sticking out a thumb worthwhile. For a brief period during the late 1970s and early 1980s, Britain's birders would develop 'hitching and twitching' into a way of life.

BIRDERS who grew up during the 1960s and 1970s are often heard to say that today's generation of youngsters has it too easy. If they want information on rare birds, they can use a pager, premium phone line or access the Internet. If they want to read the latest news and views, they can buy birding magazines from their local newsagent or get them delivered direct to their home. And if they want to meet fellow birders, with the numbers of people of all ages and backgrounds who pursue the hobby today, they don't have to look very far.

Back in the so-called swinging sixties, life for the novice birder was very different indeed. You might own a battered pair of binoculars, and you probably had a bird book or two – usually *The Observer's Book of Birds*, the Peterson *Field Guide* and later on *The Reader's Digest Book of British Birds*. You certainly didn't read any birding magazines, because the only one available was *British Birds*, which was not only very serious but also very expensive. And the chances were that unless by some major coincidence there was another birder at your school, you probably never met anyone else who shared your enthusiasm.

Growing up in a small town in Derbyshire, Mark Cocker's early experiences were typical. He recounted his formative years in the opening chapters of *Birders: Tales of a Tribe*, a detailed, funny and often moving exploration of birding culture from the late 1960s to the present day:

> Birding was for me a bid for freedom. Prior to setting off each evening I can recall that the change of dress from school uniform to my old clothes felt like shedding a more restricted identify for the unlimited spaces of the Derbyshire countryside.
>
> The second great source of happiness was a chance to go hunting. As a child my favourite forms of play were always war games, creeping around bushes with a plastic gun or stick and trying to outwit an enemy by sneaking up behind him. I'm convinced that birding at the age of twelve was a way of continuing the pleasures of an eight-year-old without appearing too ridiculous . . .

Despite his assertion that he didn't appear 'too ridiculous', he was sometimes deeply embarrassed by his participation in such a deeply uncool activity:

> It was the standard joke when people heard I was interested in birds – 'Oh, the two-legged kind, I hope!' . . . That kind of constant crass innuendo made me wary about disclosing my bird interests. I was especially terrified that the other two-legged kind would find out and I often rehearsed a nightmare scenario in which a large gang of girls stood in a scornful huddle laughing at

the nerd with the anorak and the binoculars. I don't know why
I should have had that particular childhood fantasy. At that age I
didn't even know any girls.

For a long time, the young Mark Cocker imagined that birding was a purely personal childhood interest – just something he
did because he liked it. Then, at the age of twelve, he discovered
that other people enjoyed watching birds too. In spring 1972 he
joined the Buxton Field Club, travelling with them on coach outings as far afield as Leighton Moss in Lancashire, where he saw his
first Bittern. But his most enduring memory of the period came on
a trip to the local moors, where the group encountered a Short-
eared Owl:

> Before that moment I had, like every young keen birder,
> compensated for experiences of the real thing with long hours
> poring over bird books and bird pictures. But on Goldsitch Moss
> I realised, perhaps for the first time, by how much life can exceed
> imagination. A Short-eared Owl had entered my life and for those
> moments, as it swallowed me up with its piercing eyes, I had
> entered the life of an owl. It was a perfect consummation.

The 1960s and 1970s saw the peak of activity for local bird
clubs and natural history societies, which played such an important part in the lives of young birders such as Tim Cleeves and
Mark Cocker. Most had been founded in the decades either side of
World War II, at a time when community spirit was perhaps at its
height. Writing in *British Birds* in 1958, in a celebration of the
centenary of the London Natural History Society, Max Nicholson
pointed to one of the reasons behind the increase in popularity of
local clubs:

> The role of local natural history societies and bird clubs in the
> modern world is an important one. More and more people are
> becoming divorced from close association with the land as it
> becomes increasingly difficult to get away from cities and suburbs,
> and it is the local organisation which is in the best position to
> foster an interest in things of the countryside.

Five years later, in 1963, Richard Fitter observed that outdoor field meetings 'are probably the biggest single factor in teaching bird-watching beginners their birds . . .' and predicted that as the hobby continued to grow, so would the fortunes of bird clubs.

What an exciting time this must have been, with fleets of cars and coaches heading out every Sunday morning, ferrying keen birders of all ages to Britain's birding hotspots: Cley and Chew, Minsmere and Martin Mere, Filey Brigg and Flamborough Head. Yet less than half a century later, despite a rapid growth in interest in birds and birding, many local clubs and societies are struggling to survive, as fewer and fewer people are willing to come on trips, attend indoor meetings, or pay their annual subscriptions.

More worryingly still, the clubs suffer from the combination of ageing membership and a lack of new blood; and at a time when everyone seems to be busier than ever before, not as many people are willing or able to carry out the sometimes thankless (and unpaid) task of being club treasurer or membership secretary.

It is not hard to see why. Private car ownership is now the norm rather than the exception, and most people prefer the flexibility of their own transport rather than relying on lifts from others, or going on a coach. And today, the unwillingness of parents to allow their teenage children to go out unsupervised, especially with a group of adults, means there are fewer junior members than before. Besides, for most youngsters, it is just not cool to go off on coach trips with a load of 'oldies'.

ANOTHER REASON why bird clubs were so popular in the 1960s was a practical one: the senior members knew where to go to find birds. Today, when there are guides to bird-finding in every part of the British Isles (and indeed most regions of the world) it is hard to remember that until 1967, the only way to find out about a new birding site was either to stumble across it yourself, or be told about it by a more experienced birder.

One example illustrates this point well. Today the nature reserve at Upton Warren, between Bromsgrove and Droitwich, is one of the best-known inland birding sites in the country. But back in the early sixties, it was virtually unknown outside the immediate local area, even to a keen young birder like Bill Oddie. Despite growing up just a few miles away, he only discovered Upton Warren in 1961, at the age of twenty, when he came across a reference to it in an old West Midland Bird Club annual report.

Once he and a friend finally visited Upton Warren, they had it more or less to themselves for a few precious years, until its growing fame eventually attracted birders from far and wide. In his autobiography *Gone Birding*, Oddie mused on the change that occurred between the early 1960s and the late 1970s, and the mixed feelings he had when he visited the site again while leading a group of young birders:

> I confess I felt rather proud at the idea that I might have been one of the people who, over fifteen years before, had been involved in putting Upton on the map . . . On the other hand, I had to admit, I also felt a little sad. I remembered Upton in the early sixties . . . no nature trails, hides or information boards and virtually no other birders. I'll be honest, that's how I prefer to remember it. The ideal local patch.

Upton Warren's growing popularity was partly due to a young man from Sussex named John Gooders. He was the author of a book which first appeared in 1967, simply entitled *Where to Watch Birds*. This compact little volume was a guide to more than 500 sites in England Scotland and Wales, from Scilly to Shetland and almost everywhere in between. Like all great ideas, it was so simple it seemed incredible that no-one had thought of it before. In fact they had, but only on the other side of the Atlantic, where Olin S. Pettingill's *Guide to Bird Finding East of the Mississippi* had appeared in 1951. Once again, as with the development of field guides and optics, it seems that the British were more than a decade behind their American cousins.

The genesis of *Where to Watch Birds* came from another young British birder, Bruce Coleman, who by this time was running a successful photographic agency (see Chapter 15). On a business trip to the United States, Coleman came across the

Pettingill guides, and determined to organize a similar guide to British birding sites. On his return, he contacted his friend the publisher André Deutsch, and Gooders himself: 'John was ideal for the *Where to Watch Birds* project. He had enthusiasm, terrific energy, and the ability to do fast research.'

Soon afterwards, in 1967, the book appeared, with an introduction from the great Roger Tory Peterson:

> Bird watching, bird-finding, bird-spotting, tick-hunting, or birding – call it what you will – has come of age. It is moving beyond the stage of identification guides into the era of Baedekers ... This valuable book will not only enhance the thoroughness of coverage of bird-spotting in Britain (few transient waifs or strays will escape scrutiny!) but it will also aid the conservationist in his perennial fight to preserve key wildlife areas against deterioration or outright destruction.

Publicizing bird 'hotspots' had already reaped benefits in the US, where the growing popularity of Hawk Mountain in Pennsylvania had enabled conservationists to protect it against hunting and development. In his preface, John Gooders reinforced this argument, stressing the need for birders to be vigilant in preserving important sites as competition with other leisure activities, such as fishing and sailing, grew.

In his *British Birds* review, D. I. M. Wallace praised Gooders for his 'remarkable degree of accuracy'; though in fact sometimes the information was a little too general to be useful. Another problem was that many birders, especially impressionable young ones, treated the book as the equivalent of Holy Writ, expecting to see virtually every bird mentioned in the text. When they did not, they were often disappointed.

Nevertheless, the guide became a best-seller, and influenced a whole generation of birders to explore new places to watch birds. It also saw the beginning of birds as a consumer product: just as people were buying *The Good Food Guide* to seek out a reliable restaurant, so they bought *Where to Watch Birds* – and its many subsequent imitators – in order to minimize the hassle involved in seeing 'good' birds.

Not everyone thought that bird-finding guides were a good idea. There were mutterings amongst the old guard that not only was a book like this creating a rather too 'professional' approach to the pastime, but also that it might draw unwanted attention to rare breeding birds, which could be disturbed as a result. Both author and reviewer refuted such concerns. Gooders pointed out that: 'those who have purchased this book to find rare breeders have wasted their money'. 'For those who may wish that books like this guide should never be written', added Wallace, 'the caution displayed by Mr. Gooders in clearing his draft with local and national bodies is part answer. The rest . . . must come from responsible bird-watchers disciplining their freedoms in the light of the needs of their quarry'.

In fact, as Bruce Coleman recalls, the ornithological establishment of the day was against the book being published at all. Fortunately the RSPB's Director, Peter Conder, took a more enlightened view, and gave it his official blessing.

Looking back, Bruce Coleman views the book's legacy as the beginning of the democratization of birding:

> *Where to Watch Birds* opened up birding: rather than relying on local contacts or news on the grapevine you could now plan trips farther afield, with some expectation of what you were likely to see. It enabled you to get to the right spot quickly, it provided information about restricted access, or if permits were required, and it reduced trespassing.

The perennial problem faced by authors of site guides – what you can and cannot reveal – has not gone away. Nevertheless, virtually every birder owns at least one site guide, and for many it is the only sensible way to plan their birding trips in an increasingly busy world, where time is at a premium.

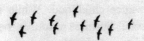

B Y THE LATE 1960s, birding horizons were finally beginning to widen. The second edition of the Peterson, Mountfort and Hollom *Field Guide*, published in 1966, continued to open up the continent of Europe. But the publication with the greatest global impact on the domestic scene in the UK was another brainchild of Bruce Coleman, *Birds of the World*.

Birds of the World was one of the many weekly magazine 'part-works' that came out during this period. Appearing from 1969 to 1971, it built up volume by volume into a complete set, at the cost of three shillings and sixpence per issue – roughly three pounds at today's prices. By the standards of the time it was an extraordinary work: packed with full colour photographs, which were complemented by a clear, authoritative and readable text written by a wide range of experts. It opened the eyes of many British birders to a range of species that they could not even imagine existed, let alone that one day they might actually travel to see them.

Birds of the World came about, like so many other projects, when Bruce Coleman took a friend out to lunch. Alan Smith had just been headhunted by IPC Magazines to establish a range of part-works. He called Bruce Coleman early one morning to ask if he had any ideas. By mid afternoon, after the consumption of lunch and a bottle or two of wine, the deal was sealed.

The project needed an editor, and Coleman and Smith did not have to look far. Despite the commercial success of *Where to Watch Birds*, John Gooders was still working as a teacher. After a discussion over a few drinks in a pub he made the momentous decision to leave teaching and take up the post.

The public interest in *Birds of the World* came about partly because many British birdwatchers had taken advantage of the package holiday boom of the 1960s, and were now heading abroad in ever greater numbers. One of these was Lawrence Holloway, a keen birdwatcher since childhood. While taking a break from running various small business ventures, he decided to go on a birdwatching holiday to Lake Neusiedl in eastern Austria with a friend. They chose an organized tour which, although successful in terms of seeing new birds, was less so in other areas, as

Holloway recalls: 'Unfortunately, the holiday was not well organised. Indeed, at times it seemed to us a complete shambles.'

On returning to Britain, Holloway began to look around for paid employment, attending interviews with Campbell's Soups and for a job as an encyclopaedia salesman. In the meantime, while on a birding trip to Pagham Harbour in Sussex in autumn 1964, he had bumped into his holiday companion:

> 'What are you doing now?' he asked.' I replied to the effect that I was 'having a holiday' and looking round for something worthwhile to do. 'Why don't you organise bird-watching holidays?' he asked. We both thought for a moment and then burst out laughing. After our experiences on the Austria tour, coping with all the disorganisation and shambles which had come about largely through lack of forethought by the organisers, the idea of becoming involved in such a venture seemed ridiculous.

But the seed had been sown. By the spring of 1965 he was still looking for work, and the idea of running bird tours came back to him. He mentioned the idea to his father, who was full of enthusiasm for the idea, and even came up with a name for the prospective new venture. And so Ornitholidays, Britain's first and longest established birding tour company, was born.

In their first full season, 1966, Ornitholidays took customers back to Lake Neusiedl, as well as to the Camargue in France, Falsterbo in southern Sweden, and various British locations including Orkney, Shetland and the Farne Islands. Prices ranged from just over £50 to under £90, inclusive of all transport, board and lodging – equivalent to between £1000 and £1800 today. Although not as cheap as the typical package holiday at the time, this still represented good value to a growing clientele of affluent middle-class birdwatchers.

In those early days, Holloway ran the one-man business from his Sussex home, and later from a room in a private residence in Chichester. It was a slow but steady start, as he points out:

> It was a very limited programme, of course. To have been too ambitious would have been a mistake. As it was, that first season

saw a total of some seventy people placing their bookings with me. How brave they must have been. After all, this was a time when there was little protection for people's money. I could have been anyone, just taking folks' money and then pushing off!

Holloway remembers the first tour, to the Camargue in April 1966, very well indeed:

We stayed at the Hôtel de la Poste in Arles and from there made excursions out around the Rhône Delta each day. It was fabulous: flamingos and Egyptian Vultures, and an Alpine Accentor on the roof of the local abbey. It was in the days when one travelled by train across Europe (none of this air business) and the only mistake I made was to book in our luggage at the Gare du Sud while we went sightseeing in Paris. When we came back to connect with our overnight train to Arles, there was no sign of our luggage – it had been sent on ahead. There's efficiency for you – can you imagine it today in Britain?! To my relief, it was all there when we arrived in Arles next morning, heaped up in a waiting room and simply awaiting our collection and transfer to the hotel.

During the next few years Ornitholidays went from strength to strength, helped at first by the lack of competition in the field, and later by a growing loyalty from customers who returned again and again. The programme expanded to include tours to the Canadian Rockies, India, Trinidad & Tobago and more 'off the beaten track' destinations such as Mozambique and Ethiopia. Today the company still runs about seventy-five trips each year, to locations in all seven continents.

For Lawrence Holloway himself, that off-the-cuff remark from a friend changed his life completely. Not only has he travelled the world and had a successful career in the travel business, but one of the young women he took on to help in the office later became his wife: 'Ann appeared to think that acquiring a job in a travel office would open far-flung foreign doors! In fact, the only trip she ever did was with me to Vancouver and the Rockies, way back in 1974! Our son Adrian was born that October, effectively putting paid to any more trips for her for a while!'

Despite the early success of Ornitholidays, foreign travel was still out of reach for most Britons. As a result, many chose to concentrate on birds closer to home, participating in regular bird surveys. These included the most ambitious of all, the first national *Atlas of Breeding Birds*, an extraordinary project carried out by between 10,000 and 15,000 amateur observers during the five breeding seasons from 1968 to 1972.

During this period the dedicated fieldworkers visited every single one of the 3,862 10-kilometre squares in Britain and Ireland, and surveyed the birds found breeding there. The resulting records – more than 285,000 of them – were verified, analyzed, and depicted on maps which showed the breeding distribution for each species. The comprehensive coverage was far greater than even the organizers of the 'Atlas' survey had predicted, as James Ferguson-Lees noted in his foreword to the resulting book, which appeared in 1976:

> There was a seemingly irreconcilable division of opinion between the optimists and enthusiasts on the one hand and the pessimists and diffidents on the other, the latter believing that such a project was doomed to failure through inadequate coverage. Even the optimists said that, because of the uneven spread of observers and their scarcity or absence in remoter areas, the best coverage that could be expected was 90% in England, 50% in Wales and a mere 25% in Scotland; the pessimists were putting these estimates much lower. Furthermore, nearly everyone thought that the coverage would be so thin in Ireland that nothing should be attempted in that country. How wrong we all were.

Such an extraordinary project could perhaps only have been brought to fruition in Britain and Ireland, with the long tradition of co-operation between professional scientists and amateur bird-watchers. As Max Nicholson had written in 1963:

> One of the outstanding features of British ornithology today is the continuous flow of energy from watching to systematic

identification, from investigation to serial conclusions, and from conclusions to practical action, while action in turn reveals fresh questions and problems which once more call the watchers to investigate and restart the cycle. This tendency is strong enough to suck into the vortex bird-watchers who never intended their hobby to become a scientific duty.

If anyone wondered why such a survey were required, we need only look back from the perspective of a single generation to see how much Britain and Ireland's birdlife has changed in the intervening period. Much of the hard data which has helped prove declines of species such as the Skylark or House Sparrow has come from this kind of survey – organized by scientists, but carried out by amateur birdwatchers. Even at the time of the first *Atlas* survey, though, it was already clear that bird populations and ranges were not as stable as had previously been assumed, with examples such as the rapid colonization by the Collared Dove fresh in people's minds.

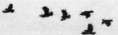

THERE ARE many parallels between people's experiences of birding in Britain and North America. But at certain periods of history the sheer disparity in scale between the two countries really does make a difference. In *Birders*, Mark Cocker related several tales of epic hitchhiking journeys by pioneering British twitchers in the 1970s: 'Back then, if you could have got into some hypothetical control module in space where you could monitor birders' movements around Britain's road networks, the screen would have appeared as an endless chaos of random blips, each one representing young twitchers hitching back and forth across the country . . .'

In 1976, at the age of sixteen, Cocker and his companion 'Tog' were on their way to the famous East Bank at Cley, and stopped off for the evening at a pub in Lincolnshire:

Sleeves rolled, we were celebrating the day's varied achievements with a pint and a game of darts. On our taste buds was the raw, satisfying, bitter-sweet blend of lager with lime and cheap cigar smoke. A quarter of a century later I cannot recover the sensations of that evening exactly. But one flavour still rings clear as on the day itself. It was the unmistakable taste of freedom.

But however hard he tries, the picture of two lads thumbing a lift on the B-roads of East Anglia simply does not have the glamour of the experiences of their American counterpart, Kenn Kaufman. In 1970, at the age of sixteen Kaufman took the momentous decision to drop out of high school – despite having good grades and being student council president. Chasing his own version of the American Dream, he hit the road – in search of birds:

> There was a day at the end of August that held a special symbolism for me. Not that I did anything unusual that day: like the day before and after, I spent it looking at birds. That day was significant because I knew that, back at home, kids my age were going back to school.
>
> They had the clang of locker doors in the halls of South High in Wichita, Kansas. I had a nameless mountainside in Arizona, with sunlight streaming down among the pines, and Mexican songbirds moving through the high branches. My former classmates were moving toward their education, no doubt, just as I was moving toward mine, but now I was travelling a road that no-one had charted out for me . . . and my adventure was beginning.

More than a quarter of a century later, in 1997, the middle-aged Kaufman recounted the story of his youthful birding experiences in *Kingbird Highway*. The overwhelming sentiment evoked by the book is one of nostalgia for a time when a young man could walk out of his front door in Kansas with only fifty dollars in his pocket to survive the next month:

> All my travel was by hitchhiking. I never slept in motels – literally never; I slept outside, regardless of the weather. For food, I tried to get by on a dollar a day. Going to grocery stores, I would buy

cans of vegetable soup, cans of hominy, perishables marked down
for quick sale. Later I discovered that dried cat food was palatable,
barely; a box of Little Friskies, stuffed in my backpack, could keep
me going for days.

At first Kaufman simply birded randomly, wherever in the
United States his lifts took him. But at the start of 1972, inspired
by Fisher and Peterson's *Wild America* (see Chapter 11) he decided to have a go at the 'Big One' – Stuart Keith's record of 598
species in the USA and Canada in a single calendar year. An expatriate Englishman, Keith had established his record a decade and a
half before, in 1956, narrowly failing to reach the 600 mark. As a
result, like the athlete's four-minute mile or the test pilot's sound
barrier, this figure had acquired an iconic status.

So in January 1972, the seventeen-year-old Kaufman packed
his bag and headed south to the Texas coast, on his quest to break
the 600 mark. He lasted just one month, when he heard the crush-
ing news that the record had not just been broken, but shattered,
in the previous year of 1971. What made it even worse was that the
new record holder, with an extraordinary total of 626 species, was
barely older than Kaufman himself; a college kid from
Pennsylvania named Ted Parker.

No account of the history and development of birding could
fail to mention Theodore A. Parker III, known to his friends and
birders the world over simply as Ted. In the forty years he spent
on this planet he became the acknowledged world expert on the
birds of that incredible continent, South America, home to almost
two-fifths of the world's bird species.

Roger Tory Peterson once described Parker as having 'the
best ears I've ever known . . . one in a million', and it was said that
he could recognize four *thousand* species of bird by sound alone.
Even in the early 1970s, Parker was already showing the energy,
skill and above all ability that would make him one of the world's
top birders.

Despite Parker's 'big year' record, and Kaufman's growing
sense of inferiority at this renaissance man of birding, the two
young men became great friends, and Parker himself encouraged

Kaufman to have a go at beating his record in 1973. So once again, as New Year dawned, Kaufman embarked on his quest. His first bird was a Ruby-crowned Kinglet, flitting nervously outside the bedroom window of a log cabin in Portal, Arizona. He got up, dressed, and went out into the snowy mountain landscape – and didn't stop for another twelve months.

Kingbird Highway is all about discovery: not just of America's birds, but that of a young man learning about the ups and downs of life. Today, it seems to come from a lost age of innocence, where, despite the occasional hazard of hitchhiking with drunk drivers, America was a much safer, friendlier place than today.

By the close of the year, Kaufman had travelled 69,000 miles, and seen 671 species: 45 more than Ted Parker's 1971 mark. However, his close rival that year, Floyd Murdoch, beat him, because despite recording two fewer species in total, under the arcane rules of listing he had seen more species than Kaufman in the area recognized by the American Ornithologists' Union.

Kaufman did break one record, however: along the way he spent less than a thousand dollars – more birds per buck than anyone would ever achieve again. He ended up in Freeport, Texas, where while taking part in the local Christmas Bird Count he was washed off the town's pier in a storm and almost drowned. Having been bandaged up by the kindly waitresses in the local Shrimp Hut diner, he went straight back out on the jetty again.

In the book's epilogue, he reflects on this extraordinary, driven obsession:

> Now, when I look back many years later, as though from a great distance, I can still see that young man standing out on the jetty. And at least on my better days, I can see myself standing there with him: shaken by experience, perhaps, but still confident that the light will be better, that the birds will come in closer, that we will see everything more clearly at last, before the day is over.

Kenn Kaufman went on to become one of North America's most respected birders, writing several books including the Peterson guide to *Advanced Birding*. Tragically, Ted Parker and his companion Alwyn Gentry were killed on 3 August 1993, when

A Bird in the Bush

their light aircraft crashed into a mountainside in Ecuador. Their loss to conservation and birding was quite simply incalculable: it was said that they carried in their heads two-thirds of the unpublished knowledge of South America's birds. 'Ted Parker was not destined to slow down, ever', runs the touching dedication of *Kingbird Highway*, Kenn Kaufman's tribute to his old friend: 'He was like a runaway train, except that he was running on tracks that he had planned out for himself, and he knew exactly where he was going.'

THIS SENSE of freedom – of every possibility being open – was not, however, uppermost in the minds of most young people on the other side of the Atlantic. By 1973, just six years after the 1967 'summer of love', Britain had exchanged a mood of heady optimism, in which anything and everything seemed possible, for the gloom of the oil crisis: petrol rationing, power cuts, and the three day week. If the sixties was the wild party, the seventies was the morning after – complete with a raging hangover.

The early 1970s was not a good time to be growing up in Britain, especially if you had an interest which marked you out from the crowd, like birdwatching. In a backlash against the 1960s, conformity and intolerance were now the watchwords for Britain's youth. Tribal allegiances were in, and any departure from the convention, in appearance, dress or habits, was very definitely out. If you did spend your spare time doing something as deeply unfashionable as watching birds, you certainly did not admit it, as birder Neil McKillop recalls:

> When I left (or should I say dropped out of) school, there were many distractions to take my mind off birding. At the time (the early 1970s), sex, drugs and rock'n'roll were far more alluring and as old passport photos bear witness, I was a full paid-up weekend hippie. As such, the last thing I would mention to anyone was that I enjoyed watching birds – it just wasn't, well, cool!

What undoubtedly *was* cool was music. Music defined 1970s youth better than anything: if you liked the same music, you could be mates, if you didn't, you couldn't. What could be more natural than to discuss song lyrics? But for McKillop and another local lad named Phil Hurrell, this proved to be a seminal experience. At the time, McKillop was working in a local record shop in his home town of Watford, and Hurrell was one of the regular clientele.

One day, McKillop put on a record by Roy Harper called *Stormcock*, which featured a photo of a Mistle Thrush nest on the back cover, together with a sleeve note reference to *The Observer's Book of Birds*. He casually mentioned this to Hurrell, and also referred to another song which featured a recording of the song of a Blackcap.

> Phil looked at me curiously, and then, in a low voice, mumbled, 'Are you interested in birds, then?'
>
> That moment, I recognised a fellow enthusiast – albeit a closet one. I admitted my passion, and the rest is history. The two of us travelled the length and breadth of Britain in search of birds – at least until Phil decided that he needed something more exotic and headed off on a world birding tour!

During the dark days of the early 1970s, any young, aspiring birder must have felt as if they would spend their whole life in the closet, afraid to admit their passion for fear of ridicule from their peers. But in society as a whole, a more tolerant mood was gradually beginning to emerge.

For this generation of birders, who came of age in the late 1970s, the world was for a brief but glorious spell their oyster. Over the following decade, the pastime was to undergo an extraordinary explosion, led primarily by these baby-boomers. Eventually, after many adventures, false starts and blind alleys, they would help create the world of birding as we know it today.

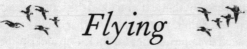

CHAPTER THIRTEEN

Flying

How Birding went Global

Farnes and Bass Rock, inclusive of travel, board and lodging.
7 days for £51 10s.

Ornitholidays catalogue (1966)

Travelling from Chile, you will fly on to the Dawson-
Lambert Glacier and spend days with breeding Emperor
Penguins in their icy home. 15 days from £15,169.

WildWings catalogue (2003/4)

I N EARLY AUTUMN 1978, two friends set off from suburban
Surrey on the 'hippie trail', an epic, overland trip of more
than five thousand miles from Britain to Nepal, via Europe,
Turkey, Iran, Pakistan, Afghanistan and India.

Nigel Redman and Chris Murphy were no different from the
thousands of other young people who, still influenced by the 'tune
in, turn on and drop out' ethos of the 1960s, had decided to give
up their day jobs and head off in search of eastern promise. Aged
twenty-five, Redman had been working as an accountant for a
publishing firm, and was still living with his parents in the Surrey
commuter belt. Chris Murphy, born in Liverpool but of Irish
origin, was a couple of years younger.

These young men were typical of their generation: with
ordinary backgrounds but extraordinary dreams. As they
embarked on their ten-month odyssey around Asia, only one thing
marked them out from the rest of the long-haired, casually
dressed crowd. Stowed away in each of their rucksacks, along
with a route map, water bottle and a change of underpants, was a
pair of binoculars.

For as well as the obvious attractions of foreign travel, Nigel
and Chris planned to see as many different species of bird as

possible. This they did. After seeing the first new bird, a Black Stork at Istanbul, they achieved a final total of almost 1000 species, most of them 'lifers'.

They were not the first to embark on such a trip: twelve years earlier, in 1966, Richard Porter had walked into his local station and asked for a single to Istanbul: 'The clerk didn't bat an eyelid, but just asked for the 18 pounds and ten shillings. I went on the Orient Express'.

Redman and Murphy did not travel by quite such luxurious means. They began by hitch-hiking down to Dover, then after taking the ferry to Ostend they hitched across Europe to Turkey, where they spent a month enjoying the spectacle of raptor migration across the Bosphorus. But the lure of adventure was still strong, so they paid sixty US dollars each for a place on a 'hippie bus' travelling to India via Afghanistan.

For two well-spoken, middle-class boys from England, the bus was a major culture shock – though a very agreeable one, as Redman remembers:

> There were 35 people on the bus, of 10 nationalities, plus one dog! It was a brilliant time – tremendous fun and a strong community spirit. At nights, we stopped in small towns, where most people found cheap hotels, but Chris and I slept on the bus each night to save money. An American-Armenian was the self-styled cook and concocted wonderful meals in a huge pan on a camping-gas stove in the bus – sometimes while we were travelling! Loud rock music prevailed, and I particularly recall 'Hotel California' by the Eagles. People hung out their washing inside the bus to dry, and sometimes the bus got so dusty that you could not see from back to front.

And in those free and easy times, even their interest in birds was not considered all that eccentric: 'Most people were intrigued that Chris and I were birders and often asked us what the more obvious birds were. We were even allowed to make the odd emergency stop to see a good bird. And at border checkpoints we told customs we were all birders – despite having only two pairs of bins between us!'

True to the spirit of the time, one female Scandinavian passenger 'played the field' with most of the bus's passengers, though as Redman wistfully recalls, 'She didn't appear to fancy birders'.

In Teheran, the bus stopped for a three-day break, and the two lads visited an old friend of Redman's who lived and worked there. This was a volatile time – growing tensions meant the authorities had introduced a night-time curfew, there were daily riots, and just six weeks later the old regime finally toppled and the Shah left the country.

Once the bus reached the border with Afghanistan, the acquisition of (legal) hashish lightened the mood of the bus and its passengers. Then Murphy got very bad dysentery, which temporarily reduced their opportunities for birding. Soon afterwards the bus reached Kabul, where the two lads parted company with their fellow travellers. They had a one-month visa for Afghanistan, and were determined to use it to the full. Highlights included seeing the country's only endemic species – Afghan Snowfinch – and watching the local sport of Buzkhashi, which involved warriors on horseback dragging around a beheaded calf.

After another epic journey by bus and taxi, and a difficult moment when they were briefly arrested in Jalalabad for birding too close to an army camp, in late 1978 the pair finally reached India. During the next few months they did some serious birding throughout the region, including visits to the famous wetland reserve at Bharatpur in northern India, the Kathmandu Valley and Chitwan National Park in Nepal, all over Thailand, then back to Nepal again.

The trip was packed with highs and lows. The latter included having Murphy's money-belt slashed and all his money taken; Redman having his boots stolen while he was using them as a pillow; and the usual hazard of 'Delhi belly' from time to time. But this did not deter them from birding: 'I reckon we suffered from the usual shits about 1-2 days per month, but it never stopped us going out birding. On one occasion in Afghanistan, I was so weak that I could barely walk, but I still went into the field, in case I missed something.'

An even worse moment came when Redman was chased by a pack of dogs on a Thai beach and bitten by one of them:

> I was concerned about rabies and went to a doctor who told me not to worry. I sought a second opinion, and the doctor said I should have the anti-rabies jabs. He fixed this up for me. He wrote a letter in Thai which I had to take to a hospital each day and this got me my injections, free of charge. I had to have daily injections in the stomach for fourteen days (a huge needle of vaccine!). So as not to disturb my birding, I used to go in the middle of the day so that I could bird in the morning and late afternoon.

Despite these discomforts and setbacks, Redman's abiding memories of the trip are the camaraderie of his fellow travellers (they bumped into a group of four young British birders in a bookshop in Delhi, and teamed up for the next three months), and the extraordinary hospitality shown towards them by the local people. Looking back, it is hard to believe that two scruffy-looking, penniless young men attracted such kindness and generosity.

For example, someone had given them the name of a friend who was a British major at a Gurkha army camp, but when they arrived it turned out the major had been posted elsewhere. Fortunately, the guards contacted his successor:

> It turned out that this major was slightly interested in birds (and also in golf which Chris played), and as their children had just returned to school in England, they invited us to stay with them for a few days. It was heaven! We birded the forests with the major and Chris played golf with him. We had a free run of their fridge which was well stocked with cold beer, and they even threw a splendid garden party, with us as the guests of honour!

Local ornithologists were also very generous with their knowledge and contacts. Redman had written to Thailand's leading conservationist, Dr Boonsong Lekagul, who not only took them on birding trips, but also gave them his business card on the back of which he had scribbled a few words in Thai:

We were told to show this to park staff at the various reserves around the country that we were to visit and they would look after us. It worked a treat! We never had to pay for any accommodation outside Bangkok, often got free meals and at one reserve were even loaned a small motorbike!

After almost a year on the road, money was finally running out, and they were feeling pangs of homesickness. The overland route was now closed, so they took a flight with the cheap Soviet airline Aeroflot, via Baghdad and a two-day stopover in Moscow, to Amsterdam. In July 1979, after a gruelling ten months away, they finally arrived back on British soil.

While Nigel Redman was in Nepal, he received a letter forwarded by his father. It came from Mark Beaman, a young Lancashire based birder who was planning to set up his own bird tour company specializing in out of the way places, who wanted information on good birding sites:

> When I got back, I met Mark and as a result he asked me to co-lead a tour to Morocco for the newly formed travel company Birdquest. I did another that year (1982) and two more tours in 1983. From 1984, I went full time. At that time, my experience of Asian birds was relatively unusual, and it stood me a good stead as a Birdquest leader. I haven't looked back!

He certainly has not. Since then he has made about eighty-five trips as a tour leader, visiting seventy countries in all seven continents. Including a few private tours and the odd business visit with a spot of birding attached, he has made almost 100 foreign birding trips – and seen about 4,500 different species – almost half the world's total. There can be few better examples of how a passion for birds transformed the life of a man who, in his early twenties, was destined to remain an accountant for the rest of his days.

ALTHOUGH Nigel Redman and Chris Murphy's overland trip was exceptional in its length and scope, it was not all that unusual for birders to be travelling abroad during this period. Changes in society had opened up opportunities for people of all social classes to travel abroad for the very first time.

Foreign travel, for so long beyond the reach of the average Briton, had undergone a massive expansion during the 1960s and 1970s. This was partly a response to the changes in work patterns during the twentieth century, during which working hours had been gradually reduced, and the five-day week had become established as the norm. At the start of the century, holidays were also very rare, but by 1945 ten million people had won the right to two weeks paid leave a year. By the late 1980s this had become the standard, and ninety-nine per cent of full-time workers were entitled to at least four weeks paid annual leave.

Along with more free time came more money in people's pockets – what eventually became known as 'disposable income'. Until World War II only the so-called 'leisured classes' holidayed abroad; by 1983, more than 18 million people travelled abroad on holiday every year (a figure that by 1994 almost doubled to more than 34 million – well over half of Britain's total population).

Birders, too, had taken up the new opportunities for foreign travel. Many combined birding with a family holiday, taking advantage of the fact that many of the most popular and accessible package destinations – such as Mallorca, the Algarve and the Greek islands – were also top sites for watching birds. The pages of *World of Birds*, a magazine which appeared in the early 1970s, included articles like the one by S. G. Perry, about a family holiday to the Greek island of Rhodes:

> Family holidays present a challenge to the ornithologist –
> namely to strike a fair balance between sightseeing, beach
> activities and bird-watching.
>
> The first impressions we gained of the birdlife were from our
> hotel balcony. Tired and hot from our flight, we sipped refreshing
> ice-cold beer, with the sun beating down and the cruise liners
> lying idly offshore. Swifts and House Sparrows filled the air, a few

Collared Doves pattered around the flat roofs, and over the harbour, the occasional Herring Gull flew by, all relatively English.

It was left to the sight of lizards on the ramparts of the old palace to confirm what the heat and plants told us – that we were in foreign parts.

Things soon improved, however, and by the end of his holiday the author had seen a good range of the exotic wonders the island had to offer. Nevertheless, his total of 'just short of sixty species' is well below what birders would expect today, even with a family in tow. But to really get to grips with foreign destinations and their birdlife, something more formal was required: the organized bird-watching tour. And following the early success of Ornitholidays back in the 1960s, several more companies had now entered the market.

By the early 1980s, the bird tour industry had developed beyond the wildest dreams of its pioneers. *British Birds* published its first directory of ornithological tours in October 1982, featuring seven companies, which between them visited destinations in six continents. Costs were still relatively high, but the tour companies could claim, with some justification, that the advantages of a tour led by a top birding guide with extensive local knowledge, which might more than double the number of species seen compared with a 'DIY trip', made them excellent value.

Travelling abroad not only lengthened birders' life lists, it also drew their attention to an example of very British parochial-ism: the use of English bird names. Until Britons began to venture abroad, it simply did not occur to them that referring to a species simply as 'Swallow', 'Heron' or 'Wheatear' might be confusing – especially in an area where several species from the same family might occur. Eventually, as a result of the rise in foreign travel, several names received qualifying adjectives such as 'Northern Wheatear' and 'Barn Swallow'. Even in today's 'global birding 'village', however, the British still use 'diver' and 'skua', while the Americans prefer 'loon' and 'jaeger'.

Another effect of foreign travel was that the notion of what constituted a 'British' bird began to expand. When the replacement for Witherby's famous *Handbook* was announced, it did not simply cover the birds of Britain, or even Europe, but a new zoogeographical area known as the 'Western Palearctic'. The first volume of *The Handbook of the Birds of Europe, the Middle East, and North Africa: the Birds of the Western Palearctic* (usually known by its acronym *BWP*) finally appeared in 1977.

Like all great projects, *BWP* had a slow and difficult birth, with the first volume appearing much later than planned. Hugh Elliott's review in *British Birds* summed up the scale of the operation:

> With the publication of the first volume of *BWP*, the size and scope of the enterprise can at last be fully appreciated . . .
>
> A book, which like its predecessor, sets out to 'review and present clearly the entire up-to-date knowledge' of the birds of a whole region, can scarcely fail to have very wide appeal. *BWP* will – and indeed must – serve as the major source book for ornithologists until well into the twenty-first century.

However, not everyone was quite so impressed. Criticisms focused on the variable standard of the colour plates, and the almost impenetrable text. In attempting to include everything known to science, the editors had managed to produce a work which was far less accessible than the *Handbook*. Their dilemma was almost impossible to solve: the vast expansion of knowledge, together with the increased geographical area (and therefore number of species) that required coverage, meant that the spare, clear prose of the *Handbook* was impossible to reproduce.

The ninth and final volume of *BWP* finally rolled off the printing presses in the late 1990s, twenty years after the first. Soon afterwards, the cost of a complete set had plummeted to just £200 – less than a quarter of the recommended retail price. With hindsight, it can be said that *BWP* was a victim of bad timing: appearing just before a technological and communications revolution which threatened to make such encyclopaedic works redundant; at a time when the information contained in several weighty volumes could be stored on a single CD-ROM; and when the explosion in detailed specialist bird books meant that unlike the original *Handbook*, much of the information it contained could be found elsewhere.

That might be a fair assessment, were it not for the fact that another expensive, weighty, multi-volume set of books – a series which did not begin until 1992, towards the end of the *BWP* cycle – has been a huge commercial and critical success.

Fifteen years after the first appearance of *BWP*, another major project was launched. *Handbook of the Birds of the World* (also known as *HBW*) is probably the most ambitious undertaking ever in the field of natural history publishing: by the time the sixteenth and final volume appears, around 2010, all ten thousand or so of the world's species of birds will have been covered.

When news of this project leaked out in the early 1990s, most birders were frankly sceptical. Many thought that a series which attempted to cover all the world's 10,000 or so species (compared to fewer than 1000 featured in *BWP*) would be either superficial, or cumbersome, or both. But the real belly-laugh came when they heard who would be producing the series: an unknown publishing house based in Barcelona, Lynx Edicions, run by two Catalans and a Scotsman.

Ten years later, we can see how wrong the sceptics were: *HBW* has been a huge success. The story of how it came to be published is an extraordinary tale of persistence and vision. In the early 1980s, Josep del Hoyo, a country doctor from Catalonia, called his friend Jordi Sargatal and told him of his idea to produce a comprehensive work covering all the world's birds. Sargatal's reaction was short and sweet: he told del Hoyo that he was completely crazy. The idea was put on the back burner, but five years later, during a wild goose watching trip to Holland, Josep nagged his friend solidly for twenty-four hours. Finally, he agreed, and the epic project was underway.

Lacking the funds to launch the project themselves, the two men approached a friend, Ramon Mascort. A lawyer and entrepreneur, Mascort promised them financial backing. With the recruitment of Scotsman Andy Elliott – not only an ornithologist but also an expert linguist – the project was underway. *HBW* has not been without its problems. The editors soon discovered that for many of the world's bird species there was little or no reliable information. So they became pioneering researchers, travelling the world to unearth new information.

The success of the project is, quite simply, down to professionalism. There are very few mistakes; the texts are well written, authoritative and interesting to read; and the illustrations (especially the photographs) are superb. Even more importantly, by drawing attention to their plight, *HBW* is contributing to saving some species from almost certain extinction. As del Hoyo remarked, in an interview with *BBC Wildlife Magazine*:

> We have a saying in Spain: you cannot love what you do not know. If a bird goes extinct before anyone has ever photographed it, or written about it, you do not really care. But once you have seen how beautiful and fascinating it is, you do care. We hope that now people have the facts, they will do something to save the species before it is too late.

THE PUBLICATION of *HBW* and innumerable other bird identification and bird finding guides means that birders exploring remote areas are far better equipped than in the early days of global travel. Nevertheless, they still face a myriad of risks, hazards and even life-threatening dangers when travelling abroad, especially when they venture – as so many do – off the beaten track.

In their passion to see ever more elusive species, and travel to more and more inaccessible places, birders have always run greater risks than the average package tourist. Add to this the false sense of invulnerability that comes from looking at the world through a pair of binoculars, and the single-minded obsession to get the bird at all costs, and you have a potentially lethal combination.

Sometimes they have simply been the victim of bad luck – in the wrong place at the wrong time. In May 1976, ornithologist Stephanie Tyler, her husband and young children were captured by rebel forces in northern Ethiopia, and held hostage for eight months. Characteristically, she made good use of her time by watching bird behaviour – later publishing her observations. Her only regret was that her binoculars were confiscated by the rebels.

A few years later, in the early 1980s, two Britons were arrested while birding in Turkey, near the military zone by the border with Greece. Incidents such as this have always been a hazard for birders travelling in countries where people have little or no appreciation of the notion of watching birds for pleasure. Birders are not the only people targeted: in autumn 2001 a group of British plane spotters was arrested and tried in Greece on charges of espionage, which they hotly denied.

Like so many birders abroad, the plane spotters failed to understand that what may appear perfectly normal to them can be received with blank incomprehension by people from another culture. As journalist Ian Jack commented in the *Guardian*:

> The idea must be remarkable in Greece that grown men – they are almost always men and 'grown', with that word's implication of physical rather than mental development – would travel to a distant country simply to see a rare kind of aeroplane for no other reason than to record the fact that they had seen it. In Greece, this isn't normal behaviour, and when behaviour isn't normal it tends, in the minds of the witness, to head towards other categories: the suspicious, the criminal.

It was precisely this lack of awareness of how their actions would be perceived which led to the tragic deaths of two young British birders in Peru, in 1991. Timothy Andrews and Michael Entwistle had crossed a river by ferry to look for Oilbirds (an elusive and mainly nocturnal species) – despite having been warned that this would take them into the territory of one of the world's most ruthless guerrilla organizations, 'Sendero Luminoso', or the Shining Path.

Suspected of being Drug Enforcement Administration agents,

one of them was shot and killed trying to avoid capture, while the other was held captive for two days before being shot in cold blood. A similar fate was narrowly avoided by British birder Tim Cowley a few years later, when he was held for nearly four months by a guerrilla group in Colombia, before finally being rescued by a police anti-kidnapping unit. Cowley was well treated, his captors even allowing him to use his binoculars. During captivity he managed to record eighty-eight species, including twenty-nine lifers and six birds new to the region. He also kept detailed notes on feeding patterns of hummingbirds, but unfortunately these were lost during his dramatic rescue.

Some people, like Jonathan Evan Maslow, go out of their way to seek out danger. In July 1983 the American writer and his companion, a professional photographer, set out on a trip to Guatemala. At the time this was one of the most dangerous places in the world, where corruption and guerrilla warfare thrived, and any travellers – especially two Americans carrying photographic gear – were in potential danger as soon as they set foot in the country. Their quest was to see the bird which is the national symbol of Guatemala, the rare and beautiful Resplendent Quetzal.

The pair not only survived but succeeded, and the resulting 'essay in political ornithology' was published in 1986, under the intriguing title *Bird of Life, Bird of Death*. The juxtaposition referred to the contrast between the rapid and potentially irreversible decline of the Quetzal – the bird of life – and the equally rapid growth in the population of the 'Zopilote' or Black Vulture – the bird of death. In a funny and moving episode, Maslow engaged in conversation with a young boy he nicknames 'Ratón Mickey' (the Spanish for Mickey Mouse):

> He asked, 'Did you get good photos of the Zopilotes here?'
> 'Plenty'.
> 'There are more Zopilotes here now than there used to be.'
> 'Is that so? Why, do you think?'
> 'I don't know,' he said. 'But I think the Zopilote has a great future in our country. It eats the dead things. And here we have more and more dead things all the time.'

For others, danger could come completely out of the blue. Alan Turner from Leeds died from heatstroke while trekking through the Australian desert in search of a rare bird. And in December 1984, three Midlands birdwatchers were among four people who died in the Gambia, when a river-boat hit a sand-bank and overturned. The survivors sat on the upturned hull for more than six hours before rescue came. Two months later, another well-known birder also met his death, killed by a tiger in India.

David Hunt summed himself up in the title of his (posthumously published) autobiography, *Confessions of a Scilly Birdman*. The dreadful pun was justified by the fact that, since first arriving on the Isles of Scilly in the mid-1960s, he had firmly established himself as 'the man on the spot', giving slide shows and guided tours for locals and visitors. In his *British Birds* obituary, Peter Grant observed that 'living in Scilly, David was probably known personally by more birdwatchers than anyone else'.

Hunt was, as his friend Bill Oddie noted after his death, 'pretty abrasive' – a man who spoke his mind and did not suffer fools gladly. He was also a fine field birder and an experienced tour leader. Like many people who earn their living from birding, he had a colourful past. He had brought his young family to Scilly as a last resort, after working as an under-gardener on the roof of Derry and Toms department store in London, and before that, having a career as a jazz musician. Looking back, it is tempting to say that he made a habit of being in the right place at the wrong time. For instance, he had formed his own group, Dave Hunt's Rhythm and Blues Band in the early 1960s, at the very time that the musical world was turned upside down by the arrival of the Beatles.

Indeed, he played his own small part in rock history. first, Ray Davies (the genius behind the Kinks, and 'father of Britpop'), and then Charlie Watts (soon to become the drummer of the Rolling Stones) appeared briefly in his band. Then, during the bitter winter of 1962-63, he finally decided enough was enough, and surrendered the band's regular Richmond gig to a newly formed group playing in a style detested by the jazz purists. The new band's lead singer, whom Hunt liked despite their difference in musical tastes, was a peculiar-looking chap named Michael Philip Jagger; the band, the Rolling Stones.

A couple of decades later, in February 1985, David Hunt had matured into an experienced bird tour leader, on his umpteenth visit to India. One morning, while leading the group around Corbett National Park, he wandered off the path, telling his companions to walk on towards the waiting coach. Minutes later, there was a terrifying scream. After a brief search, his body was found. He had been killed by a single bite to the neck from a tiger.

The definitive story of Hunt's last moments was eventually revealed by Bill Oddie in his book *Follow That Bird!* It was already known that he had seen fresh tiger prints on the path, and had gone off, apparently to try to photograph a bird. In fact, he was hoping to see – and photograph – a wild tiger:

> When David's body was recovered, so was his camera. Later on, the slides were developed . . . The first one is a nice close-up of a Spotted Owlet sitting on a branch . . . Then he must have heard a noise behind him, or maybe just sensed that he was not alone. Keeping crouched, he turned and saw a tiger pacing to and fro at the edge of the clearing. The next slide is of the tiger. It is some way away, walking to the right. On the next picture it is walking to the left. In the next one, it is facing the camera. In the next, it has begun to move forward, still looking straight at the lens. The next is closer. Then closer. And closer still. The final picture is of a frame-filling shot of the tiger's head, eyes blazing and teeth exposed in a snarl. If David had kept shooting on his motor-drive, the whole thing must have happened in barely ten seconds. Crouched behind a camera, looking through the viewfinder and especially when using a telephoto lens, you don't realise how close your subject has got. Neither, at the time, do you care. All you are focusing on is the picture. Press cameramen in war situations call it 'camera blindness'. It has proved fatal before.

No doubt it will again. Just as it did for the two young birders who ignored the warnings of Peruvian villagers and crossed into enemy territory; just as it did for the young man from Leeds who died of dehydration in the Australian bush. And just as it has so nearly done for so many birders, who can look back on narrow escapes from danger and wonder what might have happened. Most are like David Hunt – oblivious to danger when pursuing their quarry – but with one important difference: they get away with their lives.

Not all foreign birding experiences are quite so sombre. Monthly bird magazines are full of traveller's tales of visits to exotic parts, together with long lists of potential species found there. Today, there is a whole industry of professional bird tour companies which offer trips to virtually every part of the world. To take just a few examples from their lavishly illustrated catalogues: Birdquest travel to Madagascar, Burma and Antarctica; Limosa visit Namibia, Bhutan and Arctic Lapland; while Sunbird go to Papua New Guinea, Ethiopia and the Dominican Republic. One travel company, WildWings, even offers journeys into outer space, though at more than £13 million a trip the return in terms of 'ticks per buck' is not all that good.

Closer to home, Bedfordshire-based company Sunbird has pioneered two developments in foreign bird tours. In the 1980s the company launched a series of relatively low-cost packages to holiday destinations that are also excellent bases for birding, such as Eilat in Israel, Goa in India and even (stretching the 'package tour' concept a little!) Beidaihe in China. These offered a halfway house between the fully organized bird tour and a self-organized trip, giving participants the advantage of some expert guidance with the freedom of exploring on their own.

The other concept, the programme of 'Birds & . . . ' trips, acknowledges both the fact that not all birders are accompanied by equally obsessive partners; and that even the keenest birders may want to experience other aspects of the country they are visiting. As a result, Sunbird now runs 'Birds & History' in Egypt or India; 'Birds & Music' in Austria, Finland or Hungary; and 'Birds & Butterflies' in northern Spain. The notion that birders might actually want to stop watching birds to visit the Pyramids, the Taj Mahal, or the opera in Prague was a gamble, but one that has clearly paid off for the company, as their brochure reveals:

> Most birdwatchers have interests other than birds . . . there are few who would not pause to admire a bright-coloured butterfly or an unusual mammal if they were to encounter one on a birding trip. Others equate the beauty of birds with art or music, while for some it is the intriguing reminders of history to be found at many good birdwatching sites that inspire them to a greater appreciation of the environment, and perhaps allow them to look at birds in a slightly different light, seeing them as common living witnesses that have been present through the ages.

The leader of many of these tours is Bryan Bland, who combines a voracious enthusiasm for birds and birding with a breadth of appreciation for other aspects of culture not always found amongst birders. With his bushy beard, and usually clad in a pair of shorts and an artist's smock – whatever the weather – Bland is an unmistakable figure. But judging him on appearance alone would be a great mistake: he is one of the best field birders alive, and delights in showing groups of American birders a range of rare British birds, historical buildings and cultural curiosities on his annual tour of Britain.

He is also a brilliant speaker and raconteur: he once gave a lecture at the BTO on the perils of misidentification, in which he told a story against himself, illustrated with his own cartoon drawings. While in Morocco, he had finally identified a distant figure as a displaying Houbara Bustard, but not before misidentifying the bird twice: first as two dogs fighting, then as an Arab on a bicycle!

Bryan Bland is a man of great depth and contrasts, proving that birding does not have to be a one-dimensional experience: despite having seen more birds in Britain than almost anyone else, for five years in the 1960s he restricted his birding to within a five mile radius of his Surrey home. He also recognizes that although birds are a vital component of his life, other things are important too. As he once said: 'I've managed for 49 years without a White's Thrush. I doubt if I could last a month without Mozart'.

Nᴏᴛ ᴀʟʟ birders are quite so well-balanced in their approach to life. In recent years a new breed has emerged, known as 'world listers', whose aim is to see as many of the world's bird species as possible. Some are genuinely skilled birders, with years of experience visiting far-flung parts of the world, often while leading organized tours. But others are wealthy amateurs known disparagingly as 'dudes', with little or no expertise in the field.

These single-minded men (and occasionally women) hire the services of expert guides in order to 'clean up' – to see every possible rare and sought-after species at a particular locality. They pay handsomely for the privilege – sometimes handing out thousands of dollars in the quest to see a single elusive bird. For the guides themselves, who are often struggling to earn a living as artists or tour leaders in order to support their birding travels, world listers offer an opportunity to visit inaccessible places while being paid above the odds for doing so.

Bird artist Clive Byers spends part of the year guiding wealthy American birders around the jungles of Peru in search of ever more elusive species. He compares their constant need to see new species to a drug habit: 'They just need to see new birds – if a few hours pass without a tick they start getting all twitchy! They see it and they are happy – for a while. Then, a few hours later, the buzz has gone and they need another hit.'

At times Clive has questioned whether he wants to carry on doing the job at all, as despite the rewards it can reduce birding to a sterile quest for individual 'ticks', to the exclusion of all else. How much did one particularly difficult – and extremely wealthy – client pay for the privilege of Clive's expertise? 'Not enough!'

World listing has a long history. On his 'worldtwitch' website, US birder John Wall has suggested that the first example of a birder travelling abroad to see a particular species (as opposed to simply wanting to see as many different species as possible) dates back to the early 1950s, when an unnamed birder travelled to the high-lands of north-west Mexico in order to see the Imperial

Woodpecker – now almost certainly extinct. Clive Byers himself achieved a similar one-upmanship when, in December 1978, he and a group of friends travelled to Lake Atitlan in Guatemala to see the eponymous Atitlan Grebe. Ten years or so later, the species had finally become extinct.

According to John Wall, the first person to set out specifically to try to see all the world's birds was Stuart Keith. Born in Hertfordshire in 1931, Keith first became interested in birding towards the end of World War II, when he borrowed a monocular from his sister to watch birds in their garden. During the early 1950s, military service in Korea gave him an opportunity to see more exotic birds, and he became hooked. After graduating from Oxford in 1955 he travelled to the USA, where the following year he and his brother Anthony successfully broke Fisher and Peterson's record for the number of species seen in a single year.

A career back in the City of London was put on hold – at first temporarily, then permanently – and he eventually settled in New York City, where he worked in the ornithology department of the American Museum of Natural History, and became a founder and first president of the American Birding Association. Of his many achievements, perhaps the greatest was to oversee, along with Hilary Fry and Emil Urban, the mammoth seven-volume book series *The Birds of Africa*, which he finally finished in 2002, a few months before his death.

He began world listing seriously in the 1960s, helped by several visits to Africa. By 1973 he became the first person to reach the halfway mark – roughly 4,300 of what was then recognized as approximately 8,600 species. At the time his nearest challenger was Peter Alden, an American bird tour leader, with roughly 3,850 species. But although Keith carried on seeing new species around the globe, this eventually took second place to his busy life as a professional ornithologist, and by the time of his death his final total of 6,500 or so had been overtaken by several other world listers. Unlike some more obsessive birders, he also found time to enjoy life's other pleasures, including playing the piano, appreciating art, and conversation with friends.

Stuart Keith died doing what he loved best – birding in a new and exotic location. He was on his first trip to the Micronesian islands of the Pacific, aiming to see several new birds. He saw his final 'lifer', the Caroline Islands Ground-dove, the day before he died.

STUART KEITH's journey, from watching birds on the lawn as a child to his final trip to the other side of the world, sums up the way in which birding went global in the span of a single lifetime. Until the 1960s and 1970s, few British or American birders ventured beyond their native shores in search of birds; and when they did, it was usually to safe and predictable destinations such as France or Spain, Costa Rica or the Caribbean. When Nigel Redman and Chris Murphy set off on their great adventure a quarter of a century ago, they were pioneering a new form of travel – with the emphasis on seeing birds whatever the discomfort and inconvenience to themselves.

Today, a birder wishing to add a range of Asian species to his or her world list can simply sign up for a tour to Goa in India or Beidaihe in China, costing around £1000 for two weeks. Even the former Soviet Union has opened up: in the late 1970s, Mark Beaman recalls having to endure mind-numbingly dull visits to collective farms, in the hope that they could persuade their official guide to stop off on the way back to look for birds. Today, his company Birdquest does regular trips to places such as Kazakhstan, Ussuriland and Sakhalin Island – destinations once beyond even the most ambitious birder's imagination.

So as the world has shrunk in terms of ease of travel, so the opportunities available to the global birder have multiplied. But is the world lister, struggling to see the two or three species they 'need' while ignoring any other birds around them, happier than the two lads coping with the perils of dysentery and wild dogs in order to get out and watch birds? One suspects not.

CHAPTER FOURTEEN

Twitching

How Birding became an Obsession

Twitcher (n). A bird-watcher whose main aim is to collect
sightings of rare birds.

Oxford English Dictionary

IN FEBRUARY 2001, on ITV's hit quiz show *Who Wants to
be a Millionaire?*, host Chris Tarrant posed the following
question:

Which of these is a popular term for birdwatcher?
a) Twitcher; b) Jerker; c) Blinker; d) Jumper

The contestant was not absolutely sure of the answer, so
took advantage of one of the show's three lifelines, and asked the
audience. As background music built up the tension, heads were
scratched, brows furrowed, and fingers pressed electronic keypads.
Then the audience's answers were revealed. An extraordinary
ninety-three per cent of them got the answer right – proof, if
any were needed, that birding is firmly embedded in the national
consciousness.

However, it also raises a perennial problem: the fact that
'twitcher' is now generally used – by the press and public – as a
synonym for 'birdwatcher', with little regard for its actual meaning. In fact, as the *Oxford English Dictionary* confirms, the word
twitcher has a very specific definition: someone who spends a large
proportion of their free time travelling long distances to see a rare
bird.

The reasons they do so include the hunting instinct, the competitive urge, the satisfaction of 'collecting' by ticking species off
a list, the novelty of seeing something new and unfamiliar, and the
urge to 'complete a set' which can never be truly fulfilled, as

another rare bird will always turn up. There is also a spiritual aspect to the quest, as American birder Leonard Nathan reflected in his witty, personal memoir, *Diary of a Left-handed Birdwatcher*. Having just failed to see a Vermillion Flycatcher, a rare vagrant from Mexico, he pondered why people have the urge to go to see such a bird:

> I mention to Dan that this would have been a first for me. He, of course, has seen the bird many times but never minds seeing it again, particularly out of its normal range.
>
> 'Why out of its normal range?' I ask.
>
> 'Maybe because you see it better that way. Maybe you see a bird more sharply where you don't expect it, where it doesn't belong. It's sort of like seeing it for the first time again.

In an article in *The Times* in March 2000, British twitcher Rupert Kaye gave a more existential reason why he continues to chase after rare birds, despite having a girlfriend, and a business to run: 'I have been into this since I was four years old. It's about dreaming of seeing a certain bird, and then hearing that there is one such mythical creature nearby. But ultimately, I guess you're looking for rational answers to something that just isn't rational.'

People go twitching for social reasons, too. Lifelong friend-ships have been forged on the way to and from twitches – hardly surprising when you consider that four or more people might squeeze into a small family car; spend many hours driving (often overnight) to some far-flung destination; share the anticipation, excitement and eventual failure or success of their quest; and then return home forged by a common bond.

Seeing (or even missing out on) a rare bird creates a sense of camaraderie, and the atmosphere at some twitches is more like a good-natured sporting event than anything normally associated with watching birds. Indeed, the tribal nature of twitching, and its ability to produce a polar opposition of sensations and emotions, is remarkably similar to the obsessive support for Arsenal football club described by Nick Hornby in his celebrated book *Fever Pitch*.

But whether they are eccentric or existential, sad or mad, or simply indulging in an extreme version of a perfectly normal hobby, twitchers continue to travel the length and breadth of Britain in search of rare birds. So how and when did twitching begin?

B EFORE World War II, the few people who did chase after rare birds were known as 'pot-hunters' or 'tally-hunters'. By the 1950s, the term had been refined into 'tick-hunter' or simply 'ticker'. At about this time, a group of young birders based in Sussex started using the term 'twitcher'. One of those involved, Bob Emmett, explained the origins of the word in a letter to *British Birds*:

> 'Twitcher' was coined in the middle 1950s to describe our good friend Howard Medhurst, alias 'The Kid'. Birdwatching transport was very much a two-wheeled affair in those days. John Izzard and his girlfriend, Sheila, rode a Lambretta, whilst Howard rode pillion on my Matchless. On arrival at some distant destination, Howard would totter off the back of my machine and shiveringly light up a cigarette. This performance was repeated so regularly up and down the country that it became synonymous with good birds, and, as we all felt a slight nervous excitement at the uncertainty involved in trying to see a particular bird, it became a standing joke, and John and I would act out a nervous twitch to match Howard's shiverings. This led us to describe a trip to see a rare bird as 'Being on a twitch' . . . It is pretty safe to say, however, that Howard Medhurst was . . . the original twitcher.'

But the concept of 'twitching' is much older than the word itself. It could be argued that it began in the Victorian era, when instead of ticking off rare birds on a list, people shot, stuffed and collected them. Later, as collecting declined, a few hardy souls began to visit distant migration hotspots such as Fair Isle, to seek out rarities for themselves. Even so, as H. G. Alexander recalled in his autobiography, the ordinary birdwatcher simply did not consider the possibility of travelling to see a bird that someone else had found:

Before 1945, the only way to see a rare bird in England was to find it for yourself. The modern practice of rushing off for week-ends to tick off the latest rarity . . . was out of the question. There may have been fifty ardent ornithologists who would go exploring for rare birds, though I doubt if they even numbered fifty; there were certainly not five hundred or a thousand as there are in 1970. And not many bird-spotters had fast cars.

Even after World War II, little had changed. When school-boys Frank Hamilton (later director of RSPB Scotland) and Keith Macgregor found a Wilson's Phalarope in Fife in 1954 – the very first record of this elegant North American wader for Europe, which would nowadays attract a crowd of hundreds – only ten people turned up to see it!

But the following year, an event occurred which would change the face of birdwatching in Britain, and for the first time opened up the possibility of travelling long distances to see rare birds.

With a plumage that looks like it was designed to mimic Joseph's coat of many colours, and a habit of swooping acrobatically through the air in pursuit of its insect food, the European Bee-eater is simply unmistakable. Very rare visitors to Britain, Bee-eaters occasionally overshoot in spring, overflying their breeding grounds around the Mediterranean and turning up in southern England.

So imagine the excitement felt by Sussex birder E. A. Packington, when on 12 June 1955 he came across three of these beautiful birds. In the standard practice of the time, he notified his fellow birdwatchers by post, and it was not until 3 August, more than seven weeks after the initial sighting, that news finally reached James Ferguson-Lees. By then, two active nests had been discovered in a quarry near Brighton.

This was incredible news. Bee-eaters had only attempted to breed in Britain once before, near Edinburgh in 1920, so when the news of the Sussex birds leaked out there was unprecedented interest. People soon began to visit the site; at first in ones and twos, then small groups, and finally in specially organized coach-parties. The nests were guarded round-the-clock by a team of volunteer watchers organized by the RSPB, in order to foil potential egg-collectors, for whom a clutch of British-laid Bee-eater eggs would have been the ultimate prize.

Rare birds had always attracted one or two people eager to add a new species to their list. What made the Bee-eater experience different was the sheer number of visitors: estimated at more than 1000 during their six week stay, including 148 on a single day. The six adults and seven young were seen for the last time on 24 September – in a neat coincidence, by E. A. Packington, the original finder.

The main reason people were prepared to travel long distances to see the Sussex Bee-eaters was that, because they were breeding, there was a good chance they would be there for some time. Most other rarities would have disappeared before news of their presence could be spread, so birdwatchers were generally reluctant to travel very far to see them, and 'crowds' of more than a dozen or so people were unusual. Indeed, even if a rare bird turned up in your local area, you might not hear about it until long after the event.

So when a Dusky Thrush turned up in Hartlepool in December 1959 (only Britain's second record of this Siberian species), just a handful of birders managed to hear about it in time to visit – even though the bird itself stayed for more than two months. Local birder Brian Unwin recalls his frustration when he finally heard the news:

> I had been bird-watching since about 1957 and lived just six miles from Hartlepool, but until later in 1960 I never encountered another birdwatcher in the field, and I did not hear about the Dusky's visit until autumn 1961, about twenty months after it disappeared!

Writing in *British Birds* in 1993, another long-standing birder, Barry Nightingale, pointed out how much things had changed since he had first became interested in seeing rare birds: 'In November 1966, a Brown Thrasher, the first and so far the only Western Palearctic record this century, turned up in Dorset. It stayed for over two months, but I still managed to arrive too late to see it.'

The main reason was that there was no system for communicating news of such rarities, even though as long ago as 1953 James Ferguson-Lees had been broadcasting 'hot news' of rare birds in Eric Simms' *Countryside* radio programmes. As he recalls: 'On the same sort of relationship as that between stagecoaches and present-day communication methods, I like to think of them as the forerunner of all the bird lines and pagers that people use now.'

Sadly for Britain's early twitchers, the idea did not catch on until many decades later.

D URING THE 1960s, rare birds continued to turn up, and people still went to see them, though they usually arrived in ones and twos rather than large crowds. But during the Christmas and New Year holiday of 1970 to 1971 all that changed, when two rare Arctic seabirds – Ivory and Ross's Gulls – were found at the mouth of the River Tyne near Newcastle. This time Brian Unwin heard the news almost instantly, and immediately went along to see the birds – and the birders: 'Before that I'd rarely seen more than ten bird-watchers gathered together – suddenly there were hundreds from all over the country.'

As a journalist, Brian reported on the phenomenon for the *Northern Echo*, and in the RSPB's *Birds* magazine, where he recalled what happened after the second bird arrived on Christmas Eve:

> The floodgates opened. With most of Britain on holiday ... the gulls couldn't have chosen a more crowd-pulling occasion. By midnight most birdwatchers on the Northumberland, Durham and North Yorkshire 'grapevine' knew of the discovery. By Boxing Day the vanguard of what are often referred to in the North East as 'the London tickhunters' were bombing up the motorway.

For the next ten days or so, from dawn to dusk, birders held a permanent vigil on both sides of the river mouth. Four young Londoners even camped on the beach for four nights – despite freezing temperatures and three inches of snow. By the time the birds finally disappeared in early January, many hundreds, perhaps even thousands, of birders had seen them. But not everyone was in luck: one group drove all the way from Exeter, only to fail to see both birds. Such incidents, and the growth in popularity of twitching at this time, gave rise to a whole new vocabulary amongst the aficionados of the new sport: people no longer simply saw, but 'got' or 'connected with' the bird; while those who failed to see it were said to 'dip out'. Later, in the early 1980s, Bill Oddie documented the twitchers' slang in *Bill Oddie's Little Black Bird Book*; but for now the language was simply a way of telling whether someone was part of the elite 'in crowd' who had dedicated their lives to chasing after rare birds.

News of the Ross's and Ivory Gulls had travelled via an informal system of personal contact known as the 'grapevine'. As we have seen, this originally involved the finder of a rare bird sending postcards to various friends, who would then weigh up the risk of travelling to see a bird which might have long since departed. But by the late 1960s, the telephone had taken over from the Royal Mail as a faster and more effective means of spreading the news. Suffolk birder Derek Moore explains how the grapevine worked:

> The Friday night phone round was essential. You needed good contacts in the best parts of the UK. Each birder had his own private grapevine. In turn, as recorder for Suffolk I (and my wife Beryl) would be inundated with Friday night calls, often from total strangers, asking what was about.

But leaving the duty of answering the phone to a non-birding partner had its pitfalls: 'When I was out on a Friday my notepad would make interesting reading. Poor Beryl – she got so confused! "Long-tailed something" at Benacre – is that Duck, Shrike, Rosefinch or Skua, I would demand!'

Tim Cleeves, still based in Bristol, faced a different problem – his parents did not yet own a telephone:

Before we had a phone I gave my neighbours' number out to people. Mrs Palmer ran the corner shop, and was useless at taking messages about birds. I went there one night to see what she had written – 'Cheddar - ping flamant still there tonight'. It turned out to be an escaped Chilean flamingo at Cheddar Reservoir!

Contacts were made and reinforced at every new twitch. Because so few people were involved – a hard core of perhaps a couple of hundred, even in the mid-1970s – the sense of community spirit was strong, and as Cleeves recalls, some extraordinary characters would regularly turn up:

It was great in those days because when you went on a twitch you knew everyone there. My address book bulged: if we wanted to know about Teesside we would phone Tom Francis; if we wanted to know about the Midlands it was Eric Fortey and his mate (known, inevitably, as Eric and Ernie); and Norfolk had Spiny Norman. Norman had dropped out from life in Staines and lived in a barn on Walsey Hills near Cley. He made rabbit stews, scraped dead coypus off the beach road and smoked dope – he was free!

Another way to share information was to gather at a well-known birding hotspot such as the East Bank at Cley, or the public footpath which crossed Staines Reservoirs in Surrey. The ritual of meeting every Sunday morning on the wind-blown causeway at Staines continued throughout the year, even when there were precious few birds to be seen. Like a comfort blanket, it allowed birders to stay in touch with what was going on elsewhere, even if they had no intention of actually going to see anything.

Some people didn't bother to leave home at all. In a letter to *British Birds*, Mary Waller, chairman of Dungeness Bird Observatory, made a plea for people not to ring up observatories constantly to ask 'What's about?' Already, it seems, people were staying put and waiting for a rare bird to turn up, rather than going out and looking for one themselves.

THE FIRST published reference to the newly-acquired label of 'twitcher' appeared in April 1972, in the magazine *World of Birds*. It was in the introduction to an article entitled 'Tick Hunting 1971', written by a twenty-six year-old rare bird enthusiast, David Holman.

Holman related the story of his mission to see as many species of birds as possible in a year in Britain and Ireland – a similar quest to Kenn Kaufman's in North America (see Chapter 12), though given the shorter distances involved, rather more manageable. Nevertheless, his travels were pretty impressive for the time. In January alone he visited Tyneside, Slimbridge, Dorset, Norfolk and the Solway Firth, and totted up 126 species. By the end of April he was close to 200; a good summer (including King Eider, Trumpeter Bullfinch and Slender-billed Gull) took the list up to 245; and by the end of the year, trips to Shetland, Scilly and Cornwall (almost missing his niece's wedding) brought Holman to a grand total of 266 species – probably the highest annual total ever recorded in Britain and Ireland at that time.

Nowadays, when even novice twitchers regularly top the 300 mark in a year, and the record stands at over 380 species, Dave Holman's total may seem rather meagre. But remember that he achieved it without the benefits of modern communications technology such as phone lines or pagers, with limited transport, and by finding a high proportion of the birds himself.

Other birdwatchers also tried to find their own birds, with mixed results. In 1972, *British Birds* departed from its usual diet of scientific papers with D. I. M. Wallace's mouth-watering account of a month on Scilly – rapidly becoming the place to be if you wanted to see rare birds in autumn. 'An October to remember on St. Agnes in 1971' was written with his characteristic verve and enthusiasm, as this extract reveals:

> The bird flew into weeds only a few yards from me, clambered into sight, called almost into my ear and finally gave an excellent flight view as it bounced to the next line of plants . . . The large, deep bill, magnificent supercilium and yellow and buff underparts could only belong to Radde's [Warbler], the first of its kind in

Scilly. In that splendid moment, the Nighthawk was for me
eclipsed completely and Asia beat America hollow.

Readers were divided between those that found this sort of
account entertaining and inspirational, and those appalled by its
informal tone, which actually dared to reveal how much the
author enjoyed finding and watching rare birds. Wallace has never
been afraid to stick his neck out, and the account included several
records that were later rejected by the Rarities Committee as
unproven.

A further, unforeseen consequence was that the following
year Wallace was followed round by an eager band of disciples.
Unfortunately, autumn 1972 proved to be the worst for trans-
atlantic vagrants for years, and many of them left the islands
disappointed.

Whatever the misgivings of the old guard of British birdwatching, rarity hunting was the new obsession. The 'Scilly
season' soon became the focal point for Britain's new band of
twitchers: for a month or so each autumn they would descend on
the Isles of Scilly, first by the dozen, then by the hundred.

The islanders, used to a summer season of well-behaved
families enjoying a quiet seaside holiday, were at first appalled by
this invasion of binocular-toting hordes. But very soon, the
islanders began to realize the benefits: not least the extension of
the holiday season by a month or more. A 1997 RSPB report,
Working with Nature in Britain, suggested that by 1990 a substantial proportion of the £30 million annually spent on tourism to the
islands came from birders, and pointed out: 'The value to the
economy of wildlife in general, and birdwatching in particular, is
especially significant in that it attracts visitors outside the peak
months.'

By the early 1970s, visiting birdwatchers set up an unofficial
headquarters in the Mermaid Inn, on St Mary's, where they would
meet each evening to discuss the day's events over a few pints.
This scene was entertainingly described by R. J. Mynott in the
magazine *World of Birds*:

I soon discovered that there were two mutually suspicious groups in the Mermaid, characterised by one side as the birdwatchers and the twitchers, and by the other as the gentlemen and the players. The birdwatchers dismissed the twitchers as credulous counters of ticks (but did not stop asking them for hot news), and the twitchers dismissed the birdwatchers as mere dilettantes (but still welcomed their confirmation of identifications) . . . Be that as it may, by the Tuesday relations between them were definitely strained. The birdwatchers had seen virtually nothing, while the others had made heavy inroads into the British list. Against the two Firecrests, Hobby and Peregrine of the former, the latter had clocked up some eight Hippolais warblers of four species, Spotted Crake, Calandra Lark, Arctic and Greenish Warblers, Isabelline Wheatear and Bluethroat, to name but a few.

Mynott also noted the speed at which information criss-crossed the islands simply by word of mouth, in these days before the use of CB radios, pagers and the now-ubiquitous mobile phones. He also predicted the coming of bird information phone lines, which did not appear until more than a decade later:

Communications are so good that I once heard of a Black Redstart on Wingletang, St Agnes, while I was at Bar Point, St Mary's, only about thirty minutes after the bird had been seen. An Arctic Skua was tracked on its leisurely flight from Bryher to St Martin's and the report and the bird reached Peninnis just about simultaneously. I suppose one day Ornitholidays may refine this service – dial-a-Bluethroat – but by then we will all be doing our birdwatching in zoos.

BY THE LATE 1970s, twitching had become a firmly established part of the British birding scene. All it needed now was a permanent venue, which appeared in the north Norfolk village of Cley, long celebrated as a haunt of rare birds.

It all started when a local woman with the appropriate name of Nancy Gull decided to open a café in the dining room of her home. Birders soon discovered the joys of strong tea, beans on toast and her legendary bread pudding, all served with brisk efficiency by Nancy and her staff. In a generous gesture, Nancy also agreed to allow her private telephone to be used to spread news about rare birds – not just in north Norfolk, but anywhere in the country. As Mark Cocker recalls in *Birders – Tales of a Tribe*: 'Nancy's, which is what everybody called it, was legendary. Every birder knew of it. Most birders of sufficient age visited it . . . Some almost lived there. One or two actually did. And even those who never went there spoke to its occupants on a regular basis.'

To those who never went to Nancy's, it is hard to convey the extraordinary magic of the place. For the young birder, it was an initiation into the arcane rules of twitching etiquette, as Cocker remembers:

> The worst seat in the house was the one next to the phone stand because its occupant could spend the entire visit answering the same questions, sometimes every few seconds – 'Hello, can you tell me what's about?' 'Hello, can you tell me if the . . . is still there?'

The callers might be ringing from Nottinghamshire or Northamptonshire, Devon or Strathclyde, and wanting information on possible sightings of rare birds from Shetland or Scilly, and more or less anywhere in between.

Nancy's served another vital need, too. Most twitchers were not particularly well off. Some were even sleeping rough so as to maximize the time they could spend chasing rare birds. And all appreciated the fact that they could sit in a warm room for an hour or two, nursing a pot of tea and munching something tasty, nutritious, and above all cheap.

During the late 1970s and early 1980s, a time when community values were breaking down across much of Britain, Nancy's provided a focal point where birders could gather, swap stories, and simply feel part of a wider group – or as Mark Cocker has described them, a 'tribe': 'We usually took it in turns. That way everyone got to eat while maintaining the news service. But it was essential to do so. It was part of the unspoken protocol of Nancy's and, indeed, of being a birder.'

When Nancy's finally closed in December 1988 – an event reported on national television and in the press – an extraordinary era had come to an end. But even before then, the telephone in the corner of the dining room had become more or less redundant. For thanks to new technology, twitching had been propelled into the modern world.

D URING THE late 1980s, there was a telecommunications revolution, in which the state monopoly British Telecom was finally exposed to competition from outside. This coincided with the arrival of new technology, which made new kinds of communication possible. One consequence of these events was the introduction of 'premium rate' phone lines.

Predictably, the first '0898 numbers', as they were known from their prefix, were launched by the soft porn industry. Very soon the phone lines got a bad name, not least because of well-publicized cases of teenage boys running up astronomical bills on their parents' telephones.

Following this first rush of sex lines came information services with up-to-date weather reports, cricket scores and traffic news. It was at this time that a group of avid twitchers in north Norfolk came up with the notion of putting rare bird information on a premium rate line.

The original 'Birdline' had humble beginnings, far removed from state-of-the-art technology: it was a simple answer phone in the hut at Walsey Hills near Cley, manned by warden Roy Robinson. A rival, the Bird Information Service (BIS), soon appeared, and shortly afterwards Birdline became part of that service. The driving force behind the BIS was a partnership which has dominated the bird information scene ever since: Steve Gantlett and Richard Millington, who had birded together since their schooldays in Hampshire.

The key to running a successful phoneline, whether it concerned cricket scores, the weather, or rare birds, was the accuracy of information. Giving out the wrong information – either wrong directions to a location; or worse still, a case of mistaken identity – might involve twitchers travelling hundreds of miles on a wild goose chase. Located at the hub of Britain's twitching community, both geographically and socially, Gantlett and Millington soon acquired an unrivalled reputation for delivering 'good gen'. Birdline pursued a rigorous policy of confirmation by a known observer before any sighting was put out as definite, and as a result soon gained the confidence of their customers. Also integral to the success of Birdline and BIS was Richard's wife, Hazel Millington, whose voice announcing the arrival of a major rarity soon became familiar to Britain's twitchers.

The trio also hit on a brilliant marketing idea: soon after Birdline began in 1987, they launched a new magazine, with the self-explanatory title *Twitching*. Both the information line and the magazine (soon renamed *Birding World*) flourished, the latter providing a much-needed rival to the rather staid publication *British Birds*, which until then had enjoyed a monopoly for more than eighty years, and was beginning to show its age. During the peak seasons of spring and autumn, when most rare birds occurred, Birdline was getting hundreds of calls a day.

It was inevitable that the wide availability of up-to-the-minute information would lead to a major event. It occurred in February 1989, when Kent birder Paul Doherty made an extraordinary discovery near his home on the outskirts of Maidstone. While out to post a letter, he stumbled across Britain's first Golden-winged Warbler, a vagrant from North America. The combination of the rarity and beauty of the bird, the time of year (when there were few other rare birds to be seen), and the accessibility of the location, meant that on the weekend after he found the bird more than three thousand people turned up to see it. The fact that one of its favourite spots was the bushes on the edge of the local Tesco's supermarket car park only added to the bizarre nature of the event, which duly appeared on the television news bulletins.

During the following decade several other bird information services, including regional birdlines, made an appearance. Some flourished, others disappeared, but by the mid-1990s most birders had, at one time or another, rung them up to find out what was going on in their area. Bill Oddie found another use for them: before he went birding in Norfolk he would first telephone Birdline East Anglia to check out the locations of the major rarities. Then he would go elsewhere to seek out his own birds. In an increasingly crowded countryside, this made perfect sense.

By 1990, Britain was in the last, decaying days of the long reign of the Thatcher government – a time, according to the title of a book by social commentator Michael Bracewell, *When Surface was Depth*. Thatcherism had spawned a culture where possessions took on an almost iconic status, and technological gadgets in particular were the standard uniform of the high achieving 'yuppie'. About this time, a new device came onto the market: the personal pager.

Originally designed for workers in the emergency services such as doctors and nurses, these enabled a personal text message to be sent to an individual at any time of the day or night, wherever they were. At this time mobile phones were still both prohibitively expensive and as heavy as a housebrick, so the portable pager was a real communications breakthrough.

As often happens with new technology, pagers were not always put to the use for which they were originally designed. In 1991, Norfolk birder Dick Filby, founder of Rare Bird Alert, had the bright idea of sending messages about rare birds direct to individuals via a pager. This meant that twitchers no longer had to leave the field and find a functioning public phone box. At a cost of about one pound per day, the really keen twitcher could also save a considerable amount of money on his or her telephone bill.

Pagers were first introduced in October 1991, and initially had a few teething troubles. Many twitching hotspots, such as Fair Isle and Scilly, were out of range at least some of the time, while early garbled messages included some real gems, including 'Palace's Wobbler at Tesco's' (which should have read 'Pallas's Warbler on Tresco'). According to Tony Marr, there was also a message that reported a Wryneck at 'post 31, Spurn' (in Yorkshire). The pager continued to issue updates confirming the bird's presence for several hours, until its true identity was discovered. The final message read simply: 'The Wryneck at post 31 is a stone.'

Meanwhile, many an important business meeting was interrupted by the bleeping and buzzing coming from the trouser pocket of a keen twitcher, though most soon discovered that they could switch the pager mode to 'vibrate only' when required.

The obvious advantage of pagers was that unlike the telephone information lines, they allowed people to receive news of rare birds twenty-four hours a day. Rare Bird Alert even introduced a special 'Mega-Alert' service, designed to override the pager's off switch and alert the obsessive twitcher about a 'mega-tick' – an extremely rare, perhaps once-in-a-lifetime visitor. But though fine in principle, this might not be so welcome in practice, especially if the recipient was sitting in a crowded theatre, or waiting for their bride to walk down the aisle. But even though they may occasionally cause unexpected problems for their users, pagers are definitely here to stay, as an article in *Birdwatch* magazine in September 2000 pointed out:

> Love it or loathe it, there's no going back. It's a much-aired
> complaint that 'birding isn't what it used to be', or that these days
> 'birders have it too easy', but how many of us would rather go
> back to the hit-and-miss days of old? In the old days it wasn't
> what you knew, it was who you knew – and unless you were part
> of a rather elitist grapevine the chances are that you would never
> get to hear of that mega-rarity until it was too late.

O NCE LARGE crowds of enthusiastic people were able to converge without warning on a single site to see a rare bird, it was inevitable that problems would occasionally occur. Indeed, conflicts had arisen from the very start, as a *British Birds* editorial observed in 1955, following incidents at the Sussex Bee-eater site:

More and more bird-watchers, aided by modern communications
of all kinds, are able to gather with vulturine speed and efficiency
at points where some unfortunate rare bird is attempting to breed
or to rest on passage. While most are considerate and reasonable
enough to use their field-glasses for watching from a proper
distance without causing disturbance, a minority rush in and harry
the rarity from place to place quite unnecessarily . . .

The editorial also pointed out that the eventual breeding
success of the Sussex Bee-eaters was only due to careful guarding by
the RSPB's team of watchers, 'against sometimes almost unbeliev-
ably inconsiderate intrusions', and concluded with a warning:

Like all movements which have grown big quickly, birdwatchers in
particular are in danger of irritating and alienating other sections
of the community unless they can develop attitudes which allow
for the . . . legitimate interests of those who still cling to the odd
practice of not watching birds . . .

Criticism continued during the following decade. In 1969,
another *British Birds* editorial noted that a common complaint was
that chasing rare birds provides 'little of scientific value'. In reply,
reader A. F. Mitchell defended the rarity hunters:

Is not birdwatching a hobby, an interest, a pastime, any more?
I have yet to learn of the additions to science from the players
of golf or the devotees of angling . . . I am a tally-hunter, a
tick-hunter, a list-grubber, who owes no-one any explanation,
and I will not stoop to pretend that I am ashamed to be so.
Anyone else is free . . . to spend all his spare time advancing
science by observing minutely how a House Sparrow preens,
but it bores me stiff . . . Like dentistry, I am glad someone is
prepared to do it, but I want no hand in it myself.

Nevertheless, genuine problems did occur. Large crowds of
mainly young men, converging on a single location at the drop of
a hat, inevitably caused concern amongst local people – especially
farmers and private landowners on whose land rare birds
frequently appeared.

In the most celebrated incident in twitching folklore, one unfortunate individual was deliberately sprayed with semi-liquid pig manure by an irate farmer. More seriously, another twitcher ignored calls from his fellow birders, and trespassed onto the reserve at Rutland Water to get closer views of a Bridled Tern. Inevitably, not only did the rare bird fly away, but the intruder frightened off nesting birds whose eggs were then taken by crows.

On another well-publicized occasion, twitchers searching for a Great Bustard in Kent trampled crops, abused a local game-keeper, and committed the ultimate crime of flushing the bird so that late arrivals were unable to see it. As a result, two local birders wrote to *British Birds* proposing a more cautious approach to the broadcasting of rare bird news, suggesting that anyone who finds a rare bird should carefully consider their responsibilities before releasing the news.

This hinted at the notorious practice of 'suppression', in which news of a rare bird's presence was kept quiet until after it had gone, so that only a few local birders were able to see it. Amongst twitchers this was a cardinal sin, as it went directly against their code of 'share and share alike' which was so essential for twitching to work.

The most infamous incident of suppression occurred in March 1983, when a Tengmalm's Owl, a very rare visitor from Scandinavia, was discovered at Spurn Head on the Yorkshire coast. After much discussion, the Yorkshire Naturalists' Trust decided not to release the news, as high spring tides meant a mass invasion might cause irrevocable damage to this fragile site. This view cut very little ice with the twitchers, who considered any act of suppression beyond the pale.

One way in which twitching could gain at least some respectability, and to smooth the relationship between visitors and locals, was to take a collection, the proceeds going to a charity or good cause. So when, in February 1984, a rare vagrant turned up in a suburban garden in Berkshire, the householders decided to make the news public.

The bird, an Olive-backed Pipit from Siberia, stayed put for almost two months, during which time an estimated three thousand people made the journey to Bracknell to see it. Following the bird's departure, householders Dave and Maggy Parker reflected on the experience in *British Birds*, offering advice to anyone who might find themselves in the same position:

> Before doing anything, think very seriously about releasing the news and about its implications on you, your family and your neighbours . . . It is not just like living in a goldfish bowl, more like having everyone in the bowl with you . . . the constant telephone calls in the evening were very wearing . . .

Nevertheless, they were glad that they had gone ahead: 'Mad? Quite possibly, but if you could have seen the pleasure given to so many people I think you might begin to understand.'

The Parkers raised a substantial sum for charity, but twitchers have not always been quite so generous. When a Rose-coloured Starling appeared in a North Yorkshire garden in 2002, the non-birding householder was delighted to open her doors to twitchers, in return for a small donation towards the building of a local bus shelter. Unfortunately, several hundred visitors only donated the tiny sum of £16.50, despite having consumed tea and cakes for free. Fortunately, as a result of an appeal on the *BirdGuides* website, the sum was later increased by more than £50.

TWITCHING is a subject that inevitably evokes strong emotions: both for and against it. One of its most passionate defenders is Norfolk-based birder Mark Golley, who began twitching while still at school, and by the age of twenty was the youngest person ever to reach the coveted milestone of 400 different species in Britain and Ireland.

Golley's enthusiasm was sparked off when he was a teenage schoolboy in rural west Devon. In 1981, when he was aged fourteen, his father bought him a copy of *A Twitcher's Diary*, written by the co-founder of Birdline and *Birding World* magazine, Richard Millington. This was a mouth-watering account of a year travelling around Britain in search of rare birds, and galvanized the young

Mark into signing up for a Young Ornithologists' Club holiday to north Norfolk. There, he remembers making the statutory pilgrimage to Nancy's Café, where to his delight he bumped into his hero Richard Millington, tucking into a bread-and-butter pudding.

His fellow YOC members shared his obsession with the book, and each night after lights out, they would get out their copies of *A Twitcher's Diary* and test each other on which species Millington had seen on a particular day! Even now Golley can still recall whole passages, dates and events from the book. This was a golden age of YOC membership, with many of those on the same course still active today, more than twenty years later.

Later, he would regularly play truant from his school in Devon to go on twitches, often accompanied by an older schoolboy named Richard Crossley. Such a friendship – between two boys five years apart in age – was considered highly unusual in the unwritten code of schoolboy life; yet the two lads' shared passion for rare birds made it perfectly normal. Even so, led astray by the older Crossley, Golley remembers getting into trouble with his father (himself a teacher at the same school) for missing lessons to twitch a Franklin's Gull in Plymouth. He also spent every available half-term holiday visiting the bird observatories at Portland Bill and Dungeness. At the latter site, he met the late Peter Grant, who took him and his friend out on birding trips – a kind gesture that many other keen young birders experienced.

Once he left school in the mid-1980s, Golley's main aim was to see as many rare birds as possible. Like his contemporaries he regularly made epic journeys in order to do so: including a round trip via the island of Lundy (to see Britain's first Ancient Murrelet), then on to Shetland (to see a Pallas's Sandgrouse) and finally back to Norfolk, costing around £400.

Not all Golley's quests were quite so successful. On a twitch to Filey, in North Yorkshire, it soon became clear that the object of the twitch, a singing male Spectacled Warbler, was not going to show. Rather than stand about moaning, he and his mates organized a kickabout with a football – earning them the disapproving looks of various older twitchers. Fortunately the bird did appear on the following day.

His biggest 'dip' came when he was working as a shorebird warden at Gibraltar Point in Lincolnshire. One Sunday, news came that a Blue-cheeked Bee-eater had been found just down the road at Cowden. However, because of a staff shortage Golley had to stay at work, and had to wait an agonizing twenty-four hours before he was able to go for the bird, by which time it had moved on. A few days later, he had a second chance: and had the further agony of seeing the bee-eater at a distance through heat-haze, only for it to be scared off by a crop-spraying plane. It was never seen again: and under the rules of twitching, he was unable to 'count' the bird due to what twitchers call 'untickable views' or 'UTVs'. He was inconsolable: 'I'm not ashamed to say that I cried. Big tears. Totally and utterly gutted.'

Some may consider this to be an over-reaction: but, like your favourite football team winning the FA Cup, or better still scoring the winning goal for your Sunday team, the joy of finally seeing a wanted bird is the high point of many twitchers' lives. And just as the joy of winning at sport is always improved by a run of losses beforehand; so 'dipping out' on a bird is an essential component of the joy of twitching.

Mark Golley's greatest moment came on a damp evening in May 1993, when he was working as an assistant warden at Cley. As the rain began to clear, he decided to take a walk along Blakeney Point in search of migrants grounded by the bad weather. As he approached the end of the long, hard hike along the shingle, he took a diversion to look through a small patch of bushes. He noticed a movement, then caught a glimpse of a small bird which he immediately recognized as something out of the ordinary. When it finally appeared, he could not believe his eyes: it was a Desert Warbler from North Africa, the very first to be seen in Britain in spring.

Like an Olympic sprinter awaiting the results of a photo-finish, he then had an agonizing twenty minute wait for another observer to arrive and confirm his sighting. For had the bird flown away without anyone else seeing it, he knew that not only would he never be believed, but his whole reputation would be at risk. Fortunately, people did arrive, and in fact the bird stayed for several days and was seen by hundreds of twitchers. For Golley, it was the culmination of his twitching career: 'The Desert Warbler is my headed goal in the last minute at Wembley – the only way I could ever top that would be to find a first for Britain, which would be like winning the World Cup!'

This is where the analogy between football fans and birders breaks down: for by being participants as well as observers, twitchers – especially those, like Golley, who find their own rarities – are 'players' as well as 'supporters'.

Now in his mid-thirties, Golley can look back on his youthful highs and lows with a more phlegmatic attitude, though he is glad that he went to physical and emotional extremes in pursuit of birds: 'I wouldn't turn the clock back for a minute! I have absolutely no regrets at all.'

Golley still goes twitching, though since he had seen the vast majority of British rarities by his early thirties, there are not all that many species he still 'needs'. He does believe the twitching scene has changed – not necessarily for the better. Manchester United footballer Roy Keane once criticized the 'prawn-sandwich brigade' who now dominate the football scene, allegedly at the expense of lifelong supporters who have followed the team through bad times as well as good. Mark Golley draws the same analogy with the new band of casual twitchers, who have all the paraphernalia of the sport such as pagers and expensive optics, but who perhaps lack the driven passion and in-depth knowledge of the lifelong rarity hunter. Not that Golley is a twitcher to the exclusion of all else: he works for Anglia Television as a sports producer, and has a vast collection of recorded music, with a burning passion for Neil Young. But as he says:

> Sport is my job, music is my obsession, but birds are my life.

Having been a mass participation sport for over thirty years, it is hardly surprising that twitching has attracted its fair share of extraordinary anecdotes and incidents. One of the most epic feats took place in October 1980.

Steve Webb is one of Britain's leading listers, and is currently number two on the all-time chart behind the legendary Ron Johns, with well over 500 species seen in Britain and Ireland. So when a rare Siberian vagrant, the Yellow-browed Bunting, turned up on Fair Isle in October 1980, he obviously had to 'go for it'. The problem was that at the time he was with hundreds of other rare bird enthusiasts on the Isles of Scilly. Undeterred by considerations of geography, finance or stamina, he and his four companions decided to embark on the longest, and at the time most expensive, twitch possible within the borders of the United Kingdom.

The journey from Scilly to Shetland – a distance of almost a thousand miles – took over twenty-four hours, and involved a passenger ferry from Scilly to Penzance, a VW Polo from Penzance to Aberdeen, a scheduled flight from Aberdeen to Lerwick on Shetland, a charter flight from Lerwick to Fair Isle itself, and finally a taxi to the site where the bird had last been seen. Along the way the group rode a rollercoaster of emotions and problems, including almost missing their flight, being diverted to the wrong airport, and searching in the wrong place.

The story had a happy ending: the group of intrepid (or mad, depending on your view) twitchers 'connected' not just with the bunting but with two other rarities as well. They returned the next day, exhausted but elated, to regale their less committed companions with the tale of their success. Later the story reached a wider audience via the book *Best Days with British Birds*.

Other legendary long-distance twitchers include Tony Vials, who is said to have spent well over £900 to see a Caspian Plover on Shetland in 1996. This included a taxi ride from his Nottingham home to Heathrow; a flight to Aberdeen and back to London when news came through the bird had not been seen; a second flight to Aberdeen and on to Shetland and, having finally seen the bird, a flight home.

Of such amazing feats is the mythology of twitching built. It is largely an oral culture, and apart from Steve Webb's account, few of these tales have appeared in print. It has been left to a modern-day Boswell, a.k.a. Lee Evans, to chronicle the successes and failures of Britain's top listers in the bi-monthly bulletin of the elite UK 400 Club. As its name suggests, qualification is straightforward: to become a member, you simply have to have seen 400 or more species of bird in Britain.

Lee Evans runs the club as a one-man judge, jury and accounting service. He spends countless hours working out not only which species are 'countable' (and with the problem of escaped birds, 'lumps' and 'splits', and the constant arrival of new records, there are more and more decisions required). More controversially, he also decides what each member of the club is 'allowed to count'. This enters the murky and complex world of the Data Protection Act, and has caused controversy, as many twitchers dispute Evans's verdict, including Steve Webb, who has had his name removed from the UK 400 Club website in protest against the way it is run.

If there is such a thing as a typical twitcher, then Lee Evans is not it. For a start, his appearance and dress mark him out from the crowd: he generally wears a light suit, has blonde highlights in his hair, an earring, and usually sports a pair of natty crocodile leather shoes – even when out birding. Then there is his obsessive nature: even when he has seen a bird many times before he has a compulsion to tick it off again, and has been known to weep with frustration if he fails to do so.

He also has an uncanny ability to get publicity for himself and his work. Over the past decade or so he has probably had more column inches of press coverage than the rest of Britain's birders put together. Some has been merely wondering in tone, while much has been downright hostile – not helped by Evans' own outlandish behaviour. For example, he has claimed to have driven 3.8 million miles in search of birds – which works out at well over 400 miles every day of the year for twenty-five years! He also became paranoid about a rival year lister, rubbishing him on his website, which ended up with Evans almost being sued for libel. He has also claimed to have driven at a record 142.3 miles per hour on the way to secure a tick, and to have been involved in at least eleven major car crashes which have resulted in several fatalities. As a result, many people from both ends of the birding spectrum believe that the public image of the pastime has been distorted.

You might think that Lee Evans – who has boasted of going twitching on his wedding day (not surprisingly, the marriage did not survive); who lost the sight of one eye as a result of one of his many car accidents; and who has been observed in a state of almost manic distress at the prospect of missing a rare bird – is to be pitied rather than envied. As he once said about his obsession, 'I have to have everything. If I don't, I get miserable'. When the best that you can expect is 'not failing', life can hardly be full of fun.

Yet birders are a pretty tolerant lot: as one observer of the twitching scene, Rob Lambert, has commented: 'On balance he is good for birding. Every hobby has and needs a character like him!'

And although extreme in his attitudes and behaviour, Evans is far from alone in his emotional engagement with rare birds. When a Red-flanked Bluetail (a Siberian relative of the Robin) appeared in Dorset in autumn 1993, it was widely reported that some of the assembled twitchers actually burst into tears of joy and relief when, after hours of waiting and queuing patiently in line, they finally got to see the bird. No wonder the satirical magazine *Not BB* mocked the twitcher's obsession, in a parody of a contemporary government information campaign against the use of heroin:

> OK, so I do birding most weekends. I can handle it.
> OK, so I miss a few days off work. I can handle it.
> OK, so I've written off two company cars this year. I can cope.
> OK, so the mortgage payments are a bit behind. No problems there.
> OK, so the wife has taken the kids to her mother's. It happens.
> OK, so I'll be unemployed next week.

TWITCHING SCREWS YOU UP.

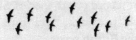

It was only a matter of time before someone would take twitching to its logical conclusion, and turn it into a team sport. In 1980, David Tomlinson, then assistant editor of *Country Life* magazine, started an event which would go on to raise a considerable sum for charity: the FFPS/Country Life Annual Bird Race.

Bird-racing, as it is generally known, has a long pedigree: dating from at least the 1930s in the USA (where it is known as a 'Big Day'), and arguably going back to the very first Christmas Bird Count of 1900. The earliest recorded Big Day in Britain took place in the early 1950s, when a group of Scottish birders managed to break the century mark in East Lothian and Berwickshire, with a score of 101 species. An English team took up the Scottish challenge, and reached a figure of 107 species in Suffolk, despite having chosen a day when the RSPB reserve at Minsmere was closed to visitors.

That record stood for a few years, until on May Day 1957, two schoolboys named David Pearson and Peter Smith totted up a total of 111 species in east Suffolk – using their pushbikes for transport. Two years later, they were at it again – but this time they had a secret weapon. Though starting off on their bicycles, they had persuaded their French mistress to meet them during the afternoon, and, more importantly, bring along her car. In his book *The Big Bird Race*, David Tomlinson showed his amazement at the young birdwatchers' powers of persuasion:

> Just how Miss Hawtin . . . had been persuaded by two Leiston
> School sixth-formers to join this bizarre exercise remains a
> well-kept secret – a secret that discretion has prevented me from
> investigating further . . . Anyway, armed with the speed of an
> upright 1950s vintage Ford Escort the lads were up to 118 by 18.00
> and finished with Stone Curlew at 21.20 for a grand total of 120.

During the next few years Pearson and Smith progressed from bikes and lifts to their own cars. On 13 May 1965 they set out well before dawn, birded solidly until after dusk, and set a new British 24-hour record of 126 species. Shortly afterwards they both went abroad to work, and bird racing temporarily disappeared from the British scene.

Fifteen years later, David Tomlinson introduced a competitive factor by setting up a match between two teams, and enlisted celebrity birder Bill Oddie to attract TV and press coverage. Since then, bird-racing has become a firmly-established annual event in the British birding calendar, only stopping when foot and mouth disease effectively closed the countryside in spring 2001. The British record now stands at 159 species, set by a team including Bill Oddie and Mark Golley in Norfolk in the early 1990s. Although this has been approached since, it has not been equalled or surpassed – and with the current serious declines in many farmland species and long-distance migrants, it may never be reached again.

In North America, bird racing has gone even further. With the self-assurance that allows them to hold a 'world series' in baseball, a sport virtually confined to the North American continent, in 1984 the first 'World Series of Birding' took place. It was the brainchild of New Jersey birder Pete Dunne, and introduced an important modification to the usual 'Big Day' rules: to enter the contest, a team had to have found a sponsor who would pledge cash for each species seen. As a result of this simple but imaginative idea, the World Series of Birding is now the biggest fund-raising event in the global bird racing calendar, and every year raises thousands of dollars for conservation.

Yet despite its obvious benefits, bird racing has attracted its fair share of criticism over the years. In 1982, one correspondent to *British Birds* condemned it as 'team twitching', while another critic complained about: 'The crude pursuit of birds for the purposes of one-upmanship . . . whose antics are beginning to cause widespread offence and give the name "birdwatcher" a bad smell.'

But most birders, whether they went twitching or not, took a more relaxed view, summed up by another correspondent to *British Birds*: 'I'm sick to death of people who seem to think that they are the only genuine birdwatchers and that everyone else should adhere to their viewpoint. Birdwatching is a hobby, and hobbies don't have to be useful, simply enjoyed, by each person in his own way.'

NEVERTHELESS, as modern birding becomes more and more frenetic in its approach, some have sought out alternatives forms of the pastime. One such was 'The Big Sit', which involved staying put in a single place (usually a hide) for twenty-four hours, and counting all the species seen or heard during that time. The first Big Sit took place in 1995, when Peter Wilkinson and Alastair Berry counted sixty-two species at Wicken Fen, Cambridgeshire.

In May 1999 four teams, including one from Scotland, took part in the first entirely sedentary 'bird race'. Although one Scottish participant became 'stir crazy' by mid-afternoon, and drove off to twitch a rare Collared Flycatcher nearby, they still managed 65 species, as well as sightings of several mammals including a stoat. But their total was soundly beaten by a team at Northward Hill RSPB reserve in Kent, who clocked up an extra-ordinary total of 77 species from a single spot.

Meanwhile, another more relaxed pastime has also grown in popularity, again as a reaction against the manic nature of twitch-ing and bird-racing: birding at one's local patch. Many birders have a favourite place within easy access of their home, which they visit regularly throughout the year, keeping a note of the birds they see there. But by the early 1990s local patch watching was being acknowledged as a valid pastime in its own right, rather than simply something you did when you could not get away to see the latest rarity.

Patch work, as it is known, has its advantages: even the commonest species can be a local rarity – bringing some of the excitement of twitching without the attendant frustration, time or expense. *Birdwatch* magazine, in particular, encouraged local patch work, partly because its editor, Dominic Mitchell, had always enjoyed birding on his own patch at Walthamstow Marshes in east London. His dedication was rewarded in May 1994 when he discovered a singing male Subalpine Warbler, a rare visitor from southern Europe. Not surprisingly, the bird's presence attracted twitchers from all over London and beyond.

Working your local patch is regarded by its adherents as more 'spiritual' in nature than other forms of birding: putting you in touch with the daily, monthly and seasonal rhythms of life. It can be exciting, especially for those fortunate enough to stumble across a rarity; and it can also be monumentally dull, especially during quiet periods of the year. Compared to twitching it is more like a single-handed yacht race than the London Marathon. In fact the two activities are not mutually exclusive: many twitchers also have their own local patch and enjoy both kinds of birding. But for the doyen of British birders, Ian Wallace, there is simply no competition between modern, pager-led twitching and 'proper' birdwatching, as he declared on Radio Four's *The Archive Hour*:

> Now rarities are instantly available . . . There's nothing more annoying than trying to concentrate on a seawatch, to have one's calm and confidence interrupted by 'beep-beep-beep'; and then some manic idiot reads out 'Rose-coloured Starling – Bryher'. And you think, well, that's three hundred miles away for a start and I'm not bloody going!

For Wallace, even after all these years, nothing beats the joys of pounding the regular beat on his local patch: 'The buzz is tremendous, it really is – the adrenaline boost is still there, not quite so sickening and heart-jolting as it was fifty years ago, but it's still there! And if there are no birds you are never bored – you just play back your memories . . . '

Chris Harbard – another contributor to *The Archive Hour* and pioneer of the early twitching scene – looks back on those days with unconcealed nostalgia:

> There was something nice about the seventies when there was a smaller crowd of people . . . you knew them all; it was very much done by word of mouth – people would ring their friends and tell them what was about and offer lifts . . . it was a much closer, social activity. The social side of it is still there, but it's now accessible to absolutely anyone, via the Internet, via the phonelines, via pagers – all the information out there whenever you want it – and somehow that's taken a bit of the charm that there used to be out of it, for me anyway.

So where is twitching at the start of the twenty-first century? Anecdotal evidence would suggest that it has found its equilibrium: that today, most birders go twitching occasionally, some do it more frequently, and a hard core of perhaps several thousand are still more or less full-time twitchers. Certainly when Britain's first Black Lark turned up in Anglesey in June 2003, large crowds gathered to see this legendary rarity.

Rob Lambert, a keen birder who is also an environmental historian at the University of Nottingham, recalls the long journey along the A55 into north Wales. He knew he was heading in the right direction because of the number of cars festooned with stickers proclaiming that their occupants were keen birders. Just as crowds heading for a football match display their club scarves as a sign that they are all members of the same 'tribe', so twitchers heading for a bird do so by displaying car stickers, wearing T-shirts with bird-related designs, and by the definitive status symbol of the serious birder – a pair of Leica, Swarovski or Zeiss binoculars around their neck.

Not that twitchers always want to be recognized. The timing of the Black Lark's appearance, with the news first released on a Sunday evening, created a moral dilemma for those twitchers who had a nine-to-five job. Either they waited until the following Saturday to try to see the bird, during which time it would probably have gone, or they pretended they were sick and took the Monday off work. For many, the latter option won the day.

A major twitch usually attracts the attention of the local TV news, and this was no exception. Yet according to Adrian Pitches, writing in *British Birds*, the reporter had terrible trouble getting any of the crowd to be interviewed, in case they were identified by their employers and their cover was blown!

As twitching has grown in popularity, and become more widely accepted, so its participants have divided into sub-groups, each pursuing their own style of rarity hunting. So although the 'Scilly season' is still a major event in the annual twitching calendar, numbers have dropped from their peak of more than 1500 visitors each October to fewer than 1000. This is partly because as cheap foreign travel becomes easier, people prefer to go to Israel or the USA – places they can reach for little more than the cost of a fortnight on Scilly. New technology has made a difference too: many top twitchers now stay on the mainland, relying on their pager to inform them if anything of interest turns up; safe in the knowledge that they are only a drive and a helicopter ride away from the bird.

Despite this, the Scilly scene continues to be about more than simply seeing rare birds: there is the social side of the daily log (bird count), with its attendant slide shows, bird quizzes and a range of bird-related products for sale. Every Friday night there is a birders' disco, which in October 1999 saw the massed ranks leaping up and down to the sound of the B52's 'Love Shack', still carrying their binoculars around their necks. The cause of their excitement was the appearance, that day, of a Blue Rock Thrush – a species which well and truly comes under the category of 'mega-tick'.

The Scilly season may have its detractors, but there can be no doubt that the annual invasion of birders continues to make a substantial contribution to the local economy. As well as the money spent on food, accommodation and transport, the birders contribute substantial sums each year to the local lifeboat charity. There is also the boost to community relations: after initial hostility and suspicion, relations between the visitors and locals are now excellent, and the annual Birders vs. Islanders football match is a popular and well attended event.

Gradually the male bias so prevalent in twitching is also changing, with more and more women each year – though still generally as partners of keen male birders. The greater participation of women was symbolized by the wedding that took place in Old Town Church on St Mary's in October 2000. Rob Lambert and Kim Macpherson emerged from the church under an arch of tripods held up by their fellow birders, and spent the next day twitching various rare birds on the island of Tresco. The blushing bride did eventually get a 'real' honeymoon – a birding trip to New Zealand.

Elsewhere, twitchers have found new ways to inject continued excitement into their pursuit of rare birds. Some now forgo birds found by others, and keep a 'self-found list', which only includes birds that they have discovered for themselves. Using this criteria, leading rarity-finders do very well to top the 300 mark; but get a much greater sense of satisfaction from doing so.

Regionalism in birding has increased too: following devolution, many Scottish and Welsh birders now keep a country list rather than a UK one – something Irish birders have always done, reflecting their stronger sense of national identity. In 1998 the journal *Birding Scotland* first appeared, with an advertising slogan borrowed from the popular Scottish soft drink Irn-Bru: 'made in Scotland for Birders' (as opposed to the original 'made in Scotland from girders'). And although the annual autumn pilgrimage to Fair Isle continues, groups of Scottish birders have followed in the footsteps of Eagle Clarke by exploring previously untried Scottish islands such as Foula, Barra and Coll. These attempts to recapture the pioneering spirit of the early days of rarity-hunting have been surprisingly successful, and given the participants a sense of satisfaction that is harder to get from visiting the more crowded and well-known hotspots.

The English are not far behind, with an increasing focus on regions and counties. A growing number of magazines now cater for this trend, with titles such as *Yorkshire Birding*. Local and regional birdlines, regional channels on pagers, and websites such as *London's Birding*, also provide up-to-date information on local sightings. A number of top twitchers from the glory days of the 1970s and 1980s have even turned their back on UK-wide twitching, and instead keep a 'county list' – doing the majority of their birding in their local area, with the odd trip abroad. It could perhaps be said that things have come full circle, and returned to the status quo of the 1950s, though this time not out of necessity, but from choice.

As if to confirm this, in the summer of 2002, almost half a century after the first car-loads of rarity hunters headed off on an adventure to a quarry in Sussex, there was a repeat event. This time the twitchers drove north, up the A1, to a quarry in County Durham – to see a pair of nesting Bee-eaters, the first to breed in Britain since the Sussex birds.

Once again, the RSPB organized a round-the-clock guard,

and chose to publicize the event. This time the birds made the front page of several newspapers, including the *Daily Telegraph*, were shown on the BBC news, and updates on their progress were issued on several websites. In all, an estimated 15,000 people came to see the birds during their three month stay.

There was one other big difference from the events of fifty years before. This time, the twitchers got the news in a few minutes, by pager; rather than in a few weeks, by postcard.

CHAPTER FIFTEEN

Earning

The Commercial Side of Birding

Hobbies are a contradiction; they take work and turn it into
leisure, and take leisure and turn it into work.

Steven M. Gelber, *Hobbies: Leisure and
the Culture of Work in America.*

NORFOLK HAS always been a great place to watch birds. So
it is hardly surprising that many birders have chosen to
settle down and live there. A few years ago, they would
either be recently retired, or have opted out of the conventional
rat race. But now, thanks to advances in information technology
and the rise of the 'portfolio career', they have the best of both
worlds: they are able to make a living out of birding, while being
near some of the best bird sites in the country.

They are a diverse bunch, as we have already seen. Some, like
Richard Porter and Tony Marr, have left their full-time jobs at
Birdlife International and the civil service, and are now near
neighbours in the village of Cley. But they have not 'retired' in
any conventional sense: Porter is still heavily involved in conservation work in the Middle East, while Marr goes off for three or
four months each winter to lead birding tours to Antarctica.

Others are still at the start of their birding careers. Mark
Golley, the schoolboy twitcher whose feats made him the youngest
person ever to reach the landmark total of 400 species seen in
Britain, combines a job at Anglia Television with a part-time
career as a writer; while Mark Cocker, author of *Birders: Tales of
a Tribe*, pursues a freelance career as a journalist and author from
his home in Norwich.

Another Norwich-based birder, Clive Byers, continues to
make a living from his work as one of the world's leading bird

artists, as well as guiding world listers around South America in search of rare birds. His school friend and former twitching partner, Dick Filby, who had the bright idea of setting up the pager service Rare Bird Alert, now splits his time between homes in Norwich and Colorado, when he is not travelling to ever more exotic birding locations.

Other Norfolk-based birders operate full-time businesses from their homes. In the town of Holt, South African-born Duncan MacDonald runs Wildsounds, a mail-order company dealing in CDs, tapes and books. In a converted farmhouse just along the coast at Northrepps, husband-and-wife team Chris and Barbara Kightley run Limosa Holidays, one of Britain's most successful bird tour companies. And Richard Millington and Steve Gantlett still publish the magazine *Birding World*, and organize the telephone information service Birdline, from a house overlooking Cley marsh and its birds.

IN SOME ways, what they are doing is not all that new: after all, human beings have always exploited birds for commercial gain. The earliest civilizations domesticated gamebirds such as the Red Jungle-fowl, and various geese and ducks, to provide eggs and meat. In the Middle Ages, birds were bred for sport, such as cock-fighting and hunting with falcons. And throughout history, songbirds have been kept in cages for people to admire the beauty of their plumage or their song.

What is different today is that people are now making money not by exploiting the birds themselves, but by tapping into the commercial possibilities of the rise in popularity of birdwatching. A handful of people have always been able to make a living by writing books about birds, or drawing and painting them, but it was not until the decade after World War II that birdwatching became popular enough for anyone seriously to consider making money out of it.

Fortunately for the relationship between commerce and birding, this movement was spearheaded by birders themselves, who saw a golden opportunity to turn their hobby into a way of making a living. One leading player in the field, Bruce Coleman, has no doubt that this contributed to the development of birding as a popular pastime:

> Commercial birding is now big business, providing a wonderful service to anyone wishing to take up the hobby. You have superb tour companies enabling anyone to see a huge percentage of the world's species. Field and sound guides, and videos, help you quickly learn the fine art of identification. High quality lenses help you get closer to birds, and to capture them on film. Meanwhile, magazines keep you abreast with the latest news; and pagers announce new arrivals of rare birds from all over the country.

Back in the early 1950s, when Bruce Coleman was growing up, the world of work was very different from today. On reaching the school leaving age of fifteen, he left his secondary modern school in Hayes in Middlesex, and joined the publishing firm Macmillan as 'tea and office boy'. One of his first tasks was to take review copies of natural history books up to the offices of the scientific journal *Nature*.

Somehow the journal's editors came to know of the young man's interest in birds, and gave him a spare copy of the newly published *Observer's Book of Birds' Eggs*. Being a polite and well-brought-up lad, Coleman wrote them a thank-you letter, and as an afterthought also sent them a review he had written. To his amazement they published it, and as a result, the teenager was invited to his first publisher's cocktail party.

There, despite his shyness, he approached L. P. Long, editor of a popular set of guides called the Foyles Handbooks. When Coleman pointed out that there was no book in the series devoted to birdwatching, Long promptly asked him to write one. Within six months he had obtained a typewriter, learned to type, and delivered the required 30,000 words. In those days, research sources were hard to come by, and Bruce made do with *The Observer's Book of Birds*, two volumes of Coward's *Birds of the British Isles and their Eggs*, and James Fisher's *Watching Birds*. Still in full-time employment at Macmillan, he wrote the book during evenings and weekends, when, as he recalls, 'access to the Westminster Public Library was a godsend'. The finished book was published in 1956, when its author was just nineteen years old.

In return for his labours, Bruce Coleman received a cheque for the sum of £100 (approximately £5000 today) – a small fortune for a lad earning just £3 a week. Spurred on by his success, he contacted Frank Lane, a photographic agent who had already written several popular nature books, and would later co-author Eric Hosking's autobiography, *An Eye for a Bird*.

Lane gave Coleman more than just good advice; he also offered him a part-time job at the photographic agency, which he promptly accepted. Soon he had bigger ambitions: to set up his own agency. Through another lucky acquaintance – this time with a German film-maker who sold him the rights to a film on wildlife in the Alps – Coleman managed to get an appointment at the BBC's Natural History Unit in Bristol. Unfortunately, as he recalls, the producer slept through most of the film, and on waking announced that the material contained nothing very new or exciting.

The BBC's loss was Anglia Television's gain. In 1961, after a successful viewing with Colin Willock, editor of the television series *Survival*, Coleman signed a contract which not only gave him the capital necessary to set up his agency, but also paid considerably better than the publicly funded BBC.

Within a decade, the name Bruce Coleman had become synonymous with high-quality colour nature photography, his agency's products being found in every publication from *National Geographic* to the *Daily Mail*. Its success was undoubtedly due to a growing interest in birds and other wild creatures amongst the general public, fostered by the advent of colour supplements and natural history programmes on television.

Things had not gone too badly for the young man from the Middlesex suburbs: it is said that by the end of the 1960s, Bruce Coleman had become the first person whose interest in birds had enabled him to become a millionaire.

TODAY, it is not all that unusual for people to turn their hobby into a business. And while not all are as successful as Bruce Coleman, many people do manage to make a living out of birds and birding.

Most begin slowly, having the odd article or photograph published, or being asked to lead a bird tour. If things go well, and their name becomes known, they get more commissions, and before they know it they are making significant money. Then it is but a short step to turn a hobby into a business. In some cases, this allows them to escape the drudgery of a dull, unsatisfying job, and do something they really enjoy. In others, it provides a sideline to their main career, which can then provide a bridge between the worlds of full-time work and retirement.

There are risks attached to such an enterprise. One of the purposes of hobbies is to provide the practitioner with an outlet from the stresses and strains of daily life; and by turning your hobby into your career you may lose this safety valve. As the title of a popular magazine article on hobbies put it in 1933: 'Here's a Job You Can't Lose'. But despite the many stresses and strains of running your own business, most birders who have done so seem glad that they did.

There are almost as many ways to make a living out of birding as there are birders. But by and large, they fall into two main categories: freelancers and entrepreneurs. By far the larger group are the freelancers: writers, photographers and tour guides, many of whom use their skills as birders to augment their main source of income rather than replace it entirely. This is a relatively risk-free approach, as apart from the initial investment they are not risking their livelihood, home or savings.

Others set up some kind of service such as the various bird information phone lines and pager services; or something more tangible such as books, bird food or overseas tours. This is a riskier venture, requiring more capital and effort but potentially providing much greater rewards. One such example could be seen at the British Birdwatching Fair in August 2002, when two of the UK birding industry's major companies joined forces.

THE FIRMS involved in the merger were CJ WildBird Foods, a leading supplier of bird food and feeders; and BirdGuides, a specialist producer of videos and multimedia products. Both were highly successful: CJ WildBird Foods had practically invented modern bird feeding, launching a range of foods and feeders designed to meet the needs of the birds as well as satisfying their human customers.

Likewise, BirdGuides had built up a near monopoly of the multimedia market, selling videos, CD-ROMs, and booklets featuring the world's best birding sites. A couple of years earlier, CJ WildBird Foods had also taken over Subbuteo, a mail-order company selling natural history books; so with this merger the new company now dominated the marketplace, selling a wide range of products to the same core base of birding clients.

CJ WildBird Foods and BirdGuides had both been set up by keen birders who were also far-sighted entrepreneurs, and who used their skills and knowledge to create successful business enterprises. The two founders, Chris Whittles of CJ and Dave Gosney of BirdGuides, came from very different backgrounds, but shared a single-minded ambition and drive for success.

Trained as an agriculturist, Chris Whittles was also a Class A bird ringer, which brought him into close contact with common birds and their habits. Frustrated by the lack of choice in terms of bird food and feeders, he set up CJ WildBird Foods in 1987. The company rapidly went from strength to strength, and by the mid 1990s was Britain's leading supplier of these products. A fire in 1999 at the company's headquarters near Shrewsbury turned out to be a blessing in disguise, allowing the company to create a purpose-built factory on the same site; and by the time of the merger in 2002 its annual turnover was approximately £12 million. The company's success is down to a commercial strategy familiar to many successful entrepreneurs, as Whittles points out: 'We created what people wanted, even though at the time they didn't realise they wanted it!'

As a result, the practice of bird feeding has been transformed: no longer a case of people throwing out a few kitchen scraps or hanging up a bag full of peanuts; instead the birds now have the choice of a wide range of specially designed feeders and foods tailored to their needs. At the top end of the market, the 'Conqueror' feeder is well over one metre in length, and weighs almost 4kg when full – retailing at a mere £44.95!

As for the future, Whittles is optimistic, pointing out that the current UK market has risen from around £30 million to almost £200 million a year in the past two decades, and has the potential to grow still further. The scope for growth can be seen when compared to the US market for wild bird food and feeding products, which has been estimated at an annual total of $3.5 billion.

Chris Whittles' counterpart at BirdGuides, Dave Gosney, is a Yorkshireman who originally gave up teaching to run birdwatching holidays and write a series of booklets on finding birds abroad. For a while, this subsidized his travels in search of birds, but eventually he had to return to supply teaching to make ends meet.

Then, in 1994, he was contacted by former BBC television producer Max Whitby, who had seen a gap in the market, and needed Gosney's help to exploit it. He proposed that with his knowledge of production and marketing techniques, and Gosney's expertise as a birder, they should team up to make birding video guides. Presented by Gosney himself, in an informal and endearing style, these were an immediate success. As technology continued to develop, the company branched out into a range of multimedia products including a series of CD-ROMs, one of which, a guide to British birds, became a runaway best-seller. Meanwhile, the company's website won a coveted BAFTA award against very stiff competition from much larger enterprises, further boosting their profile. At the time of the merger with CJ Wildbird Foods, BirdGuides had an annual turnover of £500,000.

The new company is run on an ethical basis, so that with every product sold in the RSPB Birdcare range, five per cent goes back to the RSPB for conservation work – a total now approaching one million pounds a year. Such an apparently altruistic approach is not all that unusual: several bird tour companies donate a proportion of their profits to support conservation products around the world. This makes long-term commercial sense: if a habitat disappears, the birds will disappear with it; and if the birds disappear, so will the birders who make up the client base of the firms themselves.

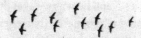

MANY BIRDERS dream of setting up a business that will allow them to watch birds while also providing a steady income – and what better way to do so than by running a bird tour company? But although it sounds simple, the reality is rather different, as Chris Kightley and his wife Barbara discovered when they set up Limosa Holidays in the mid 1980s.

Born in 1956, Chris Kightley was one of the last generation whose interest in birds began with egg collecting: 'I always had a natural curiosity about birds, butterflies, the countryside, and started to collect birds' eggs – I think this was more in vogue than birdwatching at that time. In fact, I didn't know anyone who "watched" birds.'

Like many others, he saw the light when his parents enrolled him as a member of the Young Ornithologists' Club (YOC), at the age of ten. The YOC magazine *Bird Life* carried features discouraging egg collecting, so he graduated to watching birds instead. He was encouraged by a present from his grandfather: a pair of World War I binoculars made of brass and leather. Sadly their impressive exterior was no guarantee of optical performance, so he persuaded his parents to buy him a pair of 'proper' binoculars from Boots.

Other formative influences were two seminal books of the period: *A Field Guide to the Birds of Britain & Europe*, and John Gooders' *Where to Watch Birds*, which he received as a Christmas present in 1967. The young Chris was impressed by the description of Gooders as 'a birdwatcher of boundless enthusiasm', and promptly decided to follow in the author's footsteps. So the day after Boxing Day, he persuaded his dad to drive him out to Tring Reservoirs, a location featured in *Where to Watch Birds*. He record-ed this momentous event in the back of the book, complete with spelling and punctuation errors: '19 species, including Kingfishers, Tree Creeper's, Shoveller's and Pigeons. Also a Water Vole.'

By September 1972, at the age of sixteen, his life list (neatly ticked off in the front of the *Field Guide*) had risen to the dizzy heights of 193 species – and he was well on the way to realizing his ambition of becoming a 'proper' birdwatcher.

An unusual feature of the YOC during the late 1960s and early 1970s was that many of the leaders on the regular outings were scarcely older than the members themselves. So on reaching the age of sixteen, Chris was 'promoted' into that lofty position. He recalls having to approach his headmaster, the intimidating Mr Becker, to ask for a reference. Permission was duly granted, and he became a fully fledged YOC leader. This experience would stand him in very good stead for his future career.

In 1974, aged eighteen, Chris left school and joined the Midland Bank, spending virtually his entire spare time birding. His status as a car owner – still something of a novelty for a young man in those days – made him popular with his fellow twitchers, as he was able to give them lifts up and down the country in his Mini 850. He eventually escaped from the bank, getting a job as a summer warden for the RSPB on Anglesey. He was offered another two contracts with the RSPB, but because the pay was so poor (£20 a week, equivalent to about £100 today) he turned both down. After applying for a job in the civil service, and failing to get the post he wanted in the Nature Conservancy, he ended up in the VAT office in London's Soho. He stuck this out for eighteen months, before succumbing to the lure of the far north.

It may be hard to imagine nowadays, but in the late 1970s if you wanted to make money, you headed to Britain's northernmost archipelago: the Shetland Isles. The North Sea oil boom was at its height, and Shetland was at its epicentre – coincidentally also one of the very best places in Britain to watch birds. Seduced by a fellow birder's vision of 'streets paved with gold', Chris headed north.

Unfortunately, the employment situation on Shetland was not quite as rosy as had been suggested, and it took him some time before he was taken on the payroll. His job title was 'general assistant', but the reality involved cleaning toilets, endlessly mopping corridors and making beds. The work may not have been very glamorous, but the pay was extraordinary: with overtime he could earn between £180 and £200 a week – at least £1000 today. All this with three square meals a day thrown in! Other birders employed as scaffolders (known as 'scaffs') earned even more, with one enterprising young man working round the clock by doing two jobs at the same time, and catching the occasional nap in a cupboard.

Working six and a half days a week left little time for birding, but Chris and his companions still managed to see a variety of rare birds including Bluethroats from Scandinavia, Ross's and Ivory Gulls from the Arctic, and the long-staying Black-browed Albatross, which had taken up residence in the gannetry at Hermaness.

Just before Christmas 1981, Chris was made redundant and returned south to London. He married his childhood sweetheart Barbara in September 1982, and they bought a flat together in the Middlesex suburbs. His next job, as a gardener, was a disaster, as he hated dogs, injured his back lifting a mower, and punctured a high-pressure hose to a newly filled swimming pool, inadvertently creating a water feature in the flowerbed.

As he looked around for a new career, it finally dawned on him that what he really enjoyed doing was showing birds to other people. So in May 1984, he and Barbara took the momentous step of selling their flat and moving to Norfolk. After losing out on several dream homes, they ended up buying a derelict wreck in the village of Northrepps. There, they set up a bird tour company, which they named Limosa Holidays after the scientific name of one of Norfolk's rarest breeding birds, the Black-tailed Godwit.

Before they could actually run any trips, the house needed to be completely rebuilt: a task that took more than eighteen months. Finally, in early 1986, the first group of paying guests arrived. Chris took them out birding around Norfolk and Suffolk, while Barbara cooked and catered – at the same time working as a nurse to make ends meet. Business was slow at first, with various minor disasters on the culinary and motoring fronts. But gradually customers began to book a second tour, then a third; encouraged perhaps by Chris's habit of making regular refuelling stops for coffee and homemade cake from the back of the van. By 1990, helped by a series of articles in the newly launched *Bird Watching* magazine, the business was thriving, and Limosa had become a small but significant player in the growing domestic bird tour market.

Then, another life-changing event occurred: in September 1991 Barbara gave birth to their first child, Sophie. It was immediately clear that they could no longer have guests staying at their home, so they switched to running tours elsewhere in the United Kingdom. But this soon presented another problem: British hotels were so expensive that the tours were scarcely viable from a financial point of view. Faced with this, Chris and Barbara took the bold decision to branch out overseas, competing with the 'big boys' such as Sunbird and Birdquest.

A decade or so later, Limosa is now firmly established amongst the top five bird tour companies in Britain. The full-colour brochure features more than seventy tours ranging from a long weekend 'wild goose chasing' in the Netherlands, costing £845, to much longer visits to Alaska, Japan and South America, at well over £4000 per person.

Since the birth of their second child, James, in 1996, Chris has given up full-time tour leading and now spends most of his time running the business from their now fully refurbished home. Fortunately the garden continues to provide excellent 'back window birding' experiences, especially during peak migration periods, when birds such as Firecrest, Waxwing and Yellow-browed Warbler occasionally drop in.

Looking back, Chris feels proud of his and Barbara's achievements, and would encourage any young birder with similar entrepreneurial ambitions to put them into practice. Though as he points out in a wry reference to his early career – if you want to make big money, go into banking instead!

RUNNING a company is not within everybody's reach; nor indeed their desire. Some birders have proved that it is possible to make a living out of birds without having to set up their own business, or indeed ever having a conventional job at all.

Born in Dublin in the late 1950s, Clive Byers was brought up in suburban Surrey, where after a close encounter with a Lesser Spotted Woodpecker he became hooked on birding. After cutting his birding teeth at local reservoirs and sewage farms, he became a keen twitcher, and spent the early 1970s hitch-hiking up and down the country in search of rare birds. Amongst many memorable incidents were being sprayed with liquid manure by an irate farmer and an extraordinary 1500-mile round trip with his schoolmate, another keen young birder named Dick Filby. The pair travelled to the island of South Uist in the Outer Hebrides, to twitch a Steller's Eider – an epic journey described in detail in Mark Cocker's *Birders: Tales of a Tribe*.

Not content with birding in Britain, Clive spent much of his youth travelling the world in search of even rarer birds. He financed his trips abroad in a variety of unorthodox ways, including volunteering for medical experiments at a London clinic, a lucrative if somewhat risky occupation. He also began to turn his birding skills into what would eventually become his main profession. When watching a rare bird he would often do a sketch of it in his notebook. One day a fellow twitcher offered him £5 for one of these pictures, which Clive promptly accepted. His career as a professional bird artist had begun.

A few years later, in the late 1980s, Clive was invited to lunch at Langan's Brasserie in London by a well-known figure on the British birding scene. Large quantities of fine food and wine were consumed, and when the pair finally staggered out of the restaurant in the late afternoon, Clive had been offered a contract to illustrate a book on European warblers, the first to be published in a new business venture by his fellow diner. The book received good reviews, and Clive's illustrations won special praise. He was commissioned to illustrate another book, then another; then to contribute to the major ornithological work of our time, *The Handbook of Birds of the World* – a prestigious and very lucrative commission.

As a result of this – and his other sidelines, leading bird tours

and guiding world listers around South America – Clive no longer
has to work, as he once had to, as a guinea-pig for multinational
drug companies. Indeed he is known as one of the world's leading
bird artists. He is still friendly with the man who commissioned his
first book, and set him off on his successful career. In one of those
neat quirks of fate, that man is Bruce Coleman.

THE WORLD of commerce has also shaped the development of
our leading bird conservation organization, the RSPB. Since
its humble beginnings in a Manchester suburb, more than a
century ago, the society has developed in ways that would have
astonished the respectable middle-class ladies who founded it.
Today the RSPB has more than a million members (including
almost 150,000 under 18), employs almost 1500 staff, and has an
annual turnover of £74 million. Its 150 reserves cover an area of
128,000 hectares – roughly equivalent in size to the county of
Bedfordshire, where the society has its headquarters, in a rambling
Victorian pile outside the town of Sandy.

The RSPB does everything you would expect of such an
organization, and a lot more besides. On the surface it is designed
to appeal to the widest possible membership, with a glossy catalogue selling RSPB Christmas cards, own-brand binoculars and
bird feeders; a free quarterly magazine packed with articles and
photographs; and initiatives such as 'Aren't Birds Brilliant!' which
aims to get people to watch rare breeding birds such as Ospreys,
Red Kites and Peregrines.

However, scratch the surface of the RSPB, and beneath this
benign and user-friendly exterior you will find a hard-nosed,
highly political organization, campaigning at the very highest
level to conserve birds and their habitats. So alongside the reserve
wardens and press officers, the society also employs expert lobby-
ists and campaigners in areas such as energy use, transport policy
and climate change. The RSPB has a position on subjects ranging
from wind farms to organic farm produce, and is not afraid to use

the formidable voting power of its million members to persuade the government to put environmental issues higher up the political agenda. The *Daily Telegraph* may dismiss RSPB members as 'faddish townie greens', but they should remember that many live in marginal constituencies, and if mobilized to vote one way or another could even influence the course of a general election.

The society knows this, and also knows that its power derives – both politically and financially – almost entirely from its membership. So it does everything it can to attract new members, and to retain them once they have joined. Every new recruit is invited to join their local members' group, which puts on a programme of slide shows, quizzes and outings to various RSPB reserves – usually ending with a visit to the teashop where pots of tea and home-made cakes are dispensed by a formidable brigade of women volunteers. All members, from the expert to the complete beginner, are encouraged to take part in surveys such as the annual Big Garden Birdwatch, which provides invaluable data on rises and falls in common bird populations. If you wish, you can put your monthly spending on an RSPB credit card, buy your gas and electricity from RSPB Energy, and even purchase wildlife-friendly organic rice bearing the RSPB's famous Avocet logo. Nor does death entirely sever the bond between the society and its members: adverts in *Birds* magazine encourage readers to consider leaving a legacy to the RSPB, and offer advice to those who have yet to make a will.

Looking back on the achievements of the RSPB, it is hard to imagine the state of the nation's birds had the society not existed. We have seen the return of the Osprey and Avocet, thanks to the efforts of staff and volunteers at Loch Garten in Scotland, and Havergate Island and Minsmere in Suffolk. Egg collecting, and the illegal persecution of raptors, have not quite disappeared completely, but have certainly been drastically reduced thanks to the perseverance of the RSPB's Investigations Unit. And from an international standpoint, embryonic conservation organizations throughout the world have reason to be grateful to the RSPB for their practical help and for leading by example.

It is all a far cry from the original nineteenth-century campaign against the use of bird feathers to adorn women's hats: but although the society's pioneers might have been surprised at some of the areas in which the RSPB is now involved, they would surely also have been delighted that bird protection is so high up the social and political agenda in twenty-first-century Britain.

F ROM THE early days of birding abroad, some observers have tried to give something back to the distant countries, places and people that they come across. Simply by taking a tour to a poorly developed area, individuals and companies are doing something to help the local economy. But given that most of the money spent goes back to the developed world, in the form of air fares, wages for guides and profits for the tour companies, a new approach is sometimes needed.

In recent years, this has developed into a concept known as eco-tourism. This simply involves taking a more sensitive approach to birding abroad: hiring local guides; eating and staying in independent lodges rather than chain hotels and restaurants; or leaving behind bird books and binoculars for local birders to use when the group returns home.

As a result, in some parts of the world – notably those with easy access from Western Europe or North America – a cottage industry has grown up around birding, with an infrastructure designed to meet the needs of visiting birders and the local economy. Trinidad, with the Asa Wright Nature Center and Pax Guest House, is one example. The Gambia, with its network of professional local guides, is another.

Just six hours' flight from Britain, and with a thriving tourism infrastructure already in place, The Gambia is a deservedly popular destination for British and European birders. For most, it is their first visit to Africa, and often their first trip to any exotic destination. Many go with an established bird tour company, while others travel independently on packages; but whether in a group or on their own, almost all will take advantage of the services of a local guide such as Solomon Jallow.

Born in the village of Lamin in 1969, Solomon began watching birds at the age of fifteen, thanks to the influence of an expatriate English birder named Ernest Brewer. Brewer had set up Abuko, Africa's smallest nature reserve, just down the road from where Solomon lived. One day he came to buy vegetables from Solomon's mother, and offered to take the boy around the reserve to see the wildlife. On entering, Solomon recalls that the first birds they came across were Stone Partridges, a tiny, bantam-like game-bird, which he assumed were 'wild chickens'.

His expertise and enthusiasm rapidly grew, however, and soon he could identify many species of birds. In an echo of the experience of British birders a century or so earlier, for the first few years he did so without the aid of binoculars. Like many birders in poorer countries, he turned this apparent drawback into a major asset – he is now able to identify most Gambian birds on distant views, relying purely on 'jizz' (their general appearance and behaviour) to do so.

Solomon's big break came in 1989. A British couple came to the reserve for a guided tour, but Ernest Brewer was unavailable, so Solomon stepped in and took them round. On their return to England, they sent him his first pair of binoculars. Following this he trained as a full-time bird guide, and began to lead the growing number of British and American birding groups who had discovered The Gambia and its birds.

Today Solomon works for Habitat Africa, an organization dedicated to the preservation and promotion of The Gambia's wildlife and divides his time between conservation work and leading bird tours. In recent years he has trained many of his fellow countrymen as bird guides, achieving a high standard of reliability and skill which in turn encourages more birders to visit and revisit the country. Men like Solomon can be found in virtually every other tropical birding destination, including Jamaica, Trinidad & Tobago and Goa in India. As well as the very practical advantage of having the services of a local guide, this also helps bring about a greater understanding between birders in the developed and developing worlds.

Birding not only brings prosperity to places in the developing world, but developed countries too. In places such as the Isles of Scilly in Britain, or Cape May in the USA, the local economy depends to a large extent on visiting birders, who because they come during spring and autumn, outside the normal holiday season, help keep businesses such as hotels and restaurants in profit.

Annual events can also be a big money-spinner: every September, several thousand people gather in the little towns of Rockport and Fulton, on the Gulf of Mexico in Texas, for the Hummer/Bird Celebration. They come to witness the extra-ordinary migration of the Ruby-throated Hummingbird, which in early autumn travels from Canada, via Texas, to southern Mexico and Central America, making a 500-mile trip across the Gulf of Mexico along the way.

The Celebration brings great benefits to the local community: in 1995 more than 3000 visitors spent over a million dollars during the four-day event – an average of more than $300 each. Other North American birding hotspots have enjoyed similar economic benefits from birding. In 1987, 20,000 visiting birders spent $3.8 million at Point Pelee National Park in Ontario; in 1993 roughly 100,000 birders spent $10 million at Cape May, New Jersey; while during just two months in spring 1992 6000 birders spent over $2.5 million at High Island in Texas.

Can the link between birding and commercial interests go too far? In 1991, a new species of vireo was discovered in the Chocó region of Colombia. To raise money to conserve the vireo, BirdLife International announced that it would auction the right to name the species to the highest bidder. Eventually, a private North American sponsor named Masters came forward, and in return for a donation of $70,000, the bird was given the scientific name *Vireo masteri*.

Following this, *Birdwatch* magazine invited its readers to come up with suggestions for other species which might benefit from commercial sponsorship. Proposed new names included Gillette Razorbill, Kellogg's Corncrake, Dulux Roller, Johnson's Waxwing and Burger King Eider. Less wholesome suggestions included some typical examples of schoolboy humour: Playtex Booby, and the eventual winner, Durex Shag.

ALTHOUGH some people deplore the growing commercialization of birding, it does undoubtedly bring benefits – not least to the birds themselves. Every year the 15,000 or more visitors to the British Birdwatching Fair dig deep in their pockets to buy the latest optics, books and foreign birding trips. Through the entrance fees paid by visitors, and by charging the exhibitors for the privilege of selling their products, the Birdfair makes a considerable profit, which each year is donated to a conservation project somewhere in the world. Since the fair was started in the late 1980s, it has raised more than £1 million for conservation, benefiting places as diverse as Madagascar and Morocco, Spain and Cuba, Poland and Vietnam. The format has also been successfully replicated all over the world, with similar fairs taking place in such diverse locations as Taiwan, Holland, Australia and India.

Despite its global nature, the Birdfair remains a very English occasion. Like so many events of its kind it relies on an army of volunteers, some of whom work all year round, while others turn up for the three days of intense activity every August.

Like many great events, the Birdfair arose from humble beginnings. Its genesis can be traced to a meeting of two old friends and colleagues, in a pub appropriately called the Finch's Arms, in the summer of 1986. At the time, Tim Appleton was working for the Leicestershire and Rutland Wildlife Trust, while Martin Davies was the regional officer for the RSPB. More than a decade later, both men still do more or less the same job. But everything else in their lives has changed. For their original plan of inviting a few local businesses and wildlife charities to a hastily erected marquee in the corner of a quiet field by Rutland Water, has grown into a major global event which, like painting the Forth Bridge, takes all year to set up.

Tim and Martin, along with their colleague Yanina Herridge, now spend the lion's share of their working lives running the Birdfair, though neither has ever taken a single penny in wages for doing so. The event has changed their lives in other ways, too. In 2001 the fair's profits went to a project to save forests and birds in eastern Cuba. Martin and Tim visited the island to see where the money would be going. While there, Martin met Lorasia, and they married in December 2001. Their daughter, Mervi, was born a year later.

The Birdfair has changed many other people's lives, though rather less dramatically. It has allowed businesses to flourish: providing a showcase for bird tour companies, booksellers, artists, and optical manufacturers to demonstrate and sell their wares. It has given charities such as the RSPB, BTO and the Wildlife Trusts the opportunity to recruit new members and meet existing ones. It has provided a venue for writers and publishers to get together: it is sometimes said that more bird books are commissioned outside the beer tent during the three days of the fair than during the whole of the rest of the year put together. Not surprisingly CJ Wildbird Foods, Subbuteo Books, BirdGuides and Limosa Holidays all have stalls there to promote their wares and products. And if you visit the art marquee, you can find Clive Byers displaying his paintings: works in progress as well as the finished article.

Since the British Birdwatching Fair began in 1989, it has grown into an unmissable event for birders from all over the world. But more importantly, the Birdfair has opened up birding to everyone, whatever their experience or level of knowledge. It has democratized a pastime that used to be insular, cliquey and often unwelcoming. It has created a birding community that is genuinely global, and genuinely inclusive: male or female, straight or gay, black or white, all are welcome. The creation of this worldwide birding network happened more or less by accident. No-one planned it; no-one ever dreamed it would happen. By combining the British amateur tradition with a very professional commercial awareness, the Birdfair has managed to achieve the best of both worlds.

Meanwhile, back in Norfolk, as diverse a bunch of people as you could ever wish to meet continue to organize their lives around making a living out of birds and birdwatching. Most will never make a fortune, but then again, that is not why they do it. The lucky ones have found the right balance between running a commercial venture and still being able to get out and watch birds. That is because without exception, they are birders first and entrepreneurs second – something for which other birders, who buy their products and use their services, should be truly grateful.

CHAPTER SIXTEEN

Missing Out
Women and Birding

Women like birds, whereas men like birdwatching.
C.J. Durdin, letter to *British Birds* (1987)

'OH EVIE, do come quick!' called a middle-aged woman to her companion as they were taking their regular walk around the Isle of May. 'And bring your gun – there's a dear little Piedy Fly on the lighthouse wall!'

The speaker was Miss Leonora Rintoul, her companion Miss Evelyn Baxter, and together they made a redoubtable pair. 'The good ladies', as they were always known, were lifelong spinsters and pillars of their local community – Evelyn Baxter was awarded an MBE for her work with the Women's Land Army during wartime. Their private incomes enabled them to pursue their main interest, which was the observation and collecting of migrant birds. In their lifetimes, which spanned a period from the reign of Queen Victoria to the late 1950s, they established a well-deserved reputation as two of the leading figures in Scottish ornithology. Writing in *British Birds* following Evelyn's death in 1959, fellow Scot George Waterston recalled her indefatigable energy when in pursuit of a rare bird:

> When at the age of 76 she pulled on her gumboots and took barbed wire fences in her stride to see the first Wilson's Phalarope to be recorded in Europe, I remember her enjoyment and undisguised excitement; indeed I recall wondering which gave me more pleasure – watching the bird or her in action!

What makes Baxter and Rintoul stand out from most other people involved in the development of birdwatching during the past two centuries is their gender. So far, the women mentioned in this book number less than a dozen, and half of these are primarily featured as the wife or partner of a well-known male birdwatcher or ornithologist. Even in today's age of relative sexual equality, women make up only a tiny percentage of 'leading birders' in Britain, though more and more women are now taking up birding at a beginners' level than ever before. But we have a long way to go before we can match the situation in North America, where there is a more equal balance of men and women – even so, there is still only a handful of top American female birders.

There are no easy answers as to why women remain so under-represented in the field of birding, but I shall try to shed light on at least some of the causes.

As well as the Misses Baxter and Rintoul, there have been a number of other pioneering women birders, some of whom, such as the Duchess of Bedford and Phoebe Snetsinger, have already been mentioned. In *The Bird Collectors*, Barbara and Richard Mearns include a number of women who have achieved recognition by themselves, as well as those who entered the field as a result of a professional partnership with their husband.

The latter category includes Lilian Witherby, wife of Harry Witherby of *The Handbook* fame, who, like Frank Chapman's wife Fannie (see Chapter 6), learned to skin birds while on honeymoon. Another, Annie Meinertzhagen, was already a well-known ornithologist before she met and married the soldier and collector Colonel Richard Meinertzhagen in 1921. Despite having three young children, she accompanied her husband on various bird-collecting trips to Egypt and Palestine, Madeira and northern India.

Collecting – with its emphasis on shooting, killing and skinning – was always likely to remain a predominantly male interest; but with the advent of a new method of 'capturing' birds in the field using a camera, all that changed. Bird photography was still difficult for women – it involved carrying large amounts of heavy and cumbersome equipment around the countryside – but it nevertheless attracted some notable female practitioners.

The best known was Emma Turner (1866–1940), who pioneered a new approach which she described as 'wait and see' photography. This involved putting up a hide near areas where birds were known to feed; instead of, like most of her contemporaries, concentrating on photography at the nest. Though less predictable than the latter approach, the results were usually more naturalistic and life-like, as she explained in 1916:

> Some of us are tired of photographing the eternal bird on its eternal nest . . . By the 'wait and see' method one sees so much of the inner life of birds when they are absolutely unconscious of observation. (*British Birds*)

Turner went against the conventions of the day in other ways, too: living on a houseboat on the Norfolk Broads, winning the Royal Photographic Society gold medal, and becoming one of the first honorary lady members of the British Ornithologists' Union.

In North America, one woman even managed to penetrate the male bastion of the scientific establishment. Born in 1883, Margaret Morse Nice caught the passion for birds at an early age, inspired by a book by another female pioneer, *Birdcraft* by Mabel Osgood Wright.

Having gone against her parents' wishes by attending university, where she obtained a master's degree in biology, she settled down to a more conventional life by marrying and raising four daughters. As the girls got older, she began taking them out into the field to study and count birds. But it was not until 1927, when the family moved to Columbus, Ohio, that she discovered what would become her life's passion. In a forty-acre area of scrub, just behind her new home, there was a colony of breeding Song Sparrows. Nice began a long-term study of these birds, helped by the progressive attitudes of her husband Leonard, who would frequently look after the girls while their mother was carrying out her fieldwork.

Although encouraged by some of the leading lights in American ornithology, such as Ernst Mayr (a German émigré at the American Museum of Ornithology), Nice was still denied membership of some local bird organizations – simply because she was a woman. She was also subject to snide comments that she was not a 'proper' scientist because she did not have a PhD, to which she was heard to respond: 'I'm *not* a housewife. I am a *trained zoologist*.'

Eventually, however, Margaret Morse Nice did receive the international recognition she deserved for her pioneering work in the study of bird behaviour, and for her wider work in nature conservation. She died in 1974, having proved that despite the obstacles put in her way by a male-dominated society, a woman with determination could still triumph.

Other pioneers were active in the field of bird protection, a movement that was founded, promoted and supported during its early years almost exclusively by women (see Chapters 6 and 7). They played a particularly strong role in the growing success of the RSPB: indeed, one woman, Mrs Frank Lemon, was described by writer Tony Samstag as 'the one person who can take credit for creating the Society'.

Mrs Frank Lemon (as she was known in deference to the customs of her day) lived up to the stereotype of powerful women, as H. G. Alexander recalled: 'She knew exactly what she wanted the RSPB to do, and she usually got her way . . . There was no point in fighting Mrs Lemon. She would defeat you sooner or later. I decided quite early on that the best plan was to go along with her, and try to make sure that the birds did not suffer.'

As the rise of Margaret Thatcher demonstrated, to succeed in any field where men were dominant, women needed to be tougher, more determined, and arguably more talented than their male counterparts. For a long spell during and after World War II, Phyllis Barclay-Smith occupied a key role as the assistant secretary of the RSPB and International Council for Bird Preservation – serving for an extraordinary unbroken period of fifty-six years. She needed to be tough to get to the top of the ornithological establishment – and to stay there. 'By virtue of her skill and personality, she was always the Queen bee in her global hive', wrote Max Nicholson on her death in 1980, 'always respected, widely loved, and sometimes dreaded, she rejoiced in her affectionate nickname "The Dragon".'

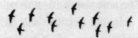

FOR MOST of the nineteenth and twentieth centuries, the barriers to women taking up birdwatching as a hobby were much the same as those preventing them taking up any other leisure activity: lack of time, lack of money and the lack of freedom to choose. In the Victorian era, women were treated as their husband's 'property' – in law as well as in practice. Middle-class women, for the most part, stayed at home and performed their household duties; if they pursued any interest at all, it was a 'ladylike' one such as embroidery or playing the piano.

A few women did go against the grain – in the pages of nineteenth-century novels, at least. Elizabeth Bennet, Jane Austen's heroine in *Pride and Prejudice*, shows her willingness to flout the customs of her day by making the journey from her home to visit her sister on foot, rather than by the more conventional means of horse and carriage. The shock felt by Mrs Hurst and Miss Bingley at her mud-spattered, dishevelled appearance is quite clear:

'That she should have walked three miles so early in the day, in such dirty weather, and by herself, was almost incredible . . . It seems to me to shew an abominable sort of conceited independence, a most country town indifference to decorum.'

Elizabeth's determination to ignore social convention is exactly what appeals to her eventual suitor, Darcy. But most women were unwilling or unable to break the rules. Her counterparts in the lower echelons of society were even worse off. Working-class women brought up their children and went to work, often labouring, like their menfolk, throughout the hours of daylight and beyond. For all women, married life was regarded as 'a woman's profession', leaving them little or no time for personal leisure.

The latter half of the nineteenth century did see some changes: a few women began to break down the male bastion of education, and professions such as medicine and the law. The same period also saw the rise of the women's suffrage movement, which finally gained the vote for women in 1918.

By the late twentieth century, women's emancipation had come a long way, but even so, they still had little time for activities outside home and work. As late as 1991, women had an average of ten hours' less free time than men per week, because of the expectation that they should perform the majority of domestic duties even when working full-time. Even when women did pursue leisure activities, these were likely to be based at or near their home, and were restricted by the limitations of time and money. So birdwatching – which often requires long periods spent far from home – was low down the list of popular pastimes for women. And unlike other leisure activities such as gyms, which have gone out of their way to become more accessible by providing crèches and facilities for young families, few if any bird reserves have made any attempt to cater for this section of society.

Perhaps the greatest barrier of all has been simple prejudice – sometimes hidden, often overt – by male birders against their female counterparts. This can be summed up in the derogatory phrase 'tart's tick', a piece of twitcher's slang which surfaced during the 1980s. Its origins and meaning were explained in an article in *GQ Magazine*:

> Political incorrectness found its apogee in the 'tart's tick'. Take your girlfriend out birding with you and she'd be pointing out chaffinches, wouldn't she, and going, 'Ah, isn't he pretty?' Thus a callow twitcher boasting of something too trivial for the rabid hard-core would be treated to scornful snorts of 'Bit of a tart's tick, innit?'

Women themselves were also mystified by, to coin a phrase, 'what makes birders tick'. Writing in December 1997, a columnist in the *Sunday Times* took a swipe at the whole range of male leisure activities: 'There are men who have hobbies and there are men who have lives. This is why I have never been out with a man who had a hobby. I prefer men to be passionate about work or their art or me. Men who have hobbies aren't passionate about anything.'

The same article lamented the fate of composer and screen-writer Julia Taylor Stanley, whose boyfriend Mark, we were told, is 'a serious twitcher', who even went away birdwatching when the couple were moving house. Apparently Julia found this preferable to 'having oily parts spread all over the kitchen table', and defended her partner's obsession by claiming that 'he needs to see something beautiful and rest his brain in the process because he has such a stressful job'.

Clearly she had never actually attended a twitch, or she would have known just how nerve-wracking the experience can be. But as in all 'twitcher's tales', there was another person who went one step further down the road to lunacy: 'At least he is not as bad as his friend who, a few years ago, was attending his own wedding reception when his bird pager went off. He told his new bride he was just going to the hotel to get changed. In the event, he was gone five hours. They have recently divorced.' 'You can always get another girlfriend,' he said in his defence. 'But you might only get one chance in your life to see a Black and White Warbler.'

With that kind of attitude prevailing, is it any wonder that so few women choose to enter the world of hard-core birding?

In the past, women who did want to become more involved were not helped by the lack of role models in the birding establishment. As Tony Samstag points out in *For the Love of Birds*, despite having been founded by women, the RSPB was as prone to sexism as anyone: a 'team photograph' of its wardens taken in 1974 did not include a single woman amongst the thirty-eight men. To be fair, major steps have been taken during the past decade or so to remedy this state of affairs, helped by the appointment in the 1990s of Barbara (later Baroness) Young as its chief executive.

Yet until recently the under-representation of women in birding was simply accepted as the norm, with few bothering to examine the reasons why. Then, in 1987, in a letter to *British Birds*, one (male) reader dared to question the status quo:

Why are there so few active female birdwatchers in comparison with the many male birders? Whereas the fairer sex would seem to have a strong aptitude for biology . . . at school or university, and, while there are certainly a good number of women birders in the upper age range, it is clear there is a disconcertingly low ratio of women to men within the younger to middle age groups. Since birdwatching does not lend itself, through physical demands . . . more favourably to one sex or the other, I find this observation most surprising. In ten years of serious birdwatching, I have come across only ten to twenty women birders toting binoculars or telescopes, and just one who actually drives to 'see' birds.

It says a lot for attitudes towards women that Philip Bentley's letter appeared under the heading 'Everything but the girl!' Not surprisingly, it unleashed an avalanche of mail – greater than on any previous topic featured in the eighty years the magazine had been going.

Correspondents suggested a number of reasons for the lack of women in birding, including the supposedly more competitive instinct of men, their evolutionary past as hunters, women's fears for personal safety, and most of all, society's expectations that they should stay at home. As C. J. Durdin observed:

> The young married male birdwatcher carries on with his 'hunting', leaving the wife behind with the children . . . The hunter role is converted into boys' and men's tendency to be involved in competitive collecting, be it of stamps, of glass marbles, or toy cars or of train or bird sightings. In the extreme, this becomes twitching.

Another correspondent, Julia Bale, agreed, and suggested that the sexist and patronizing attitudes of male birders were another key factor in discouraging women:

> First, despite our alleged liberation, women in this country are still expected to be the homemakers, and most of us conform. While it is apparently acceptable for a married man to leave his spouse and young family for birdwatching trips, the reverse is not the case . . . Second, there is, among a large section of male birdwatchers, a

refusal to take women seriously, no matter how knowledgeable they may be.

Male birders were not regarded as entirely to blame. One female correspondent suggested that women's position in society as a whole was also an important factor, and that all birders had a responsibility to persuade girls to participate as much as boys. But one woman who had made an effort to encourage girls by becoming a leader for the local YOC group noted that when she first led a weekend course she was expected to cook breakfast while her male co-leader went out birding.

Predictably, one male birder went down the 'male chauvinist pig' route, ascribing the lack of 'really outstanding female bird-watchers' to differences in mental capacity between men and women:

> Women are easily distracted, and the attention to small details
> and periods of concentration required to become a really
> competent birder seem to be more than most females are prepared
> to give to a mere hobby. Women don't make good fanatics when
> it comes to hobbies and pastimes . . . we must accept that
> there will never be more than a small minority of really good
> female birdwatchers.

Sexist and patronizing, of course. But a recent book by Cambridge psychologist Simon Baron-Cohen suggested that there may indeed be fundamental differences between the male and female brain: and that while the female brain is predominantly 'hard-wired' for empathy, the male brain is better at understanding and building systems.

In *The Essential Difference: Men, Women and the Extreme Male Brain*, Baron-Cohen was at pains to point out that this does not mean that *all* men have what he calls a 'type-S' brain, or that *all* women have a 'type-E' brain. However, if he is correct, more males than females have type-S, and more females than males have type-E. He backed this up with some observations of the differences between men and women:

We all have anecdotal impressions about typical hobbies for men and women. Men are more likely to spend hours happily engaged in car or motorbike maintenance, light aircraft piloting, sailing, bird- or train-spotting, mathematics, tweaking their sound systems, computer games and programming. Women are more likely to spend hours happily engaged in coffee mornings, advising friends on relationship problems, or caring for friends, neighbours or pets.

Michael Argyle, author of *The Social Psychology of Leisure*, has advanced a similar argument: 'Men begin collecting things obsessively from a young age – birds' eggs, butterflies, stamps. It's a genetic trait . . . Women prefer their leisure pursuits to be sociable . . . whereas men like to do something where they can measure their success.'

Along with the many practical and social barriers, this may help to explain why male birders are predominant. After all, we know that just as many women as men are interested enough in birds to join the RSPB, or to watch wildlife programmes on television.

What the majority of women may be less interested in – because of the higher proportion of 'type-E' brains amongst the female population – is the baggage that goes with being a modern birder: keeping lists, going twitching, or spending hours debating abstruse points of identification and taxonomy. If most women are more interested in the aesthetic and social sides of birding, as might be expected from Baron-Cohen's work, then by going against the prevailing male ethos they will inevitably be made to feel excluded. As a result, only the most determined women (and the minority who have a 'type-S' brain) will persist long enough to become keen birders.

This view is backed up by one correspondent to the 'Notes & Queries' section of the *Guardian*, who used Freudian psychology to answer the question 'Why don't women go fishing?'

Fishing belongs to a wide category of activities (we can include hobbies such as stamp collecting and bird watching and 'passions' such as football) which Sigmund Freud called 'displacement' activities . . . In other words, according to Freud, our true nature is being repressed and channelled into fundamentally irrelevant sideshows . . .

Freud never observed that women do not, generally speaking, share these activities. If he had, he might have concluded that women do not require such absorbing displacement activities because their true natures are not repressed to the same extent as men's.

WOMEN ARE not the only group of people under-represented in birding. As with other 'tribal' – and predominantly male – activities such as fishing, supporting football or plane spotting, some people may feel excluded simply because they are different. During the past decade or so, two groups – the Gay Birders Club and the Disabled Birders Association – have been created in response to the prejudice their members either faced, or anticipated, from 'mainstream' birders.

The Gay Birders Club was set up in 1994 by Duncan MacDonald, founder of the mail order company Wildsounds. Its website includes the following mission statement:

> Some people wonder why there is a need for a Gay Birders Club; indeed it is not obvious until you participate in your first event. Keener birdwatchers have found it suddenly brings together two very important parts of their life. They can go birding with other people and not worry about conversation which strays into non-birding matters. Other members knew they were interested in birds, but did not want to get involved in their local bird club because they felt uncomfortable with the attitudes of straight birdwatchers.

The Disabled Birders Association was founded in April 2000 by Bo Beolens, a larger-than-life figure in every sense, who also runs the eponymous website Fat Birder. Like the Gay Birders Club, the DBA aims to be inclusive, welcoming interest from all sectors of society rather than being aimed purely at disabled people:

Our society, particularly the commercial part of it, tends to cater for the average rather than the range of people who make it up. Such narrow perspectives make life difficult for the majority not just minorities. For example, the majority of people need ramps and wide door access into public buildings but the average person can cope with steps and a narrow entry. The majority is made up of disabled people, overweight people, elderly people, young people, pram pushing parents etc. Why is it that the tall, able-bodied, slim male has everything designed for him . . . simply because he is the designer!

The work of these two associations has undoubtedly begun to make birding more inclusive. So far, however, there is one group of people who remain not only under-represented, but virtually invisible. According to the 2001 census there are almost five million people of black and Asian origin in the UK, making up one in twelve of the total population. Yet if you visit an RSPB reserve or take a walk around any other birding hotspot, the chance of meeting a birder from one of these ethnic groups is very slim indeed.

Various reasons have been put forward to explain why black or Asian Britons do not generally take part in 'countryside pursuits' – for birding is not alone in its failure to attract participants from these communities. *Guardian* journalist Raekha Prasad, whose mother's family is from rural England and whose father comes from India, suggests that fundamental cultural differences may be responsible: 'My mother . . . taught me that walking was a pleasure, not just a means of getting around. She took my dad, too. As an Indian, the English countryside was a foreign land, and walking was far from his idea of fun.'

When actor and playwright Kwame Kwei-Armah was growing up in Southall in west London, more emotional factors also came into play: 'It was a very urban environment. Nearby was the suburb of Norwood Green. I always felt really frightened there because of the lack of noise. It was just too quiet. Quietness unnerved me. I didn't associate the countryside with me or anyone with an ethnic background.'

Even today Kwei-Armah feels that he does not really 'belong' in the countryside, and can never feel truly relaxed there: 'There are no signs saying "No blacks allowed". It's more subliminal than that . . . I found that people were only used to seeing black people in inner cities, so they stared. I'm not putting it down to racism. It's about what one is used to, and what one isn't.'

WHATEVER the social and cultural barriers that make certain groups of people feel excluded from the mainstream, there will always be someone who is an exception to the general rule. In the birding world, that person was a small, unassuming American woman named Phoebe Snetsinger. At the time of her death in 1999, she held the greatest prize of all – the birding equivalent of the 100 metres world record, or being the first man on the moon. By virtue of having seen more different kinds of bird than anyone else in the world – more than 8500 species – Phoebe Snetsinger was on top of the pile.

Her story, told in her posthumously published autobiography *Birding on Borrowed Time*, is a truly remarkable one. Born in 1931, she did not even take up birding until the age of thirty-four, when she saw her first Blackburnian Warbler in the woods behind her Minnesota home. At the time she was busy raising four small children, so for the first few years she merely enjoyed birding as an occasional break from her family duties. Gradually, though, she extended her boundaries with trips abroad, and by the late 1970s had become a keen lister.

Then in 1981, at the age of forty-nine, she was diagnosed with terminal cancer, and given less than a year to live. But she refused to go down without a fight, and was determined to continue birding in exotic places for as long as she could. Even she could not have imagined just how long she would manage to go on doing so, and where this quest would lead her.

Using money left by her fabulously wealthy father (who had founded the eponymous Leo Burnett advertising agency) Snetsinger began to travel the globe in search of birds. By 1992,

The Guinness Book of Records acknowledged her as the 'world's leading bird spotter', with just over 7500 species. In the meantime she had experienced the highs and lows of birding abroad, including shipwrecks, earthquakes, and being brutally attacked and gang-raped on a trip to Papua New Guinea in 1986. Despite these ordeals, she continued to travel to far-flung and exotic locations. In September 1995, despite stiff competition from the world's top male listers, she became the first person to reach the coveted 8000 mark when she saw a Rufous-necked Wood-rail at a mangrove swamp in Mexico.

Her single-minded determination to stay ahead of the pack was not without its difficulties. As well as several health problems, including periodic recurrences of her melanoma, her family life began to suffer as a result of her almost constant absences abroad. While on a trip to Colombia she missed her daughter's wedding, and at one point it looked as though her forty-year marriage would end in divorce. Fortunately, she and her husband David worked through their problems, and she continued on her mission. But something had changed. Maybe it was the realization of how close she had come to losing her husband, or the fact that she had finally reached the 8000 milestone: whatever the cause, in 1996 she announced her retirement from competitive listing.

However, she continued to travel the world in search of new birds for her own, personal satisfaction. So she was delighted when, on a trip to Madagascar in November 1999, she managed to add no fewer than five precious lifers to her list. Then tragedy struck. Thirteen days into the trip the tour minibus overturned, and while the rest of the party escaped with minor injuries, Phoebe Snetsinger, asleep in the back, was killed. Her final 'life bird' was a male Red-shouldered Vanga, seen on the morning of her death – as the writer of her obituary in *The Times* commented, 'she died with her boots on'.

To have survived what she called the 'death sentence' of cancer, yet die in such a freak accident, was both sad and deeply ironic. But in some ways it summed up her life, and the way she lived for the moment. In his foreword to her autobiography, fellow world lister Peter Kaestner recalled the first time he went birding with Phoebe, on a tour of the Malayan highlands in 1991. At the end of a long day in the field, they went in search of one final species, the elusive and enigmatic Long-billed Partridge. But things did not look good: a dense fog had rolled in and the light was rapidly fading. They were just about to give up when they heard a piercing call from the nearby ravine:

> Phoebe did not hesitate for a second as she plunged off the trail and down into the thick undergrowth that filled the steep ravine. I hustled after her, and we swiftly picked our way into the darkness and unknown. In the end, the bird did not call again, and the fog was too thick, so the partridge evaded Phoebe that night. Regardless, I shall never forget the wonderful time we shared. The sight of her disappearing down the ravine sums up Phoebe for me – committed, fearless, and never looking back.

NOTWITHSTANDING the extraordinary story of Phoebe Snetsinger, women have yet to make the impact they deserve on the world of birding. It would be nice to think that in a couple of decades' time, when a new generation of men and women have replaced those at the heart of today's birding establishment, this will have changed. Perhaps, by then, the debate about the participation and status of women birders – and indeed of gay, disabled, black and Asian ones – will seem as arcane and old-fashioned as last century's dispute about the ethics of egg collecting.

The last word on the subject should go to one (female) contributor to the *British Birds* debate, who pointed out that as well as the social and cultural barriers, there are practical ones as well: 'Have you ever tried finding a non-existent bush to pee behind on Cliffe marshes on a cold Boxing Day morning?'

CHAPTER SEVENTEEN

Watching Again

Birding now and in the future

British naturalists are going to be increasingly out of doors, enjoying, and assessing the wealth of British birds . . . The British countryside will be their playground. For the study of birds is play, an art sometimes, but still play. And who shall stop the British at their honest play?

The Birds of Britain, James Fisher (1941)

I N APRIL 2003, in his ninety-ninth year, Max Nicholson finally departed his long and extraordinarily productive life. Tributes poured in from the worlds of ornithology, conservation and birding, paying homage to the man who, more than any other, laid the foundations for birdwatching as we know it today.

One word kept cropping up, in the many obituaries and at his memorial service: 'vision'. And perhaps the most remarkable example of Max Nicholson's vision came from a book he wrote at the age of twenty-seven, entitled *The Art of Bird Watching*:

With his television outfit set up in a Devon heronry or at a lek of a blackcock in Northumberland the bird-watcher of the fairly near future may check, without leaving his house, or perhaps without leaving London, detailed observations painfully secured by isolated pioneers cramped, wet through, at dawn under flimsy canvas hides. It may be shocking that the acuter discomforts of bird-watching should be abolished for those willing to command increasingly intricate apparatus, but that undoubtedly is the way we are going.

This was written in 1931 – only five years after John Logie Baird invented television, more than a decade before the first working computer, and almost seventy years before Nicholson's prediction finally came true, in the form of web-cams which provided a live broadcast of an Osprey's nest in Scotland to anyone with access to the Internet.

Technological and social developments creep up on us, and it is easy to forget just how much the world of birding has changed in the past decade or so – let alone during the century since Max Nicholson's birth. Who now, as a novice birder, needs to go bird-ing alone because they have never met a fellow enthusiast – as Nicholson himself had to do? Who spends their first ten years watching birds without the aid of binoculars, like H. G. Alexander? And who, in this age of instant mobility, is unable to travel a couple of hundred miles to see a rare bird, or fly abroad on a birding trip – both of which were almost inconceivable only a generation or two ago?

The *pace* of change has accelerated remarkably too. When I began birding, in the late 1960s, I only needed two or three bird books. I had a good pair of East German binoculars, but did not own a proper telescope until the 1980s. I made do with one maga-zine (*British Birds*), one field guide (Peterson, Mountfort and Hollom), and one site guide (*Where to Watch Birds*). Until 1989, when I was in my late twenties, I had never seriously watched birds abroad – instead I spent my formative years trudging round the local gravel pits or reservoirs, with the occasional visit to Dungeness, Minsmere and Cley. The first time I went on a twitch, to see the Ross's Gull at Christchurch in 1974, I cycled there and back – twice, because I missed the bird the first time! And apart from my schoolmate Daniel, who accompanied me on that trip, I did not get to know any other birders for at least ten years after taking up the hobby.

At the risk of sounding like one of Monty Python's Four Yorkshiremen, I can truly say that my experiences were pretty typical. Birdwatching in the 1960s and 1970s was not all that different from birdwatching in the 1950s, or even the 1930s, apart from marginally better optical equipment and a wider range of bird books. And for most of this period it was not a passion you freely admitted to, as Brian Unwin, who grew up in the coal-mining village of Horden in County Durham, recalls:

I thought about this the other day while again watching the film *Billy Elliot*, which was made in the neighbouring pit village of Easington Colliery. The sort of antagonism Billy faced because of his passion for ballet was similar to what I experienced as the only person interested in watching wild birds in a rough, tough environment where life revolved around coal. It was a society in which keeping racing pigeons was an honourable pursuit, but watching wild birds was regarded with contempt – once the local hard lads discovered my secret I had to take care to avoid them.

Yet as Unwin points out, less than forty years later, when the Durham coalfield was finally closed down, a number of miners used their redundancy cash to buy binoculars and telescopes so that they could take up birding.

By that time, the pastime was undergoing a technological revolution as well as a social one. In a remarkably short period – just five years or so from the late 1980s onwards – there was an unprecedented explosion in the choice of products and services available to birders. There were more birding magazines, more bird books, more holidays abroad, the start of the British Birdwatching Fair, and the rapid rise of twitching.

Soon afterwards, in the mid 1990s, came popular television programmes such as *Birding with Bill Oddie*, a massive expansion in the scope and variety of bird tours throughout the globe, and the arrival of the Internet, which continues to transform the way birders communicate with each other in Britain, North America and around the world.

Much of this revolution was driven by information technology; which also helped to bring about a more commercial approach to birding, and allowed many more people to make a full-time or part-time living from watching birds. And improvements in optical design have meant that the binoculars, telescopes and digital cameras now available are light years ahead of those on sale even a decade ago.

As a result, today more people are spending more time watching birds in more places than ever before – so surely everything is for the best, in the best of all possible worlds?

Or is it? Correspondents to birding magazines and participants in website chat rooms bemoan the lack of young people taking an interest in birds. Women still face chauvinism from their male counterparts, while the very fact that there was a need to set up special clubs for gay and disabled birders suggests that prejudice still exists. Meanwhile, the gulf between the professional ornithologist and the amateur birder is growing ever wider, as more and more abstruse ways of classifying the various species of birds are being developed.

Egg collecting has still not been entirely eradicated; many bird clubs are failing to recruit younger members to their ranks; and fifty years of government-sponsored environmental degradation have led to parts of the British countryside becoming virtually a bird-free zone. And as if that were not enough, we and the birds now face the problem of global warming, which has the potential to devastate habitats and wildlife throughout the world, and has been described by the government's chief scientist as 'a greater threat than terrorism'. Against this background, how is birding likely to change and develop during the next fifty years or so?

BIRDING has always been driven by technological innovations. In the eighteenth and early nineteenth centuries, the development of accurate guns, and new techniques of preserving bird skins, led to the collecting boom. Then, in the early to mid twentieth century, advances in optical technology and colour printing produced binoculars which allowed better views of the birds, and field guides to help people identify them. And as we have seen, at the start of the twenty-first century, the telecommunications revolution now allows birders to receive up-to-the-minute information via mobile phones and pagers.

So how will the ever-increasing pace of technological development affect birding during the next half-century? The availability of cheap and user-friendly digital cameras has already allowed twitchers to post a digital image of a rare bird onto the Internet for instant verification by their peers, thus effectively by-passing the slow and tedious circulation of records around a committee by post. The advent of wireless mobile-phone technology and portable computers means that it is now possible to distribute an image around the globe almost as soon as the bird has been sighted. But there is a downside: digital technology also means that images can be altered, increasing the potential for fraud.

Another benefit of the Internet is that birders can communicate freely with each other wherever they are in the world, either by e-mail, via chatrooms and forums, or by setting up personal homepages. Nowadays, a birder planning to visit a new region or country can download trip reports and get in touch with local contacts within minutes, rather than days or weeks. This also has a downside: there may be more information available than ever before, but how can we be sure of its accuracy?

On balance, though, new technology is proving to be an asset, especially for organizations such as the British Trust for Ornithology. Today, amateur observers can send in their observations of newly arrived migrant birds from all over the country, which are then collated and posted on the web virtually in real time. For some time now, tracking devices have been placed on migrating birds such as Ospreys to follow them on their journeys to and from their African winter quarters, or wild swans migrating to Britain from Russia. As the technology becomes both more compact and more powerful, the possibility of tracking tiny songbirds on migration is coming ever closer.

Meanwhile, the new approach to taxonomy, which relies on analysing the DNA of bird specimens to reach a definitive diagnosis and identification, is beginning to lead to a huge multiplicity of different forms, so that what was once considered to be a single species may be split into several different ones. This may have its drawbacks: eventually ordinary birders could become so baffled by the range of possible 'new species' on offer that they lose interest, thus widening the gulf between the 'scientific birders' and the rest. A few years ago, in the pages of *Birdwatch* magazine, Anthony McGeehan revealed that scientists had managed to develop an instrument which could scan a bird in the field and read its DNA, providing an instant and indisputable identification. It was only when readers reached the end of the page that they realized, to their dismay, that the article had been written on April Fools Day!

Yet although we now live in a world of computer-based technology, the number of new bird books being published shows no signs of abating. The past decade has seen an exponential growth in their number, length and complexity. The keen birder can now find a volume covering every possible area of interest in almost obsessive detail: from bird sites in Ecuador to the identification and taxonomy of *Sylvia* warblers. James Fisher's 1966 prediction, that by the end of the twentieth century the ten-billionth word on birds would be printed, became reality long ago.

This is despite the fact that as the information revolution speeds up books become out of date almost as soon as they are published. The growing popularity of computer-based guides, such as DVD-ROMs, may solve this problem, as it is now possible to buy a product which can be updated via the Internet. Nevertheless, 'the death of the book', so confidently predicted for at least the past two decades, seems as far away as ever.

I T IS WORTH remembering that just as technological changes have driven the progress of birding, social changes have played a crucial part as well. Major developments such as the Industrial Revolution and the movement towards the recreational use of the countryside; cataclysmic global events such as the two world wars; and more gradual social changes such as the emancipation of women and the growth of leisure time – all have contributed to changing the way in which we watch birds.

The first half of the twenty-first century is likely to see social change on a far wider scale, and at a faster pace, than ever before. One major shift in western society is that the population as a whole is getting older. In Britain, the proportion of people over sixty rose from one in twelve in 1900 to over one in five by 1991, and continues to rise. At the same time, better healthcare and greater mobility allows people to remain active well into their 'retirement', while many continue to have a portfolio of careers and interests which keep them at the centre of society rather than on its periphery. This 'grey brigade', as one younger birder has described them, have the time, money and motivation to dominate the birding scene in the decades to come.

One appeal of birding is that, like golf and rambling, it can provide an instant social life – increasingly important in a society where almost half of all households are single-person ones, and as one recent headline put it, 'friends are the new family'. Birding does not just provide an opportunity to meet like-minded souls and companions; it may also offer the possibility of meeting a life-long partner. Indeed, one magazine runs a 'birdwatching buddies' column in its small ads, encouraging readers to find a companion who shares their love of birds.

Meanwhile, at the other end of the age scale, birding may be finding it harder to recruit new adherents. The number of children as a proportion of the general population is falling dramatically: from an average of 3.5 per family at the start of the twentieth century to less than 2 by the end. Moreover, today's children do not have the freedom that we enjoyed: their leisure time is strictly organized, and the kind of unstructured 'wandering about' outside the home that led so many people to become interested in birds in the past is now frowned upon. 'Nature tables' are no longer allowed in schools, for largely spurious health and safety reasons, while the national curriculum has forced nature study into the sidelines in both primary and secondary schools. And the notion that a teacher could take his or her pupils out birding after school or at the weekend, which encouraged so many of today's birders to take up the pastime, is now almost impossible to contemplate. Are we about to see the birding go into a terminal decline because of lack of interest amongst the younger generation?

One factor that may keep birding going is that people are better off financially than they used to be. It was recently reported that three million Britons have liquid assets of at least £50,000, and that this figure will rise to one in ten of the adult population by 2005. Moreover, people in this so-called 'mass affluent' group do not hoard their money, but prefer to spend it on 'life experiences' such as foreign travel and hobbies – good news for anyone who runs a business for which birders are the customers.

In the USA, too, birders tend to be in the older, more affluent sectors of society: the 22,000 members of the American Birding Association have an average age of 55, and an annual income of almost $100,000 (1999 figures), putting them at the upper end of the economic scale. And they spend much of their income on watching birds: a 1991 survey by the US Fish & Wildlife Department revealed that birders spent an annual total of $14.4 billion (approximately £8 billion) on their hobby. Just over half went on equipment such as optics, clothing and bird feeding, while most of the remainder went on travelling expenses. To put this sum into perspective, it is roughly equivalent to the annual gross domestic product of Costa Rica, and more than thirty times the GDP of The Gambia, two popular destinations for American birders.

The same survey attempted to count the number of birders in the USA. It discovered that roughly one in four Americans fed wild birds at home, one in five described themselves as 'backyard birdwatchers', while one in ten were 'casual birdwatchers', taking at least one birding trip a year. 'Serious birders' only accounted for 0.5 per cent of those polled: which would give a figure of 125,000 for the US as a whole. This may be an underestimate: the total of committed birders in the US has been put at between 300,000 and 1.3 million.

In the UK, the RSPB can still boast more than one million members: roughly one in thirty of the adult population. But figures on bird feeding, and the popularity of television programmes on birds such as those presented by Bill Oddie and David Attenborough, suggest that many more people have at least a passing interest in birds.

Another reason for the continued popularity of birding may be that it is good for our health – even helping us to live longer! The benefits are not confined to our physical well-being: several birders who have suffered from clinical depression, including Bill

Oddie himself, have revealed that their interest in birds helped sustain them during their illness, and speeded their recovery.

A paper entitled *The Benefits of Leisure*, from the Academy of Leisure Sciences in the USA, has pointed to the economic, physiological, environmental, psychological and social benefits of engaging in a regular outdoor leisure activity which involves meeting other people, such as birding:

> Evidence is mounting that systems of social support and companionship contribute to a longer, more disease-free, and higher quality life. Certainly many of these systems rely, or are highly dependent, on leisure opportunities . . . the 'social good' of leisure is truly staggering.

The paper also called for a new 'leisure ethic' to balance the puritan 'work ethic' which so dominates our society on both sides of the Atlantic. But this is nothing new. Birders have always understood the benefits of their pastime, as W. D. Campbell revealed back in the 1950s: 'The point of a real hobby is that a change from our normal routine is good not only for the body, but also for the soul and mind.'

ONE ASPECT of modern birding, the ability to travel the world in search of ever more esoteric experiences, may already have reached its limits. In the September 2003 issue of *Birdwatch* magazine, leading Israeli birder Hadoram Shirihai described 'the ultimate pelagic odyssey': a month-long, six-thousand-mile voyage from the southern tip of South America, via the Antarctic Peninsula and the remote and isolated islands of the south Atlantic, ending up on Ascension Island near the Equator. For seabird enthusiasts it was the trip of a lifetime.

Although unusual in its scope and ambition, this Atlantic odyssey is not unique: today, as we have seen, birders can travel the globe either on organized birding tours, or bespoke private trips aiming to see specific target species. An example of the latter appeared in *Birding World* in October 2002, where expatriate British birder Barry Walker described an expedition to the inaccessible region of southern Loreto, in Peru. The particular mountain they wished to climb was so remote that it did not even have a name – it was known simply as 'Peak 1538':

> This unromantic name records the altitude above sea-level of this Lost World-like mountain. Conan Doyle could have used an image of 1538 for the dust-jacket of his famous novel and, to us, it looked like it might still be home to dinosaurs, or some other species lost in time.

Their quest was to see a species of barbet (a close relative of the toucans) which had only been discovered in 1996. Now, this small band of British and American birders was determined to find the bird again. After an epic river trip, a soul-destroying hike up the mountain (often climbing for several hours before slipping back down the mud-covered slope to where they started), and a final climb through thick undergrowth, they achieved their goal, a pair of Scarlet-banded Barbets in all their glory:

> It was like a press conference. Video and audio recorders, microphones, binoculars and still cameras were all focused on these glamorous creatures as they performed their bizarre display routine . . . We soaked it all up, exchanging thumbs-up signals and broad grins. We've done it! The ultimate neo-tropical twitch in the bag!

Just a couple of generations ago, even a visit to a bird observatory or reserve was a major expedition. It is incredible to think that birders can now go 'global twitching' in search of a single rare bird, many thousands of miles from home. Will this state of affairs continue? Increased social and political unrest, and the threat of terrorism against Westerners, may soon make it unwise to travel to many destinations in the Middle East, Asia, Africa and South America. Meanwhile, although we are currently enjoying historically low air fares, in the near future carbon taxes imposed to combat global warming are likely to lead to restrictions in air travel. Foreign birding trips to any but a few safe and popular destinations may soon become too expensive or dangerous for any but the really committed birder.

I N THE MEANTIME, what of the birds themselves? As we concentrate on ever more varied ways of watching them, are they in danger of being forgotten? Birds all around the world face unprecedented threats to their survival, and the future looks bleak, as shown by the inclusion of a total of 1111 species in the recent BirdLife International publication *Threatened Birds of the World*. Global climate change, population pressures, habitat destruction, persecution and simple ignorance will be difficult to overcome, and there is no doubt that the number of bird species that will fail to survive the twenty-first century will be much greater than in any previous era.

Writing in 1999, in the introduction to Volume 5 of *Handbook of the Birds of the World*, Nigel Collar of BirdLife International pointed to the fundamental paradox facing birding today: that as we get to know more about the world's birds, and have better opportunities to watch and study them, so we contribute to their decline – perhaps even hasten their extinction:

> Birdwatchers and biologists get to ever more remote places by virtue of new airports, new logging roads, new tourist facilities. They arrive as tiny components of the great machinery of economic development which, in a few short years, mutilates natural landscapes and human cultures beyond recognition and brings Coca-Cola, television, chainsaws, DDT and debt to every cultivable corner of the planet.

He ended with a bleak prediction: 'By the year 2010 not only will we know more about birds than ever before . . . we will also have most of them *completely surrounded*.'

It is not only rare birds in remote places that have suffered major declines. On both sides of the Atlantic, common and familiar species are also disappearing. Leading US birder Pete Dunne, who began birding around his childhood home in the late 1950s, wonders if he would have taken up the pastime at all if he came from a younger generation:

> Were I growing up in Whippany, New Jersey, today, it is unlikely that I would have the benefit of those experiences to anchor the poles of my life.
>
> Why? Because now in spring there is no river of birds sweeping through the trees around my parents' house. There is not even a steady stream. What passes in May is hardly a trickle ... This prompts me to wonder what this means to birding's future.

An equally bleak view comes from nonagenarian British ornithologist Richard Fitter, who believes that the dawn chorus of today pales into insignificance compared with the one he used to hear when a child in suburban London, in the years between the two world wars. Like Dunne, he also wonders if he would have taken up birdwatching at all if he were growing up today.

However, maybe it is not all doom and gloom. One of the benefits of the rapid rise in the number of birders is that they now represent a major political force, both in Britain and the USA, able to influence the course of government policy. At the eleventh hour, we could still find the political will to change our priorities, and as a result the future for the world's birds may be better than we think.

So although there will undoubtedly be problems ahead, nevertheless we have a lot to look forward to. True, the golden age following World War II, when birdwatching was the preserve of a small community of like-minded souls, has gone, never to return. But we have also gained a lot. Better equipment, superior facilities, improved communication, new technology and, above all, a much greater democratization of the birding scene, all outweigh the passing of an era when watching birds was still essentially a minority interest. If you have any doubts that this is the case, a visit to the British Birdwatching Fair may help to convince you.

During the past century birding has grown from humble and uncertain beginnings into a mass participation leisure activity, which now brings pleasure and satisfaction to millions of people throughout the world. Long may it continue to do so.

REFERENCES

CHAPTER ONE
Observing

Much of the information about White, Bewick and Montagu comes from Barbara and Richard Mearns's excellent reference work *Biographies for Birdwatchers*, and Mullens and Swann's equally comprehensive *Bibliography of British Ornithology*.

Details of Gilbert White's life and writings come directly from *The Natural History of Selborne*, as well as a variety of other sources including works on social history by David Allen, G. E. Mingay, Raymond Williams and Patrick Armstrong, whose *The English Parson-Naturalist* is a fascinating history of the intertwining of religion and natural history.

John Clare's writings come from a variety of published sources from Oxford University Press, including works edited by Margaret Grainger and Robinson & Fitter. The John Barrell quote comes from *The Idea of Landscape and the Sense of Place, 1790-1840*.

As always James Fisher's *The Shell Bird Book* was an invaluable source of fascinating information and opinions, several of which I have quoted.

CHAPTER TWO
Believing

My sources for information on encounters with birds in the ancient world included J. H. Gurney's *Early Annals of Ornithology*, Jacob Bronowski's *The Ascent of Man*, Richard Inwards' *Weather Lore*, A. Landsborough Thomson's *A New Dictionary of Birds*, P. Houlihan's *The Birds of Ancient Egypt*, Max Nicholson's *The Study of Birds*, and James Fisher's *The Shell Bird Book*.

The various Biblical quotes can be found in the books of Genesis (chapters 1 and 9), Job (chapter 39) and Jeremiah (chapter 8); other classical quotes come from Homer's *Iliad*, Aristotle's *Historia Animalium* and Pliny's *Historia Animalis*.

For a portrait of the medieval world, I would highly recommend William Manchester's fascinating work *A World Lit Only By Fire: The Medieval Mind and the Renaissance*.

CHAPTER THREE
Understanding

The key works, on which much of this chapter is based, are Keith Thomas's seminal study of the links between human culture and wildlife, *Man and the Natural World*, and David Allen's superb social history, *The Naturalist in Britain*.

Details of the life of John Ray come from C. E. Raven's biography, while the background to the seventeenth and eighteenth centuries comes from Roy Porter's recent study *The Enlightenment*, together with works on social history by G. M. Trevelyan. Another useful insight came from Simon Schama's television series *A History of Britain*, broadcast on BBC2 on 28 May 2002.

Information on the growth of ornithology and birding in North America came from a variety of sources, including Jen Hill's anthology of writing on birds *An Exhilaration of Wings*, Barbara and Richard Mearns's biographical study, *Audubon to Xantus*, and Felton Gibbons and Deborah Strom's very readable book on the development of birding in the USA and Canada, *Neighbors to the Birds*. Paul Farber's more academic study, *The Emergence of Ornithology as a Scientific Discipline*, was also very useful.

Finally, two opinions on the way the development of ornithology led to a new interest in birds come from Max Nicholson's 1929 work *The Study of Birds*, and Austin Rand's popular Pelican book, *Ornithology: an Introduction*, from 1964.

CHAPTER FOUR
Collecting

By far the most comprehensive study of the history of bird collecting is *The Bird Collectors*, by Barbara and Richard Mearns, from which much of the information in this chapter is taken. Biographical information on the North American collectors, especially Elliott Coues, is taken from another of the Mearns's works, *Audubon to Xantus*. Coues's own work, *Handbook of Field and General Ornithology*, was also invaluable – and a fascinating insight into the mind of the collector.

Lynn Barber's *The Heyday of Natural History* is an excellent and very readable work on the phenomenon of collecting in the Victorian era, as is Allen Jenkins' *The Naturalists*. Other information in this section came from A. N. Wilson's seminal study *The Victorians*, J. H. Gurney's *Early Annals of Ornithology*, and David Allen's *The Naturalist in Britain*.

Details of the life of H. N. Pashley come from his posthumously published memoirs, *Notes on the Birds of Cley*, edited by B. B. Riviere.

Information on collecting in North America also came from Mark V. Barrow's scholarly yet readable study *A Passion for Birds: American Ornithology after Audubon*.

Finally, the quotation from Gosse's diaries comes from *The Life of Philip Henry Gosse*, written by his son Edmund.

CHAPTER FIVE

Travelling

Stories and quotations in this chapter come from a very wide range of sources, including several already quoted in earlier chapters, such as the studies by Keith Thomas, David Allen, Lynn Barber, Patrick Armstrong, A. N. Wilson, Mullens and Swann, and various works by Mearns and Mearns.

Quotations, references and statistics on the development of the transport system, including railways and roads, come from works by Simon Garfield, Thomas Carlyle, Alfred Lord Tennyson, J. H. Balfour and William Borrer; while those on the English enthusiasm for forming clubs and societies can be found in Jeremy Paxman's popular work *The English: A Portrait of a People*.

John Muir's works are still widely available, and make fascinating reading for anyone visiting North America's wild places.

For those interested in polar exploration and its links with the development of birding, I would highly recommend both the original work by Apsley Cherry-Garrard, *The Worst Journey in the World*; and Sara Wheeler's excellent biography, *Cherry: The Life of Apsley Cherry-Garrard*.

If you want to explore the continued link between religion and natural history, then Edward Stanley's *A Familiar History of Birds*, and F. O. Morris's *The History of British Birds*, offer plenty of source material.

CHAPTER SIX

Protecting

Once again, works by Keith Thomas, David Allen, Mark V. Barrow, Gibbons and Strom, Jen Hill and Mearns and Mearns were invaluable sources of original quotations and critical insight, notably on the lives and works of the pioneering bird protectors on both sides of the Atlantic.

Tony Samstag's history of the first hundred years of the RSPB, *For the Love of Birds*, offers a sceptical account of the influence of the Society on the development of bird protection and birding in Britain. A more academic account comes from Robin W. Doughty's *Feather Fashions and Bird Preservation: A Study in Nature Protection*.

Jeremy Gaskell's account *Who Killed the Great Auk?* offers a useful insight into the extinction of one of our finest birds.

The works of W. H. Hudson give an insight into the mixture of science and sentimentality that characterised interest in birds at the turn of the twentieth century.

CHAPTER SEVEN

Watching

The main source of first-hand information for this chapter was H. G. Alexander's delightful autobiography, *Seventy Years of Birdwatching*, which has the benefit of viewing the early days of birdwatching through a lifetime's hindsight. Ian Wallace's verdict on Alexander comes from the pages of *British Birds*. Other memoirs of this period came from E. W. Hendy's *More About Birds*.

Original writings quoted include works by Florence Merriam, Edmund Selous, W. Percival Westell and William Eagle Clarke, as well as the pages of *British Birds* (from its foundation in 1907), and D. W. Snow's history of the British Ornithologists' Club. Literary references include works by Siegfried Sassoon, E. M. Forster's *Howards End* and Edward Grey's classic work *The Charm of Birds*. I also found much useful information on Grey in a four-part BBC Radio Four series, also called *The Charm of Birds*, broadcast in November and December 1999.

Useful comments on the period came from works by Sharrock and Grant, Kenneth Williamson and David Lack (1965), and on the other side of the Atlantic, Arthur C. Bent's 'Life Histories' series.

Works already quoted by Mearns and Mearns, A. Landsborough Thomson, Mark V. Barrow, James Fisher, David Allen and Jen Hill were also used, as were the writings of W. H. Hudson.

Finally, the data on the Christmas Bird Count came from the National Audubon Society website: www.audubon.org

CHAPTER EIGHT
Fighting

References to, and quotations from, Edward Grey come from *The Oxford Dictionary of Thematic Quotations*, and Grey's own *Fallodon Papers*. The Kipling quotation is widely available.

Many of the contemporary accounts of life in the trenches, and all the obituaries, were taken from the pages of *British Birds* from 1915 to 1918. Others came from Charles Raven's autobiography *In Praise of Birds*, J. C. Faraday's letter to *The Times* (28 July 1917) and Paul Fussell's excellent and fascinating work on the subject of literature and World War I, *The Great War and Modern Memory*, from which Alexander Gillespie and Siegfried Sassoon's quotations are taken. H. G. Alexander's comment on the effect of the war on his enthusiasm for bird study comes from his autobiography, while his tribute to his brother Christopher appeared in *British Birds*.

Statistics on the number of people wounded or killed in the war are from Peter Clarke's *Hope & Glory: Britain 1900-1990*.

CHAPTER NINE
Counting

This is the first chapter in which I was able to quote directly from a living source. Sadly, the great Max Nicholson died in April 2003, before this book was published. I interviewed him at his Chelsea home on 15 February 2001, and despite being in his ninety-seventh year he was as sharp and fascinating as ever. It was a privilege to meet him.

I have also quoted from several of Max's books, including *Birds in England* (1926), *How Birds Live* (1927), *The Study of Birds* (1929), *The Art of Birdwatching* (1931), and a work written in the 1920s but not published for seven decades, *Birdwatching in London: A Historical Perspective* (1995). If you want a first-hand account of how birdwatching developed from an amateur hobby into a full-blown science and leisure activity, then these are essential reading.

Literary and autobiographical works which helped give me the social background of the period immediately following World War I included *Goodbye to All That* by Robert Graves, *My Country Right or Left* and *The Lion and the Unicorn* by George Orwell, and *Brideshead Revisited* by Evelyn Waugh.

Contemporary bird books mentioned include Coward's *British Birds and their Eggs*, Witherby's famous *Handbook of British Birds*, *Bird Reserves* by E. C. Arnold, and the long-standing *Observer's Book of Birds* by S. Vere Benson. Peter Marren and John Carter's *The Observer's Book of Observer's Books* was also invaluable. Much other material came from the pages of *British Birds*, reflecting its growing influence during this period.

Differing views on the acceptability of egg collecting came from *Birds Nesting* by J. G. Black, J. C. Squire (in his introduction to a work by E. W. Hendy), and the history of the British Ornithologists' Club edited by D. W. Snow.

Judith Heimann's biography of Tom Harrisson, *The Most Offending Soul Alive*, was a fascinating account of a remarkable man; and while *The World of Roger Tory Peterson* by Devlin and Naismith was a little too hagiographic for my tastes, it did contain useful information on the great man. Paul Erlich's tribute to Peterson appeared on a facsimile version of the original *Field Guide to the Birds*.

Other important sources, already mentioned, are works on social history by David Allen and G. M. Trevelyan, Gibbons and Strom's *Neighbors to the Birds*, and works by Mearns and Mearns. I also consulted *The Countryside Companion*, a contemporary work edited by Tom Stephenson. Another fascinating, though rather more academic, work was Steven M. Gelber's study of the importance of hobbies in the United States: *Hobbies: Leisure and the Culture of Work in America*.

The late Eric Hosking was one of my childhood heroes, and it was a great pleasure to re-read his delightful autobiography, *An Eye for a Bird*.

Finally, I also met another great British ornithologist and bird-watcher who is still looking hale and hearty despite having reached his nineties: the incomparable and deeply modest Richard Fitter, whose life story will continue to be told in later chapters. I interviewed Richard at his Oxfordshire home on 6 March 2001.

CHAPTER TEN

Escaping

As with the previous chapter, anecdotes came directly from interviews with Richard Fitter and Max Nicholson, as well as from various obituaries including those in *BTO News* and the *Daily Telegraph*, and the excellent website devoted to Max, set up by his son Piers: www.maxnicholson.com. Richard Fitter also wrote about his recollections of the war in the 2000 edition of the *London Naturalist*, journal of the London Natural History Society.

Richard Richardson's diaries are quoted at length in Moss Taylor's thorough and fascinating biography of him, *Guardian Spirit of the East Bank*.

Contemporary accounts and memoirs which give a detailed and vivid picture of life during the war include Alex Bowlby's *The Recollections of Rifleman Bowlby* (quoted in Fussell's work *The Great War and Modern Memory*); Eric Parker's book *World of Birds*, Dick Homes writing in *New Dictionary of Birds*, and Norman Moore, writing in a booklet published to celebrate seventy-five years of the Cambridge Bird Club (edited by Roger Clarke and Bill Jordan).

I would also single out E. H. Ware's book *Wing to Wing: Bird-Watching Adventures at Home and Abroad with the R.A.F.*, a fascinating depiction of the joys and setbacks of birdwatching while on active service.

Two very different accounts of life in the war, Eric Hosking's *An Eye for a Bird* and Field Marshal Lord Alanbrooke's *War Diaries*, created a fascinating juxtaposition when both men recalled the same incident in rather different ways.

Regarding the Collins New Naturalist series, and its place in the historical development of birdwatching in Britain, *The New Naturalists* by Peter Marren was invaluable. Individual works also quoted included *The Redstart*, by John Buxton; *The Yellow Wagtail* by Stuart Smith; and *The Wren*, by E. A. Armstrong. James Fisher, also intimately connected with the New Naturalists, is quoted extensively, from *Watching Birds*.

Of all the accounts and memoirs of life in the war, the most unusual and arguably also the most fascinating is a work of fiction: Kenneth Allsop's *Adventure Lit Their Star*.

CHAPTER ELEVEN

Learning

The main primary sources for this chapter, concerning the period following the end of World War II, were interviews and correspondence with James Ferguson-Lees, Richard Porter and Tony Marr (interviewed together) and Bruce Coleman.

I also drew on a previous interview I had done with Eric Simms, and correspondence or conversations with Frank Hamilton, Ian Collins, Roger Norman and Brian Unwin. I have also made use of reminiscences from Bill Oddie in *BBC Wildlife* magazine and Mike Everett in the RSPB's *Birds* magazine.

Much of the material included in this chapter, including some of the direct quotations, comes from BBC Radio Four's *The Archive Hour: A Lesser-spotted Love-song*, broadcast in the late 1990s.

Two county avifaunas, *Birds of Hampshire* (edited by Clark and Eyre) and the *Birds of Sussex* (edited by Paul James) also contained useful information on the development of birding in these two areas.

David Lack's radio lecture on bird migration and radar is reproduced in his book *Enjoying Ornithology*; while the history and development of bird observatories is covered very thoroughly in *Bird Observatories in Britain and Ireland*, edited by Roger Durman.

The parallel development of the science of ethology is covered by a variety of sources, including the original works by Tinbergen and Lorenz, and a paper by Edward Armstong in *British Birds*. Another publication, *Bird Study*, was the forum for the dispute between the scientists and the amateur birdwatchers described here.

The three volumes in Guy Mountfort's famous *Portrait* series provide an excellent contemporary account of the exciting early days of foreign travel in search of birds, as does Fisher and Peterson's epic *Wild America*, which remains for me the single most readable travel book about birdwatching.

Other works already quoted or referred to include those by Peter Marren and Eric Hosking.

On the Hastings Rarities Affair, I have drawn on the contemporary accounts of the exposé in *British Birds* (from 1962 onwards), as well as James Harrison's spirited but misguided defence, *Bristow and the Hastings Rarities Affair*. Unfortunately the two men at the heart of the revelations of the fraud, Max Nicholson and James Ferguson-Lees, would not comment on the details of the affair.

CHAPTER TWELVE

Driving

The definitive social history of the turbulent decade of the 1960s, Arthur Marwick's *The Sixties*, was a very useful background to an era which I only faintly remember!

From the birding point of view, a work by my contemporary Mark Cocker, *Birders: Tales of a Tribe*, was not only very useful but also highly entertaining.

Contemporary sources include Richard Fitter's *Collins Guide to Birdwatching* (1963), John Gooders' seminal *Where to Watch Birds* (1967), and *Birds of the World*, the part-work edited by Gooders (1969-1971).

Memoirs written many years later provided an even greater insight into the rapid changes in the field of birding that have happened during the course of a single lifetime or less: in Britain, Bill Oddie's *Gone Birding* is an amusing and deeply honest look at the period; while on the other side of the Atlantic, Kenn Kaufman's *Kingbird Highway* is just as honest and moving. Both are also highly entertaining to read. The biographical details of Kaufman's friend, the late Ted Parker, are from *The Bird Collectors* by Barbara and Richard Mearns.

I also interviewed or corresponded with Tim Cleeves, Bruce Coleman and Neil McKillop.

CHAPTER THIRTEEN

Flying

The main primary sources for this chapter were interviews and correspondence with Nigel Redman, Lawrence G. Holloway, Clive Byers, Josep del Hoyo and Richard Porter. *British Birds*, *Birdwatch* magazine, *BBC Wildlife* magazine, the *Guardian* and *The Times* also provided source material.

Contemporary sources included the magazine *World of Birds* (1973), *The Handbook of the Birds of Europe, the Middle East and North Africa* (1977-1994) and the monumental *Handbook of the Birds of the World* (1992 onwards).

The account of David Hunt's death came from his posthumously published autobiography *Confessions of a Scilly Birdman* and Bill Oddie's *Follow that Bird!* Jonathan Evan Maslow's *Bird of Life, Bird of Death* also explores the dangers associated with birding abroad.

John Wall's website on world listing is at www.worldtwitch/virtualave.net.

Statistics on travel come from Cassell's *Companion to Twentieth Century Britain*, edited by Pat Thane.

CHAPTER FOURTEEN
Twitching

The main primary sources for this chapter were interviews and correspondence with Mark Golley, Brian Unwin, Frank Hamilton, Derek Moore, Tim Cleeves, Bill Oddie, Tony Marr, Steve Webb, Bo Beolens and Rob Lambert. Rob Lambert also provided very useful background information and references.

I also used a wide variety of written sources, including articles, letters and other items in *British Birds*, *Birdwatch*, *Birds*, *Birding Scotland* and *World of Birds* magazines; *The Times*, *Guardian*, *Daily Telegraph*, *Independent* and *Sunday Mirror*; and BBC Radio Four's *The Archive Hour*. I also quoted from, and greatly enjoyed, the spoof magazine *Not BB*.

Other works used included *Diary of a Left-handed Birdwatcher* by Leonard Nathan, the *Bird Notes Bedside Book* edited by Gwen Davies, and *The Big Bird Race* by John Gooders. Works already quoted or referred to include those by Mark Cocker and H. G. Alexander.

The full title of the RSPB report on the effect of bird tourism on local economies is *Working with Nature in Britain: Case Studies of Nature Conservation, Employment and Local Economies*.

CHAPTER FIFTEEN
Earning

The main primary sources for this chapter were interviews and correspondence with Bruce Coleman of the Bruce Coleman photographic agency, Chris Whittles of CJ Wildbird Foods, Dave Gosney of BirdGuides, Chris Kightley of Limosa Holidays, freelance illustrator and tour guide Clive Byers, Solomon Jallow of Habitat Africa, and Tim Appleton of the British Birdwatching Fair.

Written works referred to include those by Mark Cocker and Josep del Hoyo. Statistics come from a variety of sources, including *The Value of Birds* (published by BirdLife International).

CHAPTER SIXTEEN

Missing Out

Works already quoted of referred to include *The Bird Collectors* by Barbara and Richard Mearns, *For the Love of Birds* by Tony Samstag, *Seventy Years of Birdwatching* by H. G. Alexander; and various editions of *British Birds*.

More general works include Jane Austen's *Pride and Prejudice*; while statistics come from *Mastering Economic and Social History* by David Taylor; Cassell's *Companion to Twentieth Century Britain* (edited by Pat Thane) and *Women's Leisure in England, 1920-1960* by Claire Langhamer.

The quotations from the Gay Birders Club and Disabled Birders Association can be found on their respective websites: www.gbc-online. org.uk and www.disabledbirdersassociation.org.uk.

The quotations on the under-representation of black and Asian people in the countryside come from an article in the *Guardian* Society section on 28 January 2004.

The correspondence regarding the reasons why women are under-represented in the birding field comes from the pages of British Birds in 1987; while possible psychological and physiological reasons for this are from Simon Baron-Cohen's work *The Essential Difference: Men, Women and the Extreme Male Brain*; Michael Argyle's *The Social Psychology of Leisure*, and the *Guardian*'s Notes & Queries page on 3 December 2003.

Phoebe Snetsinger's extraordinary story is told in her posthumously published autobiography, *Birding on Borrowed Time*.

CHAPTER SEVENTEEN

Watching Again

Many of the interviews and informal discussions I have had with the contributors to the rest of this book informed this final chapter.

Other sources include *The Art of Birdwatching* by Max Nicholson, *Birdwatching as a Hobby* by W. D. Campbell, *Small-headed Flycatcher* by Pete Dunne, articles in *Birding World*, volume 5 of *Handbook of the Birds of the World*, and *Threatened Birds of the World* (published by BirdLife International).

Statistics and other figures are from the World Bank website; a 1991 survey by the US Fish and Wildlife department; and a White Paper entitled *The Benefits of Leisure* from the US Academy of Social Sciences.

ACKNOWLEDGEMENTS

Many people have helped with the genesis and production of this book. First, I would like to thank all the people who gave me the benefit of their personal experiences. In roughly chronological order (in terms of their place in the book) these were: the late Max Nicholson, Richard Fitter, James Ferguson-Lees, Tony Marr, Richard Porter, Eric Simms, Frank Hamilton, Ian Collins, Roger Norman, Bruce Coleman, Tim Cleeves, Brian Unwin, Derek Moore, Lawrence G. Holloway, Neil McKillop, Nigel Redman, Clive Byers, Mark Golley, Steve Webb, Chris Whittles, Dave Gosney, Chris Kightley, Solomon Jallow, Graham Mee and Tim Appleton. Sadly, Guy Mountfort and Phil Hollom were both unable to speak to me due to ill-health.

Bruce Coleman, James Ferguson-Lees, Rob Lambert, Tony Marr, Richard Millington, Dominic Mitchell, Richard Porter and Nigel Redman also read various parts of the text and made helpful comments and suggestions, as did my wife Suzanne – as always, any errors that remain are of course my own.

In addition, many people responded to my appeals for anecdotes and information: and even when their names do not appear directly in the text, their stories helped guide the tone and content of the book. They include John F. Burton, Shelley Dolan, Trish Gibson, Andrew Howard, Helen Macdonald, Robin Morden, the late Ken Osborne, R. J. Raines, K. G. Spencer, Tony Vittery and Michael Ward. If I have missed anyone out, many apologies.

My editor at Aurum Press, Graham Coster, has been one of my closest friends since we first met at the Cambridge student newspaper *Stop Press* in the early 1980s. He first suggested that I write a book which answered the question 'Why watch birds?' at least fifteen years ago, though he was not in a position to commission it himself until more recently! He has worked tirelessly to correct my grammar, remove my clichés, improve the meaning and flow of the text, and to keep my attention fixed on the central question of the book – how did people watch birds at each point in history? It has been a delight and a privilege to work with him.

In addition I should thank Madeline Weston who copy-edited the text, and Peter Ward who designed it.

Finally, I must thank two women, without whom this book would never have been written. The first is my late mother, Kay Moss, who encouraged me to take an interest in birds from an early age. She trailed after me as I dashed around Shepperton Gravel Pits in search of Great Crested Grebes, Staines Reservoirs (Black Terns), Minsmere (Marsh Harriers) the Isles of Scilly (Buff-breasted Sandpipers) and mid-Wales (Red Kites). She was a fine woman, and I miss her.

Last of all, my dear wife, best friend, and lifelong companion Suzanne. We met through our shared love of birds, fostered in such diverse locations as Surrey, Trinidad & Tobago and The Gambia, where we spent our honeymoon. Suzanne has opened up my eyes to the magic, beauty and wonder of birds, so that after almost forty years as a birder I can now see them afresh. This book is dedicated to her, with all my love and gratitude.

Hampton, Middlesex; November 2003

PS: ... and of course to young Charlie, who arrived on 11 November 2003, almost three weeks early – thus making this book a month or so late!

BIBLIOGRAPHY

ALANBROOKE, Field Marshal Lord. *War Diaries 1939-1945* (eds Alex Danchev and Daniel Todman). Weidenfeld & Nicolson, London, 2001.

ALEXANDER, H. G. *Seventy Years of Birdwatching*. Poyser, Berkhamsted, 1974.

ALLEN, David Elliston. *The Naturalist in Britain*. Allen Lane, Harmondsworth, 1976.

ALLSOP, Kenneth. *Adventure Lit Their Star*. Macdonald & Co., London, 1949.

ARGYLE, Michael. *The Social Psychology of Leisure*. Penguin, London, 1996.

ARMSTRONG, E. A. *The Wren*. Collins, London, 1955.

ARMSTRONG, Patrick. *The English Parson-Naturalist*. Gracewing, Leominster, 2000.

ARNOLD, E. C. *Bird Reserves*. (Publisher unknown), 1940.

AUSTEN, Jane. *Pride and Prejudice*. Penguin, London, 2003 (originally published T. Egerton, London, 1813).

BANNERMAN, D. A. and LODGE, G. E. *The Birds of the British Isles* (12 vols). Oliver & Boyd, Edinburgh and London, 1953-1963.

BARBER, Lynn. *The Heyday of Natural History, 1820-1870*. Cape, London, 1980.

BARON-COHEN, Simon. *The Essential Difference: Men, Women and the Extreme Male Brain*. Allen Lane, London, 2003.

BARRELL, John. *The Idea of Landscape and the Sense of Place, 1790-1840*. Cambridge University Press, Cambridge, 1972.

BARROW, Mark V. *A Passion for Birds: American Ornithology after Audubon*. Princeton University Press, Princeton, 1988.

BENSON, S. Vere. *The Observer's Book of Birds*. Warne & Co., London, 1937.

BEWICK, Thomas. *A History of British Birds*. Beilby & Bewick, Newcastle, 1797-1804.

BIRDLIFE INTERNATIONAL, *Threatened Birds of the World*. Lynx Edicions and BirdLife International, Barcelona and Cambridge, 2000.

BLACK, J. G. *Birds Nesting*. (Publisher unknown), 1920.

BORRER, William. *The Birds of Sussex*. R. H. Porter, London, 1891.

BOWLBY, Alex. *The Recollections of Rifleman Bowlby*. Corgi, London, 1971.

BRIGGS, Asa. *A Social History of England* (new edn). Weidenfeld & Nicolson, London, 1994.

BRONOWSKI, Jacob. *The Ascent of Man*. BBC, London, 1973.

BROWN, Leslie. *Birds and I*. Michael Joseph, London, 1947.

BUXTON, John. *The Redstart*. Collins, London, 1950.

CAMPBELL, Bruce. *Finding Nests*. Collins, London, 1953.

CAMPBELL, Bruce and FERGUSON-LEES, James. *A Field Guide to Birds' Nests*. Constable, London, 1972.

CAMPBELL, Bruce and LACK, Elizabeth (eds). *A Dictionary of Birds*. Poyser, Calton, 1985.

CAMPBELL, W. D. *Bird-watching as a Hobby*. S. Paul, London, 1959.

CHERRY-GARRARD, Apsley. *The Worst Journey in the World, Antarctic 1910-1913*. Penguin, Harmondsworth, 1999.

CLARK, J. M. and EYRE, J. A. (eds). *Birds of Hampshire*. Hampshire Ornithological Society, Hampshire, 1993.

CLARKE, Peter. *Hope and Glory: Britain 1900-1990*. Penguin, London, 1996.

CLARKE, Roger and JORDAN, Bill (eds). *Seventy-five Years of Bird-watching and Bird Studies in Cambridgeshire (and beyond): A History of the Cambridge Bird Club*. Cambridge Bird Club, Cambridge, 2001.

CLARKE, W. Eagle. *Studies in Bird Migration* (2 vols). Gurney & Jackson, London; Oliver & Boyd, Edinburgh, 1912.

COCKER, Mark. *Birders: Tales of a Tribe*. Jonathan Cape, London, 2001.

COUES, Elliott. *Handbook of Field and General Ornithology*. MacMillan & Co., London, 1890.

COWARD, T. A. *The British Birds of the British Isles and their Eggs* (3 vols). Frederick Warne & Co., London, 1920.

COWARD, T. A. *Bird Haunts and Nature Memories*. Frederick Warne & Co., London, 1922.

CRAMP, Stanley and SIMMONS, K. E. L. *The Handbook of the Birds of Europe, the Middle East and North Africa: The Birds of the Western Palearctic*. Oxford University Press, Oxford, 1977-1994.

DALGLISH, Eric Fitch. *Name That Bird*. (Publisher unknown), London, 1934.

DAVIES, Gwen (ed). *The Bird Notes Bedside Book*. RSPB, Sandy, 1962.

DEL HOYO, Josep, ELLIOTT, Andrew and SARGATAL, Jordi. *Handbook of the Birds of the World*. Lynx Edicions, Barcelona, 1992 onwards.

DES FORGES, G. and HARBER, D. D. *A Guide to the Birds of Sussex*. Oliver & Boyd, Edinburgh and London, 1963.

DEVLIN, John C. and NAISMITH, Grace. *The World of Roger Tory Peterson*. David & Charles, Newton Abbot, 1978.

DOUGHTY, Robin W. *Feather Fashions and Bird Preservation: A Study in Nature Protection*. University of California Press, Berkeley and London, 1975.

DUNNE, Pete. *Small-headed Flycatcher. Seen Yesterday, He Didn't Leave His Name*. University of Texas Press, Austin, Texas, 1998.

DURMAN, Roger (ed). *Bird Observatories in Britain and Ireland*. Poyser, Berkhamsted, 1976.

FARBER, Paul Lawrence. *The Emergence of Ornithology as a Scientific Discipline, 1760–1850*. Reidel, Dordrecht and London, 1982.

FISHER, James. *Watching Birds*. Penguin, Harmondsworth, 1941.

FISHER, James. *The Birds of Britain*. Collins, London, 1942.

FISHER, James. 'The Birds of John Clare' in *The First Fifty Years. A History of the Kettering and District Naturalists' Society and Field Club*.

FISHER, James. *The Shell Bird Book*. Ebury Press, London, 1966.

FITTER, R. S. R. and RICHARDSON, R. A. R. *The Pocket Guide to British Birds*. Collins, London, 1952.

FITTER, Richard. *The Collins Guide to Birdwatching*. Collins, London, 1963.

FORSTER, E. M. *Howards End*. Edward Arnold & Co., London, 1947.

FUSSELL, Paul. *The Great War and Modern Memory*. Oxford University Press, New York and London, 1975.

GARFIELD, Simon. *The Last Journey of William Huskisson*. Faber, London, 2002.

GASKELL, Jeremy. *Who Killed the Great Auk?* Oxford University Press, Oxford, 2000.

GELBER, Steven M. *Hobbies: Leisure and the Culture of Work in America*. Columbia University Press, New York, 1999.

GIBBONS, Felton, and STROM, Deborah. *Neighbors to the Birds: A History of Birdwatching in America*. Norton & Co., New York, 1988.

GOODERS, John. *Where to Watch Birds*. André Deutsch, London, 1967.

GOODERS, John (ed). *Birds of the World* (partwork). IPC Magazines, London, 1969-1971.

GOSSE, Edmund. *The Life of Philip Henry Gosse*. Kegan Paul & Co., London, 1890.

GRAINGER, Margaret (ed). *The Natural History Prose of John Clare*. Oxford University Press, Oxford, 1983.

GRAVES, Robert. *Goodbye to All That*. Cape, London, 1929.

GREY, Edward. *The Charm of Birds* (2001 edn). Weidenfeld & Nicolson, London, 1927.

GREY, Edward. *Fallodon Papers*. Constable, London, 1928.

GURNEY, J. H. *Early Annals of Ornithology*. H. F. & G. Witherby, London, 1921.

HARRISON, James M. *Bristow and the Hastings Rarities Affair*. A. H. Butler, St Leonards-on-Sea, 1968.

HEIMANN, Judith M. *The Most Offending Soul Alive*. Aurum, London, 2002.

HENDY, E. W. *The Lure of Bird Watching*. Jonathan Cape, London, 1928.

HENDY, E. W. *More About Birds*. Eyre & Spottiswoode, London, 1950.

HILL, J. (ed). *An Exhilaration of Wings*. Viking Penguin, New York, 1999.

HOLLOM, P. A. D. *The Popular Handbook of British Birds* (3rd edn). H. F. & G. Witherby, London, 1962.

HOSKING, Eric, with LANE, Frank W. *An Eye for a Bird*. Hutchinson, London, 1970.

HOULIHAN, P. *The Birds of Ancient Egypt*. Aris & Phillips, Warminster, 1986.

HOWARD, H. Eliot. *The British Warblers – A History with Problems of their Lives*. Porter, London, 1907-1914.

HUDSON, W. H. *Adventures Among Birds*. Hutchinson, London, 1913.

HUGHES, Ted. *Collected Poems* (ed Paul Keegan). Faber & Faber, London, 2003.

HUNT, David. *Confessions of a Scilly Birdman*. Croom Helm, London, 1985.

JAMES, Paul. (ed). *Birds of Sussex*. Sussex Ornithological Society, Sussex, 1996.

JENKINS, Alan C. *The Naturalists: Pioneers of Natural History*. H. Hamilton, London, 1978.

KAUFMAN, Kenn. *Kingbird Highway*. Houghton Mifflin, Boston and New York, 1997.

LACK, David. *The Life of the Robin*. H. F. & G. Witherby, London, 1943.

LACK, David. *Enjoying Ornithology*. Methuen & Co., London, 1965.

LANGHAMER, Claire. *Women's Leisure in England, 1920-1960*. Manchester University Press, Manchester, 2000.

LORENZ, Konrad. *King Solomon's Ring*. Methuen & Co., London, 1952.

MacGILLIVRAY, William. *A History of British Birds* (5 vols). Scott, Webster & Geary, London, 1837-1852.

MANCHESTER, William. *A World Lit Only By Fire: the Medieval Mind and the Renaissance*. Macmillan, London, 1993.

MARREN, Peter. *The New Naturalists*. HarperCollins, London, 1995.

MARREN, Peter and CARTER, John. *The Observer's Book of Observer's Books*. Peregrine Books, Leeds, 1999.

MARWICK, Arthur. *The Sixties*. Oxford University Press, Oxford, 1998.

MASLOW, Jonathan Evan. *Bird of Life, Bird of Death*. Viking, Harmondsworth, 1986.

MEARNS, Barbara, and MEARNS, Richard. *Biographies for Birdwatchers: The Lives of Those Commemorated in Western Palearctic Bird Names*. Academic Press, London, 1988.

MEARNS, Barbara, and MEARNS, Richard. *Audubon to Xantus: The Lives of Those Commemorated in North American Bird Names*. Academic Press, London, 1992.

MEARNS, Barbara, and MEARNS, Richard. *The Bird Collectors*. Academic Press, London, 1998.

MERRIAM, Florence. *Birds through an Opera Glass*. Houghton Mifflin, Boston, 1889.

MILLINGTON, Richard. *A Twitcher's Diary*. Blandford Press, Poole, 1981.

MINGAY, G. E. *A Social History of the English Countryside*. Routledge, London, 1990.

MONTAGU, George. *An Ornithological Dictionary of British Birds* (2nd edn by James Rennie, 1831) Hurst, Chance & Co., London, 1802.

MORRIS, F. O. *A History of British Birds*. Groombridge & Sons, London, 1851-1857.

MOSS, Stephen. *Birds and Weather: A Birdwatchers' Guide*. Hamlyn, London, 1995.

MOSS, Stephen (ed). *Blokes and Birds*. New Holland, London, 2003.

MOUNTFORT, Guy. *Portrait of a Wilderness*. Hutchinson, London, 1958.

MOUNTFORT, Guy. *Portrait of a River*. Hutchinson, London, 1962.

MOUNTFORT, Guy. *Portrait of a Desert*. Hutchinson, London, 1965.

MOUNTFORT, Guy. *Memories of Three Lives*. Merlin, 1991.

MUIR, John. 'Among the Birds of the Yosemite' *The Atlantic Monthly*, Boston, Dec. 1898, vol. 82, issue 494.

MUIR, John. Our National Parks. Houghton Mifflin, Boston and New York, 1901.

MULLENS, W. H., and KIRKE SWANN, H. *A Bibliography of British*

Ornithology, from the earliest Times to the end of 1912. Facsimile edn, 1986, Wheldon & Wesley, Hitchin, 1917.

NATHAN, Leonard. *Diary of a Left-handed Birdwatcher.* Graywolf Press, Saint Paul, Minnesota, 1996.

NETHERSOLE-THOMPSON, Desmond. *The Snow Bunting.* Oliver & Boyd, London, 1966.

NICHOLSON, E. M. *Birds in England.* Chapman & Hall, London, 1926.

NICHOLSON, E. M. *How Birds Live.* Williams & Norgate, London, 1927.

NICHOLSON, E. M. *The Study of Birds.* Benn's Sixpenny Library, London, 1929.

NICHOLSON, E. M. *The Art of Bird Watching.* The Sports & Pastimes Library, London, 1931.

NICHOLSON, E. M. *Bird-watching in London: A historical perspective.* London Natural History Society, London, 1995.

ODDIE, Bill. *Bill Oddie's Little Black Bird Book.* Eyre Methuen, London, 1980.

ODDIE, Bill. *Gone Birding.* Methuen, London, 1983.

ODDIE, Bill. *Follow That Bird!* Robson Books, London, 1994.

ODDIE, Bill and TOMLINSON, David. *The Big Bird Race.* Collins, London, 1983.

OGILVIE, Malcolm and WINTER, Stuart (eds). *Best Days with British Birds.* British Birds, Blunham, 1989.

ORWELL, George. *The Collected Essays, Journalism and Letters* (4 vols). Penguin Books, Harmondsworth, in association with Secker & Warburg, 1970.

PARKER, Eric. *World of Birds.* Longmans & Co., London, 1941.

PASHLEY, H. N. *Notes on the Birds of Cley, Norfolk.* H. F. & G. Witherby, London, 1925.

PAXMAN, Jeremy. *The English: A Portrait of a People.* Michael Joseph, London, 1998.

PEMBERTON, John (ed). *Who's Who in Ornithology.* Buckingham Press, Buckingham, 1997.

PETERSON, Roger Tory. *A Field Guide to the Birds.* Houghton Mifflin, Boston and New York, 1934.

PETERSON, Roger Tory, MOUNTFORT, Guy and HOLLOM, P. A. D. *The Field Guide to the Birds of Britain and Europe.* Collins, London, 1954.

PETERSON, Roger Tory, and FISHER, James. *Wild America.* Houghton Mifflin, Boston, 1955.

PORTER, Roy. *Enlightenment: Britain and the Creation of the Modern World*. Allen Lane, London, 2000.

RAND, Austin. *Ornithology: an Introduction*. Pelican Books, London, 1964.

RATCLIFFE, Susan (ed). *The Oxford Dictionary of Thematic Quotations*. Oxford University Press, Oxford, 2000.

RAVEN, C. E. *John Ray, Naturalist*. Cambridge University Press, Cambridge, 1942.

RAVEN, C. E. *In Praise of Birds*. George Allen & Unwin, London, 1950.

RICKS, Christopher (ed). *The Oxford Book of English Verse*. Oxford University Press, Oxford, 1999.

ROBINSON, Eric and FITTER, Richard (eds). *John Clare's Birds*. Oxford University Press, Oxford, 1982.

ROBINSON, Eric and POWELL, David (eds). *The Oxford Authors: John Clare*. Oxford University Press, Oxford, 1984.

SAMSTAG, Tony. *For the Love of Birds*. RSPB, Sandy, 1988.

SASSOON, Siegfried. *Memoirs of an Infantry Officer*. Faber & Faber, London, 1937.

SELOUS, Edmund. *Bird Watching*. J. M. Dent, London, 1901.

SHARROCK, J. T. R. (ed). *The Atlas of Breeding Birds of Britain and Ireland*. BTO/IWC, Tring, 1976.

SHARROCK, J. T. R. and GRANT, P. J. (eds). *Birds New to Britain and Ireland*. Poyser, Calton, 1982.

SIELMANN, Heinz. *My Year with the Woodpeckers*. Barrie & Rockliff, London, 1959.

SMITH, Stuart. *How to Study Birds*. Collins, London, 1945.

SMITH, Stuart. *The Yellow Wagtail*. Collins, London, 1950.

SNETSINGER, Phoebe. *Birding on Borrowed Time*. American Birding Association, Colorado Springs, Colorado, 2003.

SNOW, D. W. (ed). *Birds, Discovery and Conservation: 100 years of the British Ornithologists' Club*. Pica Press, Robertsbridge, 1992.

STAMP, Sir Dudley. *Nature Conservation in Britain*. Collins, London, 1969.

STANLEY, Edward. *A Familiar History of Birds*. SPCK, London, 1865.

STEPHENSON, Tom (ed). *The Countryside Companion*. Odham's Press, London, 1939.

SUMMERS-SMITH, Denis. *The House Sparrow*. Collins, London, 1963.

TAYLOR, David. *Mastering Economic and Social History*. Macmillan Education, Basingstoke, 1988.

TAYLOR, Moss. *Guardian Spirit of the East Bank*. Wren Publishing, Sheringham, 2002.

THANE, Pat (ed). *Cassell's Companion to Twentieth Century Britain.* Cassell, London, 2001.

THOMAS, Keith. *Man and the Natural World: Changing Attitudes in England 1500-1800.* Allen Lane, London, 1983.

THOMSON, A. Landsborough. *A New Dictionary of Birds.* Nelson, London, 1964.

TINBERGEN, Niko. *Curious Naturalists.* Country Life, London, 1958.

TREVELYAN, G. M. *English Social History.* Longmans & Co., London, 1942.

WARE, E. H. *Wing to Wing: Bird-Watching Adventures at Home and Abroad with the R.A.F.* The Paternoster Press, London, 1946.

WATSON, Fred. *Binoculars, Opera Glasses and Field Glasses.* Shire Publications, Princes Risborough, 1995.

WAUGH, Evelyn. *Brideshead Revisited.* Chapman & Hall, London, 1945.

WESTELL, W. Percival. *British Bird Life.* (1908 edn) T. Fisher Unwin, London, 1905.

WHEELER, Sara. *Cherry: The Life of Apsley Cherry-Garrard.* Jonathan Cape, London, 2001.

WHITE, Gilbert. *The Natural History and Antiquities of Selborne.* Penguin, Harmondsworth, 1977 (originally published G. White & Son, London 1789).

WILLIAMS, Raymond. *The Country and the City.* Chatto & Windus, London, 1973.

WILLIAMSON, Kenneth. *Fair Isle and its Birds.* Oliver & Boyd, Edinburgh and London, 1965.

WILSON, A. N. *The Victorians.* Hutchinson, London, 2002.

WITHERBY, H. F. et al, *The Handbook of British Birds* (5 vols). H. F. & G. Witherby, London, 1938-1941.

YARRELL, William. *A History of British Birds* (3 vols). John Van Voorst, London, 1837-1843.

INDEX